YEARNING FOR YOU

The Bible in the Modern World, 46

YEARNING FOR YOU

PSALMS AND THE SONG OF SONGS IN CONVERSATION WITH ROCK AND WORSHIP SONGS

William Goodman

SHEFFIELD PHOENIX PRESS
2012

Copyright © 2012 Sheffield Phoenix Press
Published by Sheffield Phoenix Press
Department of Biblical Studies, University of Sheffield
45 Victoria Street, Sheffield S3 7QB

www.sheffieldphoenix.com

A CIP catalogue record for this book
is available from the British Library

Typeset by the HK Scriptorium
Printed by Lightning Source

ISBN 978-1-907534-61-4 (hbk)
ISSN 1747-9630

*For
Sara,
Matthew
and
Anna*

CONTENTS

ABBREVIATIONS   xi

PRELUDE: 'FROM YOUR LIPS SHE DREW THE HALLELUIAH'   1
    Questions of Culture   2
    On Songs   4
    Biblical Songs   6
    Texts in Conversation   7
    Outline   10

1. 'LET THERE BE LOVE': YEARNING FOR you/You
    IN CONTEMPORARY MUSIC   11
    Can Rock Be Read?   11
    Music Acclaimed in Mainstream Culture   17
        Beyoncé: I Can Feel your Halo   17
        Leonard Cohen: Hallelujah   19
        Coldplay: You Are, and Nothing Else Compares   23
        Florence and the Machine: I Know my Saviour's Love Is Real   24
        Whitney Houston: I Look to You   26
        Annie Lennox: Your Heavenly Connection   28
        Madonna: Just Like a Prayer, your Voice Can Take Me There   30
        Oasis: Maybe You're Gonna Be the One That Saves Me   36
        Sinéad O'Connor: I Long for You   38
        Prince: The Sensual Everafter   39
        Cliff Richard: I Still Believe in You   41
        U2: But You're Gone and So Is God   43
        The Best of the Rest   49
    Music Acclaimed in Some Church Circles   51
        Delirious?: We Are God's Romance   51
        Matt Redman: Jesus, I Am So in Love with You   55
        Stuart Townend: I'm in Love with You my Beautiful   57
        Toronto Airport Christian Fellowship: Come Away, my Beloved   58
        Darlene Zschech and Hillsong: The Kiss of Heaven   59
        What More Shall We Say of ...   62
        Yearning, Then and Now   65
    Conclusion   66

2. 'LET HIM KISS ME … HAVING YOU, I DESIRE NOTHING ELSE':
   YEARNING FOR YOU/YOU IN THE HISTORY OF INTERPRETATION
   OF THE PSALMS AND THE SONG OF SONGS   69
   Psalms   71
      The Sweetness of Poetry   72
      Philo of Alexandria's Therapeutae   73
      Athanasius of Alexandria   74
      Jerome   75
      Augustine of Hippo   77
      Flavius Cassiodorus   80
      Bernard of Clairvaux   81
      Martin Luther   82
      John Calvin   83
      Francis de Sales   85
      Historical Criticism and Beyond   86
   Song of Songs   88
      Early Jewish Approaches to the Song   88
      Origen of Alexandria   90
      Origen's Heirs   94
      Augustine of Hippo   95
      Rabbi Shlomo Yitzhaki (Rashi)   96
      Bernard of Clairvaux   98
      Medieval Mysticism   101
      Martin Luther   106
      After the Reformation   107
      Modern and Postmodern Analysis   108
   Conclusion   112

3. 'MY GOD … MY BELOVED': YEARNING FOR YOU/YOU
   IN THE PSALMS AND SONG OF SONGS   115
   Desiring you/You: Song 3.1-5 and Psalm 63   117
      Song 3.1-5   117
      Psalm 63   118
      The Language of Desire   120
      Summary   125
   Missing you/You: Psalm 42–43 and Song 5.2-8   125
      Psalm 42–43   125
      Song 5.2-8   129
      All You Love Is Need?   134
      Summary   136
   Admiring and Enjoying you/You: Song 1.9–2.7 and Psalm 84   136
      Song of Songs 1.9–2.7   136
      Psalm 84   139

The Physical Delight of Zion	142
The Anatomy of God	144
Mysterious Encounter	145
Summary	147
Hearing and Speaking to you/You: Psalm 119 and Song 2.8-17	148
Psalm 119	148
Song 2.8-17	152
Mutuality and Delight?	153
The Language of Love	155
Summary	159
Forever Devoted to you/You: Song 8.5b-7 and Psalm 136	159
Song 8.5b-7	159
Psalm 136	164
ḥesed (חסד)	167
Summary	171
Of Lords and Lovers: Psalm 45 and Song 3.6-11	171
Psalm 45	172
Song 3.6-11	174
Allusions of Grandeur	176
Marrying the King	181
Summary	183
Conclusion	183
4. 'MY SOUL THIRSTS FOR YOU ... YOU ELEVATE MY SOUL': ALL THE VOICES, CONTEMPORARY AND BIBLICAL, IN CONVERSATION ABOUT YEARNING FOR you/You	185
On the Ambiguities of Language	187
Parallels: Yearning for you as Similar to Yearning for You	189
Contrast: Yearning for you as Distinct from Yearning for You	191
Agency: Yearning for you as a Means to Fulfil Yearning for You	195
Sacrament: Yearning for you as an Expression of Divine Yearning	199
Figurative: Yearning for you as a Metaphor for Yearning for You	203
Yes, But ... : Issues Raised by a Metaphorical Understanding	208
A Range of Meanings	208
Tension: 'Is' and 'Is Not'	209
Interaction: Seeing As	210
Cutting God Down to Size	212
The Sacred Self	214

Words in Context	216
Intent on Intimacy	219
Multiple Metaphors, and How to Handle Them	221
Embracing Multiplicity	221
U2: Suggestive Metaphors	223
Delirious?: Mingled Metaphors	225
YFriday: Favoured Metaphors	226
Paul Ricoeur: Intersecting Metaphors	227
Conclusion	229
FINALE: 'YOU'VE GOT THE LOVE I NEED TO SEE ME THROUGH	232
BIBLIOGRAPHY	236
DISCOGRAPHY	255
INDEX OF BIBLICAL REFERENCES	258
INDEX OF AUTHORS	265
INDEX OF MUSICIANS	268

ABBREVIATIONS

AB	Anchor Bible
ABD	*Anchor Bible Dictionary*. Edited by David Noel Freedman. 6 vols. (New York: Doubleday, 1992)
BibInt	Biblical Interpretation
CBQ	*Catholic Biblical Quarterly*
DCH	*Dictionary of Classical Hebrew*. Edited by David J.A. Clines. 8 vols. (Sheffield: Sheffield Academic Press, 1993-2010).
JAAR	*Journal of the American Academy of Religion*
JBL	*Journal of Biblical Literature*
JHP	*Journal of Humanistic Psychology*
JPMS	*Journal of Popular Music Studies*
JPS	Jewish Publication Society
JRPC	*Journal of Religion and Popular Culture*
JSOT	*Journal for the Study of the Old Testament*
JSOT Sup.	Journal for the Study of the Old Testament (Supplementary Series)
KJB	King James Bible
LXX	Septuagint
MT	Masoretic Text
NASB	New American Standard Bible
NCB	New Century Bible
NICOT	New International Commentary on the Old Testament
NIBC	New International Biblical Commentary
NIV	New International Version
NJB	New Jerusalem Bible
NRSV	New Revised Standard Version
OTL	Old Testament Library
PopMus	*Popular Music*
REB	Revised English Bible
SCM	Student Christian Movement
SBL	Society of Biblical Literature
SPCK	Society for the Promotion of Christian Knowledge
TDOT	*Theological Dictionary of the Old Testament*. Edited by G. Johannes Botterweck, Helmer Ringgren and Heinz-Joseph

	Fabry; translated by David E. Green. 11 vols. (Grand Rapids, MI: Eerdmans, 1974-2001).
TLOT	*Theological Lexicon of the Old Testament.* Edited by Ernst Jenni and Claus Westermann; translated by Mark E. Biddle. 3 vols. (Peabody, MA: Hendrickson, 2004).
TynB	*Tyndale Bulletin*
VT	*Vetus Testamentum*
WBC	Word Biblical Commentary
ZAW	*Zeitschrift für die alttestamentliche Wissenschaft*

PRELUDE

'FROM YOUR LIPS SHE DREW THE HALLELUIAH'

> He explained that although what she saw probably *looked* like a sex ritual, Hieros Gamos had nothing to do with eroticism. It was a spiritual act. Historically, intercourse was the act through which male and female experienced God. … Physical union with the female remained the sole means through which man could become spiritually complete and ultimately achieve *gnosis*—knowledge of the divine.[1]

A best-selling novel, for all its demerits in terms of historical accuracy, can be a useful cultural indicator. Sales figures give Dan Brown's *The Da Vinci Code* exalted status as the publishing phenomenon of the opening decade of the twenty-first century.[2] The novel claims to build on historical foundations: the very first word in it is 'Fact', introducing a preliminary page which states that the two secret societies central to the plot are real organisations, and that 'all descriptions of artwork, architecture, documents and secret rituals in this novel are accurate'.[3] The story itself weaves together seamlessly fact and fantasy; thus the (fictitious) Sophie Neveu finds in the (fictitious) library of the (fictitious) scholar Leigh Teabing two books by Margaret Starbird, which are not fictitious and are available today.[4] When authoritative figures in the novel assert that the divine name Yhwh combines Jehovah and Havah (Eve), that Jews in Solomon's day believed the Jerusalem Temple housed both God and his powerful female equal, Shekinah, and that men

1. Dan Brown, *The Da Vinci Code* (London: Corgi, 2003), p. 410.
2. Worldwide sales were estimated at 80 million in 2009; see James Kaplan, 'Life After the Da Vinci Code: Interview with Dan Brown' [http://www.parade.com/news/2009/09/13-dan-brown-life-after-da-vinci-code.html], accessed 14 Apr. 2011. Also [http://en.wikipedia.org/wiki/List_of_best-selling_books], accessed 14 Apr. 2011.
3. Brown, *Da Vinci Code*, p. 15.
4. *The Goddess in the Gospels: Reclaiming the Sacred Feminine* and *The Woman with the Alabaster Jar: Mary Magdalene and the Holy Grail*; see Brown, *Da Vinci Code*, p. 339.

would visit the Temple to achieve spiritual enlightenment by having sex
with priestesses, the reader is given no clue as to how much speculation
and pure fantasy is woven into the story alongside the sprinkling of specific
historical references.[5]

One spin-off from the success of the novel has been renewed interest in
the work of writers such as Starbird. In an interview published as part of
a popular guide to *The Da Vinci Code*, she restates her views on sex and
spirituality in the Hebrew Bible and the Gospels:

> The Song of Songs is a redaction of ancient liturgical poetry from the
> *hieros gamos* rites of Isis and Osiris. Invariably the king is executed, and
> his bride seeks him, mourning his death, and is eventually reunited with
> him. In the Song of Songs, the fragrance of the bride is nard [spikenard,
> an eastern perfume or ointment] which wafts around the bridegroom at the
> banquet table. And in the Gospel, again it is nard with which Mary anoints
> Jesus, and the fragrance "filled the house" (John 12.3).[6]

The huge success of Brown's novel and the subsequent film may be seen
in part as indicators of a desire in contemporary culture (particularly in the
Western world) to find connections between sex and spirituality. Longing
for intimacy in human relationships is sometimes combined with the suggestion that a further intimacy may be found through and beyond them,
with the mystical and transcendent. It is this current, as I perceive it in my
own culture today, that has prompted the writing of this book. The novel's
heroine, Sophie, gives one of the more memorable summaries of this tantalizing idea in the sound-bite: 'Orgasm as prayer?'[7]

Questions of Culture

Talk of 'culture' immediately raises questions of definition. Culture, particularly popular culture, is a human construct which is notoriously hard
to identify and define, but easier to observe through its expression in items
packaged for mass consumption, such as books, film, television, sport,
theatre, art, and music.[8] Thus Elaine Graham defines culture in general as

5. Brown, *Da Vinci Code*, p. 411.

6. Margaret Starbird, 'God Does Not Look Like a Man', in Dan Burstein (ed.),
*Secrets of the Code: The Unauthorized Guide to the Mysteries Behind The Da Vinci
Code* (London: Orion, 2005), p. 66.

7. Brown, *Da Vinci Code*, p. 410. On current interest in and practice of *hieros gamos*,
see Samuel Wagar, 'The Wiccan "Great Rite"—*Hieros Gamos* in the Modern West',
JRPC 21 (2009) [http://www.usask.ca/relst/jrpc/art21(2)-HeirosGamos.html], accessed
5 June 2011.

8. Some analyses of 'culture' show a bias towards the traditional and 'high-brow'
in their understanding of the term. John Rogerson's article on 'Music', in the *Blackwell*

'the entirety of human creative activity' and 'the whole framework of lived human experience', while Simon Frith sees popular culture in more concrete terms as the production of cultural objects 'of', 'by', or 'for' 'the people'.[9] Culture is a shared environment, which often appeals to people's emotions and processes of self-identification, providing a medium for the construction of self and community, and for the process of meaning-making. It also provides a language by which people may express what is most meaningful to them, a repertoire or canon which 'gives us a way to evaluate in the presence of others who we are, what we believe and do, and why'.[10] Although sometimes denigrated as simply trivial and superficial, popular culture can in fact be seen as 'cultivating' mind and spirit, providing webs or matrices of meaning and key resources for those exploring questions of belief and spirituality. The arts in particular, like theology, can open up questions of ultimate human concern and provide resources for exploring those questions.[11] Cultural practices and expressions also provide the means for religious experience, which is often constructed through engagement with liturgy and iconography, or with music, dance and other media, rather than in some mystical, privatized space.[12] Those who choose to study and write about popular culture need to recognize that we are not somehow above and aloof from it; rather, we have been shaped by the cultures which we have experienced, and remain involved with them emotionally, intellectually, and existentially.[13]

Companion to the Bible and Culture (ed. John F.W. Sawyer; Oxford: Blackwell, 2006, pp. 286-98), for example, focuses on biblical resonances in the works of classical composers, such as Handel, Bach and Mendelssohn, with discussion ending at Benjamin Britten. The glaring omission of any engagement with contemporary music, in such a wide-ranging study of culture, is disappointing.

9. Elaine Graham, 'What We Make of the World: The Turn to 'Culture' in Theology and the Study of Religion', in *Between Sacred and Profane: Researching Religion and Popular Culture* (ed. Gordon Lynch; London: IB Taurus, 2008), p. 66; Simon Frith, 'Popular Culture', in *A Dictionary of Cultural and Critical Theory* (ed. Michael Payne; Oxford: Blackwell, 1996), pp. 415-17.

10. Lynn Schofield Clark, 'Why Study Popular Culture?', in *Between Sacred and Profane* (ed. Lynch), pp. 9-11. See also Anthony B. Pinn and Monica R. Miller, 'Introduction: Intersections of Culture and Religion in African-American Communities', *Culture and Religion* 10 (March 2009), pp. 3-4.

11. Graham, 'What We Make of the World', pp. 68, 76, 79-81. See also Jeremy Begbie, *Resounding Truth: Christian Wisdom in the World of Music* (Grand Rapids, MI: Baker Academic, 2007), pp. 15-17, 306-307.

12. Gordon Lynch, 'What is this 'Religion' in the Study of Religion and Popular Culture?', in *Between Sacred and Profane* (ed. Lynch), p. 137.

13. On the need for all readers of texts (be they ancient and contemporary) to be self-consciously aware of their own baggage of personal experiences and prior assumptions, see Alastair G. Hunter, *Psalms* (London: Routledge, 1999), pp. 15-17, 33-40.

Connections between sex and spirituality are suggested and explored in various ways in today's popular culture. Hearing the song 'You Light Up my Life', Homer Simpson concludes that the singer is expressing romantic love, while his wife Marge thinks that the song is about God.[14] 'Sister Act', a hit film recently revived as a London and Broadway musical, sees a traditional Catholic hymn reinvigorated as a syncopated, soulful gospel-rock song, while the 1960s hit love song 'My Guy' is effortlessly transformed into a celebration of 'My God'.[15] In Quentin Tarantino's award-winning film 'Pulp Fiction', two hit men who are discussing oral sex show reverence towards a woman's vulva, referring to it as 'the Holiest of Holies'.[16] Bestselling Brazilian author Paulo Coelho devotes an entire novel to exploring 'the sacred nature' of sex and love, with sex at its best portrayed as the 'language of the soul' which enables people to know God; in a subsequent interview he proposes that sex is a physical manifestation of God in the world.[17] Turning to popular political writings, we find Barack Obama commenting on the role of faith in the USA's social fabric: 'I also think faith can fortify a young woman's sense of self, a young man's sense of responsibility, and the sense of reverence all young people should have for the act of sexual intimacy'. His use here of 'reverence', a term commonly associated with encounters with the divine and the holy, provides another example of the blurring of boundaries between the desire to connect deeply with the divine and the desire for intimacy at the human level.[18]

On Songs

In order to narrow my field of inquiry to something manageable, I choose to focus on one particular aspect of popular culture: songs. One of the most pervasive of human cultural activities down the centuries, music has become still more ubiquitous in recent times, especially with the development of digital recording technologies. Music functions in many cultures (including my own) as a means of profound expression and communication, even as an essential integrator of life. Some songs may be simply superficial enter-

14. The Simpsons, Episode 8F10, 'I Married Marge', 1991; cited in Michael J. Gilmour, *Gods and Guitars: Seeking the Sacred in Post-1960s Popular Music* (Waco, TX: Baylor University Press, 2009), p. 18.

15. 'Sister Act', Touchstone Pictures, 1992.

16. See the clip from Quentin Tarantino's film 'Pulp Fiction' at [http://www.youtube.com/watch?v=wTAh_ih8oCA&feature=related], accessed 1 Dec. 2010.

17. Paulo Coelho, *Eleven Minutes* (trans. Margaret Jull Costa; London: Harper Collins, 2003), pp. 141, 187, 263. See also his interview with Laura Sheahen in the appendix to *The Alchemist* (London: Harper Collins, 1995), n.p.

18. Barack Obama, *The Audacity of Hope* (Canongate, 2008), p. 215.

tainment and escapism, unoriginal and formulaic throwaway products.[19] Yet songs also provide a means by which people process and weave together life's strands, revealing deep levels of their thought life, beliefs, emotions and related behaviour, while also communicating the complexities of their experiences.[20]

As a part and product of today's Western culture, I want to understand and respond to what I find that culture saying, particularly in the influential area of music.[21] As someone with a particular interest in the Christian Bible, I wonder whether any biblical songs might point towards, or away from, a connection between sexual and spiritual intimacy. As a Christian minister, I am aware of contemporary worship songs, and look for ways in which the words of these songs may have been shaped by the ancient biblical texts, and also by the contemporary culture of the songwriters. In what follows, I seek to draw these various threads together. My aim is not simply to enjoy setting up a conversation between biblical texts and contemporary songs, but in so doing to enable a deeper understanding to emerge from the conversation, which may enrich both myself and other readers.[22]

In the contemporary aspect of my research, I narrow the scope further by primarily considering rock and pop songs from those mainstream singers/ songwriters who have the highest profile, as evidenced by volume of record sales plus high-profile awards. Similarly, I consider worship songs which are sung and sold most widely in the UK today, particularly in evangelical and charismatic church circles. Acknowledging how difficult it is to identify a construct as elusive as 'mainstream culture' or 'dominant popular discourse' (and recognizing the debates over whether such phenomena can be said to exist at all), I look to sales and awards as concrete, if limited, indicators. Defining 'popularity' by consumption is itself problematic: even

19. On Theodor Adorno's acerbic critique of popular culture, and responses to it, see Begbie, *Resounding Truth*, pp. 252-57.

20. Begbie, *Resounding Truth*, pp. 33-34. See also Roberta R. King, 'Toward a Discipline of Christian Ethnomusicology: A Missiological Paradigm', *Missiology* 33 (2004), pp. 298-300.

21. Philip Tagg claims that popular music occupies parts of the average Westerner's brain for a quarter of their waking life (P. Tagg, 'Analysing Popular Music: Theory, Method and Practice', in *Reading Pop: Approaches to Textual Analysis in Popular Music* [ed. Richard Middleton; Oxford: Oxford University Press, 2003], pp. 72, 101). We may require more evidence in support of Tagg's striking statistic, but the ubiquity today of headphones, along with CDs, radio, film scores, background music in shops and TV adverts, plus the huge growth in reception of music on-line, all testify to the weight of his assertion.

22. Cf. Athalya Brenner's remarks in her Introduction to *Culture, Entertainment and the Bible* (ed. George Aichele; JSOTSup, 309; Sheffield: Sheffield Academic Press, 2000), pp. 7-12.

assuming the sales figures are accurate, they give no evidence as to why these goods were chosen and whether or not they were really valued by the consumers (effective marketing may, for example, prompt us to buy a CD which turns out to be a disappointment).[23] Nonetheless, sales can provide at least a rough yardstick of cultural significance: these are the songs which, through their popularity and widespread dissemination, reflect some of the ways in which intimacy is perceived in popular culture and, at the same time, have an influence on the development of those perceptions. High-profile awards from within the music industry further enhance that popularity and dissemination.[24] I have restricted my range to songs which use the English language. The time-frame under consideration also needs some limitations; in order to keep the flavour genuinely contemporary, I will focus largely (though not exclusively) on songs produced or re-released since the year 2000. The songs selected will be those which seem to blur the boundaries between desire for God and sexual desire, such as Leonard Cohen's 'Hallelujah', which is cited in the title of this Prelude.

Biblical Songs

In the biblical component of my work, I choose to focus on a comparison of songs found in the Hebrew Bible which seem to provide the most striking expressions of relational intimacy: namely, the Song of Songs and the Psalms.[25] That the Psalms refer to human relationship with God has never been in dispute; yet at times they use language which may have intimations of intimacy. That the Song of Songs is primarily expressing erotic love

---

23. Simon Frith, *Performing Rites: Evaluating Popular Music* (Oxford University Press, 1998), p. 15.

24. Even advocates of other forms of music acknowledge that rock and pop remain the dominant strands in contemporary popular music. See Jeremy Gilbert and Ewan Pearson, *Discographies: Dance Music Culture and the Politics of Sound* (London: Routledge, 1999), p. 38; also pp. 158-60 on debates over the distinctions between different forms of 'popular culture'.

25. It seems certain that at least some of the Psalms were used in corporate worship with musical accompaniment; see Susan E. Gillingham, *The Poems and Psalms of the Hebrew Bible* [Oxford: Oxford University Press, 1994], pp. 45-510; Samuel Terrien, *The Psalms: Strophic Structure and Theological Commentary* (Eerdmans Critical Commentary; Cambridge: Eerdmans, 2003), pp. 26-36; John Eaton, *The Psalms: A Historical and Spiritual Commentary with and Introduction and New Translation* (London: T. & T. Clark, 2003), pp. 9-13. A recent attempt to discern original melodies for the Psalms, based on deciphering the cantillational accents of the MT, was presented at the Conference 'Conflict and Convergence: Jewish and Christian Approaches to the Psalms', Worcester College, Oxford, 23 Sept. 2010. What difference, if any, ancient authors and collectors perceived between a 'poem' and a 'song' is not clear; what is clear is that various psalms describe themselves as songs, as does the Song of Songs.

between human beings is today widely agreed—but the history of interpretation of the Song has also touched on the relationship between God and humanity to a considerable degree. Therefore these seem to be the biblical songs of greatest relevance.

The Psalter itself provides a very large body of poems/songs, far too many for each to be studied in detail in this limited piece of work. Therefore I further narrow my focus to a comparison of the Song of Songs with particular psalms. While standing out because they use language suggestive of intimacy, these particular psalms present some ideas that find wider echoes among the other psalms; thus they may serve as a lens through which light from the rest of the Psalter can be focused onto the Song of Songs, and vice versa.[26]

Texts in Conversation

Why attempt a comparative study? We might do so seeking to uncover authorial influences of one text on another; but these can be hard to demonstrate convincingly.[27] It seems more fruitful simply to compare texts in the hope that doing so may illuminate our understanding of each. No text can exist as a self-sufficient whole, for two obvious reasons. Firstly, the writer is a reader of texts before becoming a creator of texts; therefore all writing is suffused with references, quotations and influences, some overt and others unacknowledged. Secondly, each reader of the particular text in question is already a reader of texts, and thus brings to this latest text a cross-fertilization of phrases and ideas from other texts previously read. Hence the growing recognition of the importance of what Julia Kristeva has termed 'intertextuality' (or 'transtextuality', to use Gérard Genette's subsequent refinement of the terminology).[28]

---

26. I will at times abbreviate Song of Songs to 'the Song', 'Song' or 'Canticles'. All chapter and verse references refer to those used in English translations such as the NRSV, rather than those in BHS. Biblical quotations are from the NRSV, unless indicated otherwise. On the general acceptability of NRSV as an adequate translation despite the uncertainty of meaning, see Hunter, *Psalms*, pp. 2-3, 8-16.

27. In her comparative study of texts, Fokkelien van Dijk-Hemmes claims that Hosea 2.5-7 must be borrowing phrases from Song of Songs, but the evidence is far from conclusive. See Fokkelien van Dijk-Hemmes, 'The Imagination and the Power of Imagination: An Intertextual Analysis of Two Biblical Love Songs: The Song of Songs and Hosea 2', in *The Poetical Books: A Sheffield Reader* (ed. David J.A. Clines; Sheffield: Sheffield Academic Press, 1997), pp. 173-87. Suggestions that Song of Songs gives a response to the picture of sexual relationships gone awry, as depicted in Genesis 2–3, are more convincing, although dependence of one text upon another still cannot be proven; see Phyllis Trible, *God and the Rhetoric of Sexuality* (Philadelphia: Fortress, 1978), pp. 144-65.

28. Michael Worton and Judith Still (eds.), *Intertextuality: Theories and Practices* (Manchester: Manchester University Press, 1990), 'Introduction', pp. 1-2, 22-23. See

Dialogue between texts can help us shape meaning. In Danna Fewell's words, 'Texts talk to one another; they echo one another; they push one another; they war with one another. They are voices in chorus, in conflict, and in competition.'[29] The similarities between texts invite conversation, while differences allow each text to be affected by the other. Indeed, all texts are embedded in a larger web of related texts, bound only by human culture and language itself; so intertextual reading is inevitable.[30]

Which texts are best for this kind of reading, and why? Recognition of an intertextual connection is where the individuality and ideology of the reader comes to the forefront. In some cases, this methodology may seem to lack sufficient controls and boundaries, and may produce results that seem strained, if not entirely fanciful. But at its best, it can refresh and expand our understanding of both texts. In this case, it also builds on a canonical mandate for intertextual reading evident in the superscriptions of the Psalms, many of which make connections with narratives about the life of David, giving the reader access to David's inner life and intimate feelings in ways which she or he would otherwise never have considered. The continuation of a tradition of intertextual reading is evident in the frequent quotations from and allusions to the Hebrew Bible found in the New Testament. It continued in subsequent centuries, as will be seen in some of the examples cited in Chapter Two.[31]

An unusual example of intertextuality is found in Fiona Black and Cheryl Exum's reading of the Song of Songs alongside a Victorian stained-glass

---

also Stefan K. Alkier, 'Intertextuality and the Semiotics of Biblical Texts', in *Reading the Bible Intertextually* (ed. Richard B. Hays, Stefan Alkier and Leroy A. Huizenga; Waco, Texas: Baylor University Press, 2009), pp. 3-11.

29. Danna N. Fewell (ed.), *Reading Between Texts: Intertextuality and the Hebrew Bible* (Louisville, Kentucky: Westminster/John Knox Press, 1992), pp. 12, 17.

30. Intertextual allusions are also an inevitable feature of songwriting, since songwriters constantly appropriate the texts of others. For example, the image of a world where 'all the colours bleed into one' can be found in U2's 'I Still Haven't Found What I'm Looking For', Oasis's 'Part of the Queue', Coldplay's 'Square One' and K.T. Tunstall's 'False Alarm': see U2, *The Joshua Tree* (Island Records, 1987); Oasis, *Don't Believe the Truth* (Big Brother Recordings, 2005); Coldplay, *X&Y* (Parlophone, 2005); K.T. Tunstall, *Eye to the Telescope* (Virgin Records, 2006). A further allusion might be traced in Radiohead's 'Jigsaw Falling Into Place', with the multi-coloured text of the CD sleeve notes giving way to a plain white script as the song speaks of a bad day disappearing and 'all blurring into one'; see Radiohead, *In Rainbows* (Self-released, 2007).

31. See Beth LaNeel Tanner, *The Book of Psalms through the Lens of Intertextuality* (SBL Monographs 26; New York: Peter Lang, 2001), pp. 31, 35-36, 58-59, 69, 74. Her own reading of Psalm 112 alongside Proverbs 31.10-31 (pp. 141-53) provides a good model of an intertextual reading using two of the Hebrew Bible's poetic books. For an intertextual reading involving the Song of Songs with Genesis 2-3, see Trible's 'Love's Lyrics Redeemed' (*God and the Rhetoric of Sexuality* pp. 144-65).

window made up of images based on the Song. In this case there is no doubt that the biblical text has been a major influence in the creation of the window; but nonetheless the window's selective treatment of the Song (particularly its highlighting of frustration, unfulfilled desire, and violence) prompts these two readers to reconsider familiar understandings of the biblical text, which have tended to highlight the delights and fulfilment of love and perhaps to neglect the more disturbing aspects of the Song.[32] Another striking example of intertextual reading is found in Michael Fox's influential comparison of the Song of Songs with ancient Egyptian love songs. He argues that by comparing structurally or thematically related works (whether or not the observed similarities are due to the influence of one work on the other) we may discover models—of attitudes, concepts, forms of expression, literary devices, and so on—which help us fine-tune our reading of the texts. Fox further argues that comparative study is particularly effective if we look for differences at the very points where the texts show similarities: '... we can best understand the individuality of a text by discovering where it diverges from the works it most resembles. This is so even when we compare texts where there can be no question of influence of the one on the other.'[33] Paul Ricoeur proposes a similar approach in his search for 'points of intersection' between the Song and other biblical texts which use nuptial imagery, with each augmenting the meaning of the other: 'Let us therefore allow all these texts to project themselves on one another and let us gather those sparks of meaning that fly up at their points of friction'.[34] This approach seems fruitful, and is one I shall use when comparing the Song of Songs with the Psalms.

32. Fiona C. Black and J. Cheryl Exum, 'Semiotics in Stained Glass: Edward Burne-Jones' Song of Songs', in *Biblical Studies/Cultural Studies: The Third Sheffield Colloquium* (ed. J. Cheryl Exum and Stephen D. Moore; JSOTSup, 266; Sheffield: Sheffield Academic Press, 1998), pp. 337-42. For another interdisciplinary intertextual reading, involving Ps. 137 and Claude Lanzmann's film 'Shoah', see Karl A. Plank, 'By the Waters of a Death Camp: An Intertextual Reading of Psalm 137', *Literature and Theology* 22 (2008), pp. 180-94.

33. Michael V. Fox, *The Song of Songs and the Ancient Egyptian Love Songs* (Madison, WI: University of Wisconsin Press, 1985), pp. xxiii, xxvi.

34. André LaCocque and Paul Ricoeur, *Thinking Biblically: Exegetical and Hermeneutical Studies* (trans. David Pellauer; Chicago: University of Chicago Press, 1998), p. 303. At this point Ricoeur is comparing Song of Songs briefly with texts from Revelation and the Gospel according to John, along with a sustained focus on Genesis 2.23-24. See also Bakhtin's insistence on 'dialogic truth' through conversation between unharmonized voices (Jennifer Pfenniger, 'Bhaktin Reads the Song of Songs', *JSOT* 34 [2010], pp. 336-36). For a critical evaluation of various intertextual approaches from a canonical perspective, see Brevard S. Childs, 'Critique of Recent Intertextual Canonical Interpretation', *ZAW* 115 (2003), pp. 173-84.

My overall aim is to listen to particular questions which popular culture seems to be asking through today's music, and then to hear what the biblical songs may say about those questions, and whether the questions in turn may have things to say about the biblical texts. I acknowledge that attempting such a cross-disciplinary approach (involving both Biblical Studies and Cultural Studies) entails the risk of failing to do justice to the complexities and subtleties of both areas of study. But I judge the rewards to be worth that risk.

My title, 'Yearning for You', is deliberately ambiguous. The demise of the traditional pronoun 'thou' has left the English language with only the multi-tasking 'you', which may refer to relationships with another (singular) or with others (plural); and the other(s) in question may be either human or divine. This linguistic ambiguity perhaps reflects an ambivalence in our culture: what kinds of different relationships are we seeking? Is intimacy found only at an individual level, or can it also have a corporate dimension? Is it possible to have an intimacy with a divine other (whom I term 'You')? If so, how does that compare with intimacy with a human 'you'?[35]

Outline

In Chapter 1, the rationale for focusing particularly on song lyrics is explored. A survey of relevant contemporary rock and worship songs follows. Attention is given mostly to music produced since the year 2000 by the most widely known artists in their fields, highlighting the ways in which they blur the boundaries between 'yearning for you' and 'yearning for You'.

Chapter 2 examines the history of interpretation of both the Song of Songs and the Psalms, with particular attention given to interpreters who have suggested parallels between them in the areas of desire and intimacy.

The biblical texts are considered in more depth in Chapter 3. In this major exegetical chapter, passages from the Psalms and Song of Songs are set up as conversation partners. Themes such as desire, absence, longing, hearing, delight, feasting, physicality, mutuality and security are examined, highlighting both connections and contrasts between the texts.

In Chapter 4 I widen the circle of conversation, reconsidering the voices of the popular songs highlighted in Chapter 1 in the light of what has been discovered in the Psalms and the Song of Songs. Issues of ambiguity are examined, along with parallels and contrasts. Then I consider whether yearning for a human lover may be seen as a means, a sacrament, or a metaphor for yearning for God, with further reflections on the implications of a metaphorical understanding.

The Finale provides a brief summary and concluding reflections.

---

35. In what follows I use lower and upper case to distinguish between a human 'you' and a divine 'You', a distinction which is not apparent in my overall title.

1

'LET THERE BE LOVE':
YEARNING FOR YOU/YOU IN CONTEMPORARY MUSIC

Can Rock Be Read?

Writing about music can feel strangely tantalizing. Reduced to words on a page, familiar songs become pale shadows of their true selves. Songs need colour, flesh and blood, above all sound. Music needs to be heard, experienced; maybe also seen in a live performance, and shared with others. Certainly it should be felt in the body, in the guts, not simply surveyed from a safe distance by the intellect.[1]

Music-making is an embodied experience which is done through the mind, eyes, mouth, hands and sometimes other parts of the body. Listening to music is also a physical activity, involving more than just the ears; some argue that listening cannot be done without activating the whole human body, at least in tapping to the beat, if not in the full movement of dance.[2] Words on the page cannot convey the visceral impact of the thumping bass line, the emotional vista opened up by a particular chord, the tension built up by the singer's slight pause. What about the timbre of the voice, the effect on the hearer of the rasping snarl or the breathy whisper into the microphone? What is the song without the passionate intensity poured out as the voice reaches the highest note of the melody, or the fatalistic sense of

---

1. Cf. Mark Roncace and Dan W. Clanton Jr, 'Introduction: Teaching the Bible with Music' in *Teaching the Bible through Popular Culture and the Arts* (ed. Mark Roncace and Patrick Gray; Atlanta, GA: SBL, 2007), p. 10; their comment about opera's holistic demands and impact on the listener can be applied to other types of music. Sigmund Freud confessed to being disturbed by his own response to music, because his pleasure in art lay in comprehending it. Finding himself stirred by music in ways that he could not explain, his analytic mind rebelled against being moved by something without knowing what exactly it was that affected him this way, and why it did so; see Simon Frith, *Performing Rites,* p. 260.

2. On the physicality of music making and music hearing, see Begbie, *Resounding Truth,* pp. 213-19.

surrender as the melody line descends? It could be argued that an approach that focuses purely on song lyrics as texts lacks validity. Does the whole process of analysing songs ignore (or defuse) the emotional and sensual heat which gives them their power to please and to threaten?[3] Is writing about music the equivalent of 'dancing about architecture ... a really stupid thing to want to do', as Elvis Costello (among others) is reputed to have said?[4]

The fact that far more seasoned analysts than I share these misgivings but still persevere with the project gives some comfort. In seeking to establish the nature and location of the text itself in popular music, Richard Middleton acknowledges the significance of cultural contexts, social and emotional effects, and the bodily movements which accompany and perhaps generate the music. This complex mix of factors has led some studies to gravitate towards 'consumptionism'—locating the textual moment, the moment of meaning production, overwhelmingly in acts of use by listeners. Content analysis of lyrics alone may become simplistic; a superficial surface-fetishizing can be a danger. Middleton further argues that the methodological hesitations found in much of the recent work analysing the texts of popular songs suggests deep-lying doubts even among practitioners about the viability of the enterprise itself. Yet he himself continues with that enterprise, focusing on musicology, hermeneutics, performance and interpretation—but also giving significant space to analysis of song lyrics. He notes the way Mikhael Bakhtin's argument that meaning is always socially and historically situated, and generally specific, is proving increasingly influential among analysts of popular music. If meaning is produced through dialogue with previous discursive moments and also with the music's addressees, then a giant intertextuality results, between texts, styles, genres and social groups (and also within individual examples of each). If any emergent analytic paradigm possesses the potential to become dominant in popular music studies, it may be this kind of 'dialogics'.[5] This gives me encouragement in

---

3. Cf. Susan McClary and Robert Walser, 'Start Making Sense! Musicology Wrestles with Rock', in *On Record: Rock, Pop and the Written Word* (ed. Simon Frith and A. Goodwin; London: Routledge, 1990), pp. 287, 290; also Umberto Fiori, 'Listening to Peter Gabriel's 'I Have the Touch'', in *Reading Pop* (ed. Middleton), pp. 183-91; Simon Frith, *Performing Rites*, pp. 141-42.

Readers can reduce the shortcomings of text alone by hearing most of the songs I refer to at www.spotify.com, www.last.fm and www.youtube.com. Happily, this can be done on a minimal budget; concert ticket prices, alas, are a different matter.

4. See Begbie, *Resounding Truth*, p. 14; Alan P. Scott, 'Talking About Music' [http://home.pacifier.com/~ascott/they/tamildaa.htm], accessed 2 Mar. 2011.

5. Richard Middleton, 'Introduction: Locating the Popular Music Text', in *Reading Pop*, pp. 1-19, especially pp. 1, 12-14. See also Gilbert and Pearson, *Discographies*, pp. 38-53.

seeking a specific and limited dialogue between ancient and modern musical texts. The contingent nature of the interpretive process means this cannot become an attempt at univocality and hegemonic closure; but nonetheless the conversation I am pursuing can be a valid and valuable part of this much larger ongoing dialogue.

Attempting to quantify the impact of songs on those who hear them is a daunting undertaking. That which brings an epiphany for one person may simply be background sound, or a brief lifestyle choice, for another. Rock is 'resistance' to the status quo for some, but simply relaxation for others—perhaps even a mixture of the two. Messages encoded in the lyrics (or sounds) of a song may be received simply as entertaining reflections on some distant world-view, with no connection to the hearer's current realities.[6] Alternatively, those messages may resonate with the listener in ways that are oblique to the content of the lyrics.[7] We must further note that the impact of music on the listener is likely to be in the emotional dimension as distinct from the purely cognitive and rational. Jeremy Begbie notes a common view that music is (or ought to be) an outward expression of inner emotional urges and surges, sometimes with the aim of stimulating emotion. He prefers to see music as something which 'can concentrate our emotional life', representing but also educating and shaping the listener by giving voice to how they feel and how they could or should feel.[8] Furthermore, it may be factors such as melody, harmony or cadence which truly affect certain listeners, evidenced most obviously in music that is purely instrumental. Even when music does have lyrics, these may be of minimal interest to some who hear it. Sometimes the lyrics can even be in tension with other aspects of the music, as verbal and musical rhetoric seem to struggle with each other; occasionally this can create an ambiguity which invites deconstruction.[9]

However, we need nonetheless to acknowledge the priority and impact of words in particular cultures, not least our own. Jacques Derrida's assess-

---

6. P. Tagg, 'Analysing Popular Music', in *Reading Pop*, p. 98. See also Motti Regev's comments on the work of Simon Frith, *PopMus* 21 (2002), especially p. 136.

7. For example, early Black Sabbath songs have a clear emphasis on the occult; but research seems to imply that they resonate with teenage boys in terms of issues of rebellion and masculinity, rather than any specifically religious inclinations (see Pete Ward, "The Eucharist and the Turn to Culture', in *Between Sacred and Profane*, p. 91).

8. Begbie, *Resounding Truth*, pp. 214, 302-304.

9. For example, Kate Bush's early song 'Feel It' (on the album *The Kick Inside* [EMI, 1983]) depicts a sexual encounter or fantasy. The lyrics alone might suggest an enjoyable experience; yet the music seems to contradict this, with its disrupted melody and rhythm, and vocal emphasis given to words such as 'nervous', 'desperate', 'nobody else'; see Simon Frith and Angela McRobbie, 'Rock and Sexuality', in *On Record*, p. 386; also Simon Frith, *Performing Rites*, p. 182.

ment of Western culture includes his assertion that it is essentially 'logocentric': both implicitly and explicitly a privileged status is given to verbal language, particularly speech. Mainstream popular music continues to reflect this in the priority it gives to audible lyrics, along with a clear melody line. Look around you at a rock concert or on the dance floor, and you will find most people singing along with some or all of the vocal line; as we identify with the voice of the singer, we imbibe and then articulate for ourselves the words which that voice is expressing. Frith insists that words do matter to people, and these 'words in performance' remain central to how popular songs are heard and evaluated, both by ordinary listeners and by analysts assessing the songs' political and social value.[10] The act of combining words with music does not devalue them or dissipate their power; it is more likely to elevate them, adding vividness and a new depth of intensity.[11] As listeners we may find that contemporary music, through both its musical content and lyrical ideology, can produce an 'excess' which helps define our 'mattering maps', that is, our sense of what matters most, of how to develop our identity and find empowerment.[12]

So the overall importance in our culture of text, both sung and read, is not to be underestimated. The fact that we have no access to any original musical arrangements of the Psalms and Song of Songs may be a limitation and a source of regret to us, but it does not prevent us finding profit in studying the lyrics themselves. The contemporary songs which I am examining in this chapter may not be valued and preserved by subsequent generations as the biblical ones have been by our ancestors, but the basic principle still applies.

The advent and growth of music videos has brought a further dimension to the ways in which we experience popular music. The relation between the music (including lyrics) and the images of the video can be complex and subtle, with correspondences ranging from strict to enigmatic. Frith cites sur-

---

10. Frith, *Performing Rites*, pp. 71, 159, 166, 172. See also Gilmour, *Gods and Guitars*, pp. 10-17; Begbie, *Resounding Truth*, p. 3; Astor, Peter, 'The Poetry of Rock: Song Lyrics Are Not Poems But the Words Still Matter', *PopMus* 29 (2010), pp. 143-48. For an example of lyrical analysis, see Greg Watson, 'The Bedroom Blues: Love and Lust in the Lyrics of Early Female Blues Artists', *Language and Literature* 15 (2006), pp. 331-56.

11. Gilbert and Pearson, *Discographies*, pp. 33, 39-42; also p. 57 for their comments on Jacques Derrida. See also Sean Cubitt, '"Maybellene": Meaning and the Listening Subject', in *Reading Pop*, pp. 149, 155; and Yngvar Steinholt, 'You Can't Rid a Song of its Words: Notes on the Hegemony of Lyrics in Russian Rock Songs', *PopMus* 22 (2003), pp. 90, 95-98.

12. Cf. Lawrence Grossberg, 'The Media Economy of Rock Culture: Cinema, Post-Modernity and Authenticity', in *Sound and Vision: The Music Video Reader* (ed. Simon Frith, Andrew Goodwin and Lawrence Grossberg; London: Routledge, 1993). pp. 178-79.

vey evidence indicating that the primary reason why teenagers watch music videos is not to find out what performers look like, but to find out what the words mean. Alf Björnberg concludes that the music video is now such a diverse and heterogenous phenomenon that all kinds of arguments may be 'proved', depending simply on which videos are called on as support. Nonetheless, he argues that, despite postmodernist prophecies of 'the destruction of meaning', watchers of music videos continue to derive pleasure from the production of meaning induced by them (albeit a temporary and volatile meaning). Building on the work of Middleton, he concludes that the predominant syntax of popular music (and of the accompanying videos) lies between the extremes of a narrative/linear approach on the one hand, and an epic/circular approach on the other; namely, in a lyrical/elliptical form, which often has some linear movement, but ultimately tends to return in some degree to where it started. Rather than explaining a narrative inherent in a song, or introducing a narrative to the song, videos are more likely to underline the lyrical, reflective character already present within the song—and may, at the same time, open up various fields of association in the user. While focusing mostly on music rather than lyrics, Björnberg points out that some music videos offer a visual narrative, and often this is based on lyrics within the song which contain some degree of narrative.[13] This confirms the primacy of the song over the images; a music video is supportive of and ultimately constrained by the song (for example, in its length, and the inability of the characters seen in the video to say anything beyond the words of the song). The song remains the 'main event', it is not subsumed into background noise, as often happens with a traditional film score.[14] In what follows, I shall refer primarily to song lyrics, and intermittently to videos which seem to shed light on or offer some kind of interpretation of the particular song lyrics under scrutiny. I shall not argue for coherent narratives or epic dimensions in the songs (or videos), but simply for allusions and ambiguities which I perceive at various points in the lyrics and which relate to the particular theme of yearning for a human or a divine lover.

13. Simon Frith, *Performing Rites,* p. 159; Alf Björnberg, 'Structural Relationships of Music and Images in Music Video', in *Reading Pop* (ed. Middleton), pp. 259-66, 373-74. There is plenty of ambiguity and room for debate in this area. For example, Anthon Corbijn's film *Linear* presents a journey narrative for the U2 album *No Line On the Horizon*; whether this is inherent in the songs, or imposed on them, is debatable. See [www.nolineonthehorizon.com/bonus], accessed 12 May 2009. See also Carol Vernalis, 'The Aesthetics of Music Video: An Analysis of Madonna's "Cherish"', *PopMus* 17 (1998), particularly pp. 162-65, 173-75.

14. For an alternative view, which emphasizes the opaque nature of music videos and their capacity to pique listeners' curiosity and widen interpretive possibilities by adding ideas not suggested in the lyrics, see Carol Vernalis, 'The Functions of Lyrics in Music Video', *JPMS* 14 (2002), pp. 13-15, 21-23.

I shall largely ignore questions of authorial intention, except occasionally when the singer or songwriter clearly seeks to make part of their intentions known. This traditional bone of contention in biblical studies can be equally elusive when considering contemporary music. Even when the songwriters are available for interview, there are limits to what can be achieved in establishing what was in the writer's mind when creating the song. When Radiohead's Thom Yorke sings, 'You are all I need, you are all I need', the rest of the song is vivid but opaque (mirrored by the impressionistic visual artwork of the CD packaging); with no clear indication of desire for anything beyond human intimacy, is it legitimate to surmise a longing for the divine at some subconscious level of which the songwriter is himself possibly unaware? Second-guessing the subconscious is a perilous occupation. When Dido sings, 'If I don't believe in love, nothing is good for me, / if I don't believe in love, nothing will last for me, / if I don't believe in love, nothing is new for me', can we detect an echo of Paul's threefold declaration in 1 Corinthians 13 ('If I speak ... but do not have love, I am a noisy gong or a clanging cymbal. If I have ... but do not have love, I am nothing. If I give ... but do not have love, I gain nothing' [1 Cor. 13.1-3])?[15] Even if we do decide to argue for a Pauline echo, a further question arises: is the singer-songwriter aware of that echo? Perhaps she heard that chapter from 1 Corinthians read at a friend's wedding some time previously, and something half-remembered lodged in her subconscious, to emerge later while she was writing songs.[16] Or perhaps biblical texts simply provide songwriters with a "language arsenal", words and images to be drawn on without much interest in their original context or connotations. The equation is further complicated by the simple question: Does the singer mean what they say? This cannot be assumed; the artist may choose to explore a particular persona or attitude. In examining the complex ways in which the listener may experience the pop singer's personality through their voice, Frith concludes that it is virtually impossible to disentangle vocal realism from vocal irony.[17]

Analysing the creative process is notoriously difficult. Andrew Motion's description of his experience of writing poetry seems apt with reference to its creative cousin, the songwriting process:

> I've always thought that poems that work, no doubt like paintings or
> pieces of music that work, are the result of a curious relationship between
> the side of your mind that knows what's going on and is educated, alert,

15. Radiohead, 'All I Need', from *In Rainbows*; Dido, 'Don't Believe in Love', from *Safe Trip Home* (Sony BMG, 2008).

16. My own title is another case in point. Did I adapt the phrase 'yearning for you' from a similar phrase in the song 'Praise Is Rising' by Brenton Brown and Paul Baloche (Integrity, Hosanna music, 2006)? Or did I come across the song after devising my title? I simply cannot remember.

17. Frith, *Performing Rites*, pp. 198-99.

fully conscious, manipulative in the sense of structuring and organising, all those sorts of things, and the side of your mind that frankly hasn't a clue what's going on and is full of fetid bubbles that rise up from the deep, primeval swamp of your un- and subconscious.[18]

U2's Bono suggests a similar ambivalence when describing how he wrote the song 'Kite': he felt it was about himself playing with his children, but then when his father died he realized that the song was partly about his father saying goodbye to him. 'That's the thing about songwriting—you're the last to know what you're on about.'[19]

Keeping all of the above in mind, let us listen to various 'texts' (song lyrics) and respond to whatever we find there that seems to blur the boundaries between 'yearning for you' and 'yearning for You'. The quotation from Oasis's 'Let There Be Love' seems an apt heading for this opening chapter, with its allusion to the voice of the divine creator in Genesis 1 blending into the preoccupation of so many contemporary songs, the primacy of love.[20]

In what follows, as previously indicated, I focus on songs which use the English language, primarily those produced (or reissued) since the year 2000. The order followed does not seek to emphasize any particular artist, but is simply alphabetical (using stage names). I begin with mainstream rock and pop music, highlighting love songs which use the language of worship. Then I narrow the focus to Christian subcultures, looking for worship songs which use the language of romance. Although for clarity I have chosen to delineate this narrowing of focus with a separate section and heading, a clear distinction between two different kinds of music is not being suggested. Many contemporary worship songs are clearly influenced by the style and idiom of popular music. Moreover, some of the mainstream rock songs highlighted here could fit equally well under a heading of 'worship songs'; this ambiguity is the heart of what I am trying to explore.

Music Acclaimed in Mainstream Culture

Beyoncé: I Can Feel your Halo

Following huge success in the group 'Destiny's Child', Beyoncé Knowles has matched and in some ways surpassed this in recent years with her solo career. She received five Grammy awards for her first solo album, and then

---

18. Andrew Motion, Interview in *Third Way* (April 2009), p. 17.

19. Bono, interviewed by Niall Stokes, Hot Press Annual 2002 [http://www.atu2.com/news/article.src?ID=2082], accessed 20 May 2009. On different levels of meaning in U2 songs, see Robert Vagacs, *Religious Nuts, Political Fanatics: U2 in Theological Perspective* (Eugene, OR: Cascade, 2005), pp. 14-16.

20. Oasis, 'Let There Be Love', from *Don't Believe the Truth* (Big Brother Recordings, 2005).

a record six Grammys for her third solo album. Her total record sales are estimated at 75 million.[21]

One of the best known songs from that third album is 'Halo', which achieved considerable success as a single in UK and worldwide during 2008 and 2009:

> Everywhere I'm looking now
> I'm surrounded by your embrace
> Baby, I can see your halo
> You know you're my saving grace
> You're everything I need and more
> It's written all over your face
> Baby, I can feel your halo
> Pray it won't fade away
>
> I can feel your halo
> I can see your halo
> I can feel your halo
> I can see your halo
> Halo, ooh ooh....
>
> Hit me like a ray of sun
> Burning through my darkest night
> You're the only one that I want
> Think I'm addicted to your light
> I swore I'd never fall again
> But this don't even feel like falling
> Gravity can't forget
> To pull me back to the ground again.[22]

---

21. 'Record sales' includes albums, singles, compilation-albums, music videos, as well as downloads of singles and full-length albums. Wherever possible in this chapter I give certified sales figures; if these are not available, estimated figures are quoted, although these may be less reliable. See 'List of Best-Selling Music Artists', *Wikipedia* [http://en.wikipedia.org/wiki/List_of_best-selling_music_artists] and 'Top Selling Artists' *Recording Industry Association of America* [http://riaa.com/goldandplatinum.php?content_selector=top-selling-artists], both accessed 7 June 2011. My aim in quoting these figures is not to achieve total accuracy, but simply to demonstrate that huge numbers of people choose to buy and listen to this music.

22. Beyoncé—'Halo' [http://www.youtube.com/watch?v=qZ0FhVZce2o], accessed 30 June 2009. Clarifying punctuation in these and subsequent lyrics quoted in this chapter is not always straightforward. If the artist has produced lyrics on their own website or on CD sleeve notes, I follow these where available. Otherwise I generally cite lyrics as presented at www.lyricslook.com.

Religious motifs of light, praying, falling and saving grace intertwine with the addictive desire for the one who is 'everything I need and more'. Salvation is sought in the embrace. Clearly this song takes us into the realms of hyperbole, for which love songs are renowned; but what effect does the pervasive religious language have on the song and on the hearer? The recurring halo image seems to suggest a reverent devotion to this flawless other which borders on worship. In the accompanying video both she and her lover are bathed in ethereal light as she sings, suggesting a dream-like, mystical experience. Here is romance suffused with a religious aura.[23]

Leonard Cohen: Hallelujah

While never achieving the worldwide sales figures of some of the other artists mentioned in this chapter, the songs of Leonard Cohen have been highly influential.[24] Love, sex and religion have been recurring and intermingling themes in Cohen's work over many years. His Jewish upbringing, knowledge of Christianity and recent practice of Zen Buddhism all feed into his writing, where references to Jesus and allusions to the Hebrew Bible inform the struggles with relationships and search for meaning explored in his enigmatic lyrics.

One of the songs in Cohen's canon most sung by other artists, 'Suzanne', gives tantalizing glimpses of a woman with a perfect body who sees you as her love; intermingled with this are glimpses of Jesus—and then Suzanne again—touching your perfect body. In another favourite, 'Joan of Arc', the lonely heroine gives her body over to the yearning fire; wedding imagery keeps recurring, as we see her burning at the stake. Elsewhere, Cohen further explores the marital motif: 'I came upon a wedding that old families had contrived: / Bethlehem the bridegroom, / Babylon the bride.' Babylon is a recurring theme in his songs. He seems to equate it with the desires of the flesh; yet it is also a place in which he glimpses possibilities of finding both oneself and God—the unknown one who waits there to hunt for me.

In recent years Cohen's songs have reached a wider audience, as a result of his successful concert tours. A televised broadcast of highlights of the tours began with the song 'Lover, Lover, Lover'.[25] Here, the verses depict an intimate quasi-religious dialogue with a seemingly omniscient 'father',

---

23. Her lover in the video is a strangely distant, 'strong, silent type' who seems incapable of speech; proof perhaps of the Arctic Monkeys' rueful adage that 'love's not only blind, but deaf' (Arctic Monkeys, 'Fake Tales of San Francisco', from *Whatever People Say I Am, That's What I'm Not* [London, Domino, 2006]).

24. When welcoming Cohen into the American Rock and Roll Hall of Fame in 2008, Lou Reed described him as someone in the 'highest and most influential echelon of songwriters'; see [http://en.wikipedia.org/wiki/Leonard_Cohen], accessed 20 May 2009.

25. 'Leonard Cohen: Songs from the Road', broadcast on BBC4, 15 Oct. 2010.

while the choruses repeatedly cry 'lover, lover, lover, lover … come back to me'; sexual and spiritual longing seem to be adjacent, indeed, interwoven. The live album arising from the tours concludes with two songs. In 'The Gypsy's Wife', Cohen sings, 'A ghost climbs on the table in a bridal negligee / She says, "My body is the light, my body is the way"'; here a sexual invitation seems to blur into an encounter with the Johannine Jesus (Jn 8.12; 14.6). The finale is a very brief version of 'Whither Thou Goest', where lyrics drawn from the Hebrew Bible speak tenderly of following an unidentified love:

> Whither thou goest, I will go.
> Wherever thou lodgest, I will lodge.
> Thy people shall be my people,
> Whither thou goest, I will go![26]

The fact that these phrases are based on the words of Ruth addressed to her mother-in-law Naomi (Ruth 1.15) is probably unknown to the majority of today's listeners.

But one Cohen song above all has achieved widespread recognition, particularly in recent years. Originally recorded in 1984, Cohen's 'Hallelujah' was comparatively unknown in the UK until the end of 2008, when his own recording entered the UK singles chart, followed by two further versions (recorded by Alexandra Burke and Jeff Buckley), which achieved the unique feat of occupying the number one and two spots in the chart that Christmas. In total, the song has now been recorded over a hundred and eighty times by a wide variety of artists worldwide, as well as featuring as the soundtrack for films and television shows, and even in school choir concerts. A poll of songwriters in September 2007 voted it one of the fifty best songs of all time.

Cohen wrote a large number of verses for this song over a period of about a year. This accounts for the variety of versions to be heard, even from the lips of Cohen himself; he sang one of his fullest versions at the Glastonbury festival in 2008. The most widely sung versions of the song include some (but not usually all) of the following lyrics:

> Now I've heard there was a secret chord
> That David played, and it pleased the Lord
> But you don't really care for music, do you?
> It goes like this, the fourth, the fifth
> The minor fall, the major lift

---

26. Leonard Cohen, 'Suzanne', 'Joan of Arc' and 'Whither Thou Goest', from *Leonard Cohen: Live in London* (Sony, 2009); Huw Morgan, 'Just Some Joseph Looking for a Manger', *Third Way* (Dec. 2009), pp. 8-12.

The baffled king composing Hallelujah
Hallelujah, Hallelujah
Hallelujah, Hallelujah

Your faith was strong but you needed proof
You saw her bathing on the roof
Her beauty and the moonlight overthrew you
She tied you to a kitchen chair
She broke your throne, and she cut your hair
And from your lips she drew the Hallelujah … *chorus*

Baby I have been here before
I know this room, I've walked this floor
I used to live alone before I knew you.
I've seen your flag on the marble arch
Love is not a victory march
It's a cold and it's a broken Hallelujah … *chorus*

There was a time you let me know
What's really going on below
But now you never show it to me, do you?
And remember when I moved in you
The holy dove was moving too
And every breath we drew was Hallelujah … *chorus*

You say I took the name in vain
I don't even know the name
But if I did, well really, what's it to you?
There's a blaze of light in every word
It doesn't matter which you heard
The holy or the broken Hallelujah … *chorus*

Maybe there's a God above
But all I've ever learned from love
Was how to shoot somebody who outdrew you.
But it's not a cry that you hear at night
It's not somebody who's seen the light
It's a cold and it's a broken Hallelujah … *chorus*

I did my best, it wasn't much
I couldn't feel, so I tried to touch
I've told the truth, I didn't come to fool you
And even though it all went wrong
I'll stand before the Lord of Song
With nothing on my tongue but Hallelujah …

Hallelujah, Hallelujah
Hallelujah, Hallelujah *repeated* [27]

The biblical imagery is unmistakable, particularly in the chorus and title of the song, along with the reference to David and Bathsheba which blends into Samson and Delilah. Love, loss, desire, failure, hope and transcendence interweave in this remarkable gospel-ballad. The repeated 'Hallelujah' of the refrain, to which the song constantly returns and on which it closes, might reminds us of the latter part of the book of Psalms, where that word is prominent. The sense of a mystical and ecstatic encounter in Cohen's song is unmistakable, yet the nature of that encounter is highly ambiguous. Who is moving inside whom? How is the 'holy dove' involved? What is the 'holy or broken Hallelujah'? Is the Hallelujah which he will speak before the Lord of Song different from the earlier Hallelujahs? The song expresses yearning for another, an unnamed 'you', charged with sexual desire and a longing for love; yet all this is suffused with a seemingly religious reverence, expressed in terms of worship.

Two of the most successful versions of Cohen's 'Hallelujah' have been by Rufus Wainwright and Jeff Buckley. Wainwright comments that 'the melody is almost liturgical and conjures up religious feelings. It's purifying', while Buckley describes his own version of the song as homage to 'the hallelujah of the orgasm'.[28] The song has a crossover appeal beyond the boundaries of rock music, evident in Katherine Jenkins' more classical version. This first appeared alongside 'Pie Yesu', 'The Lord's my Shepherd' and 'Silent Night' on Jenkins' album entitled 'Sacred Arias', released in late October 2008 in time for the Christmas market. 'Hallelujah' then resurfaced a few months later as her contribution to 'Love, Lift Us Up—Forty Legendary Love Songs', a compilation album of various artists released (with prime time television advertising) a few weeks before Valentine's Day 2009. This album included titles such as 'You're Beautiful', 'Be my Baby', 'Just the Two of Us' and 'Baby Can I Hold You'. It also featured the songs 'I Believe', 'Up Where We Belong', 'Everlasting Love' and 'God Only Knows'—titles which would not be out of place on an album of the

27. Leonard Cohen, 'Hallelujah', from *Leonard Cohen: Live in London*; Elisa Bray, 'Hallelujah—a Song With a Life of its Own', in *The Independent* (5 Dec 2008) [http://www.independent.co.uk/arts-entertainment/music/features/hallelujah--a-song-with-a-life-of-its-own-1052178.html], accessed 14 Apr. 2011.

28. Neil McCormick, 'Leonard Cohen: Hallelujah!', *Daily Telegraph* (20 June 2008) [http://www.telegraph.co.uk/culture/music/3554289/Leonard-Cohen-Hallelujah.html]; Alan Connor, 'Just Whose Hallelujah Is It Anyway?', *BBC News Magazine* (17 December, 2008) [http://news.bbc.co.uk/1/hi/magazine/7787355.stm]; Q magazine (September 2007); 'Hallelujah', *Wikipedia* [http://en.wikipedia.org/wiki/Hallelujah_(Leonard_Cohen_song)], all accessed 30 June 2009.

latest contemporary worship songs. Once again, the blurring of boundaries between romance and worship is in evidence.[29]

Coldplay: You Are, and Nothing Else Compares
When Coldplay needed one more song to complete their third album, Chris Martin, their singer-songwriter, found himself turning for inspiration to his favourite old hymn ('a heartbreaker', as Martin himself describes it), 'My Song is Love Unknown':

> My song is love unknown
> My Saviour's love to me,
> Love to the loveless shown
> That they might lovely be.
> Oh who am I, that for my sake,
> My Lord should take frail flesh and die. ...
> This is my friend, in whose sweet praise
> I all my days could gladly spend.[30]

Drawing on the old hymn, Martin soon found his final song emerging:

> My song is love
> Love to the loveless shown
> And it goes on
> You don't have to be alone
> Your heavy heart
> Is made of stone
> And it's so hard to see you clearly
> You don't have to be on your own....
> My song is love, is love unknown
> And I've got to get that message home.[31]

Here, as in other Coldplay songs, the youthful good looks and anxiety which Martin projects chime with the lyric's sense of vulnerability and longing for human intimacy. Yet the resonance with the hymn that inspired it, which depicts an individual experiencing God's love, is unmistakable. God's love, human love—the boundaries become blurred.

Religious language and images of intimacy are regularly interwoven in Coldplay's songs. The chorus of 'Clocks', one of their most widely known

29. Katherine Jenkins, *Sacred Arias* (Universal Music: 2008); Various Artists, *Love, Lift Us Up—40 Legendary Love Songs* (Universal Classics & Jazz, 2009).
30. Samuel Crossman, 'My Song Is Love Unknown', *Mission Praise* (ed. Peter Horrobin and Greg Leavers; London: Marshall Pickering, 1990), no. 478.
31. Coldplay, 'The Message', from *X&Y* (Parlophone, 2005).

early hits, keeps returning to the phrase 'You are, you are', eventually adding 'you are—and nothing else compares'. Aside from a possible reference
to Sinead O'Connor's first hit song ('Nothing Compares 2 U'), the seemingly awkward phrasing carries echoes of the biblical divine name 'I am' in
Exod. 3.14. The song concludes by repeating 'You are / Home, home, where
I wanted to go.' Here is yearning, with the identity of the 'you' somewhat
ambiguous.

A more recent album provides further examples. Among the first lyrics
we hear are the phrases: 'God is in the houses and God is in my head ... / I
see God come in my garden, but I don't know what he said, / For my heart
it wasn't open, not open ...'. Here encountering God is possible, in the intimate setting of the garden, and seems to be a matter of the heart. Romance
and heartache are recurring themes in a number of the songs that follow. At
the centre of the album, the song 'Lovers in Japan' begins: 'Lovers, keep
on the road you're on, / runners, until the race is run' (alluding to 2 Tim.
4.7 or Heb. 12.1, perhaps via another old hymn, 'Thou Whose Almighty
Word').[32] It flows seamlessly into 'Reign of Love', where love assumes a
quasi-religious authority and is linked with prayer and a place of worship:

> Reign of love
> By the church, we're waiting
> Reign of love
> My knees go praying
> How I wish
> I'd spoken up
> Or we'd be carried
> In the reign of love.[33]

Religious undertones seep into some of Coldplay's love songs. Although
now somewhat distanced from it, Martin openly acknowledges the influence
of his church background on his songwriting; in one interview he warms to
the suggestion that Coldplay's music conveys 'a seemingly spiritual search
for The Light'.[34] With an estimated fifty million records sold worldwide, the
appetite for and influence of their music is significant.

Florence and the Machine: I Know my Saviour's Love Is Real
The flame-haired face and passionate music of Florence Welch was one of
the major new arrivals on the UK music scene in 2009-10. Her debut album,

---

32. Coldplay, 'Clocks', from *A Rush of Blood to the Head* (Parlophone, 2002);
'Kingdom Come', from X&Y.
33. Coldplay, 'Reign of Love', from *Viva la Vida* (Parlophone, 2008).
34. See interview with Q magazine (July 2008), p. 46

'Lungs', achieved quadruple platinum sales in the UK, winning the Best Album prize at the 2010 Brits Awards.

One of her biggest hits from the album is 'You've Got the Love', a gospel song which previously became a dance hit. She describes how, hearing this song in her younger years at clubs and raves, it made her 'feel love'. The euphoria she discovered when first singing the song live on stage was 'like tearing ourselves open and just exploding on the crowd, ... a feeling you couldn't express.'[35] Her version of the song went on to spend thirty weeks in the UK Top Forty singles chart.

In this song, the singer declares:

> Sometimes I feel like throwing my hands up in the air
> I know I can count on you
> Sometimes I feel like saying "Lord I just don't care"
> But you've got the love I need to see me through ...
>
> When food is gone you are my daily meal
> When friends are gone I know my saviour's love is real
> You know its real
>
> You got the love
> You got the love
> You got the love ...
> Time after time I think "Oh Lord what's the use?"
> Time after time I think it's just no good
> Sooner or later in life, the things you love you lose
> But you've got the love I need to see me through.[36]

The placement of such an upbeat and overt gospel song as the final, climactic moment on the album raises questions about what has gone before. Every one of the preceding songs explores the search for happiness in human relationships, almost always in terms of romance. 'You' language abounds, in tales of desperate desire, sexual jealousy, love-hate relationships, domestic violence, and occasional contentment. Woven into these various cameos we find passing mention of God's grace, saints, hallowed ground, prayers, church bells chiming, heaven and hell, and the soul, with 'Rabbit Heart' providing the most striking example:

> Here I am a rabbit hearted girl
> Frozen in the headlights

---

35. Florence and the Machine, *Official Website* [http://www.florenceandthemachine.net/blog], accessed 11 Mar. 2010.

36. Florence and the Machine, 'You've Got the Love', from *Lungs* (Island Records, 2009).

It seems I've made the final sacrifice
We raise it up this offering
We raise it up

This is a gift it comes with a price
Who is the lamb and who is the knife
Midas is king and he holds me so tight
And turns me to gold in the sunlight

And in the spring I shed my skin
And it blows away with the changing wind
The waters turn from blue to red
As towards the sky I offer it.[37]

The language of fear and self-sacrifice in human relationships intertwines with images of sacrificial worship, particularly in the insistent repeated phrases 'this is a gift' and 'we raise it up'.

Passionate yearning abounds throughout the album. Desire for a human 'you' is clearly predominant; but another 'You' is also consistently rumoured. The final song, with its proclamation of a 'saviour's love' that is real and that is needed 'to see me through', apparently blends the two kinds of yearning.[38]

Whitney Houston: I Look to You

Certified worldwide record sales of nearly a hundred million (estimated a hundred and seventy million) put Whitney Houston among the most successful singers in history. The passion for gospel music nurtured in her as a child was combined with soul, pop, rhythm and blues and eventually dance music as her career developed. Numerous other female artists testify to her influence on them, particularly black singers. [39]

---

37. Florence and the Machine, 'Rabbit Heart (Raise It Up)', from *Lungs*.

38. See Florence Welch's interview with Francesca Ryan, *Daily Telegraph*, 4 June 2009 [http://www.telegraph.co.uk/culture/music/rockandpopfeatures/5443013/Florence-and-the-Machine-interview-sound-and-vision.html]; 'Florence and the Machine', *Wikipedia* [http://en.wikipedia.org/wiki/Florence_and_the_Machine]; Graham Cray, 'Last Year's Music', talk given at the 'Soul Survivor' festival, Shepton Mallet, Aug. 2010 [http://shop.soulsurvivor.com/product_info.php?cPath=190_329_334&products_id=2142], all accessed 22 Nov. 2010.

39. The Official Whitney Houston website [http://www.whitneyhouston.com/uk/biography]; 'Whitney Houston: Biography', *Rolling Stone* [http://www.rollingstone.com/artists/whitneyhouston/biography]; Stephen Holden, 'Diana Ross Flirts with a Willing Audience', *New York Times* 16 June 1989, [http://www.nytimes.com/1989/06/16/arts/review-pop-diana-ross-flirts-with-a-willing-audience.html], both accessed 10 Dec.

Occasionally Houston produced albums with a clear gospel or religious emphasis, such as 'The Preacher's Wife' soundtrack and the Christmas themed 'One Wish'. But it was love songs that became her trademark and came to dominate her repertoire. Probably her most famous song, 'I Will Always Love You', was a number one single in numerous countries.

In Houston's final studio album, the focus is once again strongly on romantic relationships. But her blend of musical styles constantly hints at a blurring of boundaries, which emerges occasionally in the lyrics. In this regard the title track of the album stands out, a simple and striking ballad which begins:

> As I lay me down
> Heaven hear me now
> I'm lost without a cause
> After giving it my all
> Winter storms have come
> And darkened my sun
> After all that I've been through
> Who on earth can I turn to?
>
> I look to you
> I look to you
> After all my strength is gone
> In you I can be strong
> I look to you
> I look to you
> And when melodies are gone
> In you I hear a song
> I look to you.

The identity of this 'you' is unclear. Standing alongside numerous songs which are clearly about romance, it might simply indicate another human relationship. Yet the opening reference to heaven may hint at a greater 'You'. The sense of needing a saviour beyond the merely human builds as the song progresses through images of struggling, searching and regrets which seem to have an autobiographical element. Finally, the singer's passion breaks out in a blend of soul and gospel music:

> My levees are broken (oh Lord)
> My walls have come (coming down on me)
> tumbling down on me (All the rain is falling)

2009. Also 'Whitney Houston', *Wikipedia* [http://en.wikipedia.org/wiki/Whitney_Houston], accessed 7 June 2011.

> The rain is falling
> Defeat is calling (set me free)
> I need you to set me free
> Take me far away from the battle
> I need you to shine on me.

This leads into further repetition of the poignant chorus, 'I look to you'.[40]

In the light of this, the title track of the album, other songs alongside it become less clear cut. The identity of the loved and longed-for 'you' in 'A Song For You' and 'I Got You' may be seen in purely human terms, or else may seem more ambiguous. Similarly, the album's opening song depicts the yearning and search for a love that makes you feel like a million dollars. It turns out that 'who I'm looking for / is staring in my face'; but the identity of the lover remains elusive. Similar ambiguities can be found in other songs among her greatest hits, such as 'Run to You', 'Exhale' and 'When You Believe'. The trend can be traced in her earlier album, 'The Preacher's Wife', where love songs stand alongside worship songs, with the boundaries sometimes blurring in titles such as 'You Were Loved', 'I Believe in You and Me' and 'He's All Over Me'.[41]

Annie Lennox: Your Heavenly Connection

Numerous Brit and Grammy awards, plus an Academy award and over eighty million albums sold worldwide testify to the influence of the voice of Annie Lennox. In recent years she has released two retrospective albums of her most striking and popular songs, the first from her years as one half of the Eurythmics duo, and the second from her solo career. Both sets of songs turn regularly to themes of love and romance, often laced, particularly in the earlier years, with religious language ('The Miracle of Love', 'Thorn in my Side', 'I Saved the World Today', 'Missionary Man'.)

Occasionally the link between biblical themes and loving relationships becomes more explicit; for example, 'There Must Be an Angel Playing with my Heart', with its talk of celestial intervention leaving a 'recollection of your heavenly connection'. Another example is 'You Have Placed a Chill on my Heart', with its chorus:

> Love is a temple, love is a shrine
> Love is pure and love is blind
> Love is a religious sign
> I'm gonna leave this love behind.

40. Whitney Houston, 'I Look to You', from *I Look to You* (Arista, 2009).

41. Whitney Houston, *The Preacher's Wife* (Arista, 1996); *One Wish: The Holiday Album* (Arista, 2003); *Ultimate Collection* (Arista, 2007).

Love is hot and love is cold
I've been bought and I've been sold
Love is rock and love is roll
I just want someone to hold.[42]

Although the accompanying video adds plenty of irony (images of the singer blindfolded outside a strip club, and of Lennox-as-housewife buying cleaning materials in the supermarket, as these lyrics are heard), there is also evidence in this song of the singer expressing herself and her own views, as opposed to the various personae she presents in other songs and videos.[43]

More recently, Lennox covers a song by Ash, 'Shining Light':

My mortal blood I would sacrifice
For you are a shining light
Sovereign bride of the infinite
Yeah, you are a shining light.

Yeah, you light up my life
We made our connection
A full on chemical reaction
Brought by dark divine intervention
Yeah, you are a shining light

A constellation once seen
Over Royal David's city
An epiphany you burn so pretty
Yeah, you are a shining light.[44]

Here the beloved seems to assume mythical religious proportions and to be worthy of total self-giving by the lover; language of sacrificial worship, sacred marriage, a sexual 'chemistry' with a spiritual source, and a divine revelation suggestive of Christ's incarnation is woven into the mix.

Another song of the heart entitled 'Sing' proclaims that 'the rhythm of this beating heart ... is the song of songs'. Further religious imagery recurs as the song unfolds: 'for there is in all the world / no greater love than mine / ... Let me be the only one / to keep you from the cold, / Now the floor of

---

42. Eurythmics, 'You Have Placed a Chill on my Heart', from *Ultimate Collection* (Arista, 2005). The other songs mentioned here are also on this album.

43. See Gillian Rodger, 'Drag, Camp and Gender Subversion in the Music and Videos of Annie Lennox', *PopMus* 23 (2004), pp. 17-29.

44. Annie Lennox, 'Shining Light', from *The Annie Lennox Collection* (Sony BMG, 2009).

heaven's lain / with stars of brightest gold … Come into these arms again / and set this spirit free'. Lennox describes her experience of singing as 'a spiritual thing'; clearly in her music she is happy to use biblical language in depicting sexual longing and intimate relationships. A longing for love seems to connect with another dimension, intertwining with worship and the infinite in the language of ecstasy and reverence.[45]

Madonna: Just Like a Prayer, your Voice Can Take Me There
The unofficial 'Queen of Pop' tag still hangs around the neck of Madonna, alongside the familiar crucifix. With certified worldwide record sales of over 150 million and estimated sales twice that number, she is the best-selling female singer of all time, and was inducted into the select Rock and Roll Hall of Fame in 2008. 'Hard Candy' was her tenth number one album in the UK. Her tours continue to sell out in record time, in spite of (or perhaps encouraged by) disapproval from the Vatican and some other Christian and Jewish groups.[46]

It is no surprise that a recent biography of the singer is entitled 'Madonna—Like an Icon', and structured around headings such as 'baptism', 'confession' and 'absolution'. The name 'Madonna' is not a stage name, but given at birth; her love affair with the language and images of religion arises from her Catholic background, and has long been evident in her songs. However, she challenges the traditional image of her ancient iconic namesake with a determination to make a connection between sex and spirituality: 'Where the traditional Virgin symbolized modesty and purity, this Madonna preached sexual empowerment *and* spirituality'.[47]

This intertwining of sex and spirituality becomes apparent in the album 'Like a Prayer', which she dedicated 'to my mother, who taught me to pray'. The title track endures as a highlight of her latest live concerts; the

45. Annie Lennox, 'Sing', from *Annie Lennox Collection*; Interview with the Sunday Times, 20 March 2009 [http://www.sabotagenewmedia.com/AL/TALC/Annie%20 Lennox%20STM%2022%20March], accessed 12 May 2009.

46. 'Madonna on Madonna', Interview in *Time Magazine* (27 May 1985) [http:// www.time.com/time/magazine/article/0,9171,957025-10,00.html]; Madonna, *Wikipedia* [http://en.wikipedia.org/wiki/Madonna_(entertainer)]; 'Madonna's Hard Candy—Material Woman Restoring Her Brand', Interview with John Pareles, *New York Times* (27 Apr. 2008); [http://www.nytimes.com/2008/04/27/arts/music/27pare.html?pagewanted=2&_ r=1]; 08 Tour Leader: Madonna [http://www.chicagotribune.com/topic/entertainment/ music/popular-music/sticky-sweet-tour-EVCNC0000001.topic]; also [http://madonna. com/news]. All accessed 17 June 2009.

47. Lucy O'Brien, *Madonna—Like an Icon* (London: Corgi, 2008), see Contents and pp. 14, 39, 193. See also [http://www.rollingstone.com/artists/madonna/biography]; 'Madonna on Madonna', Interview in *Time Magazine* (27 May, 1985) [http://www.time. com/time/magazine/article/0,9171,957025-10,00.html], accessed 17 June 2009.

crucifix around her neck swings to the beat as she sings and dances, now down on her knees, now ascending towards the heavens, against a backdrop of religious text and imagery on the giant video screens. The black dancers alongside her remind us of the video produced when the song was first released. This original video blends images of her shapely figure in an ecstasy of dance (sometimes sensuous, other times celebratory) with overtly religious images—the stigmata on her hands, the gospel choirs, the endless succession of crucifixes. It begins with her calling out, 'God', and falling through the air into the arms of a smiling black woman, who throws her back into the sky and later dances with her in church. Most striking is the weeping statue of a young black Christ (or possibly saint) who comes to life at her touch and is released from his 'prison' behind bars in the church. The kisses she exchanges with him are tender and intimate; the more erotic ones were cut from some versions of the video, due to the controversy they caused. All the while, the song beats out its catchy, rhythmic dance melody with intermittent pauses for more reflective moments, as the lyrics roll on:

God ...

When you call my name it's like a little prayer
I'm down on my knees, I wanna take you there
In the midnight hour I can feel your power
Just like a prayer you know I'll take you there

I hear your voice, it's like an angel sighing
I have no choice, I hear your voice
Feels like flying
I close my eyes, oh God I think I'm falling
Out of the sky, I close my eyes
Heaven help me

Like a child you whisper softly to me
You're in control just like a child
Now I'm dancing
It's like a dream, no end and no beginning
You're here with me, it's like a dream
Let the choir sing

Just like a prayer, your voice can take me there
Just like a muse to me, you are a mystery
Just like a dream, you are not what you seem
Just like a prayer, no choice your voice can take me there

> Just like a prayer, I'll take you there
> It's like a dream to me.[48]

The 'you' to whom she sings is delightful, irresistible, unsettling, exhilarating, energizing, home. This other seems gloriously human—yet also more
than human: a mysterious figure, dream-like, muse-like, child-like yet also
in control. The ambiguity is captured in the title of the song, 'Like a Prayer'.
Is this a prayer, or not? If so, to whom is it being prayed?

In Madonna's more recent work we find 'Nothing Fails', a song of devotion to the transforming power of love with strong religious undertones. The
song makes clear that connecting with 'you' was 'not a chance meeting'. It
develops from folk ballad into something more hymnic with the arrival of
backing vocals from the London Community Gospel Choir towards the end:

> Nothing fails
> No more fears
> Nothing fails
> You washed away my tears
> Nothing fails
> No more fears
> Nothing fails
> Nothing fails
>
> I'm not religious
> But I feel so moved
> Makes me want to pray
> Pray you'll always be here.[49]

In the presence of this 'you' fears and tears are unfailingly erased, and
prayer is prompted from an unlikely source.

A couple of years later we encounter the mystical escapism of 'Future
Lovers':

---

48. Madonna, 'Like a Prayer', from *Like a Prayer* (Warner Brothers, 1989). See
also Lucy O'Brien, *She Bop II—The Definitive History of Women in Rock, Pop and Soul*
(London: Continuum, 2003), pp. 210-48. Madonna, *Like a Prayer,* [http://www.youtube.
com/watch?v=lCSK2YrEGtk&feature=related]; compare with the more recent [http://
www.youtube.com/watch?v=Lz2G0oI8PRI&feature=related]. See also J.D. Considine,
'Madonna—Like a Prayer', *Rolling Stone Magazine* (6 Apr. 1989) [http://www.rolling
stone.com/artists/madonna/albums/album/185201/review/5940859/like_a_prayer], all
accessed 18 June 2009.

49. Madonna, 'Nothing Fails', from *American Life* (Warner Brothers, 2003);
O'Brien, *Madonna*, pp. 374-75.

In the evidence of its brilliance
In the evidence of its brilliance
In the demonstration of this evidence
Some call it religion
This is not a coincidence
Would you like to try?
Connect to the sky
Future lovers ride there in mission style
Would you like to try?[50]

A clearer mix of biblical and sexual imagery appears in 'Like it or Not', where the lover seems to be identified with the serpent of Gen. 3, who is offered all of her 'fruit' for his satisfaction (echoes of Song 4.16):

You can call me a sinner
But you can't call me a saint
Celebrate me for who I am
Dislike me for what I ain't ...

I'll be the garden, you'll be the snake
All of my fruit is yours to take
Better the devil that you know
Your love for me will grow.[51]

But with Madonna, perhaps more than most other singers, seeing is as important as hearing: the songs are presented above all through the physical and visual experience of the dance routines, stage acts and videos. In the video accompanying 'La Isla Bonita' we see Madonna as a vibrant and voluptuous flamenco dancer one moment, then as a serene but colourless devotee kneeling at prayer with her rosary the next; all the while the same song continues. Is this simply the Catholic girl wrestling with a choice of two contrasting paths to follow? Or does the juxtaposition hint that there can be a blending of these two ways, rather than a choice between them? Why is the final image a glimpse of the woman at prayer, rather than the colourful dancer?[52] In her stage shows, Madonna has claimed to be attempting to present not simply a conventional rock concert but something 'more

50. Madonna, 'Future Lovers', from *Confessions on a Dance Floor* (Warner Brothers, 2005).
51. Madonna, 'Like It Or Not', from *Confessions on a Dance Floor*.
52. See Madonna, 'La Isla Bonita', [http://www.youtube.com/watch?v=opaomcV2 7os&feature=PlayList&p=A43BAD8D04337FFB&index=0&playnext=1], accessed 17 June, 2009). Also John Drane, *Celebrity Culture* (Edinburgh: Rutherford House, 2005), pp. 79-81.

like theatre, which asks questions, provokes thoughts and takes you on an emotional journey; portraying good and bad, light and dark, joy and sorrow, redemption and salvation ... a celebration of love, life and humanity'.[53] Occasionally she may be pointing her audience to her concerns for the wider world. For example, in 2006 she put on a crown of thorns and sang 'Live to Tell' while draped elegantly on a glittering cross. The song was accompanied by images and information about AIDS orphans in Africa and text from Matt. 25.35-40 (with the word 'God' substituted for the parable's 'king', thus clarifying the religious source of the words).[54] Many of her songs are clearly about human sexual love relationships. Yet as the audience listens and sings along to these songs, they are repeatedly presented with religious imagery (altar rail as stage prop, Bible verses or pseudo-religious texts on screen, dancing with a partner dressed as a priest, the ubiquitous crucifixes). During the 'Drowned World' tour (2001) a film of Jews, Christians, Muslims and others performing acts of religious devotion was projected on a large screen behind her, as she sang of the happiness of paradise which had been restored when her baby came into her life, touched her soul and shared his secret with her.[55] By this repeated combination of sound and vision, the boundaries between 'yearning for you' and 'yearning for You' are blurred.[56]

Mention of the visual dimension raises important questions about the significance (and ambiguity) of image. How much of Madonna's 'theatre' is purely emotive spectacle, used to create a stirring atmosphere for the concert? How much is simply marketing, a very effective form of packaging and selling? After all, 'Like a Prayer' was launched not as a conventional single but as a TV commercial for Pepsi—complete with a trailer commercial to advertise the forthcoming full commercial![57] For that matter, could

53. See her press statement during the video 'Madonna: Live to Tell—Truth or Dare', [http://www.youtube.com/watch?v=IVamOVZNG6U&feature=related], accessed 17 June 2009.

54. Madonna, 'Live to Tell' [http://www.youtube.com/watch?v=-R7_WJSDiL0 &feature=related], accessed 17 June 2009.

55. Madonna, 'Secret', a song she describes as about as about both love and spiritual empowerment; [http://www.youtube.com/watch?v=MmCes0arawk&NR=1], accessed 17 June 2009.; O'Brien, *Madonna*, p. 289.

56. In her controversial book, *Sex* (Warner Books/Callaway, 1992), Madonna continues blurring the boundaries with help from her favourite religious symbol: she lies, bound hand and foot, at the foot of a tall cross, like a sacrificial victim, alongside a man who lies prone with candles on his hands like the nail marks of one who has been crucified; see O'Brien, *Madonna*, p. 247.

57. See [http://www.youtube.com/watch?v=1LTwQWgIGk0]; also the ITV News at Ten summary [http://www.youtube.com/watch?v=ICkKX84odrQ&feature=related], both accessed 19 June 2009. The video/commercial was seen on the same night in at least 40 countries, by an estimated 300 million people; see Leslie Savan, 'Commercials

the passing references to religion, prophet, karma and gospel, Jesus Christ, Satan, heaven and hell, sacrifice and angels in her songs simply be part of a vivid language arsenal from her past which she plunders for effect without investing significance in them?[58] It can be argued that she takes a parasitic approach to religious themes, displacing sacred symbols from their traditional setting and reappropriating them, sometimes in ironic ways.[59]

Madonna herself talks openly about her own prayers and belief in God, including praying before she comes on stage. She describes her recent involvement in Kabbalah spirituality as affecting everything in her life, including song writing, and expresses frustration at the negative or fearful responses which she has received from some quarters, with questions such as: 'What do you mean you study the Torah if you're not Jewish? What do you mean you pray to God and wear sexy clothes? We don't understand this.' The religious influences become more overt with her 'Ray of Light' album, in songs such as 'Swim', with its evocation of baptism, the washing away of sins; in the explicit Hinduism of 'Shanti/Ashtangi'; and in the title track, an ecstatic hymn-like celebration of the heavenly feeling of home. Since that album she has continued to express her religious commitment in unmistakeable ways. When the first cut of her 2005 backstage documentary film 'I'm Going to Tell You a Secret' was shown to friends, the most common criticism was of the copious amounts of Kabbalah included in it, which gave it an almost evangelical subtext.[60] It seems clear that, increasingly in recent years, she has more in mind than simply image and marketing; indeed, more than simply making good pop or rock records. But whatever her own perception, my focus is not primarily on the artist's intention; it is on the nature of the work they produce, and its widespread dissemination in popular culture.

Go Rock', in *Sound and Vision* (ed. Simon Frith et al.), pp. 85-90. On attempts to evaluate the significance of Madonna's multiple video releases (and the occasional subsequent withdrawl of what was released), see Martin Scherzinger and Steven Smith, 'From Blatant to Latent Protest (and Back Again): On the Politics of Theatrical Spectacle in Madonna's "American Life"', *PopMus* 26 (2007), pp. 211-29.

58. From the songs 'Drowned World/Substitute for Love' and 'Sky Fits Heaven' from *Ray of Light* (Warner Brothers, 1998); 'X-Static Process' and 'Intervention' from *American Life*; and 'Isaac', from *Confessions on a Dance Floor*.

59. See Graham, 'What We Make of the World', p. 71.

60. Nick Pisa, 'Vatican Fury at 'Blasphemous' Madonna, *The Daily Telegraph* (4 Aug. 2006) [http://www.telegraph.co.uk/news/1525587/Vatican-fury-at-blasphemous-Madonna.html]; 'Madonna Defends Kabbalah Interest.' *BBC News Channel* (31 Oct. 2005) [http://news.bbc.co.uk/1/hi/entertainment/music/4393642.stm]; 'Vintage Madge—on Kabbalah' [http://www.youtube.com/watch?v=Dl_FZOfGG_Q&NR=1], all accessed 19 June 2009. Also O'Brien, *Madonna*, pp. 319, 326, 442; Drane, *Celebrity Culture*, p. 81; Madonna, *Ray of Light*.

Oasis: Maybe You're Gonna Be the One That Saves Me
A sultry sexuality was often projected in the image and songs of Oasis. The
appeal of expressing this through religious language seems to have grown
on them gradually. Their early songs offer occasional examples, some of
them oblique or suggestive: language of heaven, hell, glory and salvation
crops up from time to time, not to mention the intriguing 'you' that (maybe)
is 'gonna be the one that saves me' in the haunting refrain of 'Wonderwall'.
In the band's last three studio albums religious language grew more pervasive, with a liberal sprinkling of references to soul, belief, faith, prayer,
heaven and hell, light, falling, grace, rapture, litany, messiah, angel, Cain
and Abel, God and the devil. The inclusion of the words 'heathen', 'believe'
and 'soul' in the titles of these three recent albums highlights this preference
for religious language, and seems to suggest that it is significant for each
album as a whole. The Gallagher brothers themselves (the band's singer/
songwriters) acknowledged the pervasiveness of religious themes on the
final album, while seeming slightly bemused by it.[61]

Romantic relationships are often to the fore in Oasis songs. 'Heathen
Chemistry' opens with the song 'The Hindu Times', where the refrain, 'Cos
God gimme soul in your rock'n'roll (babe)', leads on to 'you're my sun-
shine, you're my rain' and talk of a light that shines on me and gives me
peace. This opaque religious imagery becomes more prominent towards the
end of the album, as the language of a true believer proclaims reverence for
an unnamed 'she':

> She is love
> and her ways are high and steep
> She is love
> and I believe her when she speaks.
> Love
> and her ways are high and steep
> She is love
> and I believe, I do believe her when she speaks.[62]

On the teasingly titled follow-up album, 'Don't Believe the Truth', we find
overt eroticism apparently enabling connection with an inner spiritual world:

> You turn me on
> Yer love's like a bomb

61. Oasis, 'Some Might Say', 'Talk Tonight', and 'Wonderwall', from *Stop the
Clocks* (Big Brother Recordings, 2005); also 'Oasis: The Making of Dig Out your Soul',
New Musical Express, [http://www.nme.com/video/bcid/1775769132/search/Soul%20
II%20Soul], accessed 18 Dec. 2009.
62. Oasis, 'The Hindu Times' and 'She is Love', from *Heathen Chemistry* (Big
Brother Recordings, 2002).

> Blowin' my mind.
> Am I reachin'
> The world that I want deep inside?
> Girl I mean it
> An' you hold the key to the shrine.[63]

The album concludes with a memorable ballad, 'Let There Be Love':

> Who kicked a hole in the sky so the heavens would cry over me?
> Who stole the soul from the sun in a world come undone at the
>   seams?
> Let there be love—Let there be love.
> I hope the weather is calm as you sail up your heavenly stream
> Suspended clear in the sky are the words that we sing in our dreams
> Let there be love—Let there be love
> Let there be love—Let there be love.[64]

The repeated and assured fiat of the chorus, clearly reminiscent of Gen. 1, suggests there is something transcendent about this 'heavenly' love, or the one who gives it. Meanwhile the remainder of the song speaks encouragement to 'baby blue' and assurance that 'I'll be by your side'.

The second song on Oasis' final studio album explores the language of 'soul', 'messiah' and 'hope for the turning', while urging the other to 'shake your rag doll, baby' and 'when the rapture takes me, / be the fallen angel by my side'. This leads on to a song about a magical lover, sent by heaven to 'save me from the rapture':

> I still don't know what I was waiting for
> A big love to fall down from the sky
> She took my hand and picked me up off the floor
> She put an apple in my eye.[65]

Subsequent songs on the album continue the theme of longing for a romance that is special and fulfilling, while also proclaiming that 'love is a litany, / a magical mystery' and referring to requests or prayers for 'the light'.[66]

---

63. Oasis, 'Love Like a Bomb', from *Don't Believe the Truth*.

64. Oasis, 'Let There Be Love', from *Don't Believe the Truth*.

65. Oasis, 'The Turning' and 'Waiting for the Rapture', from *Dig Out your Soul* (Big Brother Recordings, 2008).

66. Oasis, 'Shock of Lightening', 'To Be Where There's Life', 'Soldier On', from *Dig Out your Soul*.

With estimated sales of over fifty million records worldwide, the influence of Oasis is unquestioned, not least in the UK, where they have had seven number-one albums and numerous awards. A poll in 2008 saw two of their early albums voted the best British albums ever recorded. Clearly their songs have registered strongly with many music listeners.[67] Does the religious imagery simply add colour and weight to the hackneyed language of love songs? Or does it suggest that there is a spiritual dimension to romance? The listener will decide.

Sinéad O'Connor: I Long for You
In 1990 Sinéad O'Connor soared to worldwide fame and fortune with 'Nothing Compares to U', a broken-hearted love song written by Prince which alludes partly to her love for her abusive mother. Both the single and the album ('I Do Not Want What I Haven't Got') sold millions worldwide. The album begins with a prayer to God, before going on to mention, alongside unreliable friends, a 'you' who continued to affect me and whom I have always still loved. The fragility and painfulness of intimacy with a lover is a continuing theme in the songs that follow. The closing song on the album refers to having water, bread and wine, and the bread of life, which are enough for the journey through the desert. Here are clear intimations of God alongside words about human love.

In 2009 that album was re-released, as was a live version of O'Connor's most recent album, 'Theology'. Here we find a further collection of passionate songs expressing love and longing; yet these lyrics come mostly from Hebrew Bible. Sensuous excerpts from the Song of Songs sit alongside an intense version of Isaiah's Song of the Vineyard (Isa. 5.1-7), set among passionate excerpts from Psalms 33, 91, 104, 130, 137 and Hannah's psalm (1 Sam. 2.1-10). O'Connor's breathy, half-whispered repetition of the words 'I long for you, as watchmen long for the end of night' to close the song 'Out of the Depths' (her version of Psalm 130) captures the ambiguity woven into this album: sensual desire seems to blend with prayerful devotion. A similar vocal style and intonation are found in 'Dark I Am Yet Lovely', her version of the Song of Songs, in which erotic longing abounds, with no hint of allegorical interpretation. The use of (capital) 'U' in place of the word 'you' throughout the album's lyric sheet serves to highlight the ubiquitous presence of that particular word in the songs; clearly relationship with this other is a central concern in the album as a whole.

Almost every track on the 'Theology' album is based around a biblical text. One of the two exceptions is 'I don't know how to love him', a reworking of the famous hit from 'Jesus Christ Superstar', the song of a

---

67. 'Oasis Top Best British Album Poll', BBC News Channel, 18 Feb. 2008 [http://news.bbc.co.uk/1/hi/entertainment/7249473.stm], accessed 18 Dec. 2009.

woman who is in love—with Jesus Christ. The themes of longing, desire and intimacy pervade this album, as they did the earlier one. Now the focus on God has become far more explicit, yet the language of romance and *eros* is still favoured; sometimes 'yearning for you' and 'yearning for You' seem to intertwine.[68]

Prince: The Sensual Everafter

Thirty albums in as many years testify to the prolific output of Prince Rogers Nelson (Prince). With seven Grammy Awards and an Academy Award to his name, Prince has entered the Rock and Roll Hall of Fame, and was ranked number twenty eight in a list of the Hundred Greatest Artists of All Time by Rolling Stone magazine. The number of artists who have sung songs written by or with him further testify to his influence in the world of popular music.[69]

Spirituality seems to have been important to Prince from early years; and sex has always been a prominent theme in his songs. The blatant hedonism and eroticism of earlier years ('I Wanna Be your Lover', 'Little Red Corvette', 'Let's Go Crazy' and 'Gett Off') has mellowed since the turn of the millennium into more opaque lyrics, still with romantic and erotic themes, but often interwoven with biblical and theological images. Visual impact plays a major role, as witnessed by the number of music videos and film scores Prince has produced, along with the theatricality of his live shows; this aspect of his output cannot be done justice to here, so I shall continue my focus on song lyrics.[70]

The elusive 'I' of the song 'I Would Die 4 U' ('I'm not a woman, / I'm not a man, / I am something that you'll never understand / ... I'm not your lover, / I'm not your friend, / I'm something that you'll never comprehend') turns out to be some kind of saviour who will 'be your fire when you're cold'. Eventually he proclaims: 'I'm your messiah and you're the reason why', and then:

> I'm not a human
> I am a dove
> I'm your conscious
> I am love
> All I really need is 2 know that
> U believe.

68. Sinéad O'Connor, *Theology* (Rubyworks, 2007); [http://www.sineadoconnor. com], accessed 22 May 2009.

69. 'Prince', *Wikipedia* [http://en.wikipedia.org/wiki/Prince_(musician)#Discography], accessed 22 Dec. 2009.

70. 'Prince Epilepsy Cured by an Angel', Interview with Travis Smiley, *Hollywood Grind* [http://www.hollywoodgrind.com/prince-epilepsy-cured-by-an-angel]; 'Prince Says He Wants Less Explicit Lyrics', *Freemuse* 16 July 2004; [http://www.freemuse. org/sw6611.asp], both accessed 23 Dec. 2009).

This flows on to the repeated chorus:

> U—I would die 4 u, yeah
> Darling if u want me 2
> U—I would die 4 u.[71]

Here is a love to die for, with intimations of a self-sacrificing saviour. Some of the language veers away from the romantic, but other aspects (particularly the 'darling') suggest that *eros* is not far away.

'Thieves in the Temple' creates a religious setting with the constantly repeated line 'There are thieves in the temple tonight'. The singer is 'looking for my soul / like a poor man looking for gold', occasionally hearing 'voices from the sky'. He calls out:

> Love if u're there come save me
> From all this cold despair
> I can hang when u're around
> But I'll surely die
> If u're not there

This leads back into the repeated chorus:

> Love come quick
> Love come in a hurry
> There are thieves in the temple tonight.[72]

The album 'The Rainbow Children' marks the emergence of more overtly religious lyrics, with allusions to Prince's new-found beliefs as a Jehovah's Witness. The erotic becomes less prominent, yet is never far away. 'Muse to the Pharaoh' gives glimpses of a mysterious 'Muse' in a sexual embrace with 'the Pharaoh'. 'The Sensual Everafter' depicts the 'Wise One' and his 'Muse', who is praised for her growing love for God; eventually the Wise One sends everyone else to bed early and invites his Muse to join him in 'the sensual everafter'. The song that follows develops these themes, exploring a 'mellow' sexual relationship with 'she who fell in2 the sensual everafter'. Later in the album, 'She loves Me 4 Me' depicts an unnamed ideal other to whom he gives fulsome praise.[73]

---

71. Prince, 'I Would Die 4 U', from *The Very Best of Prince* (Rhino Records, 2001).
72. Prince, 'Thieves in the Temple', from *The Very Best of Prince*.
73. Prince, 'Muse to the Pharaoh', 'The Sensual Everafter', 'Mellow' and 'She loves Me 4 Me', from *The Rainbow Children* (NPG Records, 2001).

The more recent '3121' album offers a paean of praise to 'Love', with biblical overtones:

> Like a bird flyin' over the hilltops
> Love is like the sky, U know it never stops
> From the abundance of the heart the mouth speaks
> Love is whatever . . . whatever . . . U want it 2 b.[74]

A later song reveals what it means to be 'Beautiful, Loved and Blessed': to be known and loved by your creator. Meanwhile, 'The Word' insists that 'the night is calling u 2 act, / Act upon every urge' as the way to get satisfaction, and says:

> How am eye gonna sleep with this feeling
> Rushing all through my veins?
> Get up, come on let's do something
> Don't u wanna go get saved?[75]

With Prince, time and again, love is the object of devotion and the focus of hope for salvation. But the blending of romantic and religious imagery makes the focus of this longed-for saving love unclear. Is the 'u/U' in his lyrics about 'you', or 'You', or both?

Cliff Richard: I Still Believe in You

As a hugely successful singer, famous for his hit love songs and his Christian faith, Cliff Richard might be expected to bring together sexual and spiritual desire in his songs. In practice, he rarely does so; down the years, his commercial hit singles and albums have tended to be largely distinct from his gospel tours and recordings. Religious imagery is rare in his hits, while romance seems equally rare in his devotional songs.[76]

---

74. Prince, 'Love', from *3121* (Universal/NPG Records, 2006).

75. Prince, 'Beautiful, Loved and Blessed' and 'The Word', from *3121*.

76. Another evangelical Christian singer of the same generation who shows little or no inclination to fuse gospel songs with love songs is Johnny Cash. See, for example, Johnny Cash *The Gospel Music of Johnny Cash* (Gaither, 2008) and *Love, God, Murder* (Legacy/Columbia, 2000). See also Dave Urbanski, *The Man Comes Around: The Spiritual Journey of Johnny Cash* (Lake Mary, FL: Relevant Books, 2005). A further limited comparison might be made with Cat Stevens (now known as Yusuf Isalm, or simply Yusuf). Following his conversion to Islam in 1977, he abruptly ended his musical career, as Cliff Richard almost did following his conversion to Christianity. In resuming his musical career, Yusuf Islam has shown little interest in blending romance with religious devotion (see *An Other Cup* [Atlantic Records, 2006]; *Roadsinger* [Island, 2009]).

This distinction, however, is not always strictly adhered to. Richard's most recent album of original songs, most of them love songs and ballads about lost love, closes with an overt worship song addressed to 'my faithful One'. Adoration is expressed to a 'true and precious friend', who consistently guides and strengthens the singer through the demands of life. The imagery is of pilgrimage, cross and resurrection, rather than of a divine lover; yet it also celebrates 'an empty tomb, a love for all who come / and give their hearts to you, the faithful One'.[77] Here, perhaps, is a hint of romance in the divine-human relationship, a faithfulness which the human lovers depicted in the album's earlier songs may struggle to achieve. Another song on the same album celebrates a love that is eternal, perhaps suggesting something more than a relationship with another human being.[78]

Questions of belief surface in a more recent compilation entitled *Love ... the Album*, which includes as its penultimate song 'I Still Believe in You'. While discarding childhood fantasies and belief in fairy tales, the singer here declares that 'you keep shining through', leading to the high point in the chorus:

> I could never doubt your kiss
> No other love fills me like this
> If you take a chance, you'll see
> I believe in you
> Believe in me.[79]

Here is an enduring faith and love like no other. But who is the unique other, and what kind of kiss does this lover give?

If a religious aspect can be detected in Richard's love songs, it relates to the particular persona which he presents. Some of his lyrics (with accompanying visual images on album covers and in stage shows) suggest a quasi-messianic figure who offers redemption and healing to those who will respond to him. Thus, in 'Let Me Be the One', the singer offers to banish loneliness, come in and bring in the sun to shine on a hearer who is willing to open up their heart and 'let me be the one'.[80] The photo on the single sleeve shows the singer larger than life, with an aura of bright light and arms outstretched in a manner reminiscent of the way Christ is sometimes

---

77. Cliff Richard, 'Faithful One', from *Something's Goin' On* (Decca, 2004). Bruce Welch, who regularly performed with Cliff Richard as part of 'The Shadows', comments, 'When he [Cliff] found some meaning in God, it took over the area of his life that you would normally devote to wife and children'. See Steve Turner, *Cliff Richard: The Bachelor Boy* (London: Carlton, 2008), p. 128.

78. Cliff Richard, 'The Day That I Stop Loving You', from *Something's Goin' On*.

79. Cliff Richard, 'I Still Believe in You', from *Love ... the Album* (EMI, 2007).

80. Cliff Richard, 'Let Me Be the One', from *Wanted* (Papillon, 2001).

depicted. While some listeners may perceive all this as pointing away from the singer to Jesus Christ, for others the singer himself may be equated more closely with a saviour figure. In the latter case, salvation seems to be offered through romantic attachment to the singer, although it is comfort and healing, rather than sexual intimacy, which he seems to be offering.[81]

U2: But You're Gone and So Is God

While one singer steeped in the Bible seems reluctant to link romance or *eros* with the divine, another shows no such reticence. Few high-profile bands have blended biblical and relational language as consistently as U2. The opening song on their first album, 'I will follow', includes quotations from the hymn 'Amazing Grace' about blindness and being lost and found.[82] The second album begins with 'Gloria in te domine, only in you I'm complete'; the song that follows comes down to earth with a bump, as John and Julia stumble through their relationship in 'I Fall Down'.[83] On the third album, 'Drowning Man' reaches out a hand towards a love that will last forever and never let go, citing Isaiah 40.31.[84] 'The Joshua Tree' album begins with 'Where the Streets Have No Name', a song which Bono describes as 'trying to sketch a location, maybe a spiritual location, maybe a romantic location'. Next comes 'I Still Haven't Found What I'm Looking For', a relentless search 'only to be with you', in which the romantic 'I have kissed honey lips, / felt the healing in her finger tips / it burned like fire, / this burning desire' leads on to the theological 'You broke the bonds, / loosed the chains, / carried the cross / and all my shame'. The resonance and influence of this particular song is evident in the fact that it is the U2 song which has subsequently been most recorded by other artists—along with the one that follows on the album, with its impassioned cry, 'I can't live with or without you'. Clearly songs expressing a 'yearning for you / You' have a wide appeal.[85]

81. See Anja Löbert, 'Cliff Richard's Self-Presentation as a Redeemer', *PopMus* 27 (2008), pp. 78-88.

82. U2, 'I Will Follow', from *Boy* (Island Records, 1980).

83. U2, 'Gloria' and 'I Fall Down', from *October* (Island Records, 1981).

84. U2, 'Drowning Man', from *War* (Island Records, 1983).

85. U2, 'Where the Streets Have No Name', 'I Still Haven't Found What I'm Looking For' and 'With or Without You', from *The Joshua Tree* (Island Records, 1987); see also comments by Bono [http://www.u2.com/discography/index/album/albumId/4031/tagName/singles], accessed 20 Oct. 2010. On the mingling of themes of sexuality, spirituality and justice in U2's early albums, see Brian Froese, 'Comic Endings: Spirit and Flesh in Bono's Apocalyptic Imagination, 1980-83', in *Call Me the Seeker* (ed. Gilmour), pp. 61-78. On the biblical allusions in the early albums, particularly with reference to the Psalms, see Andrew Davies, 'The Bible under the Joshua Tree: Biblical

After exploring various attitudes and ironies in oblique ways through the music which they wrote during the 1990s, the new millennium saw U2 return to writing songs in which their core beliefs and passions were more prominent. The suitably titled 'All That You Can't Leave Behind' album includes on its cover a cryptic reference to Jer. 33.3 (where God says, 'Call to me, and I will answer you'). The opening song begins with 'the heart', which 'is a bloom / shoots up through stony ground'. It goes on to talk of gratitude for grace, and alludes to the end of the biblical flood and the rainbow that followed as a sign of God's covenant (Gen. 8.10-12; 9.12-17), bracketed by the refrain, 'Touch me, take me to that other place, / Reach me, I know I'm not a hopeless case'. The identity of the desired other is unclear.[86]

U2's subsequent tour took its title from the song 'Elevation', which begins:

> High, higher than the sun
> You shoot me from a gun
> I need you to elevate me here,
> At the corner of your lips
> As the orbit of your hips
> Eclipse, you elevate my soul
> I've lost all self-control
> Been living like a mole
> Now going down, excavation
> I and I in the sky
> You make me feel like I can fly
> So high, elevation …
>
> Love, lift me out of these blues
> Won't you tell me something true
> I believe in you.[87]

In urgent high tempo, sexual innuendo mingles with a longing to soar, leaving us to wonder who is the 'love/you' that the singer believes in. 'It's about sexuality and transcendence,' Bono admits, 'a playful piece about wanting to get off, or, in this case, to literally get off the ground.'[88] Another favourite song presented during this tour, 'Mysterious Ways', saw a sensuous belly

Imagery in the Music of U2', *SBL Forum* (Jan 2009) [http://www.sbl-site.org/Publications/article.aspx?articleId=795], accessed 28 Apr. 2009.

86. U2, 'Beautiful Day', from *All That You Can't Leave Behind* (Island Records, 2000); see also Bono, The Edge, Adam Clayton, Larry Mullen Jr, with Neil McCormick, *U2 by U2* (London: Harper Collins, 2006), p. 303.

87. U2, 'Elevation', from *All That You Can't Leave Behind*.

88. Bono, *et al, U2 by U2*, p. 296.

dancer performing on stage as Bono sang 'Spirit moves you / does it move you? /... she moves in mysterious ways'.[89]

After wrestling with the seductions of materialism and the threat to marital stability from the mid-life crisis, a further song ends on a calmer note:

> In the stillness of the evening
> When the sun has had its day
> I heard your voice a-whispering
> Come away child
> New York, New York.[90]

The likely allusion to Song of Songs in the phrase 'come away' (cf. Song 2.10, 13; 7.11) suggests a lover, although 'child' might suggest a parental voice. A sexual partner may, of course, play a parental role towards their lover at times.

The album concludes with a vision of 'Grace':

> Grace, she takes the blame
> She covers the shame
> Removes the stain
> It could be her name
> Grace, it's the name for a girl
> It's also a thought that changed the world
> And when she walks on the street
> You can hear the strings
> Grace finds goodness in everything . . .
>
> She carries a pearl in perfect condition
> What once was hurt
> What once was friction
> What left a mark
> No longer stings
> Because Grace makes beauty out of ugly things
> Grace makes beauty out of ugly things.[91]

Here many listeners will glimpse a woman named Grace, who is looked upon with awed admiration, as she achieves miracles with what seems unpromising material.[92] Yet this mysterious figure 'could be' something

---

89. U2, 'Mysterious Ways, from *Achtung Baby* (Island Records, 1991).

90. U2, 'New York', from *All That You Can't Leave Behind*.

91. U2, 'Grace', from *All That You Can't Leave Behind*.

92. There may be a reference here to Grace Nawakunde, an AIDS sufferer and campaigner whom Bono met in Kampala; see Christian Scharen, *One Step Closer: Why U2 Matters to Those Seeking God* (Grand Rapids, MI: Brazos, 2006), pp. 140-41.

more. She shows powers suggesting the divine, as she 'covers the shame, / removes the stain', 'carries a world' and 'changed the world'. The contrasting reference to 'karma' suggests a religious agenda, while the reference to a perfect pearl may remind biblically literate readers of Jesus' parables comparing the kingdom of heaven to priceless pearls (Matt. 13.44-45). Attraction to the song's 'Grace' seems to offer a spiritual delight and transformation which goes beyond a purely human relationship.[93] The sense of a boundary between 'yearning for you' and 'yearning for You' becomes blurred in an ambiguous impressionism.[94]

The album that followed in 2004 begins with 'Vertigo', a song which fuses biblical allusions with the dizziness of desire on the dance floor, before ending in a posture of surrender or prayer or both:

> The girl with crimson nails
> Has Jesus round her neck
> Swinging to the music
> Swinging to the music ...
>
> All of this, all of this can be yours
> All of this, all of this can be yours ...
>
> I can feel your love teaching me how
> Your love is teaching me how, how to kneel.[95]

This sets the tone for the ebb and flow of these themes throughout the rest of the album. Love, romance, God and faith all mingle in 'A Man and a Woman':

> Little sister
> I've been trying to feel complete again
> But you're gone and so is God
> The soul needs beauty for a soul mate
> When the soul wants, the soul waits.

---

93. Grace is a theme that continues to inspire U2: 'grace abounds', the singer proclaims with authority, standing beneath the cathedral-like arches of the 360° stage set (see *U2360° at the Rose Bowl* [DVD, Universal/Island, 2009], end of track 14). Both singer and fans sometimes refer to U2 concerts as 'going to church', and the band has spoken of a sense of spiritual blessing during concerts; see Scharen, *One Step Closer*, pp. 188-89; see also [http://www.u2.com/news/title/this-show-will-last-for-ever], accessed 14 Apr. 2011.

94. Some later versions of the album end with a further song in which human love and longing are yet again couched in terms of reverence and worship. Written by Salman Rushdie, 'The Ground beneath Her Feet' begins 'All my life, I worshipped her, / her golden voice, her beauty's beat'.

95. U2, 'Vertigo', from *How to Dismantle an Atomic Bomb* (Island Records, 2004).

No I could never take a chance
On losing love to find romance
In the mysterious distance
Between a man and a woman

For love and sex and faith and fear
And all the things that keep us here
In the mysterious distance
Between a man and a woman.[96]

The album culminates in an overt prayer, the song called 'Yahweh', which consciously gives each aspect of the self over entirely to the divine Other:

Take this soul
Stranded in some skin and bones
Take this soul
And make it sing
Yahweh ...

Take this mouth
So quick to criticise
Take this mouth
Give it a kiss
Yahweh ...

Take this heart
Take this heart
Take this heart
And make it break.[97]

The intimacy and intensity of this prayer is a reminder of the degree to which the Psalms have permeated Bono's thinking from his teenage years until today, particularly with the themes of lament and self-abandonment.[98]

96. U2, 'A Man and a Woman', from *How to Dismantle an Atomic Bomb*.
97. U2, 'Yahweh', from *How to Dismantle an Atomic Bomb*. On the intensely relational nature of this song, see Greg Garrett, *We Get to Carry Each Other: The Gospel According to U2* (Louisville, KY: Westminster John Knox, 2009), pp. 27-28.
98. See '40' from *War* and 'Moment of Surrender' from *No Line on the Horizon* (Rhino Records, 2009). See also Bono, 'Introduction', *The Book of Psalms* (Edinburgh: Cannongate, 1999) [http://www.guardian.co.uk/theobserver/1999/oct/31/featuresreview.review2?INTCMP=SRCH], accessed 29 Mar. 2011; Scharen, *One Step Closer*, pp. 29-41, 101.

U2's subsequent album opens with the title track, 'No Line on the Horizon' (an allusion to infinity, where sea and sky seem to blend into one), depicting 'a girl who's like the sea / I watch her changing every day for me / Oh yeah / Oh oh oh oh'. The next track continues the theme of love, but in another dimension:

> I was born
> I was born to be with you
> In this space and time. ...
> Only love, only love can leave such a mark
> But only love, only love unites our hearts
> Justified till we die, you and I will magnify
> The Magnificent, Magnificent.[99]

This in turn leads on to the third song, the more earthy but still ambiguous 'Moment of Surrender' (which became the last word of their 2009-10 concerts, as the final encore). Here the intimacy of lovers blurs into the language of faith:

> We set ourselves on fire
> Oh God, do not deny her
> It's not if I believe in love
> But if love believes in me
> Oh, believe in me.[100]

A later song with a relational flavour alludes to 'perfect love that drives out fear' (1 John 4.18), while another urges, 'Stand up for your love / Love love love love love / God is love / And love is evolution's very best day'. As so often with U2, love and faith are the goals to be sought, and the identity of the elusive other seems unclear.[101]

The ambiguous and ubiquitous 'you' pervades U2's songs, from the earliest to the most recent.[102] There seems to be more than one 'you' embedded in these songs, as in the name of the band itself. Describing the sexual nature of U2's songs as like a lover's row or an argument with yourself, Bono comments that

99. U2, 'No Line on the Horizon' and 'Magnificent', from *No Line On the Horizon*. The allusion in the title 'Magnificent' to the Lukan 'Magnificat' reflects the songwriters' attempt to modernize the tradition of Bach and choral music with a piece of 'devotional disco ... a gospel song that transforms into the carnal, then into a song for family, for children' (see Niall Stokes, *U2: The Story Behind Every U2 Song* (London: Carlton Books, 2009), p. 166.
100. U2, 'Moment of Surrender', from *No Line on the Horizon*.
101. U2, 'Stand Up Comedy', from *No Line on the Horizon*.
102. See Scharen, *One Step Closer*, pp. 98, 136.

the erotic love can turn into something much higher, and bigger notions of love, and God, and family. It seems to segue very easily from me between all those. ... I'm always attracted to subjects like you can't get a grip on, like sex or God. *[muses for a while]* I think I sometimes confuse them both![103]

There is an elusiveness about U2's allusions. There often seems to be a double coding in the lyrics which makes their religious and biblical references clearly evident to some listeners while unnoticed or opaque to others.[104] This raises questions about the nature and effect of allusions in general, which I shall return to in a late chapter. For now, it is sufficient to note that an estimated hundred and fifty million albums sold worldwide and a record twenty two Grammy Awards testify to U2's unabated popularity; the resonance and influence of these songs is quite exceptional.[105]

The Best of the Rest
Evanescence brought Gothic Metal into the limelight with their debut album, 'Fallen', which has sold fifteen million copies and led on to two Grammy awards. Throughout the album desire for intimacy mingles with the language of belief, the soul, being saved, death and finding new life. One of the most memorable songs explores the pain of wounds from an intimacy which seems to have ended, yet also speaks longing for a lingering presence which may still be close. Ambiguities abound: who is the 'you' who 'used to captivate me / by your resonating light'? We may also wonder which of the parties is speaking in the chorus:

> When you cried I'd wipe away all of your tears
> When you'd scream I'd fight away all of your fears
> And I've held your hand through all of these years
> But you still have all of me.[106]

---

103. See Michka Assyas, *Bono on Bono: Conversations with Michka Assayas* (Hodder, 2005), pp. 120, 128. Bono has also been known to blur the distinction between religious experience and drug-induced ecstasy, adding repeated cries of 'Halleluia' to a song about drug addiction called 'Running to Stand Still'. This was during live performances in the 1990s, a period when U2 were often exploring the delights of irony.

104. See Deane Galbraith, 'Drawing Our Fish in the Sand: Secret Biblical Allusions in the Music of U2', *BibInt* 19 (2011), pp. 183, 187, 196, 207-209; on the reception of the song 'Magnificent' by actual listeners, see pp. 217-22. In contrast with U2's obliqueness, the music of Johnny Cash sometimes presents explicit exegesis of biblical allusions and texts; see Jay Twomey, 'The Biblical Man in Black: Paul in Johnny Cash / Johnny Cash in Paul', *BibInt* 19 (2011), pp. 228-30, 236-49.

105. 'List of Best-Selling Music Artists', *Wikipedia* [http://en.wikipedia.org/wiki/List_of_best-selling_music_artists], accessed 7 June 2011.

106. Evanescence, 'My Immortal', from *Fallen* (Wind Up Records, 2004); also 'Evanescence', *Wikipedia* [http://en.wikipedia.org/wiki/Evanescence], accessed 21 Nov. 2009.

What kind of intimacy is this? If it is purely human, why is the song entitled 'My Immortal'?

Multi-million selling albums continue to emerge from the virtual world of Gorrillaz, offering numerous intriguing and opaque lyrics. Religious imagery is not generally prominent. But the song 'Cloud of Unknowing' speaks of 'trying to find someone you'll never know', and of 'a sinking love / on the cloud of unknowing'. We also hear a voice singing 'I was here from the very start, / trying to find a way to your heart'. The song title clearly alludes to the fourteenth century mystical work of the same name, which offers a vision of the one seeking God piercing the thick cloud of unknowing with a 'dart of longing love' from the heart.[107]

The Killers have emerged in recent years as a major name in the rock world. 'When You Were Young' depicts someone sitting in heartache, waiting on some beautiful boy to come and save them; when he comes, he 'doesn't look a thing like Jesus, / but he talks like a gentleman / like you imagined when you were young'. Other songs on the same album continue the exploration of romance; one speaks of 'the restless heart, the Promised Land' alongside 'the subtle kiss that no-one sees'. Another bemoans the lack of a lover and the lack of soul, while glimpsing 'a cinematic vision / into like the holiest dream / ...an angel whispers my name'; this leads back to the pleading chorus: 'Don't you want to come with me? / Don't you want to feel my bones on your bones? / It's only natural.' The language of *eros* repeatedly blurs into that of religious vision and experience.[108]

Nine Inch Nails (a.k.a. Trent Reznor) blend sex and religion with death and sado-masochism in a grotesque, nihilistic style. One of their best known songs, 'Closer', begins with the words 'You let me violate you, / you let me desecrate you', and goes on to bemoan a lack of faith and having no soul to sell. It seeks a 'you' who 'makes me perfect'. The song's climax comes in the chorus:

> I want to fuck you like an animal
> I want to feel you from the inside
> I want to fuck you like an animal
> my whole existence is flawed
> you get me closer to God.[109]

107. Gorrillaz, 'Cloud of Unknowing', from *Plastic Beach* (EMI Records, 2010); also [http://en.wikipedia.org/wiki/Gorrillaz] and [http://gorillaz.com/plasticbeach], both accessed 20 Jan. 2011.

108. The Killers, 'When You Were Young', 'Read my Mind' and 'Bones', from *Sam's Town* (The Island Def Jam Music Group, 2006).

109. Nine Inch Nails, 'Closer', from *The Downward Spiral* (Nothing Records, 1994); lyrics from [http://www.ninwiki.com/Closer].

The controversial video released with this song includes a crucified monkey, a naked woman wearing a crucifix mask, and other overtly erotic images; sex and religion interweave in graphic visual form. The closing lines of the song might even carry an echo of the Song of Songs, in the words 'I drink the honey inside your hive, / you are the reason I stay alive' (cf. Song 4.16–5.1). But while 'Closer' explicitly links closeness to God with sexual experience, the language of love is notably absent.[110]

Music Acclaimed in Some Church Circles

Delirious? We Are God's Romance

Despite touring with major names such as Bon Jovi and skirting around the edge of mainstream success, Delirious? never achieved a degree of recognition and influence comparable with the musicians cited earlier in this chapter. But a substantial fan-base turning out to concerts in Europe and the Americas and a Grammy nomination all testify to their presence on the musical scene from the mid-1990s until they disbanded in 2009. Their influence has been most strongly felt in church circles in the UK and USA, where a number of their songs have entered the canon of the most popular contemporary worship songs.[111]

Longing for intimacy with God has been a consistent and recurring theme for Delirious? One of their early worship songs revels in 'your river' that 'runs with love for me, / and I will open up my heart / and let the Healer set me free'; this leads on to the repeated chorus 'I could sing of your love forever'. Another sings tenderly, 'Lord, you have my heart, / and I will search for yours, / Jesus take my life and lead me on', while a third says, 'we've fallen deeper in love with you'.[112] 'Obsession' develops these themes with a greater intensity:

> What can I do with my obsession?
> With the things I cannot see

110. Nine Inch Nails, 'Closer' [http://www.youtube.com/watch?v=k7ts7jviLU0]; also [http://www.youtube.com/watch?v=cVgBuwM9zcQ], both accessed 30 Dec. 2009. On the subversive nature of the grotesque as presented in Nine Inch Nails' religious and sexual imagery, see Andrew Tatusko, 'Transgressing Boundaries in the Nine Inch Nails: The Grotesque as a Means to the Sacred', *JRPC* 11 (Fall 2005).

111. For example, 'Lord You Have My Heart', 'Shout to the North', 'Thank You For Saving Me', 'I Could Sing of your Love Forever' and 'Majesty'. These and most of the other songs I mention subsequently feature on the limited edition of *History Makers: Greatest Hits* (Furious? Records, 2009).

112. Delirious?, 'I Could Sing of your Love Forever' and 'Lord, You Have my Heart', from *Cutting Edge 1 & 2* (Furious? Records, 1994); 'Shout to the North', from *Cutting Edge 3 & Fore* (Furious? Records, 1995).

Is there madness in my being?
Is it wind that blows the trees?
Sometimes you're further than the moon
Sometimes you're closer than my skin
And you surround me like a winter fog
You've come and burned me with a kiss
And my heart burns for you
And my heart burns.[113]

In the album that launched them to a new level of success, themes of mutual desire and passionate love are further explored in the opening song, 'Sanctify':

And all I want is all you have
Come to me, rescue me,
Fall on me with your love
And all you want is all I have
Come to me, rescue me,
fall on me with your love.[114]

This leads into the following track, 'Deeper', where some of the language may indicate intimacy with a father, but the recurring refrain of the chorus uses the language of romance: 'And the wonder of it all / is that I'm living just to fall / more in love with you'.[115]

The album ends with 'What a friend I've found', which celebrates eternal friendship with Jesus in a succession of images: 'closer than a brother' and 'more faithful than a mother', but also 'I have felt your touch, / more intimate than lovers'. This juxtaposition of familial and sexual images is striking and assured; their common theme is the security of a deeply intimate relationship, in all its different dimensions. The longing to continue this relationship is heartfelt: 'it would break my heart / to ever lose each other'.[116]

The imagery of mutual relationship is further explored in the strikingly titled 'God's Romance', which begins:

There's a song that everyone can sing
There's a prayer that everyone can bring

113. Delirious?, 'Obsession', from *Live and in the Can* (Furious? Records, 1996).
114. Delirious?, 'Sanctify', from *King of Fools* (Furious? Records, 1997).
115. Delirious?, 'Deeper', from *King of Fools*.
116. Delirious?, 'What a Friend I've Found', from *King of Fools*.

> Feel the music cos it's time to dance
> People all across the world
> With a heartbeat for holiness
> Feel his pleasure
> We are God's romance.

The second verse echoes the first, but with the point of view shifting in the final phrase:

> There's a song that everyone can sing
> There's a race that everyone can win
> Leave your sadness, it's our time to dance
> Everyone let out your praise
> People with their hearts ablaze
> We've found Jesus, he's our great romance.[117]

Here the relationship is explicitly romantic, with mutuality clearly indicated by the parallelism and balance of the verses. The song's additional emphasis on the importance of holiness raise questions about the nature of this divine–human relationship, but this is not central to the lyrics; romance has the last word in each verse. Celebration is the watchword, and the experience of a living relationship with the risen Jesus. Listeners are invited to feel God's pleasure as they sing, pray and dance, enjoying both God's romance and their own, which is focussed on Jesus.

Later albums continue to explore this kind of imagery. We find a longing for God to 'reach inside of me / deeper than before', and to 'hold me tonight, / will you hold me tonight, / hold me tonight, / it feels like heaven'. Another song on the same album depicts a never-ending love which envelops like a cloud:

> Inside outside, pulling me in
> No matter where I run I know you'll never give in
> I see you in the storm, I see you in a kiss
> I've been around the world and never found a love like this
> You're all over me, you're all over me
> You're everything I want to be
> I'm all over you, you're everything I want to see
> You're all over me
>
> You, still captivate me, fascinate me
> You still captivate me, saturate me

117. Delirious?, 'God's Romance', from *Glo* (Furious? Records, 2000).

You still captivate me, liberate me
You still captivate me.[118]

In 2005 we find Martin Smith (Delirious?'s front man) singing 'We're getting closer every day / Into your arms I'm here to stay / ... Everything's beautiful when you invade my life / And I'm living just to say that I love you'. The Jesus to whom he sings is 'our great desire', the home where our heart is, the 'love of my life' who holds me.[119] A few years later, Smith is still 'happy to be lost in you', because 'there's none more beautiful than you' and 'you sing so sweetly, a song called love'. God is the 'sweet heart' who's 'broken this sweet heart', who 'stole this heart of mine / Is it any wonder that our hearts are now entwined'. This final studio album concludes with a simple prayer:

Open my eyes to see
The wonderful mystery of love
Falling into you
I'm drawn to the gravity of love
We're standing still in a moment of eternity
Where worlds collide and I feel the breath of heaven over me

My soul sings [x3]
How I love you (oh I love you).[120]

In his account of life in the band, Martin Smith talks of seeking an intimacy with a divine lover which is even greater than intimacy with his wife, and of the Song of Songs transforming his view of God.[121]

One feature of Delirious?'s albums is the way songs of worship addressed to Jesus stand alongside more ambiguous pieces, which sound like the kind of love songs one might well hear on commercial radio. The choice of capital letters in the lyric sheets supplied with their CDs reinforces the ambiguity: we are given no indicators as to whether these words addressed to 'you', or 'You', or both. Another trend in their albums

---

118. Delirious?, 'Feel It Comin On' and 'Inside, Outside', from *World Service* (Furious? Records, 2003).

119. Delirious?, 'Stronger', 'Fires Burn', 'Love is a Miracle' and 'Take Off my Shoes', from *The Mission Bell* (Furious? Records, 2005).

120. Delirious?, 'How Sweet the Name', 'Wonder' and 'My Soul Sings', from *Kingdom of Comfort* (Furious? Records, 2008).

121. Martin Smith and Craig Borlase, *Delirious: My Journey with the Band, a Growing Family and an Army of Historymakers* (Colorado Springs, CO: David C. Cook, 2011), p. 216.

is to put romantic songs alongside others which seem to indicate a very different kind of relationship with God. Some speak of bowing before the awesome majesty and holiness of God; more recently others explore the need for people who love God to share and live out God's passion for justice, particularly among the poor. The way these very different ideas of relationship with God can co-exist in their music is something I shall consider further in Chapter 4.

Matt Redman: Jesus, I Am So in Love with You
Alongside the songs of Delirious?, those of Matt Redman have also gained much currency in contemporary worship in UK and US churches since the mid-1990s, particularly among younger people. As with Delirious?, Redman's songs have developed a wide range of themes over the years, such as intimacy with God as father, bowing before God as king, trusting in God's unshakable reliability in the storms of life. But he too writes worship songs which, in striving for intimacy with God, evoke the language of romance. From the declaration on his first album, 'I've got a love song in my heart, / It is for you Lord my God',[122] this preference for the language of romance develops more fully in subsequent albums, particularly one entitled 'Intimacy':

> One thing my heart is set upon
> One thing that I would ask
> To know you, Lord, as close as one
> Could hope to on this earth
> Intimacy
> O Jesus, intimacy
> My treasure will be, O Jesus
> Your intimacy
> To look upon your beauty, Lord
> Your glory and your heart
> To know you close, and closer still
> Each day upon this earth
> Lord, since the day I saw you first
> My soul was satisfied
> And yet because I see in part
> I'm searching, more to find
>
> Lord hear the music of my heart
> Hear all the pourings of my soul
> Songs telling of a life of love

122. Matt Redman, 'I've Got a Love Song', from *Wake Up my Soul* (Kingsway Records, 1993).

Jesus this is all for you.
You've become the ruler of my heart
You've become the lover of my soul
You've become the saviour of this life
You are everything to me ...
Jesus, Jesus who can tell how wonderful you are
How wonderful you are
Oh how wonderful you are.[123]

The sense of awe-struck wonder and heartfelt romance becomes even clearer in the simple lyrics of 'Let my Words Be Few':

You are God in Heaven
And here am I on earth
So I'll let my words be few
Jesus, I am so in love with you

And I'll stand in awe of you
Yes, I'll stand in awe of you
And I'll let my words be few
Jesus, I am so in love with you

The simplest of all love songs
I want to bring to you
So I'll let my words be few
Jesus, I am so in love with you.[124]

Four years later we find further love-song imagery in 'If I Have Not Love'. Here the overflow of hearts gazing upon the beauty of Jesus leads into the chorus:

This is a love song
This is a love song
Jesus, a love song to you
A song of devotion, a reverent passion
Saviour, a love song to you
Jesus, I could pray
With a faith that moves a mountain

---

123. Matt Redman, 'Intimacy', and 'Hear the Music of my Heart', from *Intimacy* (Survivor Records, 1998).
124. Matt Redman, 'Let my Words Be Few', from *The Father's Song* (Survivor Records, 2000). An indication of the popularity of this song is seen in its presence in a collection of Redman's best known songs, *Blessed Be your Name: The Songs of Matt Redman Vol. 1* (Survivor Records, 2005).

> But if I have not love
> It is just a noise resounding, an empty sound.[125]

As often, Redman shows awareness of the greatness of the other to whom he is singing, with a passing reference to the need for reverence as well as passion; but the repetition of the evocative phrase 'love song' is what dominates this chorus.

In recent years Redman has inclined away from the language of romance and intimacy in his song writing. One reason for this move is a desire to paint a bigger picture of God in his lyrics. In addition, he voices concern that the language of intimacy may mean different things to different listeners, and that what he intends by such language may be misunderstood. I shall consider these issues in my final chapter.[126]

Stuart Townend: I'm in Love with You my Beautiful
The songs/hymns of Stuart Townend have become established favourites in evangelical and charismatic circles, and beyond, since the late-1990s. Intimacy is a theme, particularly in some of his earlier songs.

'The King of Love is my Delight' (co-written with Kevin Jamieson) emphasizes the kingship and majesty of Jesus, with particular reference to Rev. 1.9-16. But it also expresses a 'desire to have you near', a longing for close relationship; and it alludes to Song of Songs in the lines, 'My lover's breath is sweetest wine, / I am his prize and he is mine'. Here is the kiss of erotic intimacy, and a relationship which suggests mutuality.[127]

In a subsequent album, themes of intimacy are again interwoven with those of royalty. One says simply:

> Please, let me stay,
> Let me rest in your arms of love.
> Please, be my King,
> Be my love, be my everything.[128]

The album closes with words that allude to the Song of Songs ('fragrance'), combined with others suggesting the Psalms ('your words are like honey'), in a prayer to the 'gentle Holy Spirit', who is also 'my Lover':

> Your fragrance is lovely,
> Your radiance fills my gaze,

---

125. Matt Redman, 'If I Have Not Love', from *Facedown* (Survivor Records, 2004).
126. Matt Redman, response to author's question during a seminar on song writing at the 'Leadership Conference', 15 May 2012, Holy Trinity Brompton, London.
127. Kevin Jamieson and Stuart Townend, 'The King of Love' (Thankyou Music, 1997).
128. Stuart Townend, 'Please Let Me Stay', from *Personal Worship* (Kingsway Music, 1999).

> Your words are like honey,
> Renewing me, refreshing me....
> So beautiful, so beautiful,
> So beautiful the things you do.
> So wonderful, so wonderful,
> So wonderful to be with you.
> I'm in love with you, I'm in love with you,
> I'm in love with you my Beautiful.
> I worship you, I worship you,
> I worship you, my Beautiful.[129]

The author explains on the sleeve notes that this album presents songs devised particularly for the individual to use in worship. Themes of romance are not prominent in songs on other albums which he intends for corporate worship; there we find more traditional theological themes presented, such as the Father's love, redemption through the death of Christ, forgiveness, hope and discipleship. When intimacy does surface on more recent albums, it is sometimes parental rather than erotic: thus 'You are my anchor' (based on Psalm 27), expresses desire 'to gaze upon your lovely face / and rest in the Father's embrace'.[130] But listeners may still find the theme of romance suggested by the ambiguity of songs such as 'Mystery' ('If I could pierce these clouds / Could I climb up to the heavens? / Would I touch the hand of mercy? / Would I kiss the face of God?') and 'All I Want to Say' ('All I want to say is "I love you" / All I want to give is my heart / All I want to do is be near you / And walk in your ways.')[131]

Toronto Airport Christian Fellowship: Come Away, my Beloved
The name and ministry of Toronto Airport Christian Fellowship has become known in churches in various countries since the mid-1990s, due to its connection with a renewal movement sometimes called the 'Toronto blessing'. A recent CD produced by this church encourages 'love soaking', which is explained in the sleeve notes as a way of waiting on God, a kind of active rest which involves careful listening to God. Meditation on Scripture forms part of this process, and various Bible passages are recommended. The longest of these is Ps. 63.1-8, chosen for its references to longing for God and delighting in God's love. The songs on the album are intended to com-

---

129. Stuart Townend, 'Your Fragrance is Lovely', from *Personal Worship*.
130. Stuart Townend, 'You Are my Anchor', from *Creation Sings* (Kingsway Music, 2009).
131. Stuart Townend, 'Mystery' and 'All I Want to Say', from *Lord of Every Heart* (Kingsway Music, 2002).

plement the Scripture passages, which are often interwoven into them; for example, 'My Soul Longs After You' clearly draws on Ps. 42.1-2.

The opening song, 'Come Away', is apparently addressed to God, but could also be used of a human love relationship. Along with a possible allusion to Zeph. 3.17, the song makes clearer reference to Song of Songs, particularly Song 2.10-13, which is highlighted in the title. This reference is further emphasized by the overall title of the album, 'Come Away my Beloved'; other CDs in the same series are entitled 'Song of the Bride', 'Intimate Bride' and 'Passionate Bride'.

Subsequent songs on the album *Come Away my Beloved* include 'Take Me Away', where allusions of intimacy permeate the lyrics: 'Take me away with you, Lord … I want you to draw near, / nearer than you've ever been before. … Embrace me in your arms, / Hold me close and never let me go / I want to fall in love with you again.'

In the song 'It's You I Want', the singer's great desire is to 'see your beauty' and to 'behold your glory'. The track which follows seems to move away from intimacy by emphasizing God's transcendence: 'Holy, holy, holy / Lord God Almighty / Who was, and is, and is to come'. At the end of the album comes 'One and Only King', which proclaims: 'You are my first love, / You are my last love, / You are my all in all, Jesus', followed immediately by 'From everlasting to everlasting / You are my one and only King … And I surrender to you, King of kings'. The language of romance is interwoven with images of reverence for an awesome majesty.[132]

Darlene Zschech and Hillsong: The Kiss of Heaven
The iconic image of the Hillsong group of churches since the mid 1990s has been the glamorous face of worship leader Darlene Zschech. With eyes closed and arms open, face raised towards the heavens, she exudes an intensity suggesting desire and delight that approaches ecstasy.[133] The worldwide popularity of one of her early songs ('Shout to the Lord'), combined with the growth of the Hillsong churches in their native Australia and further

132. Jeremy and Connie Sinott, *Come Away my Beloved* (Brampton, Canada: Rejoice Publishing and Productions, 2006). There may be echoes here of John Wimber, the founder of the Vineyard movement, whose love song addressed to the Son of God called 'Isn't He Beautiful?' became popular in some churches in the 1980s; see *Mission Praise* (ed. Horrobin), no. 344.

133. See the CD covers of Darlene Zschech, *The Power of your Love—Symphony* (Sony, 2000) and of the Hillsong worship albums *You Are my World* (Hillsong Music Australia, 2002), *Hope* (Sony, 2003), *For All You've Done* (Sony, 2004), *God He Reigns* (Sony 2005), *Ultimate Worship Collection 1* (Hillsong, 2006), *Mighty to Save* (Emm Chordant, 2010). For an example of Zschech leading worship with the song 'Irresistible', see [http://www.youtube.com/watch?v=T5iA_f2goTY], accessed 10 Mar. 2011.

afield, has made Zschech's music and style influential in a variety of church circles.

Zschech's songwriting is showcased in her first solo album, 'Kiss of Heaven'. In the repeated chorus of the title track she sings:

> My Jesus, dream maker
> My Jesus, life giver
> I'm living under the kiss of heaven
> and I'll never, ever be the same again.
> I'm living in the embrace of heaven
> and I'll never, ever be the same again.[134]

The sense of a romance found in these words is emphasized by the pop style tune, which reminds the hearer of the kind of love songs which might be heard on the radio.

The romantic dream is glimpsed in other songs on the album, such as 'Heaven on Earth', which proclaims:

> Your love is heaven on earth
> I'll shout it out to all the world
> There's no doubt
> my greatest dream has come true
> Just to be loved by you
>
> Whom you set free is free indeed
> I've got the strength of my God in me.[135]

Here the identity of the beloved is unclear, but eventually seems to emerge as being divine, rather than human. By contrast, the song 'Everything About You', presented in the same 'pop love-song' style which pervades the album as a whole, offers devotion to a lover who sounds more than merely human, but eventually emerges as being her husband, Mark (probably—he is not actually named in the song). He is 'the love of my life', repeatedly adored in the chorus: 'And I love everything about you, / everything you are'.[136]

More overt worship of God emerges in songs such as 'Irresistible', where God is presented as 'redeemer and friend' whose mercy awakens the soul, yet also the one 'taking my breath away with your irresistible love'. A version of a traditional hymn is included on the album, and proves to be one which resonates somewhat with the romantic feel of the rest of the

---

134. Darlene Zschech, 'Kiss of Heaven', from *Kiss of Heaven* (INO Records, 2003).
135. Zschech, 'Heaven on Earth', from *Kiss of Heaven*.
136. Zschech, 'Everything About You', from *Kiss of Heaven*.

songs: 'Beautiful Saviour' begins 'Fairest Lord Jesus, ruler of all nature', and goes on to emphasize the bright, shining beauty of Jesus. The album also includes Zschech's most widely sung composition, 'Shout to the Lord', which speaks to 'my Jesus, my saviour', who gives comfort and shelter, 'tower of refuge and strength', praising him as the majestic king over all of creation. Most of the song was inspired by reading Psalms 96–100, while the phrase 'I sing for joy' is perhaps drawn from Ps. 63.7. [137] The influence of these psalms is significant in producing a song which suggests an intimate personal connection with God, while preserving a sense of awe at divine greatness and majesty.

Zschech's second solo album begins with the song 'You Are Here'. The singer is 'worshipping the love of my life', whose loving touch leaves her breathless and longing for his presence, and to whom she proclaims, 'I am yours and you are mine forever more'. The identity of her love remains unclear throughout: the repeated 'Halleluias' by the backing singers might remind some listeners of the worship of God, while others might think of Leonard Cohen's song of that name (discussed earlier), with all its sexual intimations. As the album unfolds, further love songs follow, with the beloved 'you' generally still un-named and mysterious (see 'Captured', 'Sing Over Me' and 'Where Would I Be'); occasional language about a divine or holy one may suggest God, or may simply be examples of hyperbole, for which human lovers are well known. Only in the final two songs of the album do we get a clearer sense that God is being addressed.[138]

The motif of romance emerges strongly in Zschech's book, not least its title: *The Kiss of Heaven: God's Favor to Empower Your Life Dream*.[139] She speaks of sensing God kissing her on the head at the birth of her first child, and clearly sees a kiss as an expression of intimacy (although she writes about God as 'Father' and 'Saviour', rather than lover or husband).[140] She encourages readers to seek the desire of their heart.[141] She also calls readers to identify with the woman in Song of Songs (Song 6.8-9), who is unique and loved.[142] She draws inspiration from various other Bible texts, particularly the Psalms, such as Pss. 37.3-4, 24; 96.1-3; 97.11-12; 100; 139.13-16; 145.4-5.[143]

---

137. Zschech, 'Irresistible', 'Beautiful Saviour' and 'Shout to the Lord', from *Kiss of Heaven*. See also her book, Darlene Zschech, *The Kiss of Heaven: God's Favor to Empower your Life Dream* (Grand Rapids, MI: Baker, 2003), pp. 16-17.

138. Darlene Zschech, *Change your World* (INO Records, 2005).

139. Zschech, *Kiss of Heaven: God's Favor*. Note also the strongly romantic aspect of a number of the photographs throughout the book, eg. pp. 36, 51, 106.

140. Zschech, *Kiss of Heaven: God's Favor*, pp. 31-32, 146.

141. Zschech, *Kiss of Heaven: God's Favor*, pp. 51, 58, 60-67.

142. Zschech, *Kiss of Heaven: God's Favor*, pp. 14, 25, 65.

143. Zschech, *Kiss of Heaven: God's Favor*, pp. 16-17, 43, 52, 146, 155, 212.

The ethos and language of romance in worship, personified by the influential Zschech, has extended more widely into the growing Hillsong movement, which attracts large numbers of younger people. This emerges in songs such as 'Deeply in Love', with its repeated chorus:

> You have stolen my heart
> I'm captivated by you
> Never will You and I part
> I've fallen deeply in love with you, you.[144]

Similarly, 'Keep Falling in Love with You' delights in 'your embrace' and 'your touch', with the repeated chorus:

> I keep falling in love with you Lord
> Every beat of my heart, every breath that I take
> Falling in love, falling in love with you.[145]

The boundaries are blurred, and the language of 'yearning for you/You' runs strongly in the blood of Hillsong.[146]

What More Shall We Say of ...
Other contemporary Christian worship songs could also be cited. Another recent release in the 'soaking' style is Alberto and Kimberly Rivera's 'Captured'. The title track and focal song of the album involves gentle, insistent repetition of phrases such as 'hold me', 'you have captured my heart' and 'can you feel my arms around you?'. The language of feeling and joyful passion abounds; and it is not always clear whether the speaker is the worshipper or God, as the singing voice seems to drift from one to the other.[147]

A similar ambiguity can be found in 'You Won't Relent', a song on the album 'Your Love Never Fails' produced by the 'jesusculture' revivalist

---

144. Kate Spence, 'Deeply in Love', from *One* (Hillsong Music Australia, 1999).

145. Scott Haslem, 'Keep Falling in Love with You', from *Overwhelmed* (Hillsong Music Australia, 2000). Romance and tenderness emerge less explicitly in other songs, such as Marty Simson's 'Carry Me', from *For This Cause* (Hillsong Music Australia, 2000) and Reuben Morgan's, 'Eagles Wings', from *Extravagant Worship: The Songs of Reuben Morgan* (Hillsong Music Australia, 2002). As leader of the Hillsong Creative Arts team, and co-producer of many of the albums mentioned here, Darlene Zschech's influence on other musicians within the church has been considerable.

146. In the full canon of songs from Hillsong, more begin with the words 'you' or 'your' than with any other word; see [http://en.wikipedia.org/wiki/List_of_Hillsong_songs], accessed 10 Mar. 2011.

147. Alberto and Kimberly Rivera, 'Captured', from *Captured* (Integrity Music, 2009).

movement. As the song reaches its peak, two voices intertwine, one male and one female. Lyrics taken directly from Song 8.5-7 celebrate a love that is stronger than death and unquenchable by any flood, while another voice sings, 'You won't relent / until you have it all / my heart is yours'. Passionate engagement with God is indicated: 'Come be the flame upon my heart / come be the fire inside of me / until you and I are one'. But even the intermittent use of capital 'Y' for 'You' on the album's lyric sheet does not always clarify who is being addressed; and for anyone simply listening rather than reading the lyrics, the identities of the speakers are further blurred.[148]

Brian Doerksen's exploration of his experience of songwriting includes a chapter on his 'Song for the Bride', focussing on what he terms 'the divine romance of God with his people'. Doerkson sees God as a husband, taking various roles in relation to his bride. This is expressed in the song as follows: 'I have longed to hold you in my arms, / and take all your fear away'. The divine lover promises to take away her filthy rags and make them clean, 'If you will receive my love, / if you will receive my love'. The song goes on to call for repentance and returning to God.[149] As a more recent example of this genre, Doerksen praises Steve Mitchinson's song, 'Divine Romance', which is framed in terms of marriage vows: 'I do choose you to be my husband, be my Lord, / To have and to hold from this day forward'. The singer goes on to promise, 'I do give you my heart and all that I possess, / to love and to cherish every word and each caress'. The song concludes with words (perhaps from the divine husband): 'You take my hand, I'll guide your steps, / I'll show you how to dance, this divine romance'.[150]

Tim Hughes's 'Beautiful One' places the repeated chorus 'Beautiful one, I love you, / beautiful one, I adore, / beautiful one my soul must sing' alongside verses which marvel at the cross and celebrate God's power, glory, majesty and mighty works. The bridge section proclaims: 'You opened my eyes to your wonders anew, / you captured my heart with this love / because nothing on earth is as beautiful as you', leading back round into the chorus. Images of love and beauty prevail. Is this the intoxication of romance?[151] In his book

---

148. Misty Edwards, David Brymer and Cassandra Cambell, 'You Won't Relent', from your *Love Never Fails* (Chris Quilala, Kim Walker and Melissa How; jesus-culturemusic, 2008).

149. Brian Doerksen, *Make Love, Make War: Now Is the Time to Worship* (London: David C. Cook, 2009), pp. 233-51, especially p. 240. Brian Doerksen, 'Song for the Bride' (Vineyard, 1990).

150. Doerksen, *Make Love, Make War*, p. 241. Steve Mitchinson, 'Divine Romance' (ION, 2007).

151. Tim Hughes, 'Beautiful One', from *When Silence Falls* (Survivor Records, 2004).

about worship, Hughes repeatedly affirms intimacy, romance and falling in love with God or Jesus as helpful ways to understand relationship with God.[152]

Craig Musseau's 'Here I Am Once Again' gently revels in the faithfulness, listening and speaking of a you who is never actually named in the song. The chorus keeps repeating the desire to 'pour out my heart' to say that I love you, that I'm thankful, and that 'You're wonderful'. In this, as in most other contemporary worship songs, 'heart' seems to be understood in the current Western sense of 'centre of my emotions', rather than the broader Hebrew sense of 'centre of my thoughts and will' (although the Hebrew understanding sometimes includes the emotions).[153]

Intense language of the 'heart' is also found in Marie Barnet's 'This Is the Air I Breathe', where the worshipper sings 'I'm desperate for you / I'm lost without you' and longs to hear 'your very word spoken to me'. The identity of this 'you' is unclear, apart from a cryptic reference to 'your holy presence living in me'.[154]

In Ruth Fazal's 'Maranatha', wedding imagery is prominent, and slightly confused, with the singer positioned in verse one as a bride awaiting the return of her bridegroom/king, while in verse three she or he takes on the role of one of the five wise bridesmaids depicted in Jesus' parable (Matt. 25.1-13), while the chorus takes us to the eschatological wedding of Rev. 21–22. The romantic imagery which pervades the whole song becomes clearest in verse two:

> How long until I see the One I love?
> How long until I rest within your arms?
> How long until this aching heart is stilled?
> O, I will watch, and I will wait
> And I will cry with all my heart....

Here the psalmists' familiar cry of longing blends into imagery more at home in the Song of Songs. This leads us back into the chorus, 'Maranatha! Come, O come, / Beloved Bridegroom, come!'[155]

Jars of Clay's 'Love Song for a Savior' begins with a female figure enjoying the open fields of wild flowers, and thanking her Jesus for the daisies and the roses:

152. Timothy R. Hughes, *Holding Nothing Back* (Eastbourne: Kingsway, 2007): intimacy (pp. 20, 82), romance (pp. 75-76), falling in love with God/Jesus (pp. 18, 97 twice).

153. Craig Musseau, 'Here I Am Once Again' (Mercy/'Divine Romance' (ION, 2007).

154. Marie Barnett, 'This Is the Air I Breathe' (Mercy/Vineyard Publishing, 1996).

155. Ruth Fazal, 'Maranatha', from *Joy in the Night* (Tributary Music, 2007). See also [http://www.ruthfazal.com/jin.htm], accessed 18 Nov. 2010.

Someday she'll understand the meaning of it all.
He's more than the laughter or the stars in the heavens,
As close as a heartbeat or a song on her lips;
Someday she'll trust him and learn how to see him,
Someday he'll call her and she will come running
and fall in his arms and the tears will fall down and she'll pray,
"I want to fall in love with you
I want to fall in love with you
I want to fall in love with you
I want to fall in love with you".[156]

Next the song moves to a church setting, where those sitting silent in their
Sunday best cannot feel the chains on their souls. Then it repeats most of
the section quoted above, with 'we' replacing 'she'—no longer merely
observing, the listeners are invited to participate in this romance or worship
along with the singer. Finally the singer speaks of seeking words to show
his devotion, and reverts once more to the repeated chorus, 'I want to fall
in love with you', before fading out with the added refrain, 'my heart beats
for you'.

Yearning, Then and Now
It is important to acknowledge that expressing in song a passionate desire
for God and God's love is far from being a new development. Previous
generations sang:

Come down, O love divine,
seek Thou this soul of mine
and visit it with Thine own ardour glowing;
O Comforter, draw near,
within my heart appear,
and kindle it, Thy holy flame bestowing.

And so the yearning strong,
with which the soul will long,
shall far outpass the power of human telling …[157]

Desire for some kind of intimate and personal encounter is clearly in evidence. Yet the rest of the hymn sees the welcomed Holy Spirit freely burning within 'till earthly passions turn / to dust and ashes, in its heat consum-
ing'; this Comforter brings illumination, holy charity and a lowliness of

156. Jars of Clay, 'Love Song for a Savior', from *Furthermore* (Essential Records,
2003).
157. R.F. Littledale, 'Come Down, O Love Divine', *Mission Praise* (ed. Horrobin),
no. 89.

heart that 'weeps with loathing' at its own shortcomings. Romantic hopes of finding a lover are not presented here. Nor are they apparent in:

> O, the deep, deep, love of Jesus!
> Vast, unmeasured, boundless, free;
> Rolling like a mighty ocean
> in its fullness over me.
> Underneath me, all around me,
> is the current of thy love;
> leading onward, leading homeward,
> to my glorious rest above.[158]

The singer clearly revels in a love which can envelop and exhilarate the individual; yet the hymn as a whole still preserves a sense of distance from an awesome, heavenly king. Some of Charles Wesley's hymns also express desire and longing for union with a beloved Saviour, but with a similar sense of reverence for the divine majesty.[159] What is notably absent in these older worship songs, and evident in some of the contemporary ones, is the motif of romance in the divine-human relationship.

Conclusion

When Kanye West's 2004 single 'Jesus Walks' achieved both critical acclaim and huge sales in the USA, Canada and UK, many listeners and commentators were surprised. The lyrics of the song journeyed through some of America's contemporary ills, with the chorus repeatedly asking God to show the way and claiming that 'Jesus walks with me'. Conventional wisdom in the world of rap/hip-hop (and beyond) said that a song with such overtly religious content would not be a commercial success—a view provocatively echoed by West himself in the song's lyrics: 'So here go my single dog radio needs this / they say you can rap about anything but Jesus / that means guns, sex, lies, videotape / but if I talk about God my record won't get played—huh?'.[160]

The success of 'Jesus Walks', and the debate about (and in) the song itself, reflects an ambivalence in the contemporary Western world. On the one hand, a cultural shift away from traditional expressions of religion is evident in the decline in attendance at traditional church services, and

---

158. Samuel Taylor Francis, 'O the Deep, Deep Love of Jesus', *Mission Praise* (ed. Horrobin), no. 522.

159. See 'What Shall I Do my God to Love', 'Jesus the Good Shepherd Is' and 'Love Divine' *Hymns and Psalms* (London: Methodist Publishing House, 1983), nos. 46, 263, 267.

160. Kayne West, 'Jesus Walks', from *The College Dropout* (Roc-a-Fella, 2004).

reflected in a reluctance in the music industry as a whole to market music with overtly religious themes. On the other hand, religious language and imagery continues to flourish, as I have shown by examining just one aspect of the way that language is used in contemporary music. In this chapter I have highlighted the way a variety of highly acclaimed and influential musicians use language suggestive of encounter with God in order to express experience of human sexual relationships, while others use the language of human romance to express desire for God. While the reasons for doing so cannot often be ascertained, I contend that one of the effects of this trend is to blur the boundaries between human sexual desire and desire for God.

Links between popular music and religion can be observed down the centuries and across a variety of cultures.[161] More specifically, the roots of rock run deep in Gospel music, and in its ancestor, the spirituals of earlier generations of black Americans.[162] So it should come as no great surprise to find religious themes constantly resurfacing in contemporary rock music, in a variety of forms. Some songwriters use sacred texts and religious discourse to articulate sincere convictions about God, or to advocate social justice, while others use similar terms to express alienation and independence from authority, sometimes rejecting and ridiculing religious beliefs and communities in the process. Certain songwriters choose to misread or reinterpret their religious influences, in order to display their own independence and creativity; compare, for example, the different ways in which the title 'lily of the valley' (Song 2.1) is used by different songwriters.[163] Drawing on Harold Bloom's 'Anxiety-of-Influence' theory, Michael Gilmour argues that religion is a massive and inescapable precursor from which today's songwriters (particularly those in the Western world) cannot escape. It can be further argued that the power of rock music actually depends in part on its competitive and ambivalent relationship with its religious roots: 'Contemporary songs, and the subcultures that identify with this music, define

---

161. See, for example, Begbie, *Resounding Truth*, pp. 16-19, 77-96, 141-62.

162. See Steve Turner, *Hungry for Heaven: Searching for Meaning in Rock and Religion* (London: Hodder, 1995); Jeremy Beckwith, *God Gave Rock and Roll to You* (Channel 4, broadcast 23 Dec. 2006).

163. For Johnny Cash, the 'lily of the valley' refers to Jesus as saviour and friend (Johnny Cash, 'The Lily of the Valley', from *Personal File* [Legacy/Columbia, 2006]). For Queen, the 'lily of the valley' is an elusive figure who does not know how to help the one 'forever searching high and low' (Queen, 'Lily of the Valley', from *Sheer Heart Attack* [EMI, 1974]). More recently, Alicia Keys' poem 'Lilly [*sic*] of the Valley' portrays a vulnerable and exploited individual, a stripper forced to sell herself, who has an inner beauty which needs to be recognized (Alicia Keys, 'Lilly of the Valley', *Tears for Water: Songbook of Poems and Lyrics* [New York: Penguin, 2004]; see [http://community.livejournal.com/_hotlove/5705.html], accessed 8 Mar. 2011).

themselves over and against a sacred Other. ... They need the religious precursor to define themselves.'[164]

Musical tastes and fashions tend to be transient. All the more striking, then,
is the ubiquity of the love song—still dominating popular song writing today,
as it has done throughout the past sixty years. Today's songs are less coy and
romantic, more sexually explicit than those of the 1950s, but the agonies and
ecstasies of yearning for the other still dominate the music and particularly
the lyrics.[165] Moreover, we should not be surprised to find affinities between
contemporary worship songs and popular love songs, since today's worship
songwriters have grown up listening to the popular music of their day.[166]

The extent to which contemporary musicians are blurring the boundaries
between 'you' and 'You' in regard to yearning should not be exaggerated.
Christian worship songs pursue a number of other themes, in addition to
that of intimacy with God; I shall touch on some of these in Chapter Four.
In wider mainstream culture, many current songwriters include few religious allusions in their work, or none at all. Some of those that do touch
on relationship with the divine do not make it a prominent feature of their
work.[167] Moreover, in some songs religious language depicting the 'other'
as an angel or a saviour might simply be heard as flattering hyperbole, or
the ingratiating language of seduction.[168] Nonetheless, the examples which I
have highlighted in this chapter do indicate significant engagement with the
theme of yearning for a human or divine other among a variety of contemporary musicians whose music reaches huge audiences. If we note Simon
Frith's conclusion that popular songs have become an important way in
which we learn to make sense of the world, to recognize and understand
ourselves, and to construct our identities, then their significance is not to
be underestimated.[169] Expressions of 'yearning for you', and of 'yearning for
You', are in the cultural air that we breathe today, expressing and shaping
people's self-understanding.

164. Gilmour, *Gods and Guitars*, pp. xvi, 42, 48, 116-18.
165. Cf. Frith and Goodwin, *On Record*, p. 3.
166. A Sheffield undergraduate, attending church for first time since childhood,
commented 'I was surprised to recognize only one of the songs as something I've heard
before in church: the others comprised simplistic lyrics set to pop-like melodies, the
kind of which I'd more readily expect from Coldplay'. (Lucy Boase, 'Calling the City to
God', *Forge Press*, Issue 14, Friday Oct 9 2009).
167. Arcade Fire, for example, interact with the religious backgrounds of some of
the band members in their songs, but in terms of parody and critique rather than yearning; see *Neon Bible* (Merge, 2007); see also Gilmour, *Gods and Guitars*, pp. 56-67.
168. Gilmour, *Gods and Guitars*, pp. 97-99.
169. Simon Frith, *Performing Rites*, pp. 272-76.

2

'LET HIM KISS ME ... HAVING YOU, I DESIRE NOTHING ELSE':
YEARNING FOR YOU/YOU IN THE HISTORY OF INTERPRETATION
OF THE PSALMS AND THE SONG OF SONGS

Almost all of the musicians cited in the previous chapter are children of the UK, North America or Australia. They have grown up in cultures where thinking and language have been profoundly influenced by the words of the Bible (as recent celebrations of the anniversary of the King James translation reminded us). Some of these songwriters are also professing Christians, who consciously look to the Bible as a key authority in matters of faith. Therefore it seems appropriate to turn to the Bible, to see how it may have influenced them in their song writing. Does today's blurring of boundaries between desire for intimacy with God and desire for human sexual intimacy have any roots in the Bible or in the way the Bible has been interpreted?

Surveying the history of interpretation of my chosen biblical texts, the Psalms and Song of Songs, is not a straightforward business. The vastness of the territory is daunting.[1] Therefore what follows can only be highly selective; I limit my search to themes of desire and intimacy identified in the Song of Songs and the Psalms by those who have interpreted them. I also take particular interest in those writers who refer to both these books, especially on the occasions when they suggest parallels or connections between the two. Inevitably this leads to some overlap between the two sections of this chapter; thus the opening section is primarily about the Psalms, but

---

1. For a far more comprehensive picture of the reception history of the Psalms, see the whole of Susan E. Gillingham, *Psalms Through the Centuries*, I (Blackwell Bible Commentaries; Oxford: Blackwell, 2008). For a summary of the Song's entire history of interpretation, see Marvin H. Pope, *Song of Songs* (Anchor Bible, 7c; New York: Doubleday, 1977), pp. 89-229, or Duane Garrett, *Song of Songs* (Word Biblical Commentary, 23B; Nashville, TN: Thomas Nelson, 2004), pp. 59-91; see also the whole of Richard A. Norris Jr, *The Song of Songs Interpreted by Early Christian and Medieval Commentators* (The Church's Bible; Cambridge: Eerdmans, 2003).

includes references to the Song, while the second section mirrors this pattern, making occasional reference to the Psalms while focusing mainly on the Song. In addition, while some commentators are highlighted only in one section, others appear in both, because they wrote something significant on both the Song and the Psalms. My attention in this chapter falls mostly on writers of the pre-modern era. The chapter which follows will include engagement with more recent scholarship.

As far as possible, this chapter focuses on citations or allusions to the Psalms or the Song. Both of the verses quoted in my heading, for example (from Song 1.2 and Ps. 73.25), are cited by commentators as diverse as Rashi, Bernard of Clairvaux, and Francis de Sales. But at times clear citations can seem an elusive quarry, particularly in more mystical or poetic writings. The discipline of acknowledging sources through meticulous footnotes is a recent arrival on the scholarly scene; this was not the concern of most writers in previous centuries. Consequently, it is not always clear whether a writer is referring to a certain biblical text or not. The Psalms are a particular case in point. Clergy and members of religious orders down the centuries have said and sung the Psalms daily throughout the year, until these words become ingrained. What then emerged from their Scripture-soaked minds in devotional and theological writings often included an undersong which had become linguistic second nature, 'an unconscious ventriloquism of the Scripture's voices'.[2] Precisely identifying allusions to the Song can also be difficult (Geoffrey Chaucer's 'The Merchant's Tale, for example, cites the Song clearly, while 'The Miller's Tale' seems to echo the Song in various places without ever quoting it).[3] Therefore I shall occasionally refer to writings of this nature in which a biblical allusion is not explicit and could be disputed, when this seems particularly appropriate.

2. Peter S. Hawkins, 'Singing a New Song: The Poetic Afterlife of the Psalms', in *Psalms in Community* (ed. Harold W. Attridge and Margot E. Fasler; SBL Symposium, 25; Atlanta, SBL, 2003), pp. 382, 386. The same may also be said of parts of the New Testament, particularly the book of Revelation, where not a single quotation from the Hebrew Bible is found, yet scarcely a verse would survive if all the allusions to the Psalms and other parts of the Hebrew Bible were removed; cf. John Goldingay, *Psalms 1-41* (Grand Rapids, MI: Baker Academic, 2006), p. 76.

3. F.N. Robinson (ed.), *The Works of Geoffrey Chaucer* (Oxford: Oxford University Press, 1977), pp. 48-55, 124. See James Doelman, 'Song of Songs', in *A Dictionary of Biblical Tradition in English Literature* (ed. David Lyle Jeffrey; Grand Rapids, MI: Eerdmans, 1992), pp. 728-29; he also suggests echoes of the Song to be found in the works of other poets, such as George Herbert, Andrew Marvell and Henry Vaughan.

Psalms

The importance and influence of the Psalms in Jewish and Christian circles over the centuries is well established. The Babylonian Talmud connects the Psalms with ten elders, including Adam, Melchizedek, Abraham and Moses; this testifies to the particular high standing given to this book, even by the standards of Holy Scripture. The Psalms outnumber any other biblical book found in the Dead Sea Scrolls, and the canonical Psalms seem to have influenced the composition of the so-called *Hodayot* songs found at Qumran, as well as the Psalms of Solomon. The Psalms were of great importance in midrashic proof-texting, and in Rabbinic Judaism after the destruction of the Temple in 70 C.E. they were used to help preserve communal and private worship, particularly at Passover. The early churches treasured the Psalms as a 'Bible in miniature', and enshrined them especially in the daily monastic cycle of prayers (the Office). One of the earliest extant baptism liturgies depicts candidates for baptism being examined to see if they had read the Scriptures and learned the Psalms. Numerous commentaries and homilies were written on them. Patristic witnesses testify to the huge popularity of the use of the Psalms in church worship, and praise their congregations on this account even while berating them for other aspects of their conduct in church. Medieval illuminated Psalters were used in saying the daily office and in private meditation; a few were magnificent, for the use of the nobility, but other, simpler versions circulated widely among poorer people. Luther and Calvin both treasured the Psalms; their extensive writing and preaching on them added to the demand for them. Calvin subsequently commissioned the production of the 'Huguenot Psalter', which sold in large numbers during his lifetime and proved very influential throughout Europe.[4] Clearly the Psalms have a longevity and ecumenicity which is

---

4. Klaus Seybold, *Introducing the Psalms* (Edinburgh: T. & T. Clark, 1990), pp. 5, 217-23, 247-48; Robert F. Taft, 'Christian Liturgical Psalmody: Origins, Development, Decomposition, Collapse', in *Psalms in Community* (ed. Attridge and Fasler), p. 23; Lawrence A. Hoffman, 'Hallels, Canon and Loss: Psalms in Jewish Liturgy', in *Psalms in Community* (ed. Attridge and Fasler), pp. 45, 56; Raymond J. Tournay, *Seeing and Hearing God in the Psalms: The Prophetic Liturgy from the Second Temple in Jerusalem* (trans. J. Edward Crowley; JSOTSup, 118; Sheffield: Sheffield Academic Press, 1991), p. 232; Bruce K. Waltke and James M. Houston, with Erika Moore, *The Psalms as Christian Worship: A Historical Commentary* (Grand Rapids, MI: Eerdmans, 2010), p. 117. Also Peter W. Flint, 'The Psalms and Qumran' and Elizabeth Solopova, 'Liturgical Psalters in Medieval Europe': both papers given at the Conference 'Conflict and Convergence: Jewish and Christian Approaches to the Psalms', Worcester College, Oxford, 22-24 Sept. 2010.

remarkable, appealing to Jews and Christians of different cultures, classes and denominations through the centuries.[5]

The Sweetness of Poetry

Early Christian exegetes encourage their readers to understand but also to feel the Psalms; the words of the Psalms were to be taken to heart so that one's own thoughts and emotions, desires and passions, might be purified and healed and transformed. The variety and strength of human passions was a fact of life acknowledged in the Psalms, which were themselves seen to be crucial in dealing with these passions. The combination of words with music, urged repeatedly in the Psalter's conclusion (Pss. 146.2; 147.1; 149.1, 3; 150.3-5) and continued in Jewish and early Christian worship (Eph. 5.18-20; Col. 3.16-17), added a further dimension to the emotional impact of the Psalms on worshippers.[6]

Many of these early writers find the beauty of the poetry in the Psalms captivating. Some observe that poetry not only informs, but also beguiles and diverts the reader with its 'sweetness'; thus Ambrose of Milan pronounces that 'the book of Psalms is especially sweet', while John Chrysostom declares that nothing 'so arouses the soul, gives it wing, sets it free from the earth, releases it from the prison of the body, teaches it to love wisdom, and to condemn all things of this life, as concordant melody and sacred song'. Flavius Cassiodorus delights in 'the unique *eloquentia*, the heart-transforming beauty of these biblical poems'. Similarly, Theodoret of Cyrus admires the way divine grace is mingled with the charm of poetry in the Psalms; and while he sees most people making little or no reference to the other divine Scriptures in their daily lives, 'the spiritual harmonies of the divinely inspired David many people frequently call to mind, whether at home, in public places or while travelling, gain serenity for themselves from the harmony of the poetry, and reap benefit for themselves through this enjoyment'.[7]

Awareness of the beauty of the poetry, and of its disconcerting power to move the reader, is a response to the text also found among interpreters of the Song of Songs from the earliest times and re-emphasized in recent liter-

---

5. Cf. Terrien, *Psalms*, pp. 4-5.

6. Waltke and Houston, *Psalms as Christian Worship*, pp. 39-40, 486. Gillingham notes that a tradition of singing hymns based on the Psalms can be traced back to Ephraim the Syrian (306-73 c.e.), although such private compositions were subsequently banned from public worship by the Synod of Laodicea (363–364 c.e.) (*Psalms through the Centuries* 1, pp. 34-38).

7. Brian Daley, 'Finding the Right Key: The Aims and Strategies of Early Christian Interpretation of the Psalms', in *Psalms in Community* (ed. Attridge and Fasler), pp. 192-98; Theodoret of Cyrus, *Commentary on the Psalms* I (trans. Robert C. Hill; Washington DC., Catholic University of America Press, 2000), p. 40.

ary analysis of the text. The Psalms, like the Song, do not invite dispassionate analysis; they seek to engage and stir the passions of the readers/hearers.
Poetry does not 'make nothing happen', as an elegy for a recent poet has it;
on the contrary, it changes the worlds of those who engage with it, not least
by the pleasure it brings and its effect on their emotions. The poetry of the
Psalms can both stimulate and express a deep-seated yearning for relationship with another.[8]

Philo of Alexandria's Therapeutae

The singing of both scriptural and newly composed hymns during early
Christian worship, particularly after communal meals such as the *Agape*, is
well attested from sources such as Eusebius, Clement of Alexandria, Tertullian and Hippolytus. Tertullian and Clement both warn Christians to avoid
copying the debauchery of Greek love feasts, with Clement adding 'but let
erotic songs be far removed from here; let hymns to God be our song'. Here
a clear divide is made between the sacred and the sexual in terms of the
kind of songs to be used in worship. But the fact that Clement needs to state
this may suggest that he was responding to particular practices, and that not
everyone was as clear in their minds as he was about the need to make such
definite distinctions.[9]

Clement's earlier compatriot, Philo of Alexandria, gives a striking
description of a group he calls the Therapeutae—presumably a Jewish
group, although Eusebius later co-opts them and surmises from Philo's
glowing account that they must have been Christian. While indicating his
own fierce hostility to the apparent debauchery of contemporary Greek
feasts, Philo offers the Therapeutae as a striking contrast. Depicting them as
admirably self-disciplined and self-controlled in their commitment to studying the Scriptures and their ascetic lifestyle, Philo nevertheless describes
how their worship led them into raptures and ecstasy as they sang hymns
of thanksgiving to God their saviour. The president of the meeting would
lead them in singing either a new hymn of his own composition, or one
of many inherited from earlier days. They were then 'carried away by a
heaven-sent passion of love, remain rapt and possessed like bacchanals or

---

8. J. Cheryl Exum, *Song of Songs: A Commentary* (OTL; Louisville: Westminster
John Knox Press, 2005). pp. 7-8, 45-47; Walter Brueggemann, *An Introduction to the
Old Testament: The Canon and Christian Imagination* (Louisville: Westminster John
Knox Press, 2003), pp. 283-84. See also Brueggemann's *Finally Comes the Poet* (Min-
neapolis: Fortress Press, 1989), pp. 1-6.

9. Tertullian, *The Apology (Apologeticum)* 39.16-18 [http://www.tertullian.org/
articles/mayor_apologeticum/mayor_apologeticum_07translation.htm]; Clement of
Alexandria, *The Instructor (Paedagogus)* 2.4 [http://www.ccel.org/ccel/schaff/anf02.
vi.iii.ii.iv.html], both accessed 9 May 2011. See also Peter Jeffrey, 'Philo's Impact on
Christian Psalmody', in *Psalms in Community* (ed. Attridge and Fasler), p. 176.

corybants until they see the object of their yearning'. The image of drunkenness recurs, as Philo depicts two choirs (male and female) singing hymns to
God with rapt enthusiasm after supper:

> And when each choir has separately done its own part in the feast, having
> drunk as in the Bacchic rites of the strong wine of God's love, they mix
> and both together become a single choir, a copy of the choir set up of old
> beside the Red Sea. ...
>
>   Thus they continue till dawn, drunk with this drunkenness in which
> there is no shame ... and when they see the sun rising they stretch their
> hands up to heaven and pray for bright days and knowledge of the truth
> and the power of keen sighted thinking. And after the prayers they depart
> each to his private sanctuary once more to ply the trade and till the field of
> their wonted philosophy.[10]

Philo's depiction of this group is highly idealized, which raises questions
about its accuracy; a polemical agenda is evident. But if we can assume
some historical substance behind it, we may have a glimpse of worshippers
using (or at least influenced by) the Psalms in striving for an ecstatic and
mystical experience of God's love and presence.[11] If we doubt any historical
basis to Philo's description, we are still left with his evident admiration for
this kind of worship, even if only in his own imagination, and his willingness to commend it in words which blend passion, love, rapture, ecstasy and
drunkenness in vivid and startling ways.

Athanasius of Alexandria
We know that Athanasius' 'Letter to Marcellinus' was valued so highly in
antiquity that it was included in the Codex Alexandrinus (early fifth century
C.E.) as an introduction to the book of Psalms. Athanasius delights not only
in the poetry but also in the singing of the Psalms, in which he sees more
than simply aesthetic value:

> Holy Scripture is not designed to tickle the aesthetic palate, and it is rather
> for the soul's own profit that the Psalms are sung. This is so chiefly for
> two reasons. In the first place, it is fitting that the sacred writings should
> praise God in poetry as well as prose, because the freer, less restricted
> form of verse, in which the Psalms, together with the Canticles and Odes
> [presumably a reference to other hymns such as Exodus 15.1-18, Deu-
> teronomy 32.1-43, and Habakkuk 3], are cast, ensures that by them men

---

10. Philo of Alexandria, 'On the Contemplative Life', in *Philo* (Loeb Classical
Library IX; trans. F.H. Colson; London, Heinemann, 1941), pp. 130-31, 155, 162-65,
168-69.

11. Jeffrey, 'Philo's Impact', pp. 162-63, 172-76; Eaton, *Psalms*, p. 47. Also Maren
R. Niehoff, 'The Symposium of Philo's Therapeutae: Displaying Jewish Identity in
an Increasingly Roman World', *Greek, Roman, and Byzantine Studies* 50 (2010), pp.
98-108; Susan Gillingham, personal correspondence, 21 Jan. 2011.

[*sic*] should express their love to God with all the strength and power they possess. And, secondly, the reason lies in the unifying effect which chanting the Psalms has upon the singer. For to sing the Psalms demands such concentration of a man's whole being on them that, in doing it, his usual disharmony of mind and corresponding bodily confusion is resolved, just as the notes of several flutes are brought by harmony to one effect.[12]

Clearly Athanasius sees a power in the musical expression of these sacred songs which enables passionate spiritual engagement within the singer at the deepest level. The way he brackets the Psalms with both the Odes and Canticles (the latter presumably a reference to Song of Songs) suggests that all these texts can, in his view, have a similar effect in enabling a powerful encounter with the divine.

Athanasius focuses briefly on particular psalms, such as Psalm 42, which he commends as suitable for use when one is 'aflame with longing for God'. He comments further on the Psalms' ability to help their readers become aware of their needs and longings, and subtly to reshape the inner life of thoughts and desires to conform to God's own word.

Jerome

When Jerome writes to Marcella, urging her to join him and Paula in their new life in Bethlehem, he paints an idyllic picture of life in the Holy Land, in contrast to the distractions and corruptions of Rome:

Wherever you go, the husbandman sings the alleluia over his plough; the toiling harvester refreshes himself with the psalms; the vine dresser prunes his vine to a song of David. These are the popular songs of this country; the love songs of the shepherd's whistle; the lyrics of the farmer as he tills the soil with devotion.[13]

Even allowing for the hyperbole of this idealized vision, we sense in Jerome's description a strong attachment to the Psalms as the songs of ordinary people. We also note the way he compares them to popular love songs. This may be primarily alluding to how widely known and sung they were in his new context, and perhaps a contrast to the kind of songs commonly sung in Rome. But Jerome's willingness to compare part of the sacred Scripture over which he laboured in years of translation to secular love songs is striking nonetheless. He likens songs of spiritual devotion to songs of human

---

12. Athanasius of Alexandria, *Letter to Marcellinus, Concerning the Psalms* [http://www.fisheaters.com/psalmsathanasiusletter.html], accessed 30 June 2009.

13. Jerome, *Letters and Select Works* (trans. W.H. Fremantle; ed. P. Schaff and H. Wace; The Nicene and Post-Nicene Fathers, vol. 6; Oxford: Parker and Company, 1893), letter 46.12, p. 65; see also Jerome, *Homilies on the Psalms* I (trans. Marie L. Ewald; The Fathers of the Church, vol. 48; Washington DC., Catholic University of America Press, 1981), pp. xi-xii.

love without embarrassment or qualification. He also depicts people singing them in situations of everyday life (some solitary), rather than in corporate worship.

Elsewhere in his letters, Jerome uses the language of passionate desire with reference to the Psalms. He commends the imagery of the parched soul thirsting and longing for God in Pss. 63.1-3 and 42.1-2 to Rusticus and Lucinius, who are striving for restoration of intimacy with God. Writing to Eustochium on the death of his mother Paula, he praises the latter for her perseverance, along with 'the passion of her mind and the yearning of her believing soul, both of which made her sing in David's words: "My soul thirsteth after thee, my flesh longeth after thee"'. Jerome pictures Paula at the moment of death hearing the bridegroom call: 'Rise up my love my fair one, my dove, and come away: for lo, the winter is past, the rain is over and gone', to which she answered joyfully, 'the flowers appear on the earth; the time to cut them has come', and 'I believe that I shall see the good things of the Lord in the land of the living'. Here Jerome presents the desire of the lovers in the Song for each other alongside the psalmist's confident security in being close to God (Song 2.10-12; Ps. 27.13); he sees both expressing the same glorious encounter with God after death.

Jerome's distaste for sexual relationships is clear from a number of his works, including his translation of Song 8.5 (where 'conceived' and 'gave birth' are translated 'corrupted' and 'violated'), as well as his attack on Jovinian, which became widely known in the Western Church and a key resource for those advocating clerical celibacy. Yet still Jerome embraces biblical examples of the language of *eros*. Encouraging Demetrias, a wealthy Roman who had recently embraced her new vocation as a virgin, Jerome reminds her of the ceremony in which the bishop prayerfully covered her head with the virgin's bridal veil and declared solemnly, 'I wish to present you all as a chaste virgin to Christ'. 'Thereupon the bride herself rejoices and says, "the king hath brought me into his chambers", and the choir of her companions responds, "the king's daughter is all glorious within"'. Here the delight of the woman in Song 1.4 blends seamlessly with imagery of the royal wedding from Ps. 45.12; both provide images of how Demetrias will now relate to God. 'Happy is the soul', Jerome continues, 'happy is the virgin in whose heart there is room for no other love than the love of Christ', citing as his proof text Ps. 27.4, where the psalmist seeks to live in the house of Yhwh all his days and to behold the beauty of Yhwh. Jerome urges her to occupy her mind with the reading of Scripture, 'saying with the bride in the Song of Songs "By night I sought him whom my soul loveth. Tell me where thou feedest, where thou makest thy flock rest at noon"; and with the psalmist: "my soul followest hard after thee: thy right hand upholdeth me"'. Here the determination of the bride to be close to her love is paralleled by that of the psalmist striving to come near to God (Song 3.1; 1.7; Ps. 63.8). Once again the language of desire for God stands side by side with the language of human sexual desire, even though the latter is understood figuratively.

In his Homilies on Psalms 84 and 143 Jerome again depicts the deep craving of the soul for God in terms of desperate thirst, emphasizing the need for mortification of the flesh and its desires in order to experience the love of God. His letter to Eustochium, about the life of virginity, states that it is hard for the human soul to avoid loving something; therefore fleshly love needs to be overcome by spiritual love. 'Desire is quenched by desire. What is taken from the one increases the other. Therefore, as you lie on your couch, say again and again: "By night have I sought Him whom my soul loveth"' (Song 3.1, one of Jerome's favourite verses in the Song). He seems to hope that human sexual desire will be superseded or transfigured, transposed into a higher key so as to become a means of encountering God.[14]

Augustine of Hippo

Augustine found delight in the Psalms as a vehicle for passionate expression to God. In his *Confessions,* which he famously begins with a comment about the restlessness of the human heart until it rests in God, he remembers his own experiences:

> O my God, how did I cry to thee when I read the psalms of David, those hymns of faith, those paeans of devotion which leave no room for swelling pride! I was still a novice in thy true love, a catechumen keeping holiday at the villa ...
>
> What cries I used to send up to thee in those songs, and how I was enkindled toward thee by them! I burned to sing them if possible, throughout the whole world, against the pride of the human race. And yet, indeed, they are sung throughout the whole world, and none can hide himself from thy heat.[15]

14. Jerome, *Letters,* pp. 28, 152, 207, 211, 226, 261-65, 271; *Homilies on the Psalms* I, pp. 243-44, 378; Garrett, *Song of Songs,* pp. 67-68. Compare also Ambrose's depiction of a virgin as 'ever a bride, ever unmarried, so that neither does love suffer an ending, nor modesty loss', which he supports with verses from Psalm 45 and Song 4.7 (Ambrose of Milan, *Concerning Virgins,* ch 7 [http://www.ccel.org/ccel/schaff/npnf210. iv.vii.ii.vii.html?scrBook=Ps&scrCh=45&scrV=9#iv.vii.ii.vii-p11.1], accessed 5 June 2009). Negativity about sexual desire is also evident in the Midrash Tehillim, which at least concedes that God may make use of it: 'Scripture teaches that were it not for the Inclination-to-evil, a man would not take a wife, nor beget children with her, and so the world could not endure.' Anonymous, *The Midrash on Psalms* (2 volumes; trans. William G. Braude; New Haven, Yale University Press, 1959), vol. 1, p. 131.

15. Augustine, *Confessions* (Philadephia: Westminster Press, 1955), 9.4.8; [http://www.ccel.org/ccel/augustine/confessions.xii.html], accessed 22 June 2009.

Augustine admits that looking into the depths of Scripture (particularly for hidden layers of meaning) makes him shudder with awe, 'a tremor of love'. Well aware of the power of human desire, he contends that it is given by God in order to lure creatures into the divine embrace. As a preacher, Augustine seeks to display God's beauty, so that the hearer's desires will become captivated by it. Hearing Scripture proclaimed should humble pride, increase desire and eventually incite and cultivate love for God. Christian hearers and readers seek the beauty of one who is 'fair beyond all the children of men' (Ps 45.3), for whom maidens long with love (Song 1.2). Yet they, in turn, cannot please 'Him', deformed as they are and made ugly by sin.[16]

Augustine shows caution about expressing his passion for God in sexual or romantic terms in his Expositions on the Psalms, whose popularity and influence is attested by the large number of manuscripts which have survived. In Psalm 42 (which was sung at baptisms, including his own) he sees the Psalmist attracted to the house of God, 'following the leadings of a certain delight, an inward mysterious and hidden pleasure, as if from the house of God there sounded sweetly some instrument …'. Of the thirsty soul in Ps. 63.1-2, he comments that many people thirst for the longings of their hearts: one for gold, another for silver, another possessions, another inheritance, another abundance of money, another many herds, another a wife, another honours, another sons. Thus, 'all men are inflamed with longing, and scarce is found one to say "My soul hath thirsted for Thee"'. A desire to cleave to God is to be commended. Augustine goes on to distinguish between a thirst for God, which is satisfied by the Word of Truth, and thirst of the flesh, for which God gives 'the things which are necessary, for God hath made both soul and flesh'. While not denying the physical aspects of being human, he nonetheless keeps them separate from the spiritual. Commenting on Psalm 122, which delights in Jerusalem and the Temple, Augustine proclaims the need for a passionate and holy love, but contrasts it with earthly love:

> As impure love inflames the mind, and summons the soul destined to perish to lust for earthly things, and to follow what is perishable, and precipitates it into lowest places, and sinks it into the abyss; so holy love raiseth us to heavenly things, and inflames us to what is eternal, and excites the soul to those things which do not pass away nor die, and from the abyss of hell raiseth it to heaven.[17]

16. Augustine, *Confessions*, 12.14.16, accessed 16 Feb. 2011. Jason Byassee, *Praise Seeking Understanding: Reading the Psalms with Augustine* (Grand Rapids, MI: Eerdmans, 2007), pp. 101, 108-109, 119.

17. J. Clinton McCann, 'The Book of Psalms: Introduction, Commentary and Reflections', in *New Interpreter's Bible*, IV (ed. Leander E. Keck; Nashville, TN: Abingdon Press, 1996), pp. 853-54; Walter Cahn, 'Illuminated Psalter Commentaries', in *Psalms in Community* (ed. Attridge and Fasler), p. 247; Butler, *Western Mysticism*, p. 23; Augustine, *Expositions on the Psalms*, (trans. A. Cleveland Coxe; ed. Philip Schaff; A Select

It is only in his engagement with Psalm 45 that Augustine risks embracing the language of *eros*. He sees this psalm as singing of the sacred marriage feast of the heavenly Bridegroom and his earthly Bride, the church, whose true members are 'children of the Bridegroom'. The sharp arrows of v. 5 are 'words that pierce the heart, that kindle love'; these he compares to Song 2.5, where the woman speaks of being wounded with love, 'that is, of being in love, of being inflamed with passion, of sighing for the Bridegroom, from whom she received the arrow of the Word'. The sweet fragrance of the Bridegroom's robes in v. 8 of the psalm he likens to the oils and perfume of the man in Song 1.3. The king's great desire for his bride's beauty (Ps. 45.11) is seen as Christ's desire to beautify sinners; this Augustine links with his understanding of Song 8.5, where the woman comes up 'made white', that is, cleansed and purified.[18] The marital metaphor is also briefly explored elsewhere, as Augustine declares of Christ in the Psalms: 'Charity falls in love with charity! He loved us in order to win our answering love. ... His bride must question herself, if she is chaste.'[19]

Like others before him, Augustine regards self-discipline and mortification as essential parts of the path to a deeper experience of God. Preaching on Psalm 31 (in his translation, the title reads, 'a Psalm for David himself in ecstasy', while v. 22 reads 'I said in my ecstasy: I am cast forth from thy sight'), he discusses whether the verse refers to terror or else to some joyful revelation of 'mental rapture' or 'ecstasy of soul', a concentration upon heavenly things whereby earthly things, to some extent, slip away from consciousness. 'Such was the ecstasy of the saints to whom God revealed the hidden things which so far surpass this world.' Likening these ecstatic experiences to what Paul describes in 2 Cor. 5.13-14; 12.2, Augustine goes on to discuss the unity of Christ and his body, the church, in terms of the Bridegroom and Bride, with the two becoming one flesh. He also sees the soul, weighed down by its infirmity, sinking back to the ordinary level and normal experience after brief moments of exaltation, and longing to renew the experience.[20] Here is a cycle of desire, fulfilment and then

Library of the Nicene and Post-Nicene Fathers of the Christian Church, VIII; New York: Christian Literature Company, 1888), pp. 260 (see also on Ps. 73, p. 341), 593. Compare Augustine's ambivalence about physical desire with Theodoret, who sees in Ps. 63.1 intensity of desire in which the flesh is in harmony with the soul's love; 'both my soul and my body yearn for you and long for you, like the person thirsting for the sweetest and clearest water'. (Theodoret of Cyrus, *Commentary on the Psalms* I, p. 357.)

18. Augustine, *Expositions on the Psalms*, pp. 145-53.

19. On Ps. 127, see Byassee, *Praise Seeking Understanding*, p. 125.

20. Augustine, *St Augustine on the Psalms*, II (trans. Scholastica Heben and Felicitas Corrigen; London: Longmans, Green and Co, 1961), pp. 9-10; 13-15; 363; also Butler, *Western Mysticism*, pp. 26, 52.

renewed desire similar to that sometimes observed of the lovers in the Song (although Augustine himself does not make this connection).[21]

Flavius Cassiodorus

In the preface to his commentary on the Psalms, Senator Cassiodorus savours the delight he has experienced in turning from the demands of secular life and sampling 'that honey of souls, the divine psalter', from which his longing spirit delights to drink deeply, finding sweet draughts in the words of salvation. 'In it [the Psalter] there is such great beauty of thought, such healing from the drops of words, that Solomon's phrase which he uttered in the Song of Songs is apt here: "A garden enclosed and a fountain sealed up, a paradise full of fruits"'. Seeking words to do justice to what he has experienced in studying and praying the Psalms, Cassiodorus here turns to one of the most intimate and sensuous images from the Song of Songs, the fruitful garden (Song 4.12–5.1; 6.2). But in applying the image to the Psalter, he relocates the garden; while the Song uses this image to refer to the woman, Cassiodorus presents sacred Scripture as the garden of fruit to be enjoyed by the believer.

When commenting on the Psalms in order to set forth his vision of the church, Cassiodorus also cites the Song repeatedly, with the beauty of the bride (Song 6.9; 7.8; 1.2) providing an image of the beauty of the church when it remains faithful to Christ and is not distracted by heretics such as Sabellius and Arius.

> You are a mother yet a maiden, pregnant yet virgin, a mother yet undefiled, whose mouth is fragrant with the odours of all the virtues, of whom her Betrothed says: 'And the odour of the mouth shall be like apples' and a little later 'The sweet smell of thy ointments is above all aromatical spices. Thy lips, my spouse, are as a dripping honeycomb; honey and milk are under thy tongue'. In short, you deserve Christ's kiss and the continuance of your virginal glory for ever; for these words are spoken to you: 'Let him kiss me with the kiss of his mouth'.[22]

In Psalm 45, not surprisingly, he sees the spiritual marriage of the church to Christ, the king who excels all in virtue, beauty, power and devotion. The bride is truly blessed 'to be joined to such great majesty not in the alliance of the flesh but in the unbreakable bond of love!' But consummation is still awaited: 'When will you be seen to be joined to Him who has invested you with His own most radiant light?'[23]

---

21. See Exum, *Song of Songs*, pp. 9-13.

22. Cassiodorus, *Explanation of the Psalms* I (trans. P.G. Walsh; New York: Paulist Press, 1990), pp. 23-24, 42.

23. Cassiodorus, *Explanation of the Psalms* I, pp. 440, 417.

Bernard of Clairvaux

While best known for his voluminous sermons on the Song of Songs, which I shall consider later in this chapter, Bernard of Clairvaux also ventured into the Psalter in his preaching. His fascination with the Song still shines through, in regular references to it (along with numerous other biblical passages, particularly other psalms). A good example which has come down to us is his series of Lenten sermons entitled 'He Who Dwells', on Psalm 91.

Speaking about v. 9 of the psalm, Bernard contrasts those who yearn to obtain spiritual or physical benefits from the Lord with the perfect love which thirsts after the Most High alone, 'crying out with all the might of that desire: "Whom have I in heaven, and what is there upon earth that I desire except you? God is the strength of my heart and my portion for ever."' Here words from Psalm 73 are blended with Psalm 91 to reinforce an image of loving desire to meet God, similar to the desire Bernard expresses in his sermons on the Song. The fact that God is the 'Most High' and 'in heaven' seems to be no barrier to this encounter of the heart. However, the nature of this relationship is not clear here; it could be parental, as in v. 4 of the psalm, where Bernard finds God's faithful ones enfolded like chicks in the warmth of their protective mother's body.

On the guardian angels of v. 11, Bernard similarly comments that the devout person is grateful for the angels of the Lord, but aspires to the Lord of the angels himself, not content with intermediaries, but seeking directly 'the very kiss of his mouth' (Song 1.2). Bernard urges his hearers to be like the Bride in Canticles when she met the watchmen; not satisfied at being with the watchmen, she fled to find her true love in person. Why did the watchmen beat and wound her? 'Unless I am mistaken, they were urging her to go on her way and find the beloved. Then too "they took my mantle", she says, doubtlessly so that, unencumbered, she might run more swiftly.' In this remarkable interpretation of Song 5.7, Bernard depicts the watchmen as positive, helpful figures, akin to the angels—and also metaphorical. Yet a few verses later in this sermon, looking at Ps. 91.15, he takes the same watchmen from the Song and their beating to be a literal picture of what may happen to faithful believers, who should leave their garments and run as the woman does (and as Joseph literally does from Potiphar's wife [Gen. 39.12], and the young man literally does from the crowd in Mk 14.51-52), knowing that God rescues faithful believers under persecution. Now the beating is taken literally, not figuratively, and those who give it are enemies of the faithful, not angels. Here the flexibility (not to mention inconsistency) of metaphorical and allegorical approaches becomes evident.[24]

---

24. Bernard of Clairvaux, *Sermons on Conversion* (Kalamazoo, MI: Cistercian Publications, 1981), pp. 139, 190, 240, 242, 250. See also Waltke and Houston, *Psalms as Christian Worship,* pp. 50, 384. Bernard's contemporary in Germany, Hildegard of

Martin Luther

Martin Luther delighted in and was influenced by the Psalms probably more
than any other biblical book. He opened his teaching career by lecturing
on the Psalms (1513-15), and the first book he offered for publication was
a German translation and exposition of 'The Seven Penitential Psalms'.
References to the Psalms are plentiful throughout his writings, including
his sermons, where they are often given a Christological interpretation. In
his preface to the Psalms he describes the Psalter as 'a little Bible' which
presents the death and resurrection of Christ, along with a full and colourful
picture of the Christian Church.[25] He values the singing of Psalms, including their capacity to touch and rouse the emotions of the singers.[26]

The theme of desire for personal intimacy with God is not prominent in
Luther's works on the Psalms. In his devotional works, he is more likely to
refer to the Psalms with reference to finding confidence in God and strength
to face persecution or death, needing God's strengthening word, and his
own struggle with sin.[27] But occasionally he deals with the language of love
and longing. In his lecture on Psalm 84, Luther finds the soul fainting and
pining with love, a passion for the courts of God. In this fainting, Luther
sees proof of passionate longing, which is itself proof of a passionate loving for one who is truly and passionately lovable. Thus the Temple courts
represent the divine person who inhabits them and who may be loved with
deep desire. The nature of that desire is not further explored. Writing on
Psalm 63, Luther passes over the phrase 'You are my God', but alights
on the image of thirsting for God. Noting the strong language used by the
psalmist, he points out the choice of words: not 'I thirst for Thy gifts' but 'I
thirst for Thee'. But this he explains as 'so that even the flesh is understood
as thirsting for spiritual things, namely, God's glorification'. Here Luther

Bingen, experienced herself as the bride of Christ, and mentions that her initial visionary
experience immediately gave her understanding, not only of the Gospel but also of the
Psalter; see Dan Cohn-Sherbrook and Lavinia Cohn-Sherbrook, *Jewish and Christian
Mysticism: An Introduction* (New York: Continuum, 1994), pp. 103-104.

25. See for example references to the Psalms throughout Luther's 'Word and Sacrament', in *Luther's Works*, XXXV (trans. Herbert J.A. Bouman; ed. E. Theodore Bachmann; Philadelphia, Fortress, 1960) and 'Letters 1', in *Luther's Works*, XLVIII (trans.
and ed. Gottfried G. Krodel; Philadelphia: Fortress, 1963), particularly pp. 205; 254,
256. In his 'Devotional Writings', there are almost twice as many references to the
Psalms as to any other biblical book; see *Luther's Works*, XLII (trans. Martin H. Bertram; ed. Martin O. Dietrich; Philadelphia, Fortress, 1969), pp. 203-204. Also Seybold,
Introducing the Psalms, p. 224.

26. See Begbie, *Resounding Truth*, pp. 103-105.

27. Luther, 'Devotional Writings', pp. pp. 64, 73, 112, 149, 154, 157-58, 183; 52,
56, 109; 63, 66, 70, 79, 102.

steers away from the idea of intimacy in encounter with God, or desire for it, in favour of desire for God to be honoured.[28]

Luther comments that Psalm 45 is a delightful and joyous wedding lyric—but one to be sung 'in the spirit'. He swiftly passes over the surface meaning to a purely allegorical one, about the spiritual kingdom and church. The beauty of the king (v. 2) speaks of Christ, who was without sin, full of grace and truth. In physical, human marriage Luther sees images and faint representations of the true spiritual marriage, between Christ and the church. The bride is beautified by the king's gifts of adornment, that is, Christ's gift of his own righteousness, as an alternative to her own good works. When man and woman are joined in physical marriage, one body is formed and everything is in common; similarly, Christ's bride appropriates his gifts of righteousness, grace, joy, peace, and salvation. (Taking into account Luther's repeated dismissals of the value of human good works, there seems little question here of reciprocity, with the bridegroom receiving something precious from the bride.) Marriage here simply provides a useful sermon illustration for aspects of a relationship with Christ. Desire and intimacy with God are not in focus.[29]

John Calvin
In his ground-breaking commentary on the Psalms, John Calvin seeks the literal or grammatical sense of the text, eschewing the mystical and allegorical methods of interpretation inherited from previous generations. Even the writings of Augustine (whom Calvin generally admires) are critiqued; his interpretation of the term 'life' in Ps. 63.3 is dismissed as 'philosophical and ingenious, but without foundation'.

Like Luther, Calvin values the way passion and emotional engagement may be expressed through praying and singing the Psalms. He explains his description of the Psalter as 'An Anatomy of all the Parts of the Soul' in terms of the range of human emotion expressed in it: 'all the griefs, sorrows, fears, doubts, hopes, cares, perplexities, in short, all the distracting emotions with which the minds of men are wont to be agitated'. Calvin pro-

---

28. Martin Luther, 'First Lectures on the Psalms', in *Luther's Works*, X (trans. Herbert J.A. Bouman; ed. Hilton C. Oswald; St Louis: Concordia, 1974), p. 302; Sermon *On Faith and Coming to Christ* [http://www.ccel.org/ccel/luther/sermons.vii.iii.html], accessed 25 June 2009.

29. Martin Luther, 'First Lectures on the Psalms', in *Luther's Works*, X, pp. 302; XI, p. 137; 'Selected Psalms 1', in *Luther's Works*, XII (trans. E.B. Koenker; ed. Jaroslav Pelikan; St Louis: Concordia, 1955), pp. 201-206, 260, 278. Luther gives limited approval of figurative exegesis in his 'Preface to the Glosses' (X, p. 4), where he says 'In the Scriptures, therefore, no allegory, tropology, or analogy is valid, unless the same truth is expressly stated historically elsewhere. Otherwise Scripture would become a mockery.'

moted a widespread knowledge and use of the Psalter for personal and congregational piety, including the singing of metrical versions of the Psalms. For him the Psalter makes known a privilege, 'which is desirable above all others — that not only is there opened up to us familiar access to God, but also that we have permission and freedom granted us to lay open before him our infirmities which we would be ashamed to confess before men'. Prominent in Calvin's thinking, as in Luther's, is his own experience of persecution, both in the church and in the wider world, as he candidly explains in his Preface. The chief value of passionate engagement with God through the Psalms is, in Calvin's view, to train us to bear the cross, renounce our human affections and submit entirely to God's rule.[30]

In dealing with the remarkable opening of Psalm 18, Calvin resists interpretations known to him which nuance רחם to mean 'seek mercy' or 'revere God's majesty'. Instead he chooses the straightforward translation 'I will love thee affectionately, O Jehovah, my strength', insisting that God 'requires nothing so expressly as to possess all the affections of our heart, and to have them going out towards him, so there is no sacrifice which he values more than when we are bound fast to him by the chain of a free and spontaneous love'. The thirsty deer of Ps. 42.1-2 he takes as an intense image of 'the extreme ardour of desire' for God; a similar vehemence of desire is expressed in his exegesis of Ps. 84.1-2—desire to 'enjoy the living God', who is not shut up in the tabernacle, but provides it as a ladder by which the godly may ascend heavenwards. Likewise in Ps. 143.6 David speaks of drawing near to God 'with vehement desire, as if the very sap of life failed him', like the earth cleft in a drought and opening its mouth to heaven for moisture.

While thus affirming the need for passionate desire for God, Calvin seems wary of using sexual imagery to depict this. He acknowledges that Psalm 45 is a song celebrating mutual human love, composed for the wedding of Solomon and given the ascription 'a song of loves'. But he immediately qualifies this:

> But as the word 'loves' is sometimes taken in a bad sense, and as even conjugal affection itself, however well regulated, has always some irregularity of the flesh mingled with it; this song is, at the same time, called משכיל 'maskil', to teach us, that the subject here treated of is not some obscene or unchaste amours, but that, under what is here said of Solomon as a type, the holy and divine union of Christ and his Church is described and set forth.

He defends this move into typology by highlighting the 'eternal throne/kingdom' of v. 6; this must indicate that the psalm is also about Christ and

30. John Calvin, *Commentary on the Psalms* (Authors' Preface, Geneva 1557) [http://www.ccel.org/ccel/calvin/calcom08.html], accessed 10 Aug. 2009. Also Gillingham, *Psalms Through the Centuries* 1, pp. 141-43; Begbie, *Resounding Truth*, p. 107.

his church. The ambivalence he shows in handling the language of sexual desire, added to his general aversion to using allegorical methods, may give us clues as to why, in all his voluminous work on the biblical texts, Calvin wrote no commentary on the Song of Songs (nor is the Song mentioned even once in his five volumes on the Psalms).[31]

Francis de Sales

Calvin the reformer's ambivalence is not shared by the Roman Catholic Francis de Sales. Seeking to respond to the Calvinists in his role as Bishop of Geneva in exile, Francis cites the Psalms and the Song of Songs more than any other biblical books in his famous 'Treatise on the Love of God'. Moreover, the interplay between them is striking, as he regularly brackets them together. Francis sees the human will ardently desiring the presence of the as yet absent God, 'whence the soul holily cries out: "Let him kiss me with the kiss of his mouth; my soul panteth after thee, O God"'. When faith removes the veil of ignorance, we become like an unhooded falcon which sees its prey and suddenly launches itself upon the wing (and if not unleashed will struggle upon the hand with extreme ardour)—'we then desire it in such sort that, "as the hart panteth after the fountains of waters; so my soul panteth after thee, O God! My soul hath thirsted after the strong living God; when shall I come and appear before the face of God?"'. Here the desire for the kisses of the other which begins the Song of Songs segues seamlessly into the thirst for God in the opening to Psalm 42 (two texts married in a similar way by Teresa of Avila during the previous century).

Desire of this kind seeks fulfilment, without which it languishes; the tears of Ps. 42.3 at the absence of God are the same, Francis argues, as the spouse's weeping and languishing with longing for her love in Song 5.8. The longing soul need not be reduced to despair, since the same sovereign good which prompted in us so vehement a desire also gives assurance through numerous promises in Scripture that what is desired may be obtained, so long as the means prepared and offered by God for this purpose are used.

Thus the search leads on to fulfilment and consummation, sometimes depicted in terms of loving ecstasy. For example, Francis compares the different reasons why people approach the Saviour, whether to hear him, adore him, be healed by him or to overcome their unbelief; but his 'divine Sulamitess seeks him to find him, and having found him, desires no other thing than to hold him fast, and holding him, never to quit him. 'I held him', says she, 'and will not let him go'.' Jacob, having taken hold of God, is willing let him go, provided he receives his benediction; 'but the Sulamitess will not let him depart for all the benedictions he can give her; for she wills not

---

31. Calvin, *Commentary on the Psalms*, Pss. 18, 42, 84, 143, 45.

the benedictions of God, but the God of benedictions, saying with David: "What have I in heaven, and besides thee what do I desire upon earth? Thou art the God of my heart, and the God that is my portion for ever"'. Here Song 3.4 is linked with Ps. 73.25-26; both express a worshipper's desire for God and determination to keep hold of God once he is found. Elsewhere Francis continues: 'A bundle of myrrh is my beloved to me, he shall abide between my breasts. "My soul", says David, "hath stuck close to thee: thy right hand hath received me"'. She is drawn to him by grace, but then, animated by him, chooses to run to him; the result is 'My beloved to me and I to him'. Here Song 1.13 and Ps. 63.8 illuminate each other, both depicting security and intimacy in a close encounter with God.[32]

Historical Criticism and Beyond
The development of historical critical methods in the nineteenth century C.E. brought new questions and approaches to the study of the Psalms. Following the pioneering work of Julius Wellhausen, some scholars sought to identify particular psalms as late compositions which gave evidence of an individualized spirituality superior to the corporate worship of previous centuries. Others, such as Hermann Gunkel, were motivated by a similar desire to find in the Psalms a religious piety freed from all ceremonies, a pure 'religion of the heart'. Gunkel concluded that certain psalms which gave expression to personal feelings and experiences pre-dated the Temple cult. However, Gunkel's lasting influence has been in the search for different forms and groups in which particular psalms may be placed, and the worship settings in which they were written and used. Sigmund Mowinckel then directed scholarly attention further away from individual piety onto corporate worship, in his search for the rites and festivals in which the Psalms were used, and for which many of them were originally written. This led on to preoccupation among scholars with myth and ritual and to attempts to develop Mowinckel's proposed New Year festival, or to recreate a covenant renewal ceremony. The 'I' of the Psalms became subsumed into both the 'we' of corporate worship and the much discussed role of the king in sacral kingship rituals or in leading worship as representative of all the people.[33]

---

32. Francis de Sales, *Treatise on the Love of God* 2.14, 7.2, 7.3 [http://www.ccel.org/ccel/desales/love.html], accessed 13 Aug. 2009; Teresa of Avila, *The Interior Castle* 3.12 [http://www.ccel.org/ccel/teresa/castle2.txt], accessed 15 Aug. 2009. The 'kiss of the mouth' which expresses the union of the soul with God is sometimes compared by de Sales with the intimacy of children with their mothers, rather than that of *eros*; see Cohn-Sherbrook and Cohn-Sherbrook, *Jewish and Christian Mysticism*, pp. 131-34.

33. McCann, 'Book of Psalms', pp. 643-45; Goldingay, *Psalms 1-41*, p. 46; Sigmund Mowinckel, *The Psalms in Israel's Worship* (2 volumes; trans. D.R. Ap-Thomas; Oxford: Blackwell, 1962); Steven J.L. Croft, *The Identity of the Individual in the Psalms* (JSOTSup, 44; Sheffield: JSOT Press 1987), pp. 131-32.

Attempts to highlight a mystical relationship with God in the Psalms during this period were few and received little attention. Mysticism was sometimes seen to be linked with the fertility cults and thus irreconcilable with Israel's worship at the Temple in Jerusalem. However, the sense of relationship with God expressed in the Psalms was not totally effaced. Susan Gillingham notes a continuing emphasis among some scholars during this period on a personal and individualized interpretation, in which the 'I' of the Psalms is seen as a heroic leader or prophetic figure, 'with an exceptionally personal and intimate relationship with God'.[34] Thus Gunkel saw pious individuals behind many of the Psalms. Like Gunkel, Mowinckel acknowledged that the Psalms expressed prayer to a powerful and personal God who was understood to be willing to respond; Mowinckel further insisted that the use of the Psalms in a corporate and cultic setting did not preclude emotional and relational engagement on the part of the worshippers. Artur Weiser emphasized the expression in certain psalms of the 'ardent desires of the faithful' to 'behold the face of Yahweh' in the context of worship. He understood this in terms of majestic theophany rather than intimacy, but nevertheless saw it as in some way a personal encounter. Others scholars developed Claus Westermann's focus on the Psalms of Lament, sensing a relational moment in the frequent use of 'I-you' language; they argued that the striking turn from plea to praise found in many of the laments was best explained by the insertion of an external voice: a priest or worship leader would give an oracle of assurance similar to that of Eli to Hannah (1 Sam. 1.17), or to the 'fear not' formula found in Isaiah 43.1. This hypothesis produces a performative moment of interaction with God, set in the context of corporate worship.[35]

One of the fruits of historical critical scholarship today is a near-consensus sometimes summarized in the phrase, 'Hymn Book of the Second Temple': the Psalter is seen as a repository of texts compiled for the use of the post-exilic community in its communal worship in Jerusalem. This has led to an interest in the way the Psalter is organized and whether it can fruitfully be read as a whole rather than as a collection of loosely related units. However, the failure of historical critical approaches to produce more detailed consensus about dates, festivals and usage of the Psalms has encouraged recent commentators to keep more open minds about the historical background of the Psalms.

---

34. Gillingham, *Psalms Through the Centuries* 1, p. 268.

35. H.J. Franken, *The Mystical Communion of JHWH in the Book of Psalms* (Leiden: Brill, 1954), p. 9; Mowinckel, *The Psalms in Israel's Worship*, I, p. 22; vol. 2, p. 20; Brueggemann, *An Introduction to the Old Testament*, pp. 282-84; Artur Weiser, *The Psalms* (London: SCM, 1962), pp. 39-40; Craig C. Broyles, *The Conflict of Faith and Experience in the Psalms: A Form-Critical and Theological Study* (JSOTSup, 52; Sheffield: JSOT Press, 1989), pp. 12, 19.

While affirming that the Psalms played an important role in the corporate worship of ancient Israel, writers such as Walter Brueggemann, John Goldingay and J. Clinton McCann have highlighted their ambiguity of language and lack of specific details, and the consequent variety of settings in which most of the Psalms may be placed. They acknowledge the broad validity of Gunkel's search for particular types of psalms, but use rhetorical and other literary critical tools to argue that too much focus on what is typical may lead to neglect of the individuality of each psalm.[36]

While this interest in the Psalms as texts to be studied from literary critical perspectives has grown, their identity as prayers and worship songs remains prominent; thus a section on 'Spirituality and the Psalms' (or some similar heading) is to be found in many recent commentaries. But in terms of passion and emotional engagement with God, desire for intimacy with God is not highlighted. Partly in response to perceived needs and blindspots among their contemporary (Western) audiences, today's commentators focus instead on the importance of lament in response to suffering and to the apparent absence of God; the role of anger and the desire for justice; and the importance of praise and corporate worship.[37] Furthermore, very few scholars have chosen to link the Psalms with the Song of Songs over the past hundred years, apart from a few comparative studies of Canticles and Psalm 45.[38] I shall engage further with contemporary writers in the chapter which follows.

Song of Songs

Early Jewish Approaches to the Song

'He who trills his voice in the chanting of the Song of Songs and treats it as a secular song has no share in the world to come.' These words, attributed to Rabbi Aqiba, show that there were some in the late first or early second century c.e. who regarded the Song as an erotic love song, and sang it as such. It also shows us that others, including Aqiba himself, rejected any approach

---

36. McCann, 'Book of Psalms', pp. 651-52; Walter Brueggemann, *The Message of the Psalms* (Minneapolis: Augsburg, 1984), pp. 15-23; John Goldingay, *Psalms 42-89* (Grand Rapids, MI: Baker Academic, 2007), p. 84; Ernest Lucas, *Exploring the Old Testament: The Psalms and Wisdom Literature* (SPCK, 2003), pp. 29-32.

37. Craig C. Broyles, *Psalms* (NIBC; Peabody, MA: Hendrickson, 2002), see his Introduction, especially pp. 32-34; Walter Brueggemann, *Spirituality and the Psalms* (Minneapolis: Fortress Press, 2002), pp. 25-45; Goldingay, *Psalms 1-41*, Introduction, especially pp. 60-69; J. Clinton McCann *Great Psalms of the Bible* (Louisville, KY: Westminster John Knox Press, 2009), pp. 9-10, 88-91, 112-13.

38. One example of such a study is Raymond Tournay, 'Les Affinitiés de Ps. lxv avec le Cantique des Cantiques et Leur Interpretation Messianique', in *Congress Volume: Bonne, 1962* (VT Sup., 9: Leiden: Brill, 1963), pp. 168-212.

which failed to see a different, religious dimension to the Song. Thus it seems questions about whether this text was expressing human sexuality or divine-human relationship, or both, were being asked from earliest times.[39] Martti Nissinen points out that the religious use of love poetry is amply demonstrated by Sumerian, Akkadian and biblical evidence, and argues that ancient religious readings of the Song should therefore come as no surprise to us.[40] In the literature which has survived, religious interpretations of the Song have held sway (in a variety of forms) until modern times, when the pendulum has swung the other way.

Jacob Neusner maintains that the Jewish sages who were responsible for passing on the oral Torah (which they eventually transposed into written form in the Mishnah, Tosefta and two Talmuds) were constantly in dialogue with the ancient texts they had inherited. They took it for granted that God spoke not only to one time or place or person, but everywhere and all the time, eternally, to Israel. Thus the sages' role was to mediate what God had previously spoken to the Israel of their own time and place. This prompted the development of figurative interpretations.[41]

Exactly when the Song of Songs was first interpreted allegorically is not clear. The discovery of fragments of the Song at Qumran (Cave 4) suggests that it was being read allegorically by the first century B.C.E., since it is hard to imagine the group behind the scrolls reading it literally, given their socio-religious outlook. However, we cannot say for sure how the Qumran community read the Song, since evidence is lacking. When the Mishnah was compiled (around 200 C.E.) the status of the Song may have been in doubt—there was still debate about whether it 'made the hands unclean', a phrase probably related to whether a book should be seen as sacred Scripture or not; this may suggest there was still some unease about its content at that time.[42] By the start of the seventh century C.E. we find no question

---

39. Rabbi Aqiba, *Tosefta, Sanhedrin* (trans. Herbert Danby; London: SPCK, 1919), p. 120; [http://www.toseftaonline.org/seforim/tractate_sanhedrin_mishna_and_tosefta_1919.pdf], accessed 7 May 2010; cf. Tremper Longman III, *Song of Songs* (NICOT; Cambridge: Eerdmans, 2001), p. 21. What Aqiba was rejecting may have been not the Song's literal meaning, but what he perceived as a vulgarization of its essential mysticism; see Francis Landy, *Paradoxes of Paradise: Identity and Difference in the Song of Songs* (Sheffield: Almond Press, 1983), pp. 13-14. For a general summary of early Jewish interpretation of the Song, see Pope, *Song of Songs*, pp. 93-112.

40. Martti Nissinen, 'Song of Songs and Sacred Marriage', in *Sacred Marriages: The Divine-Human Sexual Metaphor from Sumer to Early Christianity* (ed. Martti Nissinen and Risto Uro; Winona Lake, IN: Eisenbauns, 2008), pp. 214-16.

41. Jacob Neusner, *Israel's Love Affair with God* (Valley Forge, PA: Trinity Press International, 1993), pp. viii-xii, 57.

42. John Barton argues that the phrase 'defiled the hands' has been misunderstood. He finds no reason to think the Song of Songs was ever of doubtful canonicity, or that

that the Song is a holy text in a book such as the Song of Songs Rabbah, a Midrashic compilation of exegeses. Here the kisses of the mouth (Song 1.2) are understood as a picture of God encountering his people at Sinai, in the tent of meeting, and in the gift of the Torah. In the divine embrace of Song 2.6, the left and right hands depict the first and second tablets of commandments given to Moses, or the fringes of prayer shawl and the phylacteries worn by the devout, or the daily recitation of the Shema and the Eighteen Benedictions. These are the means by which Israel draws close to God. The Song is seen as a purely figurative picture of God's relationship with his chosen people.[43]

Origen of Alexandria

Since the Christian church initially developed out of Jewish roots, it was natural for Christians to take up Jewish allegorical approaches to the Song, although these were then redirected to speak of Jesus Christ and his followers.[44] Although pre-dated by his earlier contemporary Hippolytus of Rome, it is Origen who is generally agreed to be the fountainhead of Christian allegorical approaches to the Song, because of the influence of his writings and the number of them which have survived.[45] In fact he adopted a complex mixture of hermeneutical approaches in his commentary and homilies on Canticles: he describes the Song as an epithalamium (wedding song), in the form of a drama, and he gives considerably more attention to the literal meaning of the words than do many of his allegorizing successors. However, having done this, Origen goes on to a 'spiritual' exegesis, searching for a 'higher' theological meaning (or 'undersense'), which he cannot find in the plain sense of the text. What is said literally about the outer, physical person must, in Origen's view, also apply in a figurative sense to the inner person, thus assisting the soul in its desire for communion with God. Scripture discloses heavenly mysteries, while cloaking them in the language and physical manifestations of earthly reality. Thus his allegorical

---

its canonicity depended on its being understood as an allegory. 'Allegorical reading was a consequence, not a cause, of canonicity' (see Barton's 'The Canonicity of the Song of Songs', in *Perspectives on the Song of Songs* [ed. Anselm C. Hagedorn; Berlin: Walter de Gruyter, 2005], pp. 3, 6)

43. Philip S. Alexander, 'The Song of Songs as Historical Allegory: Notes on the Development of an Exegetical Tradition', in *Targumic and Cognate Studies* (ed. Kevin Cathcart and Michael Maher; Sheffield: Sheffield Academic Press, 1996), p. 15; Neusner, *Israel's Love Affair With God*, pp. 22, 28, 40, 69-72.

44. Longman, *Song of Songs*, p. 28.

45. Jerome is said to have praised Origen for surpassing all writers in his other works, but surpassing even himself in his commentary on the Song of Songs; see Rufinus' Prologue to Origen's *De Prinicpiis* [http://www.ccel.org/ccel/schaff/anf04.vi.iv.htm l?scrBook=Song&scrCh=1&scrV=4#vi.iv-p5.1], accessed 18 Aug. 2009.

approach is not so much a method as a metaphysical presupposition: 'his exegesis assumes that "spiritual" meaning is an inherent dimension of the biblical text itself'.[46]

Origen derives his approach from his reading of the apostle Paul, whom he sees departing from the plain meaning of the Hebrew Bible text in passages such as 1 Cor. 10.1-12. The term 'allegory' is itself taken from Paul in Gal. 4.21-24; the root meaning is 'another sense' beside the plain sense. Thus, significantly, the plain sense is not rejected, but a second meaning is added to it. In his search for a figurative or 'anagogical' meaning, Origen often uses a rabbinical midrashic style, assembling a succession of biblical texts each unrelated to the other except by the presence of a similar word or idea. Thus the destructive foxes of Song 2.15 lead him to seek out other foxes, in Ps. 63.9-10 and Judges 15.3-5; all these he connects as representing perverse false teachers who seek to harm the faithful (although he does confess that the passage about Samson is extremely difficult to interpret!).[47]

In his commentary on the Song, Origen raises the question of how justified it may be to use the language of *eros* to describe the human–divine relationship. He argues that *eros* and *agape* are not very distinct in meaning, and finds no theological reason to prefer the word *agape*. For him, it is of no consequence whether God is said to be the object of *eros* or *agape*. Indeed, Origen goes further; with reference to the phrase 'God is love' (1 Jn 4.8, 16), he asserts that one could not be blamed for choosing to call God *Eros* just as John called him *Agape*. For this Origen has been depicted in recent times as one who allowed Hellenistic or Platonic thinking to corrupt his understanding of the unique, self-giving love of God presented in the New Testament. This critique rests on an understanding that Plato presents *eros* as a selfish desire to possess and meet one's own needs—a view that may be found among Neoplatonists, such as Plotinus, but is not the only understanding of *eros* presented by Plato himself. However, the key question for us is how Origen himself understands *eros*, which is not entirely clear. It may be that he sees it not as a selfish desire to possess, but as

46. Roland E. Murphy, *The Song of Songs* (Hermeneia; Minneapolis, MN: Augsburg Fortress Press, 1990), pp. 20-21.

47. Norris, *Song of Songs*, pp. xi-xii, 126-27; Garrett, *Song of Songs*, pp. 64-66; E. Ann Matter, *The Voice of my Beloved: The Song of Songs in Western Medieval Christianity* (Philadelphia: University of Pennsylvania Press, 1990), pp. 27-28; Francis Young, *Biblical Exegesis and the Formation of Christian Culture* (Cambridge: Cambridge University Press, 1997), pp. 94-95. It is likely that Origen, along with Philo and others at Alexandria, was also influenced by the long-established Greek tradition of using allegory to reinterpret difficult texts, particularly myths depicting the capricious behaviour of the gods; see Ernest Lucas, *Exploring the Old Testament: The Psalms and Wisdom Literature* (London: SPCK, 2003), p. 192; Pope, *Song of Songs*, pp. 112-13.

a non-appetitive, philanthropic love, akin to the New Testament's under-standing of *agape*. Commenting on the phrase 'wounded with love' (Song 5.8), Origen develops the idea of God's arrow (from Isa. 49.2) and evokes the classic Greek image of the arrows of *eros*: God wounds the soul, but for a good purpose—to prompt love. This kind of love is inspired not by any selfish desire for the beauty or benefits of God, but simply by the wounding arrows of divine love. Clearly Origen feels confident that certain features of the Platonic tradition can fruitfully enrich Christian theology without corrupting it.[48]

While embracing the language of *eros*, Origen is aware that it raises vari-ous difficulties. Acknowledging the plain sense of the Song leads him to concern about how it may be perceived by some readers—'fleshlings', or people whose inner self is infantile. These, he argues, should not be admit-ted to study the Song, which is solid food for the mature (Heb. 5.14). 'For anyone who does not know how to listen to the language of erotic desire with chaste ears and a pure mind will pervert what he hears ... and will fos-ter carnal desires in himself, and it will seem to be the Divine Scriptures that are thus urging and egging him on to fleshly lust!' Hence the Jewish practice that only the mature may handle this book is to be commended. Origen rejoices in the faculty for passionate love which is implanted in the human soul by the creator's kindness and which cannot fail to be expressed by human nature; but he deplores the way it becomes twisted into passion for money or glory or harlots, or indeed for athletics or arithmetic. He openly admits his admiration for those learned Greeks who have sought to show that the power of erotic desire conducts the soul from earth to the exalted heights of heaven, and others who have written on how to elicit this sort of desire in the soul. 'But carnal individuals have dragged these skills down to serve vicious desires and the mysteries of illicit desire.' Thus he finds dis-cussions about desire close to being dangerous—commenting on Song 2.3-7, he cuts short reflections on the consummation of marriage with the words 'But turn swiftly to the "life-giving spirit" (1 Cor. 15.45). Set aside talk of bodily things.' At times he takes refuge in the safer imagery of childbirth;

---

48. Origen, *The Song of Songs: Commentary and Homilies* (London: Longman, Green & Co, 1957), pp. 21-22; 32-35. See the discussion of Anders Nygren's critique of Origen in Catherine Osborne, *Eros Unveiled: Plato and the God of Love* (Oxford: Clarendon Press, 1994), pp. 8-9, 52-53, and her further analysis of Plato and Neoplaton-ism, pp. 55-58, 70-72, 165-66, 171. Also Socrates' account of the words of Diotima, his 'instructress in the art of love', in Plato, *Symposium* [http://classics.mit.edu/Plato/symposium.1b.txt], accessed 10 Nov. 2009; and the examples of non-acquisitive '*eros*' in Plato, *Lysis* [http://classics.mit.edu/Plato/lysis.html], accessed 10 Nov. 2009. Origen is not alone among patristic commentators in using the language of *eros*; Gregory of Nyssa suggests a distinction of intensity, describing heightened *agape* as *eros* (Osborne, *Eros Unveiled*, p. 70).

through marriage to the heavenly bridegroom the church 'may conceive by Him and be saved through this chaste begetting of children' (that is, the conversion of unbelievers). Yet still Origen urges his readers to pray that God will enable them to find a wholesome understanding of desire.[49]

Origen points out that both the outer, physical self, and the inner, spiritual one are said in Scripture to need 'food and drink' (Jn 4.14; 6.33, 41), and so the reader/hearer must distinguish which of the two Scripture is talking about. Similarly, he argues, there is fleshly desire, and spiritual desire (Gal. 6.8):

> The soul is driven by a heavenly desire and lust when it has detected the beauty and comeliness of the Word of God, and has been captivated by him, and at his hand has received a certain dart and wound of desire. ... one will receive from him the wound that is saving and will burn with the blessed fire of the desire of him.

Thus the opening words of this drama (Song 1.2) are presented as those of a bride at her wedding, 'burning with heavenly desire for her bridegroom, who is the Word of God. For the bride desired him very deeply—whether she be identified as the soul that is made after his image or the church.' Origen describes the bride's desire in terms that suggest infatuation, as she longs for the bridegroom day and night, unable to speak or think of anything else.[50]

In his introduction to the Song of Songs, Origen makes it clear that this is a book about love. But for him and his Christian successors, the subject of this book, as of all the Scriptures, is what Cyril of Alexandria termed 'the mystery of Christ signified to us through a myriad of different kinds of things'.[51] Origen briefly compares the Song with Psalm 45, where he sees the bride forgetting her family in order that she may come to Christ. Although Eusebius and Jerome tell us that Origen wrote extensively on the Psalms, very little of this has survived apart from his homilies on Psalms 36–38, where themes of desire and intimacy are not prominent. In these homilies he affirms that Scripture should not simply be taken literally, as the heretics do; instead, the faithful should press the grapes of the scriptural vine to bring out the spiritual sense. Thus Psalms 37 and 39, when pressed for their inner depths, are found to depict the faithful Christian's calling to imitation of Christ. Yet while thus allegorizing, Origen gives priority to the plain sense of certain parts of these psalms (such as the scandal of the wicked prospering, and the danger of envying them, in Psalm 37). This lack

49. Origen, *Song of Songs*, pp. 21-22; 36-38; Matter, *Voice of my Beloved*, pp. 31-32.
50. Origen, *The Song of Songs*, p. 21; also excerpts in Norris, *Song of Songs*, pp. 2-5, 109.
51. Norris, *Song of Songs*, p. xii.

of consistency is an issue which frustrates today's readers of the ancient
allegorists, although it seems not to have disturbed them and their contemporaries as much as it disturbs us.[52]

Origen's Heirs
The allegorical path established by Origen is well trodden by his successors. Many chose to go to greater extremes than he, often ignoring his prior
concern to find the plain meaning of the text, as they strove for ever more
ingenious allegorical interpretations. Thus Apponius of Ancyra sees in the
woman's red lips (Song 4.1-8) the scarlet hue of blood, which reminds him
of Christ and the martyrs (and also of the headband worn by Aaron), while
the woman's two breasts are images of the two covenants. Theodoret spir-
itualizes each phrase in 'my sister, my close one, my dove, my perfect one'
(Song 5.2): 'perfect' means obeying Christ's commands (Matt. 5.48), while
'dove' is an image of one who is spiritual, like the Holy Spirit at Jesus' baptism; 'close one' is one who walks in Christ's footsteps (Jas. 4.8).[53]
   But the sexual imagery and innuendo of the Song will not be ignored and
sometimes slips through into the writings of the allegorists. For Theodoret,
Solomon's bed (Song 3.6-11) represents the Scriptures: 'For in the Scriptures the Bride, lying down as it were alongside the Bridegroom and receiving the seeds of his teaching, conceives, carries a child, enters into labor
and gives birth to spiritual profit'. In Song 5.2-8, Gregory of Nyssa sees the
soul stripping off the old humanity so that the Word may enter her. He also
likens the bride of Song 1.2 to Moses, who became after the face-to-face
encounter of theophany 'more intensely desirous of such kisses, praying to
see the object of his yearning as if he had never glimpsed him'. Gregory the
Great concludes that the Song uses words about bodily love to wake up and
heat up our soul, arousing it to a higher love with language of a lesser love;
'from the words associated with this sensual love we learn how fiercely we
are to burn with love for the Divine'. Intense desire for God is a feature of
Gregory's writings, which feeds into the monastic tradition; Gregory sees
desire as an essential part of clinging to the love of God and contemplating
the beauty of the creator.[54]

   52. Origène, *Homélies sur les Psaumes 36 à 38* (Paris : Les Éditions du Cerf,
1995), pp. 9-10, 14, 28-29, 183-85. Origen has also achieved notoriety for his literal
interpretation of Jesus' admonition about removing bodily members that offend and lead
to sin, leading him to self-castration—another passage he chose not to allegorize; cf.
Pope, *Song of Songs*, p. 115.
   53. Apponius, 'Exposition in the Song of Songs'; Theodoret of Cyrus, 'Interpretation of Song of Songs'; both in Norris, *Song of Songs*, pp. 162-65, 197.
   54. Theodoret, 'Interpretation'; Gregory of Nyssa, 'Homilies on the Song of
Songs'; Gregory the Great, 'Exposition of the Song of Songs'; all in Norris, *Song of*

Augustine of Hippo

Augustine also follows the allegorical tradition of Origen in his approach to Scripture; in his commentary on Genesis he cites both 1 Cor. 10.11 and Eph. 5.32 (another Pauline text which has contributed to spiritualizing interpretations of the Song down the centuries) as clear evidence that the biblical text may and should be taken in a figurative sense. Indeed, he celebrates the fact that the same words in the divine writings may be interpreted in different ways as a stimulus to the desire to learn, and a sign of God's generous and abundant provision.[55] As noted above, he wrote at length on the Psalms in a series of sermons; by contrast, he comments on the Song only in passing, in works on other subjects.

Some of these comments arise only in response to other people, such as the Donatists, who claim that the 'noon' of Song 1.7 refers to their base in northern Africa (a very sunny place), thus proving that they are the true church, where Christ pastures his flock. Augustine responds with an affirmation of the value of the Song, with its 'holy songs, love songs, songs of holy love, of holy benevolence. Be sure that I want to hear the voice of the Shepherd speaking in those Songs, the voice of the sweetest Bridegroom.' But he adds that these songs are composed of enigmas which few can understand. He then mines the passage for terms with which he outlines a convoluted ripost, whereby the Donatists are in fact those mentioned in the same verses who are 'veiled' and have 'gone out' pasturing 'goats' (as opposed to true sheep); they used to be close 'companions' of Christ and are now betrayers, like the former soul-mate of the psalmist depicted in Ps. 55.12-14. Here the ingenuity and flexibility of the allegorical method are clearly displayed; either side in a dispute can use the same text and make it say more or less what they like.[56]

Augustine seems to be aware of the beguiling power of the language used in the Song. Mulling over why it gives particular pleasure to hear truths about Christ, the church and baptism expounded in the Song, 'where the church is depicted in language one would use to praise a beautiful woman', he concludes that intriguing imagery has a particular power: 'No one disputes that it is much more pleasant to learn such things through imagery, and much more rewarding to discover meanings that are gained with difficulty'. In contrast to Origen, Augustine does not claim to be seeking a deeper spir-

Songs, pp. 148, 200, 22, 8; Jean LeClerq, *The Love of Learning and the Desire for God: A Study of Monastic Culture* (New York: Fordham University Press, 1982), pp. 29-31, 60, 68.

55. Matter, *Voice of my Beloved*, pp. 52-53.

56. Augustine 'Sermons' 46.33-37, in Norris, *Song of Songs*, pp. 48-50; see also p. xi.

itual truth beyond the plain meaning of the text; he sees his interpretation of the book (as representing Christ's love for the church and the answering love of the church for Christ) to be the plain meaning of the text—a testimony to the extent to which allegorizing had become the accepted norm by his day. Thus he can enjoy exploring the imagery of Song 4.1-8, where he finds new believers depicted as ewes coming to baptism and then giving birth without fail to spiritual twins, an image which signifies that they obey Jesus' twin commandments of love for God and neighbour. (He reverts on a number of occasions to images of sheep and teeth, the latter representing those who speak for the church.)[57]

Occasionally Augustine touches on the language of love expressed in the Song, particularly as he preaches on the Psalms. In Ps. 7.12-13 he sees God's bow as Scripture, and the arrows as the apostles (or else 'divine preachings'); anyone who is hit by these arrows becomes stricken, 'wounded by love' (Song 2.4-5), inflamed with heavenly love for God's kingdom. Here Augustine sees desire and longing for the divine—but it is for the divine rule, not for the person of God in any intimate encounter. Generally Augustine avoids imagery suggesting intimacy; in his depiction of the martyrdom of Crispina, he manages to reconfigure the intimate embrace of Song 2.6 into something much more restrained, with just the divine right hand embracing her from above (the left hand is her own). He is stirred by the Song's one generalizing abstraction, that 'love is strong as death' (Song 8.6); this reminds him of the unwavering faith of the martyrs, and also leads to reflection on dying to self. But the Song's more intimate images he generally avoids.[58]

Rabbi Shlomo Yitzhaki (Rashi)
Much of classical Jewish exposition from medieval times suggests that the Song is 'a sort of poetic prism, intentionally designed to refract the light of the Torah already revealed and enabling its spectrum of hues to be more clearly perceived and appreciated by diligent interpreters'.[59] The eleventh-century C.E. French rabbi best known by the acronym 'Rashi' continues the tradition of allegory, but in a more concrete form than that favoured by

57. Augustine, 'On Christian Doctrine' 2.11-13, in Norris, *Song of Songs*, p. 157; cf. Augustine's comments on the nursing ewes of Ps 78.71 in Augustine of Hippo, *Expositions on the Psalms* (ed. Philip Schaff; A Select Library of the Nicene and Post-Nicene Fathers of the Christian Church, vol. 7; New York: Christian Literature Company, 1888), pp. 379-80; also p. 489. On Augustine and allegory, see Mary Dove, 'Sex, Allegory and Censorship: A Reconsideration of Medieval Commentaries on the Song of Songs', *Literature and Theology* 10 (1996), pp. 320-21.

58. Augustine, *Expositions on the Psalms*, pp. 25 (on Ps. 95.7), 593 (on Ps. 121.7), 167-68 (on Ps. 48.12) and 595-96 (on Ps. 122.7).

59. Murphy, *Song of Songs*, p. 29.

many Christian mystical interpretations. Rashi affirms the words of Rabbis Akiva and Eleazar ben Azariah, which extol the Song as the holiest of all holy writings. In the tradition of the Targum and Song of Songs Rabbah, Rashi sees the story of Israel's past, particularly the events of the exodus, unfolding in the Song. It is written from the perspective of the exiles, who are the woman in the Song, while God is her lover, the Holy One, 'the Rock of my heart and my portion' (Ps. 73.26). The allegorical method enables Rashi to ignore much of the sexual imagery of the book (at different times in his commentary the woman's breasts symbolize the two stone tablets in the ark, then the staves of the ark, then suppliers of nourishment such as Moses and Aaron, Daniel and his friends, then the synagogues and study halls which nurture Israel with the words of the Torah; once again the elasticity of allegorical methods becomes evident). The embrace of the right hand (Song 2.6) Rashi sees as a reminder of how God brought down manna and quails in the desert, a memory which leaves the exiles sick with longing for his love. The garden and spice beds of Song 6.1 become for him the Jerusalem Temple, where incense is offered.

The underlying sexual imagery of the Song is not, however, totally effaced. On the opening verse, 'Let him kiss me with the kisses of his mouth', Rashi depicts the woman reciting the song with her mouth, in her exile and in her widowhood, remembering how her husband (King Solomon) used to kiss her; 'in some places they kiss on the back of the hand or on the shoulder, but I desire and wish that he behave toward me as he behaved toward me originally, like a bridegroom with a bride, mouth to mouth'. Here Rashi dispels any possible confusion about more modest and chaste kinds of kisses, proclaiming the sexual nature of the Song's imagery. Later, in Song 8.5, the woman is her husband's companion and clings to him. In the phrase 'under the apple tree I aroused you', Rashi sees the woman remembering her former encounter with her divine lover: 'So she says in the request of the affection of her beloved ...under Mount Sinai, formed over my head as a sort of apple tree, I aroused you. That is an expression of the affection of the wife of one's youth, who arouses her beloved at night when he is asleep on his bed, and embraces him and kisses him.' The picture of God's people arousing divine affection is striking, and all the more startling when the image of the amorous wife in bed with her husband is spelled out so clearly.[60]

---

60. Rashi, *Commentary on the Tanakh*, http://www.chabad.org/library/bible_cdo/aid/16263/showrashi/true], accessed 17 June 2009.

Subsequent Jewish medieval interpreters who develop the *peshat* tradition of interpretation, such as Abraham Ibn Ezra and David Kimhi, also acknowledge and explore the literal meaning of the Song. But they follow this with allegorical explanations, which they see as the true depth of the text. See Mordechai Z. Cohen, *Three Approaches to*

In his commentary on the Psalms, Rashi sees God's people expressing longing, desire and pining for God (Pss. 42.1; 63.1; 143.7), but he chooses not to explore or illustrate what this might mean. Even the desire of the king for the bride's beauty (Ps. 45.11) is emasculated into the Holy One's desire for beautiful deeds from his people. The sexual or romantic imagery of the Song finds no echoes here. Rashi's concerns are polemical (refuting Christian translations and interpretations of psalmody), rather than devotional.[61]

Bernard of Clairvaux

'Because of its excellence, I consider this nuptial song to be well deserving of the title that so remarkably designates it, the Song of Songs, just as he in whose honour it is sung is uniquely proclaimed King of kings and Lord of lords.' In comments such as this Bernard of Clairvaux sets himself in the tradition which acknowledges the plain meaning of the text, yet digs below the surface for deeper meanings. Behind the obvious stands truth not necessarily apparent, but more profound; this chimes in with Bernard's instinct to seek out a mystery, and supports his mistrust of too much explicitness. For him, the Song is 'pre-eminently a marriage song telling of chaste souls in loving embrace, of their wills in sweet concord, of the mutual exchange of their heart's affections'. But at a deeper level it speaks of the individual's union with God in a gift of holy love which gives delight and exaltation of spirit; a nuptial union with the divine partner which only those of riper years may appreciate. Bernard repeatedly cites Psalm 45, where he sees the royal wedding of Jesus, the majestic, anointed king, to his bride (see Sermon 2 in particular).[62]

Bernard delights in the Song and writes on it at great length. As a nobleman well versed in contemporary literature, it seems likely that the courtly love stories of his day are an influence on his thinking. As the leader of a group of monks from backgrounds similar to his own, we may see him creating a new kind of love literature which speaks to their valued traditions of romance and helps them sublimate their emotional energies towards engagement with this new way of life (just as the use of warfare imagery in his other writings would speak to their traditions of noble combat, and his

Biblical Metaphor: From Abraham Ibn Ezra and Maimonides to David Kimhi (Leiden: Brill, 2003), pp. 3-6, 263-64.

61. See Gillingham, *Psalms Through the Centuries* 1, p. 84.

62. Bernard of Clairvaux, *On the Song of Songs* I (Kalamazoo, MI: Cistercian Publications, 1977), Sermon 1, pp. 5, 7; Sermon 2, pp. 9-10; G.R. Evans, *Bernard of Clairvaux* (Oxford University Press, 2000), pp. 61-62, 71. Note also the influence on Bernard of Bede's commentary on the Song, and the way Bernard's sermons in turn became influential in England; see Wolfgang Riehle, *The Middle English Mystics* (trans. Bernard Standring; London: Routledge, 1981), pp. 34-35.

advocacy of the Order of Knights Templar would resonate with their aspirations to knighthood).[63]

Yet there seems to be a further, personal dimension to Bernard's passion for the Song: the way it resonates with his own experiences in prayer. In fact much of what he writes might best be described as an exegesis of his own experience, which looks to the Song for support and illustration. He describes visits of the Word who moves and warms and wounds his heart, quietening his carnal affections—but then, having allowed himself to be laid hold of, too soon the visitor slips away, as one fleeing from your embrace, leaving all to revert to slumber and grow cold like a boiling pot withdrawn from the fire. The intensity of joy and pain in these repeated experiences seem like echoes of the tension between closeness and withdrawal expressed in the Song (e.g. Song 3.1-5; 5.2-8).[64]

The Song's opening image captivates Bernard: 'that most intimate kiss of all, a mystery of supreme generosity and ineffable sweetness' (cf. Song 1.2). The kiss is given by Jesus (or occasionally he says the kiss actually *is* Jesus; or it is the Holy Spirit, the bond of love between the Father and the Son). Those who experience this mystical kiss are few, but they eagerly crave its repetition, like the psalmist who longs for God to restore the joy of salvation (Ps. 51.12), for each time the kiss brings 'an unreserved infusion of joys, a revealing of mysteries, a marvellous and indistinguishable mingling of the divine light with the enlightened mind, which, joined in truth to God, is one spirit with him'. Bernard regularly uses the Psalms to help him explain this experience. The one who desires to receive the kiss looks to God and seeks his face (Ps. 27.8), experiencing unbounded joy in God's presence, like David's delight at being close to God (Pss. 16.11; 73.28), as the soul clings tightly to God (Ps. 63.8). The language of the Psalms pervades Bernard's thinking and writings, and is what he uses to construct a world of meaning around the Song.[65]

Bernard does not avoid the erotic implications of the kiss; the one who desires a kiss is a lover, just as husband and wife are lovers:

63. Jean LeClercq, *Monks and Love in Twelfth-Century France* (Oxford: Clarendon Press, 1979), pp. 22-23, 88-89, 103; Ann W. Astell, *The Song of Songs in the Middle Ages* (Ithaca, NY: Cornell University Press, 1990), pp. 9, 133.

64. Bernard of Clairvaux, *On the Song of Songs* II (Kalamazoo, MI: Cistercian Publications, 1976), Sermon 32, p. 135. The courtly love romanticism of Bernard's day finds further resonance in how love has been perceived in subsequent eras, including Western culture today; see Tyler Blanski, *Mud and Poetry: Love, Sex and the Sacred* (Nashville, TN: Fresh Air Books, 2010), pp. 101-11.

65. Murphy, *Song of Songs*, p. 26; Bernard, *On the Song of Songs* I, Sermon 2, p. 9; Sermon 3, p. 16-20.

> They share the same inheritance, the same table, the same home, the same
> marriage bed, they are flesh of each other's flesh. ... it is not unfitting to
> call the soul that loves God a bride. Now the one who asks for a kiss is in
> love. It is not for liberty that she asks, nor for an award, not for an inherit-
> ance nor even knowledge, but for a kiss.[66]

He revels in the erotic frankness of the language, as the most appropriate
expression for the love of God; where other medieval writers were anxious
to spiritualize the carnal nature of the text, Bernard seems more concerned
with the eroticizing of the spiritual. He values the quality of language in the
Song for its capacity to move hearts and awaken desire, thus stimulating
spiritual arousal in the listener.[67]

Bernard is aware of some of the difficulties raised by the image of marriage when used of a human being's relationship with God. He depicts from
the human side 'an ardent love, blinded by its own excess to the majesty of
the beloved. For what are the facts? He is the one at whose glance the earth
trembles, and does she demand that he give her a kiss? Can she possibly be
drunk?'. Acknowledging the awesome majesty of the creator (with a reference to Ps. 104.32), Bernard concludes that the devotee has become drunk
with the power of love, through God's gracious provision of a feast and
river of delights (Ps. 36.8). In embracing, he says, two wills are united as
one; the inequality of the spouses does not damage this harmony of the will,
'for love has no care for reverence'. God, though he deserves to be honoured and admired, prefers to be loved—'They are spouses now, and what
other bond exists between spouses than that of mutual love?' But while
using this language of mutuality, Bernard retains an uneasiness, sometimes
reverting to more reverential or hierarchical pictures of the relationship.
Ultimately this cannot be a knitting together of equals. We respond to Jesus,
he teaches, by kissing first his feet (begging forgiveness), then his hand, as
he lifts us up and strengthens us so that we may produce fruit in keeping
with repentance. Only after that is it appropriate for us to kiss the mouth of
the benign bridegroom; none should rashly aspire to kiss his lips. 'O soul
called to holiness, make sure that your attitude is respectful, for he is the
Lord your God, who perhaps ought not to be kissed, but rather adored with
the Father and the Holy Spirit for ever and ever. Amen.'[68]

Ultimately union with God is not corporeal or carnal. While sometimes
alluding to the writings of Ovid popular in his day, Bernard creates a con-

---

66. Bernard, *On the Song of Songs* I, Sermon 7, p. 39.
67. Astell, *Song of Songs*, pp. 16-17, 19; Denys Turner, *Metaphor or Allegory?
Erotic Love in Bernard of Clairvaux's Sermons on the Song of Songs* (Paper presented to
the Catholic Biblical Association, Newman College, 28 April 1998).
68. Bernard, *On the Song of Songs* 1, Sermon 3, pp. 16-20; Sermon 7, p. 40; Sermon 8, p. 52; Sermon 83 (see Introduction, p. xxiv); Norris, *Song of Songs*, p. 132.

trast with the overt carnality and desire to possess which he sees Ovid presenting. In Sermon 31 on the Song, which repeatedly depicts the fire of the desiring heart to which God responds (using Pss. 20.4; 37.4; 38.7; 42.1; 88.13), Bernard insists that he is depicting a spiritual union, devoid of desire to submit to the ways of the flesh. He uses neo-Platonic images of light to contrast the immutable and eternal nature of God with human understanding. The soul seeks to become one in spirit with God (1 Cor. 6.17). 'As much as we can, we express in words the ecstasy of the pure mind in God, or rather the loving descent of God into the soul, matching spiritual things to the spiritual.'[69]

Medieval Mysticism

In medieval exegesis it became standard practice to draw on as many sources as possible while acknowledging as few as necessary. But the influence of those who followed Bernard of Clairvaux (not to mention the underlying influence of Origen) is clear. The twelfth century saw exponential growth in the number of commentaries written in Latin on the Song, particularly in the Cistercian movement. As monks, the authors of these commentaries were also well versed in the Psalms; they express no sense of tension or contrast between desire for God as presented in the Psalter and the desire for God which they discern in the Song of Songs.[70]

William of St Thierry, a contemporary and friend of Bernard, sees in the Song a drama about Solomon's marriage; what this truly depicts is the soul turning its face to God and being purified in order to be married to the Word of God, having tasted and seen how sweet the Lord is (Ps. 34.8). William wrestles with the significance of using sexual imagery about a relationship with God. He commends a desire to know God, as far as is permitted, and to be known by God, but insists that true worship needs to be in spirit and truth. Of the 'Song of spiritual love' (Song of Songs), he concludes that the Holy Spirit chooses to attire its inner, spiritual subject matter in the external garment provided by images of fleshly love, in order to enable fleshly humanity to be introduced to spiritual love and lay hold of what it is like.

> Moreover, since it is impossible for genuine love, hungry as it is for what is authentic, to rest in images and be content with them, it will the more quickly make the transition by the way made familiar in its imaginings.

---

69. LeClercq, *Monks and Love*, pp. 66-69; Matter, *Voice of my Beloved*, p. 128; Bernard, *On the Song of Songs* II, p. 129.

70. Matter, *Voice of my Beloved*, pp. 35-36; 203-10. The full extent of Bernard's influence is inevitably hard to quantify, although clear references to his writings on the Song can sometimes be identified, for example in Dante's depiction of Beatrice in 'Paradiso' (Dante Alighieri, *The Divine Comedy* [trans. Geoffrey L. Bickersteth: Oxford; Blackwell, 1981], pp. 30-31; 739-54; see also LeClercq, *Monks and Love,* pp. 137-44).

> And even though the person in question is spiritual, nevertheless the pleas-
> ures of the flesh are natural to him in virtue of his sharing in a bodily way
> of being; but once they have been taken captive by the Holy Spirit, he
> embraces them as part of his allegiance to spiritual love.

For William, it seems that 'fleshly' (i.e. sexual) love can be a helpful gate-
way into spiritual love, which alone can grasp the things of God. Since
we are physical beings, the pleasures of the flesh are to be embraced, not
rejected, as part of the spiritual journey; but they are to be seen as a means
to a greater end, the spiritual encounter with God.[71]

Rupert of Deutz, a Benedictine scholar and abbot in Germany at the
end of the eleventh century c.e., encouraged the development of a Marian
understanding of the Song. For him, the woman in the Song represents the
virgin Mary at the Annunciation. Mary is seized by overflowing joy, powerful love, a rush of delight, as she receives the news from the angel. She
is kissed by the mouth, not of a lover but of the Father; he, in a wondrous
act of speech, places deep within her womb the person of the Word and
that love which is the Holy Spirit. Rupert thus seeks to avoid specifically
sexual imagery with regard to Mary, opting instead for the maternal; but
the language of intimacy is still evident. Rupert also speaks to his audience as 'friends and daughters of Jerusalem', telling them that the closer the
Beloved is, the more deeply they will desire him, desire to see and possess
him.[72]

Richard St Victor, a twelfth century contemplative based in Paris, depicts
the bride in Song 5.2-8 complaining when her bridegroom turns away,
'because her mind thirsts for the One it has tasted and desires him; and the
more she becomes acquainted with his sweetness, the less does what she has
known satisfy her.... All of her melts for love of him whose in-breathing
she has received.' Confronted by the magnitude of his love, she dissolves
in tears, and as long as it is not granted her to see her God, 'tears become
her bread night and day' (Ps. 42.3). Richard develops the idea of spiritual
marriage, in which he sees four phases: espousal, marriage, wedlock and
childbearing; the third phase (copula) brings the contemplative into closest
union with God.[73]

During this period, a Bernardian–Franciscan mysticism of the cross
developed and culminated in the concept of the 'marriage of the cross and
the soul', sometimes using erotic imagery from the Song. The outstretched

---

71. William of St Thierry, 'Exposition of the Song of Songs, in Norris, *Song of
Songs*, pp. 11-17.

72. Rupert of Deutz, 'Commentary on the Song of Songs 1', in Norris, *Song of
Songs*, pp. 25, 139.

73. Richard St Victor, 'Explanation of the Song of Songs 5', in Norris, *Song of
Songs*, pp. 203-204; Butler, *Western Mysticism*, p. 208.

arms of the crucified Christ are seen as expressing the longing of the suffering lover to receive his beloved, and his bowed head is understood to show God's wish for the kiss of the soul. Thus Anselm of Canterbury writes of Christ inclining his head on the cross:

> He seems as it were to say to his beloved: 'O my beloved, how often hast thou longed to enjoy the kiss of my mouth, addressing me through my companions: 'Let him kiss me with the kiss of his mouth'; I am ready, I incline my head to thee, I offer thee my mouth; kiss me, and take thy fill'....
>
> For stretching out his arms he lets us know that he, ay he, desires our embraces, and seems as it were to say: 'O come to me, you that labour and are burdened, and refresh you within my arms, within my embraces; you see that I am ready to fold you in my arms ...'[74]

In some related types of mysticism, the wounds of Christ came to be regarded as a nest for the soul (references to the dove in Song 2.14), or even as the vulva, a place of mystical ecstatic union following an ecstatic dying which dissolves individuality.[75]

Other mystical writers might be included. The anonymous fourteenth century English text entitled 'The Cloud of Unknowing' (which draws on the earlier work of Pseudo-Dionysius) speaks of affection inflamed with the fire of His love; for once, discretion is to be discarded in order to experience the perfection of this passionate calling, 'which is called ravishing'.[76] The latter image became popular among English mystics, some of whom developed a preference for the verb *ravishen* which can mean 'to carry off', 'to be passionately in love' and 'to assault sexually'. English mysticism draws strongly on the language of passionate earthly love, often sharing the language of secular love literature in a developing a tradition of the spiritualizing and metaphorical use of erotic imagery. Thus Richard Rolle, the so-called 'father of English mysticism' in the fourteenth century c.e. speaks of a 'burning heat of desire' for Christ and being 'ravished' out of fleshly feeling and into contemplation, which brings delicious heavenly joy. Rolle also refers to feeling wounded, languishing, fainting for love, longing to die for love. (In addition he explores other images, such as desire

---

74. Anselm of Canterbury, *Meditations* X [http://www.ccel.org/ccel/anselm/meditations.iv.x.html], accessed 25 Aug. 2009. Pope (*Song of Songs,* p. 122) argues that Anselm's commentary on Canticles may be the work of Anselm of Laon, wrongly attributed to his namesake.

75. Riehle, *Middle English Mystics,* pp. 39-40, 46-47.

76. Anon, *The Cloud of Unknowing* [http://www.ccel.org/ccel/anonymous2/cloud.html], chapters 26, 41, 71, accessed 25 Aug. 2009. Also Dionysius the Areopagite, *On the Divine Names and the Mystical Theology* [http://www.ccel.org/ccel/rolt/dionysius.html], chapter 1, accessed 25 Aug. 2009.

for the sweetness of honey in Song 4.11 and 5.1, which he compares with Ps. 119.103.) In a letter to a nun of Yedingham, entitled *Ego Dormio* (after Song 5.2), he depicts three grades of love: beginning with holiness of life, one then forsakes all to follow Christ in poverty, before finally achieving the joyful state of being lifted up to God—a mystical rapture of languishing with love, as in Song 2.5; the letter ends with a passionate love poem to Jesus.[77] Margery Kempe in her autobiography depicts spiritual marriage as an actual event, with a wedding scene in which God says 'I take thee, Margery, for my wedded wife ...'; later she hears Christ saying to her 'thou mayest boldly, when thou art in thy bed, take me to be as for thy wedded husband'. Medieval religious love songs such as *Quia amore langueo* draw on the Song in style and vocabulary, as do the Corpus Christi play cycles.[78] English poets such as John Donne and George Herbert also explore images of marriage and sexual desire, with biblical allusions underlying (but rarely explicit in) much of their writing. Thomas Traherne marvels at the wonders of the human body, beginning with lengthy quotations from Psalms 103 and 139; by the end of this poem allusions and quotations abound from Song 5.4-5; 4.9-11; 6.12-13; 8.1-2, as he explores intimacy with God, sometimes using the word 'ravish' as he does so.[79]

Looking beyond the British Isles to Europe, we find in the Spanish Carmelite nun, Teresa of Avila, another who embraces the language of celestial marriage, as she likens the 'kiss of his mouth' to the waters sought by the thirsty deer (Song 1.2; Ps. 42.1-2). Her contemporary, John of the Cross, speaks of spiritual marriage and ecstatic love in such powerful terms that it was said of him, 'this monk can give lessons to lovers!' In seventeenth century France we find Jean Marie Guyon developing the idea of spiritual marriage in her autobiography, citing Song of Songs as part of her inspiration.[80]

77. Richard of Rolle, *The Fire of Love* [http://www.ccel.org/ccel/rolle/fire.pdf], accessed 6th Mar. 2011. Note Rolle's emphasis on spiritual song as part of his deepest experience of divine love; e.g. Book 2.2, 3, 5, 12. See also Matter, *Voice of my Beloved*, pp. 183-85.

78. Astell, *Song of Songs*, pp. 145-76.

79. John Donne, *Show me dear Christ, thy spouse so bright and clear*; also *Since she whom I loved hath paid her last debt* and *The Ecstasy* [http://rpo.library.utoronto.ca/poet/98.html], accessed 25 Aug. 2009; George Herbert, *Love I, II, III* [http://rpo.library.utoronto.ca/poet/159.html], accessed 25 Aug. 2009; Thomas Traherne, 'Thanksgiving for the Body', in *Centuries, Poems and Thanksgivings* II (ed. H.M. Margoliouth; Oxford, Clarendon Press, 1972), pp. 214-28.

80. Teresa of Avila, *The Interior Castle*, ch. 3 [http://www.ccel.org/ccel/teresa/castle2.txt], accessed 27 Aug 2009; St John of the Cross, 'The Living Flame of Love', cited in Butler, *Western Mysticism*, pp. 143-44; Riehle, *Middle English Mystics*, pp. 24, 36-38, 95; Jeanne Marie Guyon, *Autobiography of Madame Guyon* (Chicago, IL:

Jewish mystical sources from medieval times are generally more restrained than these Christian ones. Moses ibn Tibbon and Gersonides developed Maimonides' view of the individual soul (the receptive material intellect) yearning for union with God (the active intellect). Many of the Kabbalists agree that the supreme rank attainable by the soul at the end of the mystic path is that of *devekut*, mystical cleaving to God. Love of God and fear of God will lead to this. A key text for them is Deuteronomy 13.4, with its call to serve God and cleave to him. This is an intimate union, yet without entirely eliminating the distance between creature and creator. The main route to it is ecstatic rapture through prayer; the personal element in this is highly emphasized. But few memoirs or descriptions of the ecstatic experiences have been written and preserved, possibly because this was frowned upon. The revered Zohar texts on Genesis encourage physical con-jugal union as a key way for a man to experience the *Shekinah*, bringing delight both to the *Shekinah* and to his wife. The kiss of Song 1.2 is seen as an expression of 'the universal ecstasy and eternal delight experienced by every animated being in its union with the Divine, by which partially devel-oped spirits become eventually perfect'. The *Shekinah* is understood to be dwelling in the Holy of Holies, like the virtuous wife in her husband's house described in Ps. 128.3—an unusual example of the use of a female marital image in connection with God. This Kabbalistic understanding of *Shekinah* as a female aspect within the divine sometimes sees human sexual inter-course in marriage as resembling the pattern of the divine, even as stimulat-ing by example the cosmic generative forces.[81]

While Jewish mysticism tended to be more intellectual and speculative than its Christian counterparts, erotic imagery was not unknown. For exam-ple, sexual language is used in the Zohar in connection with the *Ayn Sof*, the infinite source from which ten *sefirot* emanated; the last of these *sefirot* is the indwelling *Shekinah*, whose reunion with *Ayn Sof* is often depicted using sexual terminology. Some later Hasidic works also use erotic termi-nology to describe movement in prayer, depicted in terms of copulation

Moody Press, 1960), pp. 73, 92, 104. Also Cohn-Sherbrook and Cohn-Sherbrook, *Jewish and Christian Mysticism*, pp. 109-10, 125-28.

81. Gershom Scholem, 'Kabbalah', *Encyclopaedia Judaica* 10 (Jerusalem, Keter Publishing House, 1971), especially pp. 624-32; Exum, *Song of Songs*, pp. 74; Anony-mous, *Zohar Bereshith to Lekh Lekha* (Trans. Nuro de Manhar) Genesis; ch. 21 27; 90 [http://www.sacred-texts.com/jud/zdm/index.htm], accessed 27 Aug. 2009. Also Alicia Ostriker, 'A Holy of Holies: the Song of Songs as Countertext', in *The Song of Songs* (ed. Athalaya Brenner and Carole R. Fontaine, The Feminist Companion to the Bible, Second Series, 6; Sheffield: Sheffield Academic Press, 2000), p. 39; Pope, *Song of Songs*, pp. 161-69; 179; Philip S. Alexander, *The Targum of Canticles* (The Aramaic Bible, 17a; London: T. & T. Clark, 2003), pp. 45-46; Michael Fishbane, *The Exegetical Mind: On Jewish Thought and Theology* (Cambridge, MA: Harvard University Press), p. 109.

with the *Shekinah*. Yet there is no parallel in Judaism to the rich and detailed romantic or erotic visionary experiences described in some of the Christian sources mentioned earlier in this section.[82]

The medieval period also saw a blurring of the distinctions between sacred and profane literature. Examples of this include a Latin poem *Iam dulcis amica venito*, full of imagery from the Song. Widely known in its day and possibly used as a court entertainment, it may also have been used in liturgical settings. More broadly, the widespread influence of commentaries on Canticles seems to have had an effect on medieval love poetry, some of it not primarily (or not even marginally) related to religious themes: verses from the Song became stock literary phrases in descriptions of the beauty of the courtly lady in poetry from Provence, France and Italy.[83] Here we glimpse the Song breaking free from its longstanding role as a religious text, as the artists of this era blur the boundaries between 'yearning for you' and 'yearning for You'.

Martin Luther

As a great translator and preacher who sought to enable ordinary people to understand the Bible, we might expect the reformer Martin Luther to eschew figurative understandings. This he does in a number of his works, but not in his lectures on the Song of Songs. Finding it impossible to agree with those who think it is a love song about the daughter of Pharaoh beloved by Solomon, and equally unsatisfying to expound it as an allegory of 'the union of God and the synagog [*sic*], or like the tropologists, of the faithful soul', Luther concludes that it is 'an encomium of the political order' and 'entirely figurative'. It is a song in which Solomon honours God with his praises, thanks him for his divinely established kingdom, and encourages citizens of that kingdom in their trials to trust in God who defends them. 'Thus any state in which there is the church and a godly prince can use this song of Solomon's as if it had been composed about its own government and state.'

Thus the divine kisses refer to God showing favour to this government, kissing it, honouring it with all manner of blessings and love. The left hand refers to government, the right hand to priesthood or worship of God; these come together in an embrace, enabling the precious unprotected rose/lily to endure (Song 2.6). This spouse is the people of God—Solomon's subjects, but also the church, and perhaps the individual soul. Only on the phrase

---

82. See Cohn-Sherbrook and Cohn-Sherbrook, *Jewish and Christian Mysticism*, pp. 165-67. They point out that Jewish scholars were invariably married, and viewed human sexual activity as a divine obligation, while within Christianity 'mystics were largely celibate ascetics with no other outlet for their sexual longing than in their most intense spiritual experience' (p. 167).

83. Matter, *Voice of my Beloved*, pp. 188-89; 191-93.

'sick with love' (Song 2.5) does Luther briefly touch on a more personal dimension: '... my whole being is on fire with the love of my God out of this consideration of His blessings. Therefore I yearn so greatly that all men should be aware of them and give Him thanks for them.'

Luther does hint at dissatisfaction with these particular lectures, ending them on a slightly defensive and diffident note: 'In this way I understand this book to be about Solomon's state. If I am wrong about this, a first effort deserves lenience. The musings of others have a much larger share of absurdity.'[84]

After the Reformation

The need for allegorical interpretations of the Song is an area of agreement which curiously united Protestant and Roman Catholic interpreters in the centuries following the Reformation. Some chose the path of historical allegory, developing ideas popularized by Nicholas of Lyra that the Song provided a prophetic history of the Church during various eras between the time of King David and the era of the church. Others, such as John Wesley, continued the traditional Christian interpretation of the Song as an allegory of the love between Christ and his church.[85]

Sermons and commentaries were not, of course, the only outlet for interpretation of the Song. Uses of the Song in German Lutheran piety include two of J.S. Bach's cantatas, where Bach reinterprets Jesus' wedding parables (Matt. 22.1-14 and 25.1-13) in the light of both the Song and Lutheran pietist themes; thus he depicts Christ searching for the bride, and giving her garments of righteousness. Yet Bach's medium may unwittingly add another dimension to their surface message; by presenting phrases from the Song in duets (with melodies which sometimes contrast and at other times echo each other), the cantatas inevitably present two human beings speaking words of love to each other, personified in the soloists.[86]

Luther and his fellow reformers unwittingly helped to pave the way for modern, more literal readings of the Song. By attacking the monastic ideal as the accepted paradigm for Christian character, they also undermined it as the privileged setting for correct readings of the Song, thus opening the way for new readings from other quarters. By affirming marriage as a valid option for clergy, the leaders of the Reformation helped develop more posi-

---

84. Martin Luther, 'Lectures on the Song of Solomon', in *Luther's Works*, XV (trans. Ian Siggins; ed. Jaroslav Pelikan; St Louis, MO: Concordia, 1972), pp. 192-96, 216; see also Garrett, *Song of Songs*, p. 72; Exum, *Song of Songs*, p. 75.

85. Alexander, 'Song of Songs as Historical Allegory', pp. 16-25; Longman, *Song of Songs*, p. 34.

86. John M. Rogerson, 'The Use of the Song of Songs in J.S. Bach's Church Cantatas', in *Biblical Studies/Cultural Studies* (ed. Exum and Moore), pp. 343-47, 350.

tive attitudes to sexuality in their culture, which contributed to a greater openness to the sexual language of the Song. The allegorical approach was further undermined by the reformers' stress on the plain sense of Scripture and the need for it to be its own interpreter; this too paved way for modern literal readings of Song.[87]

The tension between traditional and newer forms of interpretation can be traced in the exegetical works of clerics such as Jacques Bousset and subsequently Robert Lowth, who critiqued the excesses of allegorical and prophetic-historical interpretations. Lowth acknowledged the human sexuality presented in the Song, but framed it as the respectable marriage feast of King Solomon.[88] Occasionally artists would also explore the tension: at the start of the Victorian era, Edward Burne-Jones designed an entire stained glass window made up of twelve panels, each of which depicts a verse from the Song. The installation of this window in an English parish church would not have been permitted unless an allegorical interpretation of the images was still widely assumed and accepted. But the particular texts Burne-Jones chooses from the Song, and the way he presents them in visual form, suggests medieval courtly tales of the vicissitudes of mortals in love (which may echo the artist's own anxieties and disappointments in his experience of love and marriage). A more down-to-earth understanding of the Song is suggested; the humanity of its subject matter shines through these windows, to those who have eyes to see.[89]

Modern and Postmodern Analysis
The arrival of historical critical approaches to the Song brought a kind of death and resurrection to its celebration of intimacy and desire. Stripped of its various elaborate allegorical robes, the Song re-emerged in its pristine beauty as an erotic love poem. Understandings of it centred on intimacy with God were increasingly discarded; human sexual desire was unveiled as the Song's true subject.

Inevitably, such a generalization invites qualification. The allegorical approach never totally died out; the metaphor of Christ and his church has been upheld by some over recent centuries, while in the twentieth century it has occasionally been argued that the Song is a political tract, calling Jews to return from the exile to their homeland. Equally, the understanding of the Song as depicting human erotic love is not new; we catch glimpses of such thinking in the work of Hugo Grotius, the teachings of Calvin's associate Sebastian Castellio, the lost work of both Jovinian and the Antiochene Theodore of Mopsuestia, and in the actions of those whom Rabbi Aquiba

---

87. Cf. LaCocque and Ricoeur, *Thinking Biblically*, pp. 293-95.
88. Garrett, *Song of Songs*, pp. 71-74; Murphy, *Song of Songs*, p. 38.
89. Black and Exum, 'Semiotics in Stained Glass', pp. 315-21.

frowned upon for singing it as a secular song at the turn of the first century C.E. But these are nonetheless exceptions which prove the rule, standing out from the mass of figurative interpretations.[90]

While enjoying the new-found freedom to admire the uncovered text of the Song, some scholars developed an urge to paint the background and frame it. The new critical concern to find the 'life-setting' of each biblical text prompted speculations about the original context of the Song. Some framed it in a cultic ritual setting, explaining it as a mythic poem linked with so-called fertility cults of Canaan, Mesopotamia, or Sumeria. Others depicted it as an ancient Israelite epithalamium, to be sung during wedding celebrations; still another saw it as set in a love feast at a funeral. A different approach was to fill in the gaps within the text itself and create a story, a romantic drama involving two lovers, sometimes with a third character intruding and trying to disrupt their love. A historical background for this scenario was then developed, with the Song identified as an anti-Solomonic diatribe, or as evidence of a tension between city and countryside dwellers. In all of these theories, human desires and relationships predominated; even the fertility cult setting was one designed to manipulate the gods in order to get human beings the fertility they wanted, rather than to enable any intimate relationship with those gods.[91]

Feminist interest in the Song has continued this focus on the human relationships depicted in it. A number of writers have noted the apparent lack of androcentrism and patriarchy in the text, finding in it a mutuality and balance in male–female relations, or even a glimpse of female superiority. More recently, others have questioned whether the Song does present an autonomous female protagonist, arguing that it may alternatively reflect male consciousness and fantasies. As this debate has developed, the focus has remained very largely on sexual love and desire within human relationships, with human desire for God dismissed as an anachronistic distraction from earlier centuries when the true subject matter of the Song was repressed.[92]

---

90. Garrett, *Song of Songs*, pp. 71-72; Exum, *Song of Songs*, pp. 75-77; Pope, *Song of Songs*, p. 180; Murphy, *Song of Songs*, p. 27.

91. Garrett, *Song of Songs*, pp. 76-84; Exum, *Song of Songs*, pp. 78-81; Samuel N. Kramer, *The Sacred Marriage Rite* (Bloomington: Indiana University Press, 1969), pp. 89-90; Pope, *Song of Songs*, pp. 220-28. Murphy's conclusion that cuneiform sources yield scant evidence to support any cultic interpretation of the Song's provenance or contents would find widespread agreement today (*Song of Songs*, pp. 48-57).

92. Exum, *Song of Songs*, pp. 80-86; Athalaya Brenner, *The Song of Songs* (OT Guides; Sheffield : JSOT Press, 1989), pp. 87-97; J. Cheryl Exum, 'Ten Things Every Feminist Should Know about the Song of Songs'. in *The Song of Songs* (ed. Brenner and Fontaine), pp. 24-36; David J.A. Clines, 'Why Is There a Song of Songs and What Does It Do to You If You Read It?', in *Interested Parties: The Ideology of Writers and Read-*

In recent discussion, however, there are signs that God is making a come-back. Phyllis Trible's influential work, arguing that Song of Songs deliber-ately echoes (and gives a counter-response to) the story of Genesis 2–3, has encouraged others to consider intertextual links within the Hebrew Bible.[93] Ellen Davis proposes links between the Song's Eden motif and the Jerusa-lem Temple.[94] Developing these ideas, Edmée Kingsmill proposes that the Song is a contemplative text, written as a metaphor or allegory of the love of God for his creation and especially for the land of Israel, Jerusalem, the Temple and the people whom God chose.[95]

André La Cocque points out that the language of *eros* found a home in Israel's religious realm through figurative use in other Hebrew Bible texts, particularly prophets such as Isaiah, Jeremiah and Hosea; indeed, for La Cocque, this is essential as the background which made composition of the Song possible. He argues that a rejection of allegory need not prevent acknowledgment of analogy. LaCocque proposes that the Song is deliber-ately reclaiming erotic language for inter-human relationships, subverting the message of the prophets in the process (an approach echoed, I might add, in the way some modern scholars have sought to reclaim the Song from the traditional allegorists). For LaCocque, the Song celebrates a love that is both *eros* and *agape*; indeed, *eros* becomes a 'sacrament' of the divine love, through which human beings may experience that greater love.[96]

Alicia Ostriker sees the Song as a counter-text, subversive of the Law and the Prophets with their emphasis on hierarchy and obedience. For her, it annihilates any supposed 'sacred–secular' division, celebrating a love that is both natural and spiritual. Citing some of the views of medieval Kabbalah, she sees a spiritually elevating, divine power in human love; God is present in the interaction of the lovers in the Song, as they recognize, honour and celebrate the divine in one another. In all this she seeks to rediscover God as

ers in the Hebrew Bible (JSOTSup, 205, GTC 1; Sheffield: Sheffield Academic Press, 1995), pp. 94-121.

93. Trible, *God and the Rhetoric of Sexuality*, pp. 144-65.

94. Ellen F. Davis, *Proverbs, Ecclesiastes and the Song of Songs* (Louisville, KY: Westminster John Knox Press, 2000), pp. 240-43, 261, 270-75, 278; also Robert W. Jen-son, *Song of Songs* (Interpretation; Louisville, KY: John Knox Press, 2005), pp. 42-43, 50-52.

95. Edmée Kingsmill, *The Song of Songs and the Eros of God* (Oxford: Oxford University Press, 2009), pp. 43-44. Note also her summary of recent commentaries aris-ing from France, Italy and Spain which indicate a renewed trend to interpret the Song on both levels, as relating to human sexual relationships and also relationship with the divine (pp. 31-35).

96. André LaCoque, *Romance She Wrote: A Hermeneutical Essay on Song of Songs* (Harrisburg, PA: Trinity Press International, 1998), pp. 27-28, 55-56, 207-209.

friend, companion, co-creator, and as lover.[97] Carey Walsh shares Ostriker's conviction that ancient people lacked today's sacred–secular dualism, and that today's readers need to expand their vision of what is 'spiritual'. For Walsh, desire is an impulse to find more in life, and God is an expression of belief that there is something more to life. 'Can't these be the same?' The Song's pulsating desire for an (in her view) absent lover resonates with the readers' desire for the most absent object of all, God, if only as a phantom memory. Sexual intimacy 'approaches levels of communion, of fullness, of ecstasy, in ways that can only be described as mystical'.[98]

In many ways we might see a renewed openness to spiritualized readings of the Song as an inevitable consequence of the prevailing post-modern perspective. If no single reading may be privileged, then can any particular reading be disqualified? We may be relieved to have reclaimed the Song's plain erotic sense, and even resentful at those who suppressed this understanding in previous centuries.[99] But if our resentment then blinds us to another kind of love and desire to which the Song also has relevance, we end up guilty of denying that one kind of reading, in a kind of ironic mirror image of the allegorists of old. So we find a renewed openness to what Virginia Burrus and Stephen Moore refer to as 'a return of the divine repressed'. But the latter pair also insist that this returning God cannot be the same as the God previously evicted from the text; this God needs to be 'an infinitely malleable lover', 'in command and under command by turns'.[100] The divine may need a significant makeover in order to survive the conditions of the comeback. Ironically, an allegorical reading of the Song of Songs, with its unruly and assertive female protagonist who holds so much sway over her enthralled lover, might produce just that kind of God (although allegorists down the centuries have tended to avoid this line of thought).[101]

In spite of the growing tendency to compare the Song of Songs with other biblical texts, none of the recent works mentioned in the last few para-

---

97. Ostriker, 'Holy of Holies', pp. 39-41, 50.

98. Carey E. Walsh, *Exquisite Desire: Religion, the Erotic, and the Song of Songs* (Minneapolis: Fortress, 2000), pp. 11, 31-32, 52, 191.

99. Othmar Keel, for example, dismisses the allegorical approach as the Song's 'Babylonian captivity', from which it has finally been released, describing it as 'an elegant way of despising the text' (*The Song of Songs* [trans. Frederick J. Gaiser; Continental Commentary: Minneapolis, Fortress Press, 1994], p. 11). However, for an attack on what he terms 'the myth of repression', in contemporary critique of the Song's history of interpretation, see David Carr, 'Gender and the Shaping of Desire', *JBL* 119 (2000), pp. 233-48.

100. Virginia Burrus and Stephen D. Moore, 'Unsafe Sex: Feminism, Pornography, and the Song of Songs', *BibInt.* 11 (2003); see their final section, entitled 'Missing God', pp. 50-52; cf. also Walsh, *Exquisite Desire*, pp. 51-52.

101. Cf. Carr, 'Gender and the Shaping of Desire', pp. 245-46.

graphs has shown significant interest in the Psalms, as either inter-text or counter-text. This omission gives me encouragement to try to enable some conversation between these two biblical books.

Conclusion

The shifting currents of thought which we find in the history of interpretation of the Psalms and Song of Songs (and of other biblical books) show how successive generations of interpreters can become aware of the hermeneutical limitations of their predecessors. It would be naïve, therefore, for us to assume that we have now 'arrived', having resolved once for all the methodological problems and issues of meaning which exercised our forebears. Indeed, our own ideas and cultural presuppositions will in turn be scrutinized and critiqued by the next generation of interpreters.[102]

A sharp distinction between the sacred and the secular, of the kind found in the modern Western world, was not common in ancient times. Thus love poetry could be used in religious contexts in a variety of civilizations, and language of divine love that echoed human relationships was used by various ancient near eastern cultures.[103] Therefore religious interpretations of the Song would not have surprised readers or hearers in those times, in the way that such interpretations puzzle readers today. Love poetry can be read as a description of the relationship between God and his people without employing religious vocabulary or mentioning divine actors, particularly when a long-standing cultural memory supports this kind of reading. Recent scholarly hostility to religious interpretations should be also be viewed in its cultural context, not least from the perspective of the history of sexuality in the modern world. Those who today see non-religious readings as the 'natural' ones tend to be secular modern people from a Western background. Moreover, recent readings of the Song as affirming non-fertility-related *eros* echo the shift in industrialized societies towards non-reproductive sexuality.[104] Interpreters are always children of their own time and culture. However, while seeking to be aware of our cultural influences, we can still assess our present situation, and chart how we got here; this is what I have sought to do in this chapter.

102. Cf. Murphy, *Song of Songs*, p. 41.

103. On Sumerian and Akkadian evidence for this, see Nissinen, 'Song of Songs and Sacred Marriage', pp. 173-212.

104. Nissinen, 'Song of Songs and Sacred Marriage', pp. 212-18. Cf. Carr, 'Gender and the Shaping of Desire', pp. 233-48, esp 235; also Ricoeur in LaCocque and Ricoeur, *Thinking Biblically*, pp. 294-95. On the effect which social location may have on interpreters, see also Hector Patmore, '"The Plain and Literal Sense": On Contemporary Assumptions about the Song of Songs', *VT* 56 (2006), pp. 247-50.

Poetry at its best has always had a particular power to capture hearts and minds. Combine poetry with the interwoven framework of music, and that power is multiplied. This proves as true with ancient songs as with contemporary ones. The Psalms and the Song of Songs have beguiled and thrilled their readers down the centuries, stirring passions and giving them expression. The extent to which both books have been treasured is evidenced in the sheer number of commentaries and reflections written on them and then preserved in successive eras. Add to this the large number of medieval manuscripts with a mystical content alluding to the Psalms or the Song which have been preserved, and we seem to have evidence of a strong appetite for such writings both from religious orders and also from the lay public (the Lollards, for example, show a keen enthusiasm for mystical texts). All this indicates not simply academic interest, but a widespread desire for an authentic experience of God.[105]

This desire for encounter with God may be traced in the history of interpretation of the Psalms. The popularity and influence of this particular biblical book in both Jewish and Christian worship has been one expression of this. A number of interpreters have noted the strong emotional dimension to such desire. A few of these have explored it in terms of passion and intimacy, even connecting it boldly with the language of *eros* found in the Song of Songs. Many others, due to a veneration of celibacy and wariness of the destabilizing power of human desire, or for other reasons, have steered clear of the language of intimate relationship, particularly romantic or sexual imagery. But most interpreters acknowledge the relational nature of the language found in the Psalms, and the need to do justice to it in some way. Few, past or present, would deny that the Psalms present a 'yearning for You'; more contentious are the questions of how that yearning is experienced, and what other kinds of human yearning may help us to understand and express it. These are among the key issues which need to be addressed in the chapters that follow.

Meanwhile, a bewildering mixture of interpretations have been offered and often imposed on the vivid, sexual language of the Song of Songs. Chief among these have been the various allegories of a divine–human relationship (in which some have boldly explored the sexual imagery, while others have avoided it). More recently, scholars have offered various hypothetical scenarios as a historical background to the text. The cumulative effect of all these different approaches has been to reaffirm the beauty and mystery of the Song, and its vulnerability to abuse, as it has silently been made to acquiesce to each one of them in turn. The modern overthrow of allegory and acceptance of the Song as simply an erotic love poem has brought a

---

105. Riehle, *Middle English Mystics*, p. 166-68.

profound relief and delight to many interpreters. However, the identification of literary traits such as *double entendre* throughout the Song by some contemporary scholars has a certain irony, in that it carries echoes of the traditional allegorical interpreters, who also found two levels of meaning in the text.[106] Moreover, questions about the nature of a divine–human relationship raised by centuries of figurative interpretation still linger in the air, and are being reconsidered by a small but growing number of scholars. This mysterious love song, with its vision of love, courtship, compassion, intimacy, longing and mutual delight, still resonates with elements of God's dealings with human beings as depicted elsewhere in the Hebrew Bible. The ebb and flow of its history of interpretation suggests that the Song, in its depiction of 'yearning for you', may still have something to say about humanity's 'yearning for You'.[107] This suggests that a more detailed analysis of the biblical texts is needed. That will be my task in the next chapter.

106. Cf. Dianne Bergant, *The Song of Songs* (Berit Olam: Collegeville, MI: Liturgical Press, 2001), p. x.
107. Cf. Renita J. Weems, 'The Song of Songs', in *New Interpreter's Bible,* IV (ed. Leander E. Keck; Nashville, TN: Abingdon Press, 1997), p. 391.

3

'MY GOD ... MY BELOVED':
YEARNING FOR YOU/YOU IN THE PSALMS
AND SONG OF SONGS

In the previous chapter I briefly surveyed interpretations of the Song of Songs and the Psalms down the centuries, focusing on themes of desire and intimacy and noting ways in which some writers have sought to link these two biblical books. In this chapter I present a conversation between selected passages from the Psalms and the Song which builds on what has gone before, but with an emphasis on contemporary scholarship and the use of current literary critical methods of analysis. Can any connections or contrasts be found between the texts: for example, the 'my God' of the Psalms (Ps. 63.1), and the Song's 'my beloved' (Song 1.13)?

Inevitably this approach may raise questions. Does isolating certain parts of each biblical book give an unbalanced picture by failing to take account of the whole? Clearly, 'no text is an island';[1] any biblical text is part of a larger context, within its own book and the wider canon. Readers of biblical texts have traditionally sought to be aware of their wider context within the books in which they are set. For example, commentators on the Psalms have looked for reasons to explain the way they are ordered in the Psalter. Augustine depicted a progression which he saw echoed in the spiritual lives of believers, from penitence in the fiftieth Psalm (Ps. 51 in most English translations), through mercy and judgment in the hundredth (Psalm 101) to praise in the hundred and fiftieth.[2] Although simplistic, this scheme does reflect the fact that greater numbers of laments are found early in the Psalter, while the emphasis on praise is stronger towards the end of it. Many have sought to explain why some psalms are grouped together, such as the so-called Elohistic Psalter (Pss. 42–83), the Songs of Ascent (Psalms 120–34), and the overall five-fold division of the Psalter. Some

---

1. Peter D. Miscall, 'Isaiah: New Heavens, New Earth, New Book', in *Reading Between Texts* (ed. Fewell), p. 45.
2. Augustine, 'Expositions on the Psalms', p. 682.

recent studies have shown increased interest in looking for connections
between adjacent psalms, and in some cases attempting to read the Psalter
as a whole, rather than as a selection of isolated units.[3] While adding much
to our understanding of the shape of the Psalter and the flow of some of its
theological themes, these approaches are too broad to help with my specific
project, namely, identifying themes of yearning for another. Furthermore,
those who advocate such approaches are generally still content to focus on
particular psalms as units within a larger whole. A specific focus need not
imply ignorance or neglect of the bigger picture, nor should interest in that
bigger picture lead us to neglect the individuality of particular psalms.[4] In
what follows, I focus on six particular psalms[5] of different types and from
different parts of the Psalter, while alluding to others where appropriate.
These six all speak to my central themes of desire and intimacy, offering
both similarities and differences to what is expressed in the Song of Songs.

Finding a structure in the Song of Songs is a task which has exercised
and divided scholars, as seen in the diversity of proposals which they have
presented. The repetitions, similarities and contrasts within the Song tease
and perplex, raising numerous questions, including that of unity: should
we view this book as a single song or a collection? Is there any plot, or at
least some progression of thought in the way the book is organized? Or
is the Song better understood as an anthology of love poems loosely connected by their subject matter, a kind of 'erotic psalter'?[6] Despite scholars'
disagreements on these questions, studies of the Song still divide the text
into shorter sections which are perceived to be coherent units; the divisions
I have chosen in what follows are similar to those found in a large number
of commentaries.[7] While inevitably ignoring some parts of the Song, I have

---

3. On the Elohistic Psalter and other groupings of the Psalms, see Frank-Lothar
Hossfeld and Erich Zenger, *Psalms 2: A Commentary on Psalms 51–100* (Hermeneia;
Minneapolis, MI: Augsburg Fortress Press, 2005), pp. 3, 7; John Day, *Psalms* (Old Testament Guides; Sheffield: Sheffield Academic Press, 1990), pp. 113-14; McCann, 'Book
of Psalms', pp. 641, 662-66. On tension between wisdom/Torah and royal covenant
themes in the overall structuring of the Psalter, see William P. Brown, *Seeing the Psalms:
A Theology of Metaphor* (Louisville, KY: Westminster John Knox Press, 2002), pp.
15-17. For links between adjacent Psalms, see Goldingay, *Psalms 1–41, 42–89, 90–150*;
Konrad Schaefer, *Psalms* (Berit Olam; Collegeville, MN: Liturgical Press, 2001), pp.
xix-xxi. On reading the Psalter as a whole, see Ernest Lucas, *Exploring the Old Testament: The Psalms and Wisdom Literature* (London: SPCK, 2003), pp. 29-32.

4. Cf. McCann, 'Book of Psalms', pp. 651-52.

5. Seven, if Psalms 42 and 43 are counted separately; I view them together, as a
single psalm.

6. Longman, *Song of Songs*, pp. 43, 48.

7. For a summary of ways in which commentators have divided the Song, see
Exum, *Song of Songs*, pp. vi, 39. On recent attempts to find a plot or flow of thought,

selected passages from various parts of the book as a whole which reflect its major themes of desire and intimacy, and which can be fruitful conversation partners with my chosen psalms.

I have also opted to vary the order in which I consider the chosen texts from the Song and the Psalms, in order to avoid any unintended impression of giving primacy to one book over the other. Rather than either one being given pride of place and the first or last word, I shall keep alternating between them; a mutuality in conversation is intended.

Desiring you/You: Song of Songs 3.1-5 and Psalm 63

Desire to encounter the other is a recurring motif throughout the Song and the Psalms; indeed, it is a major theme of both books. My first pairing of texts explores this theme.

Song 3.1-5

The Song of Songs is shot through with an all-pervading passion, a longing for the other. It bursts out dramatically in the opening verses, where, in the words of William of St Thierry, 'a woman leaps forth, as if from some hidden place, and wholly without modesty, without saying who she is, or where she comes from, or whom she is talking to, cries, "Let him kiss me with the kiss of his mouth!"'.[8] This declaration of yearning generates anticipation in the reader, who looks for the realization of that yearning in the subsequent verses and chapters.[9] The urgency and exhilaration of desire exudes from all that follows: 'draw me after you ... you are beautiful ... his fruit was sweet to my taste ... O that his left hand were under my head, and that his right hand embraced me ... arise my love, my fair one, and come away ... my beloved is mine and I am his ... how sweet is your love ... your lips distil nectar ...' (Song 1.4, 15; 2.3, 6, 10, 16; 4.10, 11). Delight in and longing for the other energizes the ebb and flow of the Song's dialogue all the way to the cryptic final verse, where the plea to 'make haste ... upon the mountains' suggests both withdrawal and an invitation to renewed intimacy (Song 8.14).

Experiencing the longed-for intimacy, however, is not always easy or straightforward for the characters in the Song. Song 3.1-5 depicts a quest

---

see Garrett, *Song of Songs*, pp. 76-81; 107-114; also Michael D. Goulder, *The Song of Fourteen Songs* (JSOTSup, 36; Sheffield: JSOT Press, 1986), pp. 2-4; Eliyahu Assis, *Flashes of Fire: A Literary Analysis of the Song of Songs* (London: T. & T. Cark, 2009), pp. 266-70.

8. Norris, *Song of Songs*, p. 17.

9. Richard S. Hess, *Song of Songs* (Grand Rapids, MI: Baker Academic Press, 2005), p. 48; Assis, *Flashes of Fire*, p. 34.

for the other, who initially seems absent or unresponsive.[10] The vivid immediacy of the scene depicted in vv. 2-4 needs to be set alongside v. 1, where
'at nights' is plural; this desire and the resultant search seem to be regular
and repeated.[11] Whether what is presented in these verses should be taken
as a dream, or a metaphor-laden fantasy, as some have argued, is unclear;
we are dealing with lyric poetry rather than plot-driven narrative, and here,
as elsewhere, the language of the Song has a dreamlike 'dizzying fluidity'.[12]
What is clear is that the poet, through the woman's narration, is presenting
powerful desires which persist by night. Eventually the woman's lover is
found, grasped, and brought into a secure and intimate place. The quest that
began with the woman alone in bed ends with her bringing the man to a bedroom associated with sexual intimacy, 'the chamber of her that conceived
me'. The reader is excluded from what follows with the sudden recurrence
of the enigmatic adjuration to the women of Jerusalem (cf. Song 2.7; 8.4),
which solemnly insists either that the couple should not be disturbed in their
lovemaking, or else that love (in the abstract) does not need to be stirred up,
but will rouse itself and arrive in its own good time.[13]

Psalm 63
Psalm 63 was highly valued in the early churches, where it came to be used
regularly as a morning psalm and an introduction to the singing of other
psalms in Sunday worship.[14] Hermann Gunkel described Psalm 63 as 'one
of the pearls of the Psalter', even while struggling to interpret it, a struggle
he resolved only by considerable rearrangement of its verses. This psalm
eludes clear categorization of the kind Gunkel and his successors sought.
Is it for individual prayer, or corporate worship? Is the speaker in the Temple, perhaps for a night vigil, or far away, remembering the Temple? Does
the sudden appearance of 'the king' in the closing verse make it a Royal

---

10. The lover seems closer at hand, indeed, calling out to the woman, if we link
Song 2.8-17 with 3.1-5. There is much to suggest such a link when we note the parallels
with a later, more clearly defined unit, Song 5.2–6.3 (Exum, *Song of Songs*, pp. 122-23).
But 3.1-5 still stands out as a distinct part of a larger section of the poem, where the
man's absence is acutely felt.

11. Fox, *Song of Songs*, p. 118; Hess, *Song of Songs*, pp. 86-87, 102; against Murphy,
Song of Songs, p. 145. Note the similarity to language used of those who regularly medi-
tate and worship at night, in Pss. 16.7; 92.2; 134.1.

12. Ariel Bloch and Chana Bloch, *The Song of Songs* (Berkeley: University of
California Press, 1998), pp. 15, 180. On issues and challenges in identifying poetry, see
Hunter, *Psalms*, pp. 23-30.

13. Exum, *Song of Songs*, pp. 135-37; 117-19; Garrett, *Song of Songs*, pp. 170-71;
Landy, *Paradoxes of Paradise*, p. 115.

14. James Luther Mays, *Psalms* (Interpretation; Louisville, KY: John Knox Press,
1994), p. 217.

Psalm? Does the language of seeking (v. 1) suggest a Wisdom influence? Is it a Psalm of Lament, or a Psalm of Thanksgiving or Confidence? So this psalm stands (not alone) as evidence that Gunkel's passion for categorizing different forms, while broadly helpful, has its limitations and must not be imposed rigidly on the Psalter.[15]

The passionate intensity of Psalm 63 is difficult to probe, and has enabled it to be many things to different people.[16] It has characteristics which seem to indicate both lament and confidence. The ascription and opening verse depict crisis and urgent need, while v. 5 seems much more assured, and vv. 9-11 seem confident of vindication; the psalm's remaining verses may be read as indicating assurance and hope for the future, or alternatively anxiety and longing for past glories. It can also be argued that the predominance of imperfect tenses throughout the psalm suggests not a particular crisis but an ongoing dynamic in the suppliant's life with God—seeking, being filled, rejoicing; in this case, the enemies referred to in the closing verses are best treated as poetic symbols of all that oppresses the speaker, either externally or internally, disrupting communion with God.[17]

These uncertainties about the nature of this psalm highlight the potential for ambiguity found in Hebrew poetry. Its capacity to be opaque and suggestive can (ironically) be clearly seen, notably in the Song and the Psalms, as will become evident in what follows. These ambiguities are particularly appropriate when we consider subjects such as desire and intimacy, which can simultaneously be sources of both assurance and anxiety. The possibility that assurance and anxiety can co-exist is suggested in the way this single psalm holds together both 'profoundly intimate communion with God and the elemental yearning of a faithful heart'.[18] Schaefer notes the various oppositions in the psalm (thirsting and feasting, intimacy with God and human hostility, fainting human and God's power), finding in it both nos-

15. Hossfeld and Zenger, *Psalms 2*, pp. 120-22; see also Day, *Psalms*, p. 15; A.A. Anderson, *Psalms 1–72*, (New Century Bible Commentary; London: Marshall, Morgan and Scott, 1972), p. 455. On the historical background, see J.W. McKay, 'Psalms of Vigil', *ZAW* 92 (1979), p. 246, arguing for a generalized understanding, in contrast to Michael Goulder, who favours a very specific historical scenario: *The Psalms of David (Psalms 51–72)* (JSOTSup, 102; Sheffield: JSOT Press, 1990), pp. 162-66.

16. Robert Davidson, *The Vitality of Worship: A Commentary on the Book of Psalms* (Cambridge: Eerdmans, 1998), p. 198. Eaton's confident assertion that Ps. 63 presents a king on the eve of a battle, seeking God in the sanctuary, is an example of a scenario which fits the text well, but is unduly prescriptive (*Psalms*, pp. 32, 236).

17. Goldingay, *Psalms 42–89*, p. 255; Marvin Tate, *Psalms 51–100* (WBC, vol. 20; Dallas, TX: Word, 1990), p. 125.

18. Weiser, *Psalms*, p. 454; cf. Eaton, *Psalms*, p. 236; Broyles, *Psalms*, p. 260. LaCocque sees parallels between Song 3.1-4 and the opening of Psalm 63 (*Romance She Wrote*, p. 94).

talgia for God and intimacy with God; he entitles the whole simply 'Love Song'.[19]

This psalm introduces a number of themes found in both the Psalms and the Song, which will be explored in this chapter. It abounds with the relational language of 'I' and 'you', as does the Song; a mutuality of commitment is reflected in the overall balance of the suffixes, with you/your (-*kā* [ךָ-]) coming fifteen times in this psalm, and 'I/me/my' (-*î* [י-]) fourteen times.[20] The psalm begins with an overpowering longing for God, who is 'my God', a phrase redolent with mutual personal commitment, perhaps expressing a covenantal bond.[21] The longing is depicted in terms of thirst (v. 1), later contrasted with the image of a divinely-provided feast of rich food (v. 5); thirsting for and feasting on the other are also important motifs in the Song (see Song 2.1-7; 5.1). The psalm's contrast between thirsting and feasting highlights a tension between God's absence and presence, which we shall note in other psalms; the absence and presence of the other is also a recurring and intriguing theme in the Song (Song 3.1-5; 5.2-8; 6.1-3). The language of 'my flesh' and 'your right hand' upholding me as my soul 'clings to you' (Ps. 63.1, 8) raises questions of physicality, or lack of it, in the relationship; the Song focuses strongly on the physical (Song 1.15; 7.6-9; 8.3). The psalmist speaks of having 'looked upon you … beheld you' (Ps. 63.2); the Song abounds in references to looking at the other (Song 4.1-8; 5.10-16; 6.4-10). Longing for the other takes place when in bed at night (Ps. 63.6; compare Song 3.1; 5.2).[22] The psalmist delights at being under the shade of God's wings, while the woman in the Song delights to sit in the shade of her tree-like lover (Ps. 63.7; Song 2.3). However, the language of loving commitment introduced in the psalm (v. 3) is different from the love language used in the Song (Song 1.3, 15-16; 3.1; but see also 8.6-7). How significant these differences are needs to be carefully considered. We shall examine some of these themes in what follows. For now, I limit my focus to expressions of desire.

The Language of Desire

biqqēš (בקשׁ). Seeking the other is a significant motif in the Song. The verb *biqqēš* indicates a seeking which is connected with desire and yearning.

---

19. Schaefer, *Psalms*, p. 153.

20. Goldingay, *Psalms 42–89*, p. 260.

21. On the significance of the phrase 'my God', see Broyles, *Psalms*, pp. 17, 23 (also Eaton, *Psalms*, p. 235).

22. Comparing Song 3.1 and 5.2 with Pss. 4.5 and 149.5, Edmée Kingsmill argues that a bed can sometimes be seen as a place of prayer and revelation (*Song of Songs*, p. 212).

This verb comes repeatedly in Song 3.1-4, as well as in 5.6 and 6.1. The fourfold repetition in Song 3.1-4 emphasizes the duration of the search; perseverance is needed to keep on seeking, seeking. The emphasis on *biqqēš* in Song 3.1-4 is paralleled by a fourfold repetition of 'found' and 'the one my soul loves' in the same verses. Eventually the woman's prolonged searching has an outcome, in this case a happy one. Seeking is mutual in the Song: the man also comes in search of the woman. In Song 2.8-10 and 5.2 the language used depicts him bounding across the hills, gazing in at the windows, pounding on the door and calling to her; like her, he is an earnest seeker.

Psalm 63 opens with an image of the speaker seeking God, not in the blind groping of a stranger, but 'the eagerness of a friend, almost of a lover, to be in touch with the one he holds dear'.[23] Here *šāḥar* (שׁחר) is used, as in Ps. 78.34 (see also Isa. 26.9; Hos. 5.15); intensity might be indicated by the use of the piel. Psalm 139 also uses the image of God searching for and knowing the speaker, who is tempted to flee; in this case, the rarer *ḥāqar* (חקר) is used (Ps. 139.1, 23; cf. Jer. 17.10).[24] Although not used in Psalm 63, *biqqēš* is used of the divine–human relationship elsewhere in the Psalter. Faithful people seek God's strength and presence (Ps. 105.3-4). Those who ascend the hill of Yhwh seek his face (Ps. 24.6). True seekers experience rejoicing and delight (Ps. 70.4). The earnest worshipper seeks to dwell in God's house and gaze upon God's beauty, experiencing an inner prompting: '"Come" my heart says, "Seek his face!" / Your face, Yhwh, do I seek' (Ps. 27.4, 8). Generally this seeking comes from the human side rather than the divine, although occasionally we find the reverse: God is urged to 'seek out your servant', who has gone astray like a lost sheep (Ps. 119.176). Thus a sense of desire for the other is clearly evident in the Psalms.

nepheš (נפשׁ). A key word in both Song 3.1-5 and Psalm 63 is *nepheš*. It occurs four times in this part of the Song, in addition to its use at Song 1.7; 5.6 and 6.12. In Psalm 63 it also appears four times, at significant moments: vv. 1, 5, 8, 9.

Usually translated 'soul' in English versions of the Bible, *nepheš* is an elusive word with a wide range of meanings. The primary one of 'throat' or 'gullet' leads into the nuance of breathing as a sign of life, and also of appetite, which is often reinforced by its use with verbs of desire. In the Hebrew Bible this tends to be expressed in intense longing or craving, either for food (Pss. 78.18; 107.9, 18; Prov. 6.30), or for power and prosperity

---

23. Derek Kidner, *Psalms 1–72* (Tyndale; Leicester: Inter Varsity Press, 1973), pp. 224, 26.

24. Siegfried Wagner, 'בקשׁ', *TDOT* 2, pp. 237, 240; Assis, *Flashes of Fire,* p. 97; Pope, *Song of Songs,* p. 525. The wicked are also seeking—to harm the righteous: Ps. 63.9; also Pss. 35.4; 40.14, 16; 71.13, 24. See also McCann, 'Book of Psalms', p. 926.

(Pss. 10.3; 35.25; Prov. 13.2), or in relational desire, which can be familial (Gen. 44.30), but is more often sexual (as in Song 1.7; 3.1-4; Jer. 2.24; Ezek. 16.27). A further meaning is the 'vital self', the true essence of the person; this is evident in the repeated Deuteronomic call to love God with one's entire being, the *nepheš* (Deut. 4.29; 6.5; 10.12; 30.2, 6, 10; Josh 22.5; 1 Kgs 2.4; 8.48; 2 Kgs 23.25). Thus loving with all one's *nepheš* is the calling of worshippers, as well as human lovers. The *nepheš* touches the inner depths, signifies the person as a whole: a person does not *have* a vital self but *is* a vital self (Gen. 2.7). A related understanding sees *nepheš* as the individuated life of the person; this leads to the translation 'life' or 'soul', as in 'those who seek to destroy my life' (Ps. 63.9; cf. Pss. 19.7; 23.3; 62.1).[25]

In the Psalter as a whole, *nepheš* is a significant word, recurring in a number of the psalms I shall focus on later in this chapter (Pss. 42.1, 2, 4, 5, 6, 11; 43.5; 63.1; 84.2; 119.20, 81). In some instances it may have the meaning of 'vital self' (e.g. Pss. 103.1, 2, 22; cf. Pss. 25.1; 34.2; 62.1; 71.23); yet even here we find a clear element of passion expressed in the urge to praise and trust God from the core of the speaker's being. Elsewhere the sense of craving and desire is more prominent (Pss. 42.1, 2; 84.2; 119.20, 81; 143.6, 8), involving an active pursuit of God or desire to get to the courts of God's house.

Psalm 63 in particular opens with a striking expression of 'the intensity of desire ... It wishes to say, "Both my soul and my body yearn for you and long for you, like the person thirsting for the sweetest and clearest water"'.[26] A number of commentators note the presence of *nepheš* at the turning points in the psalm. Erich Zenger finds three major sections: the soul thirsts for God (Ps. 63.1), finds satisfaction in God (63.5), and clings to God in the face of enemies (63.8, 9). However, the fluidity of meanings attached to the word is such that they may even vary within the same text. Pointing out that, in v. 2, *nepheš* is subject of the verb 'thirst' and parallel with 'flesh', Robert Alter argues that the physicality of 'throat' is a more suitable translation here than 'life' or 'soul'. Anthony Ceresco proposes that each of the psalm's three strophes begins with a different nuance of *nepheš*—'my throat' (v. 1), 'my desire' (v. 5) and 'my life' (v. 9); the first two, he argues, suggest appetite. The neatness of his outline is undermined by his failure to account for the fourth occurrence of *nepheš* in the psalm, at v. 8; however, the motif of

---

25. Horst Seebass, 'נֶפֶשׁ', *TDOT* 9, pp. 504-17; Claus Westermann, 'נֶפֶשׁ', *TLOT* 2, pp. 743-59; Klaus-Dietrich Schunck, 'Wanting and Desiring', *ABD* 6, pp. 866-67; Day, *Psalms*, p. 129; Keel, *Song of Songs*, p. 121; Longman, *Song of Songs*, p. 129; M. Deckers, 'The Structure of the Song of Songs and the Centrality of *nepheš*', in *A Feminist Companion to the Song of Songs* (ed. Brenner), pp. 187-89. It is worth noting that *nepheš* can also be used with negative expressions (hate, detest, loathe).

26. Theodoret, *Commentary on the Psalms*, p. 357.

desire/appetite turns out to be further reinforced in that verse by the use of *nepheš* with *dābaq*, which we shall consider shortly. John Goldingay also argues that the nuance of 'desire' is probably found in vv. 2 and 5 of this psalm, as in Ps. 27.12; similarly Hans-Joachim Kraus sees in v. 5 (and Ps. 42.1-2) 'the self of the needy life, thirsting with desire'.[27]

Like Psalm 63, Song 3.1-5 also emphasizes *nepheš* through repetition; in this case it is even more evident due to the brevity of the passage. Some commentators give little attention to this usage, or render the word simply as reflexive, equivalent to 'I'.[28] But in Song 3.1-5, the rendering of *nepheš* found in many English translations as 'soul' seems appropriate: in English idiom, we can say that the woman's 'heart-and-soul' love for her beloved is emphasized. If we remember the root meaning of *nepheš* alluding not only to appetite but also to 'breath', we might say she is depicting the kind of inner emotion that makes one breathe heavily, or takes the breath away. Breath can also be seen as the very source of her life, with which she loves him.[29]

All the examples cited above refer to the human *nepheš*. Occasionally we are given glimpses of the *nepheš* of God. Although sometimes the word can be seen as simply an emphatic reference to God's very self (e.g. Jer. 6.8, 51.14; Amos 6.8), invariably it occurs in contexts where God's passionate commitment to truth and justice among his people is being expressed (e.g. 1 Sam 2.35; Ps. 11.5; Isa. 1.14; 42.1; Jer. 32.41). The language of heartfelt desire is evident here.

dābaq (דבק). The joining, holding, or clinging which forms the root meaning of *dābaq* may take various forms, most of which involve earnestness or passion. At times in the Hebrew Bible *dābaq* indicates hot pursuit, sometimes of enemies in warfare (Gen. 31.23; Judg. 18.22; 20.45; 1 Sam.

27. Hossfeld and Zenger, *Psalms 2*, p. 123; Robert Alter, *The Book of Psalms: A Translation and Commentary* (New York: W.W. Norton, 2007), pp. xxvii-xxviii; Anthony R. Ceresko, 'A Note on Psalm 63: A Psalm of Vigil', *ZAW* 92 (1980), pp. 435-36; Goldingay, *Psalms 42–89*, pp. 257, 259; Kraus, *Psalms 1–59*, p. 439. On *nepheš* as desire in Ps. 63, see also Susanne Gillmayr-Bucher, 'Body Images in the Psalms', *JSOT* 28 (2004), pp. 317-20; also McCann, 'Book of Psalms', p. 927; Mitchell Dahood, *Psalms 51–100* (Anchor Bible, 17: New York: Doubleday, 1968), p. 99.

28. Garrett, *Song of Songs*, p. 170; John G. Snaith, *Song of Songs* (NCBC; London: Marshall Pickering, 1993), p. 48.

29. Bergant, *Song of Songs*, pp. 17, 37; cf. Exum, *Song of Songs*, p. 106-107; Hess, *Song of Songs*, p. 103; Murphy, *Song of Songs*, p. 131. Deckers renders *nepheš* as 'my being' in these verses ('Structure of the Song of Songs', pp. 189-90). The fact that the Song rarely uses the word *leb* (לב) confirms that 'heart' may not be the best translation of this word in English, which links 'matters of the heart' strongly with romance. We shall consider the meaning of *leb* (לב) later in this chapter.

31.2; 2 Sam. 1.6.). It can also mean holding tightly onto one's ancestral land (Num. 36.7, 9). But its most common uses are relational. Often it conveys a passion for God, envisaged alongside walking with, listening to and obeying God, as 'holding fast' to God (Deut. 10.20; 11.22; 13.4; 30.20; Josh. 22.5; 23.8; 2 Kgs 18.6; Ps. 119.31; Jer. 13.11). It is also used of human desire for physical closeness (Ruth 1.14; 2.8, 21, 23), and more specifically of sexual relationships ('Therefore a man leaves his father and his mother and clings to his wife, and they become one flesh', Gen. 2.24; see also 34.3; 1 Kgs 11.2).

The use of *dābaq* in Ps. 63.8 suggests intimacy. While John Calvin emphasizes the nuance of pursuit with determination to apprehend, most commentators have preferred the image of clinging.[30] This verse almost depicts a kind of embrace, with the speaker clinging to God, who responds with an upholding right hand. Clinton McCann finds here an articulation of both immediacy and intimacy in the psalmist's relatedness to God, while Zenger sees the individual soul seeking intimacy with God, clinging 'with all its vital and emotional powers, with all the power and passion of its love, to its God'; like McCann, he makes comparisons with the husband and wife image in Gen. 2.24 as well as the covenant loyalty expressed in Deut. 10.20; 11.22, etc. Samuel Terrien sees here a 'mystical embrace' (which does not blur the radical distinction between the human and the divine by sliding into pantheism), as the psalmist declares his most intimate attachment to his God: 'like the swearer of an oath, he "clings" (Deut. 10.20) to his divine lover'. John Rogerson and J.W. McKay argue that this verse presents almost a definition in personalized language of the relationship between God and his people in the covenant, sometimes summed up in the words 'I will be your God and you shall be my people' (Jer 7.23).[31]

The Song never uses *dābaq* but it does use a verb with similar meaning, *āḥaz* (אחז: 'seize' or 'grasp'). This is used by the woman of catching foxes (who probably represent young men, Song 2.15), and of clinging to her own lover ('I held him and would not let him go', Song 3.4; see also 7.8, where

30. Calvin, *Commentary on the Psalms*, Ps. 63.8 (cf Augustine, 'Expositions on the Psalms' p. 262); Theodoret sees the psalmist inflamed by passion, 'attached to your memory by desire for you as though by a kind of glue'; *Commentary on the Psalms*, p. 359.

31. McCann, 'Book of Psalms', p. 927; Hossfeld and Zenger, *Psalms 2*, pp. 3, 126; Terrien, *Psalms*, p. 464; John Rogerson and J.W. McKay, *Psalms 51–100* (Cambridge, UK: Cambridge University Press, 1977, p. 67. See also Anderson, *Psalms 1–72*, p. 458; Goldingay, *Psalms 42–89*, p. 260. Note, however, Eaton, who suggests here a parental embrace (*Psalms*, p. 236). Tate sees in Yhwh's right hand upholding the speaker not intimacy but a more robust expression of strong support especially meant for kings and warriors (e.g. Isa. 42.6; 45.1; Ps. 18.35; cf .17.7; 41.12; 80.17; 89.21; 110.5); *Psalms 51–100*, p. 128.

the man desires to lay hold of the woman's body).[32] The same verb is used in the Psalms of God holding his faithful ones (Pss. 73.23; 139.10 'your right hand shall hold me fast').

Summary
If *eros* love can be described as the desire for union (or reunion) with that which is valued, as Paul Tillich has argued, this resonates with terms used in both Ps. 63 and Song 3.1-4.[33] Song 3.1-5 depicts an earnest search for a human lover, which is resolved in finding and holding the beloved. Some of the language of yearning and desire used here has echoes in Psalm 63, which expresses a passionate longing to find and cling tight to God arising from the vital self, the desirous inner being. A longing for intimate encounter with another emerges as a theme in both texts.

Missing you/You: Psalm 42–43 and Song of Songs 5.2-8

My first pairing of passages emphasized desire for the other, and gave glimpses of the challenges involved in fulfilling that desire. In my second pair, the challenges are more clearly highlighted: desire produces anguished disappointment, as the longed-for other seems to be absent.

Psalm 42–43
The striking opening verses of Ps. 42 set the tone for what follows: in the text we meet a distraught individual, thirsty and hungry with desperate yearning for 'the living God', who seems to be absent (Ps. 42.1-3). As with many other psalms, the speaker's identity and location are not clear. What is clear is a deep desire for freedom from the taunts and torments of unspecified enemies, which will be achieved through a renewed encounter with the seemingly absent God. Straining with intensity, the speaker expresses a conviction that it is possible to 'come and behold the face of God' (Ps. 42.2), a conviction based on previous experience of corporate worship, apparently in the Tabernacle or Temple at Jerusalem (Pss. 42.4; 43.3-4). The *Sehnsucht* of Hossfeld and Zenger's title for this psalm perhaps captures best the wistful looking and longing of the speaker.[34]

32. See Exum, *Song of Songs*, pp. 130, 134.
33. Cf. Paul Tillich, *Love, Power and Justice* (New York: Oxford University Press, 1960), pp. 30-31. See Sallie McFague, *Models of God: Theology for an Ecological, Nuclear Age* (Philadelphia: Fortress Press, 1987), p. 130.
34. 'Ps. 42–43: Sehnsucht nach dem lebendigmachenden Gott'; see Frank-Lothar Hossfeld and Erich Zenger, *Die Psalmen* 1 (Neue Echter Bibel; Würzburg: Echter Verlag, 1993), p. 265. See also Goldingay, *Psalms 42–89*, p. 23; Schaefer, *Psalms*, p. 108; Alter, *Book of Psalms*, p. 148.

The metaphor of thirst found in these opening verses and in other relevant psalms (Pss. 63.1; 143.6) is suggestive with regard to the speaker's feelings towards God.[35] God is likened to life-giving water, and the Tabernacle or Temple to the source of that life. Alter sees water as a stock metaphor in a semi-arid culture, but one which psalms such as this one and Psalm 63 use in distinctive ways. For him, 'these poems, even if many of them were written to be used in the temple cult, exhibit an intensely spiritual inwardness. Yet that inwardness is characteristically expressed in the most concretely somatic terms.'[36]

The craving for water is one of the most basic and powerful human experiences, which can bring torment and become all-consuming.[37] The intensity of this craving gives it some similarities to sexual desire, as we shall see in the Song, which repeatedly uses images of drinking to depict experiencing intimacy with the lover—although there it is delight, rather than desperation, that is emphasized (Song 1.2; 4.10, 15; 5.1; 7.9; 8.2). Like sexual desire, thirst is soon renewed, needing further satisfaction (cf. Sirach 24.19, 21). The image of the thirsty deer is also suggestive of a basic instinct for self-preservation which humans share with other animals. Here, as in other Psalms of Lament, we find not measured consideration, but instead an 'extravagance of language'.[38] The speaker's disappointment is evident, seeking life-giving water, but instead tasting only the salt water of tears. Images collide as the thirsty one suddenly fears drowning, being overwhelmed by a destructive flood—for which God is to blame: it is 'your waves, your billows' that threaten (Ps. 42.7).[39] Here is one of the classic tensions of Psalms of Lament, where the speaker pleads with God and, at the same time, against God; God is both the problem and the solution.[40] In Dietrich Bonhoeffer's words, the distressed one heard in such Psalms never

35. Suggestions for an alternative translation of Ps. 143.6 fail to convince; against Stefan Paas, 'A Textual Note on Psalm 143,6', *ZAW* 113 (2001), pp. 415-18.

36. Alter, *Book of Psalms,* pp. xxvii-xxviii, xxxi.

37. Noting that the psalmist chooses the image of thirst, rather than that of hunger, David Kimhi suggests this is because thirst is the greater and most urgent of desires. See Cohen, *Three Approaches to Biblical Metaphor,* p. 167.

38. Ellen F. Davis, 'Exploding the Limits: Form and Function in Psalm 22', in *The Poetical Books: A Sheffield Reader* (ed. David J.A. Clines; Sheffield: Sheffield Academic Press, 1997), p. 139.

39. We may find a glimpse here of the overwhelming waters of Sheol; see David C. Mitchell, '"God Will Redeem my Soul from Sheol': The Psalms of the Sons of Korah', *JSOT* 30 (2006), p. 376.

40. See especially Alonso Schökel, 'The Poetic Structure of Ps 42–43', in *Poetical Books* (ed. Clines), pp. 17-19; also Hossfeld and Zenger, *Psalms* 2, p. 269; McCann, 'Book of Psalms', p. 853; Peter C. Craigie, *Psalms 1–50* (Word Biblical Commentary, 19; Waco TX: Word, 1983), p. 326; Broyles, *Conflict of Faith and Experience,* pp. 201-

loses sight of the origin and the goal of all distress, namely God; thus 'He sets out to do battle against God for God'.[41] The Song of Songs provides a comparable tension in its portrayal of love-sickness: love for her beloved causes the woman to feel faint, while also being the cure for her fainting. She is faint because of her lover, yet also faint with longing for more of him (Song 2.5-6).[42] But she never depicts him as opposed to her or potentially destructive, as the psalm does.

One of the features of this and many other Psalms of Lament is the repeated use of 'my' (the possessive suffix, *yōd*) and 'I' (the aleph verbal prefix).[43] God is seen to be 'my God' (Pss. 42.6, 11; 43.4, 5), 'my help' (Pss. 42.6, 11; 43.5) 'my rock' (Ps. 42.9) and 'my exceeding joy' (Ps. 43.4). The enemies are aware of these claims, and turn them into a taunt: 'Where is your God?' (Ps. 42.3, 10). While much of the psalm seems to be internally addressed, to the disturbed inner self, nevertheless the language of 'you' is also increasingly present, as the speaker addresses God (Pss. 42.1, 7, 9; 43.1-4). A relationship of mutual and personal commitment is indicated.[44] The speaker longs to get back to the Temple or Tabernacle, yet this is mentioned only obliquely in Pss. 42.4 and 43.3-4; the central focus is not on the special place, but on the person of God, who is mentioned repeatedly in the text. Moreover, the taunting question, 'where is your God?' suggests that God is not confined to any central place of worship, but can be encountered elsewhere. Paradoxically, the God whose absence is lamented in the psalm turns out to be very much present in it, being mentioned twenty-two times in all in these sixteen verses.[45] Direct address to God in the opening verses is a characteristic of this and many other Psalms of Lament.[46]

The use of personal, relational language in psalms such as this one has prompted much discussion about the identity and location of the speaker. From initial questions about authorship, this debate moved on to questions

---

3. See also Pierre Grelot, *The Language of Symbolism* (Peabody, MA: Hendrickson, 2006), p. 157.

41. Dietrich Bonheoffer, *Psalms: The Prayer Book of the Bible* (trans. James H. Burtness; Minneapolis: Augsburg, 1970), p. 48.

42. Exum, *Song of Songs*, p. 116.

43. Cf. Anderson, *Psalms 1–72*, p. 329.

44. This personal emphasis may be increased if we consider this psalm's place at the beginning of the Elohistic Psalter, and therefore read the divine name 'Yhwh' (יהוה) behind the frequent 'Elohim' (אלהים), for example, 'Yhwh, my God' (Ps. 43.4; cf. Ps. 63.1); Anderson, *Psalms 1–72*, p. 336.

45. Schökel, 'The Poetic Structure of Ps 42–43', p. 22; Goldingay, *Psalms 42–89*, pp. 21-22, 34. Cf. Hossfeld and Zenger's comment on Ps. 63.2-5: 'God is present in the mode of being passionately desired', *Psalms 2*, p. 123.

46. Hermann Gunkel, *Introduction to the Psalms* (completed by Joachim Begrich; trans. James D. Nogalski; Macon, GA: Mercer University Press, 1998), p. 85.

about the way psalms were used. While there is now widespread agreement
among scholars that parts of the Psalter were used in corporate worship during the Second Temple period, there is still a lack of consensus about how
the 'I/my' language found in a number of them is to be understood. Some
have argued that such language should be understood in a plural sense,
being spoken by the king or some other leading individual, who speaks not
simply for himself but as representative of the whole body of worshippers.[47]
If this theory is correct, it has implications for our understanding of the
divine–human relationships being expressed in the Psalms. We may need
to infer a more corporate 'we/our' behind the text in many psalms, which
would seem to diffuse some of the personal intimacy suggested by the more
individual 'I/my' language. In Psalm 42–43, for example, we would see a
group of worshippers (rather than an individual) expressing their experience of longing for God, using the prescriptive liturgy of the psalm as a
model prayer.[48]

A growing number of recent scholars, however, conclude that some of
the individual laments probably do reflect the experience of an individual,
and may have been written and used by individuals, in addition to their use
in small groups and at the Temple.[49] Indeed, it can be argued that the distinc-

47. See Mowinckel, *The Psalms in Israel's Worship* vol. 2, pp. 85-88; Weiser,
Psalms, p. 35; more recently W.R. Bellinger, Jr, *Psalms: Reading and Studying the Book
of Praises* (Peabody, MA: Hendrickson, 1992), p. 143. Gerstenberger sees two main
social settings for the Psalms: small, organic groups (such as family or neighbourhood)
and larger organizations (such as the monarchy and Temple cult). He titles Psalm 42–43
'Individual Complaint', but, noting also this psalm's repeated refrain, he suggests a setting of liturgical (communal) discourse (*Psalms* Part I, pp. 33-34; 179-80). B.W. Anderson argues that the Psalter was the prayer book of the Synagogue, not just the Second
Temple, as suggested by the presence of Psalm 119, which praises the Torah (a key focus
in the synagogue). He insists that the Psalms give no support to the idea of any individual finding access to God outside the liturgical forms and sacraments of the worshipping
community, but undermines his argument by further commenting that God, for his own
part, can seek people as and where he pleases, as shown in the story of Jonah; this would
seem to indicate that an individual may, after all, experience God away from the regular
forms of worship. See *Out of the Depths: The Psalms Speak for Us Today* (Philadelphia:
Westminster Press, 1977), pp. 10; 120-21.

48. Broyles, *Psalms,* pp. 3-4; cf. Mays, *Psalms,* pp. 175-76.

49. Seybold, for example, sees the 'I' in the Psalms usually reflecting a single individual who has drafted the prayer for personal use, and who cannot be identified through
the generalized language of particular psalms. He concedes that some of these psalms
may have been adapted later for communal use, but shows a healthy scepticism towards
the urge to develop totally imaginative scenarios (*Introducing the Psalms,* pp. 159-60).
See also Day, *Psalms,* pp. 26-27; Gillingham, *Poems and Psalms,* pp. 189, 273; Rainer
Albertz, *A History of Israelite Religion in the Old Testament Period* 1 and 2 (trans. John
Bowden; London: SCM Press, 1994), pp. 100, 400, 407-11. Steven Croft, even while

tion between corporate and individual in these texts is blurred, as the character and destiny of Israel is often replicated in the character and destiny of individuals, who are also covenant partners with Yhwh.[50] Overall, it seems wisest to embrace a 'fruitful openness and ambiguity' in the generalized language of these poems, by which one can imagine an ordinary individual, or a leader, or an entire worshipping congregation using a particular 'I' psalm.[51] What is striking is the relational nature of that language: God may be addressed—indeed, challenged, or even accused (Pss. 10.1; 13.1-2; 22.1-2)—person to person, with an expectation of response and interaction. This lament is not lamentation over unchangeable circumstances, such as might take place at a funeral. Pain is addressed to God with 'an insistent hope that the trouble can be changed and must be changed'; this covenant-making God is not gloriously unapproachable, but one who can and must act in response to his people's cry.[52] The speaker is missing the divine 'You', and declares that unfulfilled yearning is not the end of the story.

Song 5.2-8
Numerous questions are raised when studying this particular passage in the Song. Its context puzzles those who seek connection and continuity (or even a coherent plot) in the Song: why does this scene, depicting the man and woman failing to meet, follow immediately after verses which clearly suggest a very intimate and erotic encounter (Song 4.12–5.1)? How can the woman's 'heart' be awake while she sleeps?[53] Why is the woman appar-

---

arguing that nearly half of the ninety-six psalms which mention an individual were probably recited by the king, nevertheless identifies a further eighteen psalms written for the use of private persons in Israel (but then preserved to be used in worship at the Temple) (*Identity of the Individual*, pp. 131-35).

50. Walter Brueggemann, *An Unsettling God: The Heart of the Hebrew Bible* (MN: Fortress, 2009), pp. 58-61, 99. Gunkel argues that most of the Individual Laments began with a particular individual, but may have been adapted later for community use; he finds similarities between them and Communal Laments (*Introduction to the Psalms*, pp. 122-23).

51. Goldingay, *Psalms 1–41*, pp. 42, 60. Gillingham builds on the work of Westermann and Brueggemann in proposing a 'life-centred reading' of the Psalms, seeing them as enigmatic and generalized reflections on life which can encompass a wide variety of settings (*Poems and Psalms*, p. 189). See also Schaefer, *Psalms*, p.xxv; LaCocque and Ricoeur, *Thinking Biblically*, pp. 199, 226; Patricia K. Tull, 'Bakhtin's Confessional Self-Accounting and Psalms of Lament', *BibInt* 13 (2005), pp. 48-55.

52. Walter Brueggemann, *Israel's Praise: Doxology Against Idolatry and Ideology* (Philadelphia, PA: Fortress Press, 1988), p. 141; also Broyles, *Psalms*, p. 33.

53. Kingsmill sees in this verse a confirmation that the poet was one who experienced mystical prayer, since various monastic contemplatives speak of the need to quieten the body in order to pray, and of being most able to pray when their faculties are 'asleep' (*Song of Songs*, pp. 208, 259). Her argument that the Song is thus 'the contem-

ently so reluctant at first to open to the man, and then so regretful immediately afterwards? How does this passage, with its nightmare combination of violence at the hands of the watchmen and failure to find the one she seeks, relate to the similar scenario of Song 3.1-5, which presents a far more contented outcome? Some of these difficulties arise from the mistake of reading the Song as if it were a prose narrative, rather than poetry, and they diminish if we choose to infer from Song 5.2 that this passage relates a dream, since almost anything is possible in the surreal world of our dreams. The predominance in this passage of the first person singular 'I', along with description of certain actions, does present the woman who speaks in the role of a narrator. The absence of common indicators of narrative (such as the waw consecutive with the imperfect), however, should also remind us that we are not reading a sequential narrative, but a poem, with the opacity and ambiguity which poetry entails.[54]

Certain things, however, are vividly clear in this passage. One is the presence of desire, which arises by day and night, when awake or even when asleep. The man longs for the woman, and comes to seek entry. In spite of the reluctance (or teasing banter) expressed in v. 3, she yearns for the man when he strives to come in (Song 5.4). She describes this in terms of *hāmâ* (המה);, the same verb of noisy tumult which features in the repeated refrain of our psalm: 'Why are you so cast down, my soul, / and why so disquieted within me?' (Pss. 42.5, 11; 43.5). Longing for the other creates inner upheaval, both for the psalmist who yearns for God, and for the sexually desirous woman of the Song. The *double entendre* of Song 5.4, and quickening of tempo through the shortening of lines as this passage develops, may be suggestive of sexual intercourse taking place, even while the surface message of the text indicates the reverse.[55] This could be seen as her anticipation of what opening the door will bring, and perhaps as a memory of a previous encounter: the woman, like the psalmist, might be disturbed by the memory of a past experience of the longed-for one, which prompts her to seek him again in the present. Her term for her 'inner self', *mē'â* (מעה), covers a wide range of meaning, as can be seen in the various ways it is translated elsewhere in the Hebrew Bible; in the passage that follows

plative text par excellence' (p. 44) seems to be a striking example of how an interpreter can look into the Song and find their own reflection mirrored there.

54. Hess, *Song of Songs*, p. 166; Exum, *Song of Songs*, p. 190.

55. Cf. J. Cheryl Exum, 'In the Eye of the Beholder: Wishing, Dreaming and *Double Entendre* in the Song of Songs', in *The Labour of Reading: Desire, Alienation and Biblical Interpretation* (ed. Fiona C. Black, Roland Boer and Erin Runions; Semeia Studies, 36; Atlanta, GA: Society of Biblical Literature, 1999), pp. 82-85. Iain Provan also highlights the innuendo here, in what he explains in Freudian terms as an 'anxiety dream' (*Ecclesiastes, Song of Songs* [NIV Application Commentary; Grand Rapids, MI: Zondervan, 2001], pp. 334-35, 341).

it seems to be used more generally, to describe the body as a whole (Song 5.14). The closest parallels to its use in Song 5.4 are in the anguished yearning of Lamentations and Jeremiah (Lam. 1.20; 2.11; Jer. 4.19 and 31.20—in the latter verse, it describes God's inner yearning and compassion towards his people). In the Psalms it depicts the melting heart of the sufferer (Ps. 22.14), and the heart which delights to obey Yhwh's teaching (Ps. 40.8).

After her change of heart, the woman takes action to admit the man, only to find that she is too late—he has gone. The double verb ('he had gone away, he had left') emphasizes her shock and disappointment.[56] No reason is given for his departure; the suggestion that it is connected with the arrival of the watchmen (Song 5.7) can only be speculation.[57] Her heart sinks—or more literally, 'my life came out'; acutely disappointed, she feels as if her very life has departed (compare Gen. 35.18, where the death of Rachel is described in similar terms). Soon we will find her drained of life and feeling faint with love (Song 5.8). While another occasion would prompt her to use the same language in describing the overwhelming pleasure she enjoyed from being so close to him (Song 2.5), here it is the reverse—she is suffering, faint with longing for him.[58] As we have seen, the psalm also suggests desperation when using the imagery of thirst (Ps. 42.1-2); for lack of water, life withers and quickly comes to an end. It seems that both 'yearning for you' and 'yearning for You' can feel like a matter of life and death.

Absence makes the heart grow reckless. Now the woman goes out into the night in search of her beloved, as he did recently in searching for her.[59] She seeks, but does not find; calls out, but hears no answer. She cannot find him, in spite of her attempts to enlist the help of the watchmen and the women of Jerusalem (Song 5.6-8). Failure to find him proves painful both physically (through the beating she receives), and emotionally (as she explains it to the women of Jerusalem).

The disappointment of the missed encounter in Song 5.2-8 raises wider questions about the relationship depicted in the Song: to what extent is the man depicted in the Song present, or absent?[60] If or when he is present, what

56. Longman, *Song of Songs*, p. 168.

57. Bloch and Bloch, *Song of Songs*, p. 182.

58. See Bergant, *Song of Songs*, pp. 65-67; Hess, *Song of Songs*, p. 162, 174. The *double entendre* in Song 5.6, 8 may well also suggest sexual ecstasy and *la petite mort* of orgasm (cf. Exum, *Song of Songs*, pp. 196-201; Longman, *Song of Songs*, p. 167). But this, if over-emphasized, jars too strongly with the disturbing experiences of Song 5.7. Even if we see the woman disappointed at the man's abrupt withdrawal due to his post-coital dwindling of desire (cf. Garrett, *Song of Songs*, p. 213), this does not sufficiently explain the abusive watchmen who beat her.

59. Fox, *Song of Songs*, p. 324.

60. I am identifying with those who see the Song as a broadly unified poem (or unified collection) with a coherent literary style, depicting one archetypal couple repeat-

degree of intimacy do the couple achieve? The Song's cryptic, lyrical poetry is opaque, clouding our view, enticing the reader. The preceding verse is a case in point: different commentators translate Song 5.1 using past, present or future tenses, depending on their view of what is happening in the text at this point. Exactly whether this verse indicates coitus, foreplay, or some other intimacy between the lovers remains unclear.[61] The verses that follow Song 5.2-8 raise similar questions: the woman conjures up her lover by describing him, and then reveals that he is in fact in his 'garden', which indicates sexual intimacy with her (Song 6.2; cf. 4.16–5.1); now, it seems, he is once again present. It seems as if he never really left her in the first place;[62] yet if so, what are we to make of her anguish in 5.6-8, where she clearly experiences his absence? We cannot dismiss the contrast between the affirmation of intimate presence in 6.2-3 and the absence depicted in Song 5.6-8 as simply an example of two contrasting poems placed in sequence, since one of the few points of agreement among most commentators about structure is that Song 5.2–6.3 forms a unit.[63] Somehow presence and absence are being held together.

There is wide disagreement about these questions, even among those who are like-minded. Daphna Arbel sees the whole of the Song as a poem depicting a fantasy, in which a woman imagines herself in different possible encounters with her lover, trying on various personae (sensual erotic woman, hesitant young girl, protected virgin, admired lover, seductive dancer).[64] In the same volume, Alicia Ostriker argues that the Song depicts desire which is not deferred, but already satisfied, and hence more is anticipated with confidence rather than anxiety.[65] Emphasizing the man's absence, Carey Walsh argues that desire (which abounds in the Song) is a memory of experienced pleasure, born of previous enjoyment and fuelled by current absence. Thus 'desire for an absent lover pulsates throughout eight chapters in a heady mixture of glee, frustration, exhaustion and surrender'. This, Walsh further argues, resonates with readers, reminding them of desire for the most absent object of all, God, if only as a phantom memory. She finds here a Song about delayed and frustrated desire on the part of two lovers (one unseen), which is part of the coping strategy of the exilic community

---

edly, rather than a loose collection of poems depicting various couples; see Exum, *Song of Songs*, p. 33-37; Fox, *Song of Songs*, pp. 209, 226; Murphy, *Song of Songs*, p. 67.

61. Fiona C. Black, 'What is my Beloved? On Erotic Reading and the Song of Songs', in *The Labour of Reading* (ed. Black *et al.*), pp. 42-45.

62. Cf. Longman, *Song of Songs*, pp. 175-76; Murphy, *Song of Songs*, p. 173.

63. See Robert Gordis, *The Song of Songs and Lamentations* (New York: Ktav Publishing House, 1954), p. 63; Exum, *Song of Songs*, p. 39.

64. Daphna V. Arbel, 'My Vineyard, my Very Own, is for Myself', in *The Song of Songs* (ed. Brenner and Fontaine), pp. 92-93.

65. Ostriker 'Holy of Holies', p. 49. Also Bloch and Bloch, *Song of Songs*, p. 4.

in Babylon, as they are forced to live without the felt presence of their loved God; hence, she argues, the Song's capacity to resonate with readers on both the sexual and spiritual planes.[66]

While the parallels Walsh draws between spiritual and sexual desire are suggestive and significant, she overstates the degree to which the man in the Song is absent; there is considerable evidence in the text for his presence, as we shall see later in this chapter. A more nuanced approach to the theme of absence is needed. The man in the Song does at times seem elusive, leaping across the hills, coming and going as he pleases (Song 2.8-9; 3.3; 5.1; 6.1; 8.14), but this is not the same as constant absence. Like Walsh, Eliyahu Assis emphasizes the importance of desire as the main motivating factor for the lovers depicted in the Song—their love is an infinite desire to be together. Assis does not deny the presence of the beloved, and sees the couple finally achieving an intimate rendezvous in the central part of the book (Song 3.1–5.1), after which they have to deal with the ebb and flow of their desire. Assis argues that their love is always seeking a deeper, more absolute experience, and so can never be satisfied; at times the lovers feel some sense of perfection and fulfilment, yet they still experience longing for a total love that cannot be satisfied.[67] Kathryn Harding suggests that the theme of the man's absence highlights the woman's anxieties and sense of vulnerability, along with her desire to be united with the man while also establishing her own separate identity. Thus the Song, in Harding's view, presents a vision of love which is beautiful and exuberant, yet also perceptive and realistic.[68] Cheryl Exum points out the Song's inbuilt resistance to any kind of closure, as seen in its abrupt opening and ambiguous ending. She sees the boundaries between desire and fulfilment constantly being blurred, as the poet depicts love forever in progress. In the rhythms of love which the Song mirrors, longing leads to satisfaction, which in turn leads to renewed longing, and so on. Like Keats' Grecian Urn, the Song celebrates a love that is ongoing, indeed, unending. 'Desire in the Song is always on the brink of fulfilment, has an urgency about it (come! tell me! make haste!); and fulfilment is simultaneously assured, deferred, and, on a figurative level, enjoyed.'[69] In a similar vein, Francis

---

66. Walsh, *Exquisite Desire*, pp. 22-23, 31-32, 97. Deferred gratification is also a common feature of music, found in a composer or songwriter's use of pauses, digressions etc.; see Begbie, *Resounding Truth*, p. 283.

67. Assis, *Flashes of Fire*, pp. 269-70.

68. Kathryn Harding, '"I sought him but I did not find him": The Elusive Lover in the Song of Songs', *BibInt* 16 (2008), pp. 54-59.

69. Exum, 'In the Eye of the Beholder', p. 75; *Song of Songs*, pp. 11-13; 123-24, 133; cf. Bergant, *Song of Songs*, p. 11; Hess, *Song of Songs*, p. 176. See also Michael Riffaterre on ways in which the object of desire can be represented, even visible, while

Landy sees the lovers pursuing each other across the poem, 'elusive but in touch, changing roles, parting and converging', involved in a pulse or rhythm which is characteristic of all erotic poetry and reminiscent of ballet or a courtship dance.[70]

These tensions between desire and fulfilment found in the Song can resonate with tensions found in spiritual experiences. Taking the man in the Song to represent God and the woman Israel, the Targum of Canticles maps the rhythm of communion, estrangement and reconciliation which runs through the Song onto the history of Israel; for these rabbinic readers familiar with prophetic texts (such as Hosea 1–4; Jer. 2.1-2; Ezek. 16; Isa. 54.4-8; 62.4-5), this seems to have felt like a natural way to interpret the Song. Some of the Psalms also display tension between desire to encounter God and fulfilment—or the lack of it—of that desire; the Psalms of Lament, inevitably, emphasize the lack. In Psalm 42–43 God's absence is keenly felt. Yet paradoxically this painful awareness is a means of God being present— in the mind of the psalmist, bringing grief and anxiety.[71] 'At one level of consciousness nostalgia and dismay seem to predominate; yet the repeated refrain of the psalm suggest that, at a deeper level, confidence and hope may be emerging and growing'.[72] The Song also surprises the reader with its apparent contrasts: immediately after the anguish of missed encounter, we find the woman conjuring up her lover with a vivid description that makes him seem vividly present (Song 5.9-16).[73]

All You Love Is Need?[74]

If the psalmist is 'missing You', desiring the presence of an apparently absent God, one question which arises is simply, 'why?' Is it the person and company of God that is missed, or simply God's help that is wanted? Does the psalm express a yearning for relationship with God, or simply a desire for the divine 'You' to come and help me? The couple in the Song miss each other's physical presence and company, rather than needing help: they both sense and express an urgent desire to be with the other (although on this occasion they fail to fulfil the desire), rather than to get something beneficial from the other. Thus the Song might ask whether the desire expressed by the psalmist is self-focussed rather than other-focussed.

still absent ('Compulsory Reader Response: The Intertextual Drive', in *Intertextuality* (eds. Worton and Still), pp. 63-64; 73).

    70. Landy, *Paradoxes of Paradise*, p. 57; cf. Bloch and Bloch, *Song of Songs*, p. 17.

    71. Alexander, *Targum of Canticles*, p. 27; cf. LaCocque, *Romance She Wrote*, pp. 117-20.

    72. Schökel, 'Poetic Structure of Ps 42–43', p. 21.

    73. Exum, *Song of Songs*, p. 188.

    74. I borrow this phrase from Tony Walter, *All You Love is Need* (SPCK, 1985).

It is only in the opening of Psalm 43 that the desire for rescue becomes prominent, with its call for vindication from God. Up to that point, there is no clear cry for help, only a desperate desire to be close to God, prompted by the current crisis. Hans-Joachim Kraus (with Gunkel) argues that what is expressed here is first and foremost a longing for what he calls 'the sure experience of the living God'.[75]

Similar questions can be asked of other Laments. Psalm 143 uses similar imagery to Ps. 42.1, 'I stretch out my hands to you; my soul thirsts for you like a parched land' (Ps. 143.6). This verse is set within a psalm where a sense of urgent need for rescue from enemies is paramount (Ps. 143.1, 3, 9, 12). The soul is lifted up in expectant trust, the hands stretched out by the suppliant (vv. 6, 8); but there is little sense of a desire for ongoing relationship—as we might expect, the urgency of the immediate crisis predominates. However, there are other psalms where a need for help is less evident, and a desire for relationship more prominent, as we shall see in what follows.

Challenging questions can have a disconcerting habit of rebounding on the questioner; what we ask about the psalm may also be asked of the Song. Why does the man seek entry in Song 5.2? Why does the woman grieve at her failure to connect with him, in the verses that follow? Are they expressing desires to assuage a fear of loneliness, or to fulfil a need for company, or to achieve sexual release? Do they delight in the other, or seek their own fulfilment? The immediately preceding verse (Song 5.1) gives strong indication of a desire for personal satisfaction on the part of the man: personal pronouns ('I' and 'my') predominate, as he describes enjoying his lover's body in terms of satisfying his appetite with an exotic banquet. The woman speaks in more relational terms, but ends this passage with a focus on her own need, as she asks the women of Jerusalem to help her find him; being 'faint with love' (5.8) seems to leave her feeling weak and in need of support.[76]

Unravelling human motivations is a complex task with living subjects; seeking to read them behind the lines of ancient texts is even more daunting. Osborne explores some of these intricacies, asking 'because a benefactor *might* be loved for the sake of the benefits she supplies, need it follow that that can be the only motivation for the beneficiary to love her? Need it be a

---

75. Kraus, *Psalms 1–59*, p. 441.

76. Landy sees in Song 5.1 'a song of greedy exploitation, of masculine triumph, expressive of satiety', yet combined with an assertion of the ego which verges on dissolution, as the verbs evoke intoxication and confusion (*Paradoxes of Paradise*, p. 108). Weems points out that the personal pronoun 'my' occurs more than fifty times in the Song, spoken by both the man and the woman; lovers, she concludes, are possessive ('Song of Songs', p. 393).

motive at all?' While self-interest can be a motivation, it is equally possible to treasure the promised benefits because one already loves the person who gives them. Merely identifying the benefits which each receives does not establish that desire for them is what motivates the recipient's love.[77] Alternatively, we might argue that delight in feasting on the other (Song 5.1) or on the Other (Ps. 63.5) is simply a natural, joyful outcome of experiencing intimacy in the relationship, to be welcomed rather than questioned.[78] What we can say is that both the Psalms and the Song raise questions about the extent to which desire for intimacy, be it with God or with other human beings, is driven by self-interest—'need-love' rather than 'gift-love', in the words of C.S. Lewis. There may well be mixed motives behind a 'yearning for you', and for 'You'.[79]

Summary
Parallels between yearning for a human lover and yearning for God may be found in the motif of absence. For the speaker in Psalms 42–43 and the woman in Song 5.2-8, desire sometimes results in grievous disappointment. The intense, desperate longing is not fulfilled: for the psalmist, God seems inexplicably absent, while the woman's lover in the Song seems to have suddenly departed. Both the woman and the psalmist are left in anguish, feeling as if they are dying, desperate for the situation to change. In both texts questions arise about the extent to which their longing for the other is self-focussed, as opposed to self-giving.

Admiring and Enjoying you/You:
Song of Songs 1.9–2.7 and Psalm 84

After the upheavals of desire and absence, we move on to enjoyment: the awestruck delight of encounter, especially of gazing on the other, and touching.

Song of Songs 1.9–2.7
The structure of the opening chapters of the Song is debated, although most scholars agree that a break occurs at Song 2.7. This section may begin at

---

77. Osborne, *Eros Unveiled*, pp. 8-9, 63-69 (cf. C.S. Lewis, *The Four Loves* [London: Geoffrey Bles, 1960], pp. 110, 145-51).

78. Cf. John Piper's call to worshippers to enjoy 'the feast of Christian Hedonism', as they delight in the perfection of God (John Piper, *Desiring God* [Nottinhgam: Inter-Varsity Press, 2003], p. 96).

79. Concern that desire can become coveting, and thus sinful, is found in later Judaism in texts such as 1Qs 9.25; 10.19 and rabbinic sources; see Klaus-Dietrich Schunck, 'Wanting and Desiring', *ABD* vol. 6, p. 867.

Song 1.7, or perhaps back at 1.2. The verses I have chosen highlight the particular themes of seeing, gazing and delighting in the other, along with physically enjoying each other.

In these verses we see the lovers through each other's eyes, as they exchange compliments in a dialogue of mutual admiration. The man sees the woman as 'like a mare among Pharaoh's chariots' (probably indicating a coveted and prized possession, rather than an allusion to the disturbing effect she has on him and other 'stallions').[80] He admires her bejewelled face, and imagines embellishing it further; he gazes into eyes 'like doves', and compares her to a lily (Song 1.9-11, 15; 2.2). She in turn describes him as 'like a cluster of henna blossoms', 'beautiful, truly lovely', 'like an apple tree among the trees of the wood', giving welcome shade and fruit (Song 1.14, 16; 2.3). The repetition in the mutual exclamations, 'Look at you! You are beautiful!' (Song 1.15, 16), highlights the impression that the couple cannot take their eyes off each other.[81] These lovers do not say 'I love you', but 'you are lovely' (1.15, 16; 4.1; 6.4); the emphasis is not so much on their own feelings, but much more on what is lovely about the other.[82] Terms of praise and endearment abound: 'beautiful' (1.8, 15, 16; 2.10, 13: 4.1, 7; 5.9; 6.1, 4, 10); 'lovely' (1.5; 2.14; 4.3; 6.4); 'more pleasing' (1.2, 3; 7.9; cf. 4.10); 'awesome' (6.4, 10); 'delightful' (1.16); 'sweet' (2.3); 'pleasant' (2.14).[83] The poem permits the reader, and the lovers themselves, to see with the lover's vision, which sees the other as lovable and valuable; this draws forth a response in kind, prompting the beloved to value the one by whom they are valued.[84]

Looking with delight is a recurring theme in the Song, which occurs extensively in further depictions of the other often referred to as *waṣfs*, from an equivalent found in Arabic literature, or as Praise Songs or Description Songs (Song 4.1-5; 5.10-16; 6.4-7; 7.1-5). The often opaque, metaphorical language of these declarations of admiration has long puzzled readers; most assume them to be complementary, although a few have identified them as

---

80. Exum, *Song of Songs*, pp. 108-109; Bergant, *Song of Songs*, p. 19; Murphy, *Song of Songs*, p. 131; against Pope, *Song of Songs*, pp. 338-39.

81. Exum, *Song of Songs*, p. 98; against Longman (*Song of Songs*, p. 107). On mutuality in the Song, see also Martti Nissinen, *Homoeroticism in the Biblical World: A Historical Perspective* (Minneapolis: Fortress Press, 1998), p. 133; also Bloch and Bloch, *Song of Songs*, p. 4, 145, 206-207.

82. Robin Payne, 'The Song of Songs: Song of Woman, Song of Man, Song of God', *Expository Times* 107 (1996), p. 333. A number of the Psalms show a similar tendency, with God rather than humans being the grammatical subject to whom praise is declared; see Broyles, *Psalms*, p. 34.

83. See Murphy, *Song of Songs*, p. 70.

84. Cf. McFague, *Models of God*, p. 128.

'comic', 'satirical', or 'grotesque'.[85] The reader is given a glimpse, not of the body of each beloved, but of the way the beloved is perceived by the lover. The images serve partly to convey the effect which looking has on the emotions of the beholder, as well as delight in the body of the other. They may also convey something of the lovers' anxieties and sense of vulnerability (expressed elsewhere in his feeling overwhelmed and captivated by her, while she feels weak and wounded with lovesickness; Song 4.9; 6.5 and 2.5; 5.8).[86] At the same time, they render the reader's pleasure less voyeuristic and more aesthetic, by veiling as much as they reveal, 'clothing the lovers' bodies in metaphors'.[87] The poet's ability to use language that seems both voluptuous and at the same time reticent is one of the Song's most striking features.[88]

Yearning prompts a desire to come ever closer to the loved one; thus gazing naturally leads on to touching. In keeping with the Song's delicacy of expression this is not directly stated, but repeatedly implied.[89] We see the lovers lying in embrace beneath the trees; the man's 'fruit' is sweet to her taste, and he lies between her breasts (Song 1.13; 2.3, 6). Here images of feasting and lovemaking are fused, as the woman asks for further pleasurable sustenance to strengthen her and prolong her pleasure; the nourishment which she wishes to taste above all is him, her lover. Note the contrast with Song 4.12–5.1, where she is the garden and we see him feasting on her. The rhythmic dance of mutuality in their relationship is evident in other ways: here he gives protection and pleasure to her, reversing the roles found earlier, when she seems to be sheltering and delighting him (Song 1.13; 2.3).

85. See Whedbee's chapter on 'Paradox and Parody in the Song of Solomon: Towards a Comic Reading of the Most Sublime Song', in J. William Whedbee, *The Bible and the Comic Vision* (Cambridge: Cambridge University Press, 1988), pp. 263-72; Fiona C. Black, 'Beauty or the Beast? The Grotesque Body in the Song of Songs', *BibInt* 8 (2000), pp. 311, 317-21, and her more recent *The Artifice of Love: Grotesque Bodies in the Song of Songs* (London: T. & T. Clark, 2009).

86. Fox, *Song of Songs*, pp. 271-77, 330; LaCocque, *Romance She Wrote*, pp. 24-25; Garrett, *Song of Songs*, p. 151. Also Richard N. Soulen, 'The *wasfs* of the Song of Songs and Hermeneutic', *JBL* 86 (1967), pp. 183-90; in response, Marcia Falk, 'The Waṣf', in *The Song of Songs: A New Translation and Interpretation* (San Francisco, CA: Harper San Francisco, 1993), pp. 127-35, particularly p. 131.

87. Exum, *Song of Songs*, pp. 15, 24. An interesting contrast to the Song's subtle suggestiveness is the more explicit style of erotic description found in the traditional Sanskrit lyric, *Gita Govinda*. This, Pope notes, includes in one part such graphic language that various European translators either omitted it 'or cast over it the veil of Latin so that the mystic beauties may be perceived only by the initiated'. (Pope, *Song of Songs*, p. 86; *Gita Govinda* [http://en.wikisource.org/wiki/Gita_Govinda], accessed 9 June 2010).

88. Bloch and Bloch, *Song of Songs*, pp. 4, 14, 119.

89. Robert Alter, 'Afterword', in *Song of Songs* (Bloch and Bloch), p. 122.

The alternating voices of the dialogue also convey reciprocity, as does the declaration that 'my beloved is mine and I am his', with its mirror image, 'I am my beloved's and he is mine' (Song 2.16; 6.3). The sensuous atmosphere of edenic bliss in these verses is heightened still further by references to the scent of costly perfumes; smells of blossom, grass, cedar, cypress and fruit might also waft in the reader's imagination (Song 1.12-14, 16-17; 2.3).[90] The natural world in which the lovers live is not ignored or displaced, but instead affirmed and embraced in their love-talk.[91] For those who suggest allusions to the opening chapters of Genesis, here is 'paradise regained' in the exotic garden of lovemaking.[92]

Psalm 84
Looking with delight is also a theme of Psalm 84. The expressions of longing in the opening verses remind us to some extent of how Psalms 42 and 63 began. But in Psalm 84, the speaker expresses admiration, not specifically for God, but for Yhwh's 'dwelling place' or 'house' and 'the courts of Yhwh' (vs. 1-2, 4, 10). This refers to the Temple (or possibly the earlier Tabernacle) at Jerusalem, as seen in the references to journeying to Zion (vs. 5, 7). While Psalm 42 places the speaker away from Temple, longing for it, Psalm 84 seems to be set in the Temple, with the speaker delighting in it.

> Heart and flesh resound to the living God. Here there are no tears, no taunts, no downcastness, no breakers and waves, no enemies. ... The pilgrim's consuming longing has now been fulfilled; now it is possible to resound, to make a noise, with enthusiasm.[93]

The physical reality of this place of delight is emphasized by the repetition of the terms 'dwelling place', 'house' and 'courts', and also by glimpses of doorkeepers and birds nesting near the altars, as well as mention of the highways, rain and springs experienced by the pilgrims (vs. 3, 5-6, 10). Reaching the focal point of worship on Mount Zion is the consummation of the journey. The pilgrim (or pilgrims, if we take the 'I' of this psalm to represent a group) has been consumed by the desperate yearning of the desirous *nepheš* (v. 2; a 'holy lovesickness' as Charles Spurgeon terms it, per-

---

90. Hess, *Song of Songs*, pp. 80-81; Fox, *Song of Songs*, p. 108; cf. Exum, *Song of Songs*, pp. 109, 116; Provan, *Song of Songs*, p. 284. There is also mutuality in the looking and describing of the *wasfs*, although, in the text as a whole, we find the man describing more often than the woman.

91. Alter, 'Afterword', p. 130.

92. Landy, *Paradoxes of Paradise*, pp. 57, 183-84, 201, 275; Trible, *God and the Rhetoric of Sexuality*, pp. 152-56; LaCocque, *Romance She Wrote*, pp. 78, 115; Whedbee, *Bible and the Comic Vision*, pp. 276-77.

93. Goldingay, *Psalms 42–89*, p. 588-89

haps alluding to Song 2.5).[94] It can be argued that this psalm is the lament of
one who is away from the Temple, longing to get to it, as in Psalms 42–43
and 63.[95] But in contrast to the opening of Psalms 42 and 63, here perfect
tenses probably indicate that the longing is now in the past, as desire has
found fulfilment in arrival.[96] This debate may remind us of the ambivalence
which we have noted in the Song, where scholars wrestle with the blurring
of boundaries between anticipation and achievement, desire and fulfilment.

The striking opening words, 'how loved', immediately raise questions
about the object of this love; elsewhere in the Hebrew Bible *yādîd* (ידיד)
invariably refers to a person who is loved, usually by God (Deut. 33.12;
Pss. 45 [ascription]; 60.5; 108.6; 127.2; Jer. 11.15; the exception is the love-
song/lament in Isa. 5.1, where God is the singer's beloved). The language
used also raises questions about the nature of this love. Observing the obvious associations of *yādîd* with the terms *dôd* (דוד) and *dôdîm* (דודים), which
are used for lover and lovemaking (not least, we might add, in the Song of
Songs), Alter argues that use of such a term here in the psalm conveys 'a
virtually erotic intensity in the speaker's longing for the temple on Mount
Zion'. He sees the speaker envying the happiness of the birds which live in
the Temple (v. 3), 'whereas he, like an unrequited lover, only dreams of this
place of intimacy with the divine'.[97]

Solomon's Temple (and, to a rather lesser extent, its post-exilic replacement) was undoubtedly awe-inspiring. But there is far more to the admiration expressed here than simply aesthetic pleasure in an immense architec-
tural achievement. The breathtaking grandeur and beauty of the building is
seen to express something of the one for whom it was built; it symbolizes
worship, in which God could be encountered. Thus L.J. Sabourin's title for
Psalm 84, 'Desire for the Sanctuary', is accurate, but does not say enough.[98]
The worshipper's excitement is not just at being in a place but also at the
prospect of meeting the one who dwells in that place. The Temple is a place
of encounter, as well as a metaphor for the one who works wonders from it.
The focal point of the Temple, and of the psalm, is 'the living God', the true
fountain of life and source of security, satisfaction and fulfilled existence.

94. Charles H. Spurgeon, *Treasury of David* 3 [http://www.ccel.org/ccel/spurgeon/
treasury3.i.xxx.html], accessed 29 Mar. 2010; cf. Goldingay, *Psalms 2*, p. 601.

95. So Hossfeld and Zenger, *Psalms 2*, pp. 350-52; also Kidner, *Psalms 73–150*,
pp. 303-305. Rashi sees the Psalm as composed during the exile, lamenting the loss of
the Temple (*Commentary on Psalms 1–89* [trans., Introduction and Notes by Mayer I.
Gruber; Atlanta, Georgia: Scholars Press, 1998], p. 392).

96. Goldingay, *Psalms 42–89*, p. 588.

97. Alter, *Book of Psalms*, p. 297.

98. L.J. Sabourin, *The Psalms: Their Origin and Meaning* II (Staten Island, NY: The
Society of St Paul, 1969), p. 211; cf. Schaefer's comment that 'the poet is in love with
the temple' (*Psalms*, p. 209).

The divine name Yhwh occurs seven times in Psalm 84, as does Elohim; this double septenary pattern perhaps suggests completeness and perfection.[99] Here in the Temple is a place on earth where God 'dwells', a house which God offers to human beings (and even birds) as a 'home'.[100] The exhilaration of delight is expressed in the hyperbole of v. 10: 'For a day in your courts is better than a thousand elsewhere'.[101]

Yearning for God gives energy, as seen in the determination of the travelling pilgrims (Ps. 84.5-7). They find strength renewed, and even desert places filled with refreshment, rain and springs which God has provided. Citing Isa. 40.31, where the faithful find 'an energy that gives them wings', Zenger comments on Ps. 84.5-7: 'That is the experience of all lovers. Genuine longing releases unsuspected powers—and makes the world a manifold reference to the beloved. The same is true of longing for God.' He finds here 'a metaphor for intimate closeness to God (Pss. 27.4; 42.3; 63.3)', and notes the three beatitudes at significant places in the psalm (Ps. 84.4, 5, 12) as important signs of the blessedness of being close to God, or moving towards God.[102] An interpretative crux occurs in v. 7: who is it that is (or will be) 'seen in Zion'? Most translations understand the verse to mean that the worshippers are seen by God, as indicated by the MT; but some more recent versions follow LXX and have God seen by the worshippers (NRSV, REB, NJB). The MT may be giving a short form of a technical expression for appearing at the sanctuary in the presence of God (as in Exod. 34.23; Deut 16.16). But some manuscript evidence suggests scribal corrections here, presumably in order to avoid direct reference to seeing the face of God. A similar dispute arises in Ps. 42.2: should we read the MT's *wᵉ 'ērā 'eh* (וְאֵרָאֶה) or the Targum's *wᵉer 'eh* (וְאֶרְאֶה)? The NRSV renders the phrase, 'When shall I come and behold the face of God?'; NJB agrees, with 'When shall I go to see the face of God?'. NASB and REB have 'appear before God', choosing the passive niphal 'be seen'. The NIV hedges its bets, with 'When can I go and meet with God', thus avoiding the ambiguity of the text, rather than seeking to choose one of the two alternatives. If we follow the principle of *lectio difficilior* and choose the more unlikely option, we then need to consider what is meant by 'seeing God'. In spite of the dangers sometimes associated with 'seeing God' (Judg. 6.22-23; Isa. 6.5; Exod. 33.20), a tradition of

99. Schaefer, *Psalms*, p. 206.
100. Hossfeld and Zenger, *Psalms 2*, pp. 353-56; the animals referred to are the nesting birds mentioned in Psalm 84.3. See also Goldingay, *Psalms 42–89*, p. 600; Kraus, *Psalms 60–130*, p. 171.
101. A similar phrase is used in an ancient Egyptian love poem, where an amorous woman declares to her lover 'Better indeed is one day in your arms ... than a hundred thousand [anywhere] on earth', Exum, *Song of Songs*, p. 52; cf. Fox, *Song of Songs*, p. 8.
102. Hossfeld and Zenger, *Psalms 2*, pp. 354-56.

'seeing', in which Israel is invited during cultic worship to gaze on a vision of Yhwh's presence, holiness and beauty, is found in the Psalter (e.g. Pss. 11.7; 17.15; 63.2) and beyond.[103] Since no images of God were permitted in the religious practice which the Hebrew Bible approves, 'seeing God' may be simply a metaphorical expression of what it means to have a sense of being in God's presence (where, of course, one is also seen by God; so there is some mutuality about the looking). However, in both of these psalms, this experience is clearly connected with worship at the Temple or Tabernacle. This raises the question: 'To what extent is seeing the Temple (and its worship) part of what it means to "see God?"'[104]

The Physical Delight of Zion
Delight in Mount Zion is a recurring theme in other psalms. We have already had glimpses of it in Pss. 42.4; 43.3-4; 63.2; it is spelled out more fully elsewhere. Sometimes the focus is primarily on the city as a whole, and its security with God at the centre (Psalms 46, 48, 76, 122). The distinction between God and Zion can become blurred, as if the very stones are a physical expression of Yhwh's person; for example, both God and the city seem to be 'our refuge' (Ps. 46.1, 5-7). The faithful are to walk around Zion, admiring its towers, ramparts and citadels, and then tell the next generation: 'This is God, our God forever and ever' (Ps. 48.12-14). A similar ambiguity arises in language about beauty. The beauty of Yhwh is praised in Ps. 27.4, where the parallelism of the verse links beholding this beauty with the experience of inquiring in the Temple; compare Ps. 50.2, 'Out of Zion, the perfection of beauty, / God shines forth' and Ps. 96.6, where both strength and beauty are in God's sanctuary.

Mount Zion was the location of the Tabernacle and later the Temple— which were themselves reminders of Mount Sinai, and were attempts to continue the encounter with God which had been experienced on that mountain.[105] Some psalms focus more specifically on the Temple/Tabernacle, and particularly the worship which takes place within it (Psalms 24, 84, 118,

---

103. Brueggemann, *An Unsettling God*, pp. 30-31; Eaton, *Psalms*, p. 32. See also George Savran, 'Seeing is Believing: On the Relative Priority of Visual and Verbal Perception of the Divine', *BibInt* 17 (2009), pp. 320-61.

104. Goldingay, *Psalms 42–89*, p. 23; also p. 595; and see discussion in Tate, *Psalms 51–100*, pp. 354-55, 363. An ambivalence is evident in the contradictory metaphors found in Exod. 33.11 and 33.20, 23: Moses was permitted to speak to Yhwh face to face, yet had to be shielded from seeing the face when Yhwh's goodness passed before him, lest he should die. The language of 'facing' suggests knowing Yhwh intimately, yet not exhaustively; see James Palmer, 'Exodus and the Biblical Theology of the Tabernacle', in *Heaven on Earth: The Temple in Biblical Theology* (ed. T. Desmond Alexander and Simon Gathercole; Carlisle: Paternoster, 2004), p. 18.

105. Palmer, 'Exodus and the Biblical Theology', p. 19

132, 135). Here is a divinely appointed 'sacred space', which God inhabits.[106] Yhwh is somehow both transcendent and immanent, in his holy Temple while also having his throne in heaven (Ps. 11.4). Indeed, the Temple provides a window into the heavenly realms, where human praises merge with those of the heavenly hosts.[107] The speaker in Psalm 27 declares a desire 'to live in the house of Yhwh all the days of my life, / to behold the beauty of Yhwh, and to inquire in his temple', promising to sing and offer joyful sacrifices in Yhwh's tent (Ps. 27.4-6). The Temple, and the liturgy experienced there, has a powerful aesthetic dimension; 'the God of Israel is known to be present in an environment of physical, visible loveliness'.[108]

The theme of delighting in the Temple is widely evident beyond the Psalms (for example, 1 Kgs 6-8; 1 Chron. 29.1-9; Ezra 3.8-13; 6.13-22; Jer. 7.4; Ezek. 40–48; Haggai 2.1-9). When Yhwh warns Ezekiel of the imminent death of his wife, describing her as 'the delight of your eyes', Yhwh immediately talks of the sanctuary in Jerusalem in identical terms: *maḥmad* *ênê* (מחמד עיני; Ezek. 24.15, 21; see also v. 25). The Temple sanctuary is deliberately compared to a beloved wife, and further described as 'your heart's desire'.[109] Elsewhere we find *maḥmad* used of the treasures of the Temple (Lam. 1.10; Joel 3.5) and of precious newborn children (Hos. 9.16); in Canticles, *maḥmad* is used by the woman in erotic appreciation of her lover, who is 'altogether desirable' (Song 5.16).

At the centre of the Temple was another physical token of Yhwh's presence: the ark of the covenant. The extent of its use and significance in worship has been much debated; the Psalms give hints that it was used repeatedly at festival time (perhaps the feast of Tabernacles), being brought up to the sanctuary in a procession (Psalm 132, notably v. 8; see also Ps. 24.7-10; and perhaps Pss. 47.5; 68.1, 18; 99.5, if the reference to Yhwh's footstool refers to the ark). Looking at the ark in such processions may be part of the 'seeing' to which some of the Psalms refer.[110] In addition, seeing other physical and paradisal aspects of the Temple, such as its gold and precious

---

106. Broyles, *Psalms*, pp. 23-25. Hossfeld sees Zion as 'the centre of a sacred landscape', and suggests further study is needed of the relationship of the Psalms to Zion/Jerusalem, as distinct from the Temple alone (Frank-Lothar Hossfeld, 'Problems and Prospects in Psalmic Studies'; paper given at the Conference 'Conflict and Convergence: Jewish and Christian Approaches to the Psalms', Worcester College, Oxford, 24 Sept. 2010).

107. Eaton, *Psalms*, pp. 13, 33.

108. Brueggemann, *An Unsettling God*, p. 32.

109. Chris Wright, *The Message of Ezekiel* (Nottingham: Inter-Varsity Press, 2006), p. 215, n. 10.

110. Day, *Psalms*, pp. 128-29; Goldingay, *Psalms 42–89*, p. 257; Broyles, *Psalms*, p. 262; Mays, *Psalms*, p. 274.

woods, water and carvings of cherubim, could have been part of the experience of 'seeing God'.[111]

Seeing God's face provides a metaphor for a real and immediate experience of God's presence sought by those who went to the Temple

The Anatomy of God

The Psalms make it clear that God is distinct and different from humans, particularly in greatness and power (Pss. 35.10; 70.4-5; 86.10 102.25-27). Yet the writers are not afraid to use multiple anthropomorphisms of God. God has eyes and ears, in contrast with idols which lack such things (Pss. 34.15-18; 94.9-11; 115.2-8). God has a face, which can be turned towards humans in judgment or blessing (Pss. 21.6; 27.7-9; 41.12; 88.14; 90.8). God has hands, often used for fighting (Pss. 10.12-14; 118.15-16; 136.12-15), but also for planting (Ps. 44.2). God's mouth or breath can enliven or kill when God speaks (Pss. 33.6, 9-10; 83.1, 4; 147.15-20). Along with personality come emotions, such as anger (Pss. 6.1; 7.6; 30.5; 69.24; 78.21, 31, 38, 49, 50, 58). God also shows love, for people (Pss. 97.10; 146.8), actions (Ps. 11.7) and concepts (Pss. 33.5; 37.28; 45.7); God has familial compassion (Pss. 102.13; 103.13; 116.5). God experiences delight and pleasure: in the afflicted psalmist (Pss. 18.19; 41.11; 147.9-11), in Zion, Israel and its land (Pss. 51.18; 85.1; 106.4; 149.4), in right sacrifice (Ps. 51.19), and in right discourse (Ps. 19.14). The major roles ascribed to God are king (Pss. 29.10; 47; 72.1-3; 96.6; 99) and warrior (Pss. 7.12-13; 74.12-14; 78.65-66); also parent (Pss. 2.7; 27.10; 89.25-26; 103.13-14; 131.2-3) and teacher (Pss. 32.8-9; 94.12-13; 119.4-5, 8-10). Significantly, the image of spouse or lover is never used in the Psalms. Whether this is a reaction to the erotic dimensions of other forms of worship of which the psalmists disapproved, or is something more fundamental in their understanding of God, is not clear.[112]

All these images place us in the realm of metaphor, rather than literal, physical reality; they attempt to depict God in human terms. Yet each of them also serves to remind us that God is understood to be personal, with personal attributes; as such, a God who can understand and (to some degree) be understood by human persons, and with whom they can have a relationship.[113]

---

111. Cf. Mark S. Smith, '"Seeing God"' in the Psalms: The Background to the Beatific Vision in the Hebrew Bible', *CBQ* 50 (1988), p. 181.

112. See the discussion in Zevit, *Religions of Ancient Israel*, p. 653; Tilda Binger, *Asherah: Goddesses in Ugarit, Israel and the Old Testament* (JSOTSup, 232; Sheffield Academic Press, 1997), pp. 109, 140-41.

113. See 'Anatomy of a Personal God', in Brown, *Seeing the Psalms,* pp. 167-95; also Gillmayr-Bucher, 'Body Images in the Psalms', pp. 306-308. On the Hebrew Bible's consistent depiction of God as a relational, personal agent, see Brueggemann, *An Unsettling God*, particularly pp. 2, 15, 163-70.

To behold 'the face of Yhwh' is regularly represented in the Psalms as the ardent desire and goal of the faithful (the only exception being Ps. 39.13). The image of the face, sometimes depicted as shining, is used of Yhwh's encounter with the worshipper (Pss. 4.6; 31.16; 67.1; 69.17; 80.3, 7, 19); the face also speaks of Yhwh's actual presence in the sanctuary (Pss. 96.13; 98.9); or in sacred cultic events (Pss. 44.3; 68.1; 80.16). A contrast can be seen in references to God hiding his face, which is a calamity and a cause of physical and spiritual affliction. The roots of this formula seem to lie in the cultic tradition of the theophany of Yhwh, to which I now turn.[114]

Mysterious Encounter

What kind of fulfilment can be found to the 'yearning for You'? The nature of the divine–human encounter envisaged in the Psalms is unclear and much contested. Textual reticence on the subject may be a way of guarding against the temptations of idolatry.[115] Debate about whether it involves 'mystical experience' is hampered by a lack of agreement and specificity as to what 'mystical' might involve, and by the opacity of the texts themselves. Kraus warns against speaking of 'mystical' or 'unobjective spiritualism', insisting that these are impracticable for the pious person in the Hebrew Bible, even while leaving their precise meaning unclear. Elsewhere Kraus agrees that Yhwh does somehow appear, shine, and manifest his presence, but Kraus insists that it is very uncertain how this is to be imagined.[116]

In an older study, H.J. Franken seeks what he calls 'the Mystical Communion of Yhwh in the Psalms'. For him, this communion is brought about through active co-operation on both sides of the relationship, and realized on the human side 'not by reasoning but directly and intuitively through feeling'. Exploring the use of terms such as *sôd* (סוד), indicating friendship or confidant (Pss. 25.14; 55.14; 111.1) and *maḥseh* (מחסה), 'refuge' (Pss. 62.7-8; 73.28; 91.2, 9), he concludes that there is evidence of an ardent longing for 'communion with the world of God'. For Franken, this is typified in Psalm 63, particularly in the language of *dābaq* (דבק). While making it clear that there is no question of losing the self in the union, as the two remain distinguished in *dābaq*, he sees here the most intimate unity known in the Hebrew Bible, with significant use of covenant language. Both parties keep their own individual being, while submitting to the limits given by the new relationship; but the stronger party largely decides on the nature of the covenant relationship. (Artur Weiser also notes the major disparity in power relationship with one who is addressed as 'my King and my God' [Ps. 84.3];

---

114. Weiser, *Psalms*, pp. 39-40.
115. Cf. Brueggemann, *An Unsettling God*, p. 33.
116. Kraus, *Psalms 1–59*, pp. 70-71; *Psalms 60–150*, p. 21.

this asymmetry within the divine–human relationship is an issue which I shall consider in the section following this one.)[117]

John Day is clear that if mysticism is understood as absorption into the deity, this is certainly not found in the Hebrew Bible. 'If, on the other hand, we mean intimate fellowship and communion with God, then one may speak of mysticism in the Psalter.' He further notes that the Psalter indicates God's presence being particularly apprehended in the course of worship in the Temple (cf. Pss. 23.5-6; 42.1-2; 84.1-7, 10).[118] Similarly Terrien argues that:

> The theology of the Psalms begins and ends with the theme of Divine Presence, in the sanctuary and outside, revealed and concealed, confessed when it is absent, and always anticipated. The apprehension of the Presence or the terror of its loss dominates the imagination of the psalmists.[119]

Observing that Biblical Hebrew lacks an abstract noun to designate 'presence', Terrien notes the use of terms such as God's 'face'. This, he suggests, could speak not only of a cultic presence, but also of 'an immediate and intimate encounter', which could even be termed 'a mystical ecstasy'.[120] Seeing God's face provides a metaphor for the culminating experience of God's presence sought by those who went to the Temple.[121]

Tension between perceptions of personal and corporate piety is one issue which raises its head in this discussion. Lewis argues that the poet of Ps. 27.4 probably draws no distinction between seeing God's fair beauty and the acts of worship themselves, since seeing the events of Temple festivals and seeing God were indistinguishable from the holistic perspective of the ordinary worshipper.[122] Zenger, while confirming the importance of communal worship, particularly at the Temple, sees in Psalms such as 63 and 84 an impressive testimony of personal devotion, in which official and private religion become fused.[123]

Another concern which emerges in discussions of mystical encounter is the potential for adopting an excessively inward gaze which is alien to the biblical texts. Goldingay cautions against viewing the sense of God's presence in the Psalms as simply an internal spiritual experience. For him, the final verses of Psalm 63 make this explicit, with their reference to the king's enemies immediately following verses which delight in God's protection

---

117. Franken, *Mystical Communion*, pp. 11-12, 34-36, 41; Weiser, *Psalms*, p. 357.

118. Day, *Psalms*, pp. 128-29. Similarly, Mays speaks of 'encounter with the Presence in the sanctuary' (*Psalms*, pp. 217, 275).

119. Terrien, *Psalms*, p. 57

120. Terrien, *Psalms*, pp. 46-47, 351, 354-55.

121. Smith, '"Seeing God" in the Psalms', p. 181.

122. C.S. Lewis, *Reflections on the Psalms* (London: Collins, 1973), p. 45.

123. Hossfeld and Zenger, *Psalms 2*, p. 357.

and closeness. The psalmist expects to experience Yhwh's care through Yhwh's intervention and action in the physical stuff of life: 'The God of the Psalms is not one who is merely involved in people's inner lives, as readers whose outer lives are quite comfortable may be inclined to infer'.[124] But this, we might add, does not preclude an inner experience of communion with God, in addition to looking for divine intervention in the outer life.

We have limited understanding of what individuals expected to experience when they worshipped; as to what they actually did experience, we know even less. As we have already seen, the worshipper's experience can be described in the Psalms as the *nepheš* being deeply satisfied with 'a rich feast', literally, 'fat and fatness' (Ps. 63.5). This reference to enjoying the cuts of meat which were such a rare privilege suggests experiencing something precious and satisfying; here is a lavishness expressive of utter well-being.[125] The metaphor of feasting could remind us of its usage in the Song, to convey the delights of sexual intimacy. Alternatively, it could point us towards a special family or community meal, or even a royal banquet; these kinds of occasion could also involve intimacy, but of rather different kinds.

The language of gazing in admiration at the other raises major questions about 'yearning for you' and 'yearning for You'. Can we really compare these two kinds of desire, when the divine 'You' is disembodied, while the human 'you' is flesh and blood? Can any kind of intimacy be achieved without living, tangible physicality (a question of growing importance in today's world, with the growth of online interaction devoid of physical proximity)? The issue of physicality needs further exploration. It will arise again in what follows, as we consider what is involved in hearing and speaking.

Summary
Admiring and enjoying the other is a feature of parts of the Song and of the Psalter, such as Song 1.9–2.7 and Psalm 84. The lovers in the Song delight to gaze at each other, and this leads on to erotic touch. The psalm speaks of seeing God, who is identified closely with the physical reality of the Temple/Tabernacle and the worship which takes place there. God is portrayed by psalms such as this one in anthropomorphic terms, which indicates that any encounter in worship must be in some sense a personal and relational one; however, the physical intimacy of erotic contact is not involved. Moreover, the language of *eros* is not used to describe the worship experience, the nature of which seems powerful and stirring, but remains opaque to the reader.

---

124. Goldingay, *Psalms 42–89*, pp. 261; see also pp. 413, 419.
125. Hossfeld and Zenger, *Psalms 2*, pp. 124-25; Brueggemann, *Praying the Psalms*, p. 33.

Hearing and Speaking to you/You:
Psalm 119 and Song of Songs 2.8-17

The voice of the loved one elicits pleasure when heard, and raises the prospect of an encounter. For a voice to be heard, a speaker must be present, or at least nearby. My next pairing of texts explores this dimension of relationship.

Psalm 119

By its repetitive, formulaic structure and sheer length, Psalm 119 provokes commentators to voice a variety of assessments. A few pass over it without much comment (e.g. Weiser), some decrying its tedious repetition and lack of inspiration (Sabourin); others admire the ingenuity of the acrostic structure (A.A. Anderson), proclaiming the author's freshness of thought and felicity of expression (Dahood) and massive intellectual achievement (Brueggemann), while still others hedge their bets (Terrien).[126] If the eight lines in each strophe suggests totality (eight being one more than seven, the number of completion found in the Sabbath principle), this sense of totality and wholeness is confirmed by the presence in the psalm's acrostic structure of one strophe for every letter of the Hebrew alphabet. Through its mesmerizing repetition, the psalm conveys an impression of overwhelming, comprehensive perfection; this in turn says something about its subject matter, the words of God.

Exactly what is being praised in this psalm? The opening verse speaks of Yhwh's *tôrâ* (תורה); what follows in the opening strophe mentions Yhwh's 'decrees' (*'ēdōtāyw*, עדתיו), 'ways' (*dᵉrākāyw*, דרכיו), 'precepts' (*piqqudêkā*, פקדיך), 'statutes' (*ḥuqqêkā*, חקיך), 'commandments' (*miṣwôtêkā*, מצותיך) and 'ordinances' (*mišpᵉṭê*, משפטי). This sets the pattern for what follows, with these terms used in broadly interchangeable ways, along with 'words' and 'word' (*'imrātᵉkā*, אמרתך) and *dᵉbārᵉkā*, דברך). Most commentators see the psalm focussed on God's *tôrâ*; while this could be interpreted in narrow terms as a reference to a particular written work of 'law', the range of synonyms used throughout the psalm argue for a broader understanding. Thus Goldingay translates *tôrâ* as 'teaching', which could refer to the content of particular books, but could also cover the teaching of a prophet, or the instruction of a priest or a wisdom teacher.[127] While it may have

126. McCann, 'Book of Psalms', p. 1166; Goldingay, *Psalms 90–150*, pp. 377-78; Brueggemann, *Message of the Psalms*, p. 39; Terrien, *Psalms*, p. 805.

127. Goldingay, *Psalms 3*, p. 761. Although wisdom is not mentioned in this psalm, many commentators note significant similarities with the other acknowledged 'Wisdom Psalms', Pss. 1 and 19; see Day, *Psalms*, p. 57; Brueggemann, *Message of the Psalms*, pp. 38-41.

been inspired by written texts such as Deuteronomy or Proverbs, this psalm delights in the full range of divine revelation, as expressed in the abundance of broadly synonymous terms mentioned above.[128] 'Yearning for You' finds some degree of fulfilment in this experience of revelation.

The psalmist expresses delight in divine speech (vv. 16, 24, 47, 70, 77, 92, 143, 174) and proclaims a wholehearted commitment to receiving and responding to it (vv. 36, 58, 69, 80, 112, 145; note that the first mention of wholeheartedness is in seeking not 'it' but 'you', v. 10). Indeed, the language of love abounds to a striking degree: again and again the speaker proclaims a love for Yhwh's commandments, teaching and decrees (vv. 47, 48, 97, 113, 119, 127, 140, 159, 163, 165, 167; v. 132 has love for Yhwh's name, which signifies God's person and identity). Calvin finds in the phrase 'O, how I love your law!' (Ps. 119.97) evidence of an ardent love of God's law which can 'inflame and ravish the heart with the love of it'.[129] Terrien suggests that in this verse we hear 'the language of a lover' rather than of an ethicist.[130] McCann understands the zenith of the poem to be found at the centre, in vv. 89-96 and 97-104, and here in particular he finds the language of romance:

> The exclamations in vv. 97, 103 are downright sensual. The psalmist is in love with God's revelation (v. 97a; see vv. 47-48, 113, 119, 127, 132, 159, 163, 165, 167). As is always the case with a beloved person or thing, the psalmist has God's revelation always in mind (v. 97b). ... Not surprisingly, v. 103 employs the sensual language of the Song of Solomon (see Song 2.3; 4.11; 5.1, 16; 7.9; see also Ps. 19.10; Prov. 24.13-14).[131]

The metaphor of God providing delicious sweetness to the faithful does recur in the wisdom traditions, as McCann rightly observes. However, while the source of that sweetness is wisdom in Proverbs, and Yhwh's words in Psalms 19 and 119, in the Song it tends to be the beloved in person, his 'fruit', her 'lips', 'honeycomb' and 'kisses', rather than any words spoken by the beloved.[132] Can words be separated from their speaker, or are the two indistinguishable? Certainly the couple in the Song delight in words as they speak and listen to each other, as we shall see below.

---

128. Cf. A.A. Anderson, *Psalms 73–150* (New Century Bible Commentary; London: Marshall, Morgan and Scott, 1972), pp. 805-806; Kraus, *Psalms 60–150*, p. 413; Leslie C. Allen, *Psalms 101–150* (Word Biblical Commentary, 21; Waco TX: Word, 1983), pp. 142-43.

129. Calvin, *Commentary on the Psalms*, Ps. 119.97.

130. Terrien, *Psalms*, p. 802.

131. McCann, 'Book of Psalms', pp. 1168; 1171-72.

132. NRSV renders Song 5.16a 'His speech is most sweet', but the more literal 'mouth' seems appropriate and preferable (as in JPS, KJV, REB, NIV, NASB).

As with the delight in Zion/Temple/Tabernacle which appears in some of the psalms examined earlier, questions of physicality arise here. Is physicality needed in expressing a divine–human relationship? If so, do these words of Yhwh provide that physicality? If we understand *tôrâ* in terms of teaching given by a priest, prophet or wisdom teacher,[133] that individual might be seen as a spokesperson physically representing God to the worshipper. Alternatively, if we associate *tôrâ* with the scrolls which came to be treasured in the later development of synagogue traditions, we could see here a physical expression of the beloved in the tangible form of those holy books, preserved in special buildings. Created beings live in a physical world, and that physicality is bound to impinge on any relationship they may seek to have with their creator; any act of prayer or worship involves use of one's body. However, the key issue here is not so much physicality as audibility: words are heard, which are understood to be originating in the divine speaker.

As in the other psalms we have already examined, so also in Psalm 119 personal language abounds: the psalmist speaks in terms of 'I' rather than 'we', and the object of delight is not 'Yhwh's teaching', but 'your teaching'. The psalmist speaks not about but to God; apart from vv. 1-3 and 115, the whole psalm is addressed directly to Yhwh. There is a dynamic quality to the divine 'teaching' that enables the psalmist to hear in it what is perceived by the psalmist to be the very voice of the living God speaking directly. This Torah is not just a set of rules, but 'a mode of God's life-giving presence'.[134] The whole psalm has a personal, relational flavour, as if the speaker were standing close to God; in praising the *tôrâ*, the speaker praises the one who gives it, the one whose name is loved and whom he or she seeks so wholeheartedly (v. 10).[135] Longing for the commandments blurs into longing for the gracious one who gives them (vv. 131-32). Continuing with the language of romance, McCann finds at the heart of this psalm 'the happiness of a person who is in love with the one who truly offers life … The psalmist has an emotional attachment to God's word that is indicative of his or her love for and commitment to God.'[136]

While acknowledging the very personal relationship with Yhwh indicated in this psalm, Goldingay steers clear of using the language of romance in his analysis. He points out that 'heart' in the Hebrew Bible is more often

---

133. Goldingay, *Psalms 90–150*, p. 761.

134. Brueggemann, *Message of the Psalms*, p. 40; cf. Kraus, *Psalms 60–150*, p. 413; Allen, *Psalms 101–150*, p. 142.

135. Rogerson and McKay, *Psalms 101–150*, pp. 89-90; Schaefer, *Psalms*, p. 296. On the Torah as a surrogate for the person of God in Psalm 1, see McCann, *Great Psalms of the Bible*, pp. 6-8.

136. McCann, 'Book of Psalms', pp. 1171-72.

connected with thinking and decision making (as in the English 'mind') than with the emotions. In this psalm and others he consistently translates *'āhab* (אהב) not as 'loves/loved' but as 'is/was dedicated to', arguing that it indicates as much a commitment of the will as a feeling; loving Yhwh's commandments involves obeying them rather than liking them. Noting this psalm's emphasis on obedience (e.g. vv. 2-8, 11, 63, 80, 121, 167-68) and how this fits with the ubiquitous term 'servant' (vv. 17, 23, 38, 49, 65, 76, 84, 91, 122, 124, 125, 135, 140, 176), Goldingay presents a master–servant relationship between God and the psalmist. Here he sees a relationship of mutual commitment, but between two very unequal parties: the servant is pledged to obey the master, who in turn is obliged by previous promises to take care of the servant; this gives the servant confidence in appealing for help (vv. 122-26).[137] This motif is underlined by frequent references to enemies (vv. 42, 51, 53, 61, 69, 78, 84-85, 95, 110, 115, 122, 139, 150, 157-58), from whom the psalmist needs to be saved by God (vv. 94, 134, 146, 153). However, we might ask whether the directness shown by the speakers in some of the Psalms of Lament undermines this hierarchical understanding. If God can be accused to his face of abandoning his own (Pss. 22.1; 88.14), called to wake up from his sleep (Pss. 35.23; 44.23; 59.4), and depicted as doing so like a drunken warrior (Ps. 78.65), this suggests a frankness and even a shrill assertiveness from the suppliant beyond what we would expect from a mere servant. The hierarchical relationship suggested in psalms such as Psalm 119 could, alternatively, fit that of parent and child in an ancient Near Eastern culture. However, the image of God as 'father' is rare in the Psalms, found only in Pss. 68.5 and 103.13 (plus 2.7 and 89.26, of the king in particular).[138] The issue of asymmetry in the divine–human relationship is important; I shall consider it further in the section that follows, when examining the significance of *ḥesed* (חסד).

137. Goldingay, *Psalms 90–150*, pp. 424, 427, 754, 757; see also *Psalms 42–89*, pp. 619-20; 629-70. Compare Anderson, *Psalms 73–150*, p. 822. Broyles similarly sees a mutual bond between God and the psalmist expressed in the personal language of the Psalms (such as the phrase 'my God'), with different expectations laid on each (*Conflict of Faith and Experience*, pp. 121-22). For a stronger emphasis on the servant's deference and total dependence on the master, see Edward J. Bridge, 'Loyalty, Dependency and Status with YHWH: The Use of *'bd* in the Psalms', *VT* 59 (2009), pp. 366-70, 377.

138. See Eaton, *Psalms*, p. 31. The image of God's sheltering wings in the Psalms (Pss. 17.7-8; 36.6-8; 57.1; 61.4-5; 63.7-8; 91.1-4) could possibly suggest a mother bird, perhaps drawing on mother goddess traditions from other ancient Near Eastern cultures; see Siliva Schroer, 'Under the Shadow of your Wings: The Metaphor of God's Wings in the Psalms, Exodus 19.4, Deuteronomy 32.11 and Malachi 3.20, as Seen through the Perspectives of Feminism and the History of Religion', in *Wisdom and Psalms* (ed. Athalaya Brenner and Carol Fontaine; A Feminist Companion to the Bible, Second Series; Sheffield, Sheffield Academic Press, 1998), pp. 265, 280-81.

Song 2.8-17

In Song 2.8-17, as in Psalm 119, a beloved voice is celebrated: we are told
that the voice of the other has been heard and is prompting a strong response.
The poet suddenly turns one of the major characters, the woman, into a narrator.[139] She announces, dramatically, 'The voice (or sound) of my beloved'.
Then she depicts her lover approaching from a distance, bounding across
the countryside, seemingly oblivious to all obstacles, until he arrives where
she is and can peer inside. In this way his physical presence is emphasized:
this is no disembodied voice, still less a love letter delivered by another; he
has come in person. Now the emphasis shifts to his speech: 'My beloved
speaks and says to me, "Arise my love, my fair one, and come away"', and
she reports his words at some length (vv. 10-14).[140] If the sound she reported
in v. 8 may have been a cry from a distance, vv. 10-14 are the words of one
who is close at hand, enticing her to come out from behind the walls and
lattice. He woos her with a vivid evocation of the delights of spring, which
they can experience together if only she will come out from the security of
home to join him.[141] Later, in Song 5.2, we again hear his voice through her
voice, as she describes him knocking on her door and urgently pleading for
admission. In that incident, she has not seen him approaching, but instantly
knows it is he when she hears him speak. She knows his voice and treasures
his words, quoting them. His voice speaks to her 'yearning for you'.

Voices abound throughout the Song, right from the opening verse, where
we suddenly hear an unidentified voice (Song 1.2). The way the poet has
structured Song 2.8-17 gives emphasis to not one but two voices, which in
turn are set among other voices. Throughout we hear the woman's voice;
her repeated use of the particle *hinneh* (הנה), meaning 'look!' (vv. 8, 9;
see also v. 11), emphasizes that she is speaking, either to herself or to the
poem's audience. Thereafter her words direct us to the man's voice, which
she quotes at length. In her presentation of his voice, we hear him proclaiming not only the sights, smells and tastes of spring, but also the arrival

---

139. Exum, *Song of Songs*, p. 123.

140. There is some dispute as to who speaks in v. 15: Hess assigns this verse to both
the man and woman together, while Garrett gives it to a chorus (the women of Jerusalem); Bloch and Bloch somehow ascribe it to the woman's brothers. I follow Murphy,
Longman, Provan and Exum in assigning it to the woman in her own right, after she has
finished quoting the man's words and is giving her response to them; the various plural
forms in this verse are not a problem if she is speaking to a wider audience, namely, the
women of Jerusalem (and, by implication, the poem's readers; cf. Exum, *Song of Songs*,
p. 125).

141. The created world, which in Proverbs and Job is scrutinized in order to find
wisdom, is seen in the Song as something to be participated in rather than analysed; it
provides a kind of 'musical accompaniment to the inner stirrings of the human heart'
(Murphy, *Song of Songs*, p. 68).

of 'the time of singing', when 'the voice of the turtledove is heard in our land' (v. 12).[142] Indeed, she herself is described by him as a 'dove', and he delights in the delicious sweetness of her voice, which he longs to hear along with seeing her face (v. 14). Then we hear her speak, perhaps to the audience of the poem, the women of Jerusalem (and thus implicitly to its readers), or else to herself, in her cryptic exhortation to catch 'little foxes'.[143] This is followed by her affirmation of the mutuality of their relationship: she declares to her audience that she and the man are entirely given over to each other (v.16). Finally, for the first time in this passage, she speaks to the man himself, telling him to 'turn' either away from her or (more probably) towards her.[144]

Mutuality and Delight?

The spoken word has a central place in the Song of Songs. The whole book abounds in words of love; it is 'a work of tender, affectionate speech' in which each of the lovers caresses the one they love with words, seeking to touch the inner depths of the other in this way.[145]

These spoken words are ordered by the poet in various ways, one of which is the exhilarating dialogue which is a distinctive hallmark of the Song. As a whole it presents a dialogue between two voices, with a third voice (that of the women of Jerusalem) occasionally added. The voices echo

142. 'Singing' is probably the best translation of *hazzāmîr* (הזמיר), suggesting parallelism with the voice of the dove in the line that follows. 'Pruning' is possible as a secondary meaning, linking with the previous line, but the arrival of blossom is not usually the time for pruning (see the discussion in Gordis, *Song of Songs*, pp. 6-7 n. 30, and Garrett, *Song of Songs*, p. 159).

143. 'Fox' is probably a metaphor for lustful young men; for discussion of this verse, see Exum, *Song of Songs*, pp. 128-30; Fox, *Song of Songs*, p. 114; Landy, *Paradoxes of Paradise*, pp. 240-41; also Anselm C. Hagedorn, 'Of Foxes and Vineyards: Greek Perspectives on the Song of Songs', *VT* 53 (2003), pp. 339-42. Murphy's suggestion that she is teasing him with a saucy reply to his wooing (pretending to be wary while in fact highlighting her readiness for intimacy as a 'vineyard in bloom') could link with the *double entendre* of v. 17, where she seems to be sending him away while actually inviting him to spend the night with her (*Song of Songs*, p. 141-42). Whatever these puzzling 'little foxes' are, the use of the diminutive in describing them, and the fact that they are passed over so briefly, suggests that this is not a major concern for the couple. Their relationship seems blissfully (naïvely?) uncluttered with threats or anxieties.

144. J. Cheryl Exum, '"The Voice of my Lover": Double Voice and Poetic Illusion in Song of Songs 2.8–3.5', in *Reading from Right to Left: Essays on the Hebrew Bible in Honour of David J.A. Clines* (ed. J. Cheryl Exum and H.G.M. Williamson; JSOTSup, 373; Sheffield: Sheffield Academic Press, 2003), pp. 134-35. In the passage that follows, which is clearly connected to 2.8-17, we hear the woman's voice again, as she speaks to herself (3.2) and then to the watchmen (3.3).

145. Garrett, *Song of Songs*, p. 163; cf. Exum, *Song of Songs*, pp. 13-14.

and respond to each other, sometimes interacting with what the other has said (e.g. 1.15-16; 2.1-3; 4.12–5.1; 5.2-3; also 7.10-13, in which the woman takes up some of the spring imagery expressed by the man in 2.10-15). The rapid interplay of dialogue conveys exhilaration, urgency, impatience, ardour.[146] Reported speech within the poem, such as we have noted in Song 2.10-15, is not the norm; usually the poet presents the words of each speaker directly, conveying a vivid sense of immediacy in the dialogue (which even the reported speech shares).[147] The way the reported speech is introduced in Song 2.10 (using not *dābar* [דבר] but *ānâ* [ענה], which normally means 'answered') itself seems to suggest interaction: he is responding to her, perhaps having caught a glimpse of her or sensed her as he looked in.[148] The poet presents further lengthy passages of direct speech, almost entirely from the man, in Song 4.1-5.1 and 6.4–7.9.

The Psalms, by contrast, do not present dialogue. Usually we hear the psalmist's voice, addressed to God (as in Psalm 119) or to self and others (as in Psalm 42–43). God's voice is also heard. Just as *qôl dôdî* (קול דודי) is highlighted in Song 2.8, so *qôl Yhwh* (קול יהוה) is prominent in Ps. 29.3-9; but the psalm presents an awesome, thunderous 'voice' or 'sound', which does not engage in conversation (cf. Pss. 18.13; 46.6; 77.17-18; 93.3-4). Significantly, Psalm 119 indicates that God's voice can be heard through the words of the Torah; but it does not suggest that this process involves a dialogue with God. We are told much in the Psalms about God, but only rarely does the psalmist mediate God's speech directly to us. On a few occasions this does happen, notably Psalms 50, 81 and 89 (also possibly Psalm 82 if we take God to be the principal speaker).[149] The impression in Psalms 50, 81 and 89 is of a formal speech given by God, without any interaction with the psalmist or any other character. In Psalm 89 the psalmist gives a response to what God is quoted as having said, but the impression is of speeches given in a formal dispute; there is no real sense of dialogue.[150]

---

146. Fox, *Song of Songs*, pp. 317, 321. Fox contrasts this vigour in the Song's dialogue with the more contemplative and passive nature of that found in some of the ancient Egyptian love poems.

147. Exum, *Song of Songs*, p. 125.

148. Cf. Hess, *Song of Songs*, p. 90.

149. God's voice is also heard more briefly in Pss. 2.7-9; 12.5; 35.3; 37.13; 46.10; 91.14-16; 95.8-11. Noting the sudden movement from plea to praise in various Psalms of Lament, some scholars also posit a divine voice at the turning point of these psalms, with the intervention of an authorized worship leader to bring an oracle of reassurance (Brueggemann, *Introduction to the Old Testament*, p. 282).

150. The tone in Pss. 50, 81 and 89 is one of disputation, rather than mutual delight. In Pss. 50 and 81, Yhwh accuses his people of breaking their covenant commitments to him through their behaviour. In Ps. 89, the roles are reversed, as the speaker accuses Yhwh of reneging on his covenant commitment to David and his descendants by allow-

The Language of Love

If the magisterial voice of God which we occasionally hear in the Psalms seems to present a divine–human relationship different from that which we sense from listening to the voices of the lovers in the Song, what are we to make of the language of love prominent in certain psalms, such as Psalm 119? Does this psalm's use of language have any connections with that found in the Song?

A feature of Canticles is the distinctive use of terms of endearment by the man and the woman. She calls him *dôdî*, which is usually translated 'my love/lover/beloved'. This word occurs in different forms thirty-two times in the Song, usually a reference to the man in person by the woman (or by her companions). Occasionally it is used in a more abstract sense, referring to his love for her (Song 1.2, 4) or her love for him (4.10; 7.12), and once it depicts the pair of them as 'lovers' (5.1). In the rest of the Hebrew Bible the word occurs only twenty times, usually meaning 'uncle', or occasionally 'cousin'; only Proverbs and Ezekiel use it with clear sexual connotations (Prov. 7.18; Ezek. 16.8; 23.17).[151] Meanwhile, the man in the Song has his own even more distinctive term of affection, choosing to call the woman *rayātî* (רעיתי). Usually translated as 'my love/darling', this epithet is used nine times in the Song (e.g. 1.9, 15; 2.2, 10, 13), and nowhere else in the Hebrew Bible.

Alongside these particular terms, the Song consistently presents the sexual relationship between the man and the woman in terms of *'ah°bâ* (אהבה; Song 2.4, 5, 7; 3.5; 5.8; 7.6; 8.4, 6, 7) or *'āhab* (אהב; Song 1.3, 4, 7; 3.1, 2, 3, 4).[152] This high concentration of usage of these two words is echoed by their repeated use in the Psalms, particularly Psalm 119, where *'āhab* is used eleven times of the psalmist's love for Yhwh's Torah, and once of love for Yhwh's name. Here we face a problem similar to that experienced by users of the English language when speaking of 'love': a wide range of meaning has been invested in one small word. The etymology of *'āhab* is unclear, although Ugaritic parallels may suggest a root meaning which is linked with sexual desire, and was used of human relationship with Baal or El. This leads to a suggested understanding of the word involving 'passionate desire to be intimately united with a person (in all of life's relationships, not only inwardly, but also outwardly) with whom one feels himself [*sic*] united in his affections';[153] note the emphasis here on desire and affection. Over time

---

ing the destruction of the Davidic monarchy. In these three psalms it is confrontation and recrimination that are foregrounded through formal complaint, rather than any sense of mutual delight.

151. Use of the term in Isaiah's שיר about Yhwh's relationship with his people should probably also be understood as a sexual or romantic metaphor; see Isa. 5.1.

152. Cf. Bloch and Bloch, *Song of Songs*, p. 138.

153. Gerhard Wallis, 'אהב', *TDOT* 1, p. 103.

the word developed a range of uses in Hebrew (possibly reflecting in part a desire to distance it from any sexual–mythical connotations which linked it with Baal religion).[154] Thus we find it referring variously to love between human beings (including sexual love, but also parent–child relationships, as well as love for a friend, or a patron), love for things or for qualities, human love for God, and God's love for individuals and for groups; about twelve percent of all these occurrences refer to erotic love. A slave might love his wife, as well as his children and master (Exod. 21.5). Deuteronomy speaks of a love which can be commanded from another, specifically that required by Yhwh from his people (e.g. Deut 6.4-5; 10.12, 11.1, 22; 30.16). This usage seems to have its roots in the rhetoric of international relations in the ancient Near East, rather than in metaphors of conjugal intimacy. Rulers would write to equals with whom they were in treaty relationship about the importance of love, and would command subject vassals to show love to their ruler as an expression of their faithfulness to the treaty. Here loyal obedience rather than intimate affection seems to be what was called for: love is an activity rather than an emotion.[155]

Thus it can be argued that the meaning of *'āhab* in the Hebrew Bible when used with reference to inter-human relationships is different from its meaning when speaking of divine–human relationships. Susan Ackerman argues that the 'political love' which characterizes the divine–human covenant relationship differs significantly from the emotional love shown in interpersonal relationships. She further proposes that a hierarchical dimension persists, with the 'superior' person in the relationship (be it God above human, male above female, or parent above child) depicted as the one who is 'loving'; mutual affection may be suggested in some of these relationships, but a one-sided pattern is maintained, reflecting a hierarchical understanding of a suzerain–vassal relationship. However, while what she presents may be broadly accurate, particular verses bring it into question. Deuteronomy presents God as giving love to his people, but also indicates a wholehearted love for God from his people (Deut. 10.12; 11.13; 30.6), and even depicts a slave choosing to reject the offer of freedom because of love for his master (Deut. 15.16). Here

---

154. There has been heated debate in recent years about whether any religious practices in the Ancient Near East involved ritual sexual acts. While talk of 'cultic prostitution' now seems inappropriate, some forms of sexual activity may still be argued from particular texts arising in Mesopotamia, Egypt and Ugarit; see Richard M. Davidson, *Flame of Yahweh: Sexuality in the Old Testament* (Peabody, MA; Hendrickson, 2007), pp. 85-97.

155. Wallis, 'אהב', p. 107; Katherine Doob Sakenfeld, 'Love', *ABD* 4, p. 376; Ernst Jenni, 'אהב', *TLOT* 1, pp. 45-54; *DCH* 1, pp. 138-41. See also Athalaya Brenner, *The Intercourse of Knowledge: On Gendering Desire and 'Sexuality' in the Hebrew Bible* (Biblical Interpretation Series, 26; Leiden: Brill, 1997), pp. 13-18; G. Lloyd Carr, *Song of Songs* (Tyndale; Leicester,UK: Inter-Varsity, 1984), pp. 62-63.

any hierarchical understanding of *'āhab* seems to be subverted. Ackerman does concede that a politically-based conception of divine–human love gives way in some prophetic texts (Hosea, Ezekiel, and Jeremiah) to images of God's affectionate love more typically found in stories of men's relationships with women and parents' relationships with their children. She admits that the word 'love' as it is used throughout the Bible of both interpersonal relationships and the divine–human relationship is 'a concept tinged with ambiguity and a certain fluidity of meaning'. Significantly, she also concedes that the Song is anomalous in regard to what she is proposing, in the non-hierarchical way in which it depicts the relationship between the man and the woman.[156] We might further point to another passage reminiscent of the Song: the adulterous woman in Prov. 7.18 invites the man to a mutual enjoyment of sexual desire which she expresses as both *dôdîm* and *ᵉhābîm*; if there is any hierarchy in this relationship, it seems to be the woman who is the stronger and is using her seductive powers over the weak man.[157]

Ancient Hebrew thought did not make some of the distinctions favoured by modern Western thinking. For example, the biblical *lēb* (לב), often translated 'heart', is clearly connected with thoughtful decision making, but is also the source of some strong emotions, which cannot be separated from the mind and will of the individual.[158] In his commentary on Song of Songs Rabbah, Jacob Neusner argues that the theology of Judaism regularly expresses itself in images of love, using language of emotion and sentiment. 'Judaism' he insists, 'is a religion that conducts a love affair with God, and in such a love affair, people do not describe the one they love, so much as express their feelings for the one they love'.[159] This may remind us again of the passion expressed in Psalm 119, which we have already examined, and the contrary views expressed about it by two of today's leading interpreters of the Psalms. Is the psalmist in love with the divine revelation, and

---

156. Susan Ackerman, 'The Personal Is Political: Covenantal and Affectionate Love ('āhēb, 'ahăbâ) in the Hebrew Bible', *VT* 52 (2002), pp. 439, 447, 457. Similarly Grelot, *Language of Symbolism*, p. 159. Ellen van Wolde also argues that the Song of Songs provides an exception to the general rule that אהב expresses a hierarchical relationship lacking mutuality (*Reframing Biblical Studies: When Language and Text Meet Culture, Cognition and Context* [Winona Lake, IN: Eisenbrauns, 2009], pp. 45-50; her discussion is about language used of human sexual relationships).

157. See also Helen Leneman's discussion of the power of sexually active women over men as presented elsewhere in the Hebrew Bible ('Portrayals of Power in the Stories of Delilah and Bathsheba: Seduction in Song', in *Culture, Entertainment and the Bible* [ed. Aichele], pp. 139-55).

158. Hess, *Song of Songs*, pp. 33.

159. Neusner, *Israel's Love Affair with God*, p. 122. Neusner's overtly romantic choice of language finds an echo in the JPS translation of Hos. 11.1: 'I fell in love with Israel'.

with the God who has given that revelation, as McCann puts it? Or is the relationship with God indicated in the psalm that of master and servant, as Goldingay argues? The fact that this and other psalms choose the language of master and servant, not husband and wife, must be a significant factor in the argument. Yet the master–servant language is hard to reconcile with the warmth and passion of the love language used, even if we picture an affectionate relationship with a particularly benevolent master. We may need to probe further. If Yhwh's sovereignty is truly 'governance-in-relation', marked by fidelity as much as by power,[160] we must ask whether different types of relationship may overlap and become blurred. Is it not possible to fall in love with the boss? If so, hierarchical differences may be subverted, or may simply be unnoticed by the ones so affected. At times in Psalm 119, with its abundant language of loving, delighting, and treasuring that which is sweeter than honey and better than silver and gold, we sense the praise of a servant who is also a lover, who feels intoxicated and overwhelmed, 'ravished by a moral beauty'.[161] We do not hear a corresponding voice in this psalm indicating that the master has reciprocal feelings towards the servant; but neither does the psalmist show any hesitancy in expressing this love, as if it might be seen as inappropriate by Yhwh, or by other worshippers who may hear and participate in the psalm.

The ambiguities inherent in 'love-language' extend more widely. When God promises in Ps. 91.14 to deliver those who love him, *ḥāšaq* (חשק) is used; the same term is used elsewhere for human sexual desire (Gen. 34.8; Deut. 21.11), and also for God's loving desire for his people (Deut. 7.7; 10.15; Isa. 38.17). The unusual use of *rāḥam* (רחם), expressed to Yhwh in the opening words of Psalm 18, is also intriguing: many translate this as 'love' (KJV, NASB, NIV, NRSV, NJB, REB). Alter renders it 'I am impassioned of You, LORD, my strength!'. Goldingay chooses the more subdued 'dedicate myself', to emphasize commitment rather than intimacy, while others suggest emending of the text to read 'elevate' (Gerstenberger) or 'lift up' (McCann). What follows in Psalm 18 is clearly a grateful testimony to the faithfulness and awesome power of Yhwh, who has rescued the speaker from grave danger.[162]

---

160. Brueggemann, *An Unsettling God*, p. xvi; also pp. 22-24 on the emotion and affection evident in Yhwh's attitude towards Israel.

161. Lewis, *Reflections on the Psalms*, p. 53, 81-82

162. Alter, *Book of Psalms*, p. 52; Goldingay, *Psalms 90–150*, pp. 257-57; Erhard S. Gerstenberger, *Psalms Part I* (Grand Rapids, MI; Eerdmans, 1988), p. 97; McCann, 'Book of Psalms', p. 747.

Summary

Hearing the voice of the other, and making one's own voice heard, are important to those who yearn in both the Psalms and the Song. For each of the lovers in Song 2.8-17, that voice is heard directly and informally, bringing affirmation and delight. For the psalmist in Psalm 119, it is heard particularly through God's teaching. At times this brings rebuke, which may be heard in a formal speech; yet it can also be a source of joy and delight which the psalmist expresses in language of direct, personal relationship. The language of love is evident in the Song and in the longest of the Psalms, but there is ambiguity about how this language is to be interpreted: in the Song it is clearly expressing a mutuality of sexual desire, whereas in the psalm it seems to indicate a benevolent master–servant relationship. Even here, however, a romantic understanding of the experience from the human side cannot be entirely ruled out.

Forever Devoted to you/You: Song 8.5b-7 and Psalm 136

The language of love, which I began to explore in the previous section, is also prominent in my next pair of texts. Striking contrasts are evident between Song 8.5b-7 and Psalm 136, not merely in length but also in content. In addition to their differences, however, each provides a sharpness of focus, succinctly distilling its vision of the true essence of love.

Song 8.5b-7

As the Song draws towards its close, a different tone is heard in this brief passage. From the words which the archetypal lovers speak to each other, our eyes are lifted to a broader horizon, with a reflective and didactic comment about love (*'ahᵃbâ*) which is the crucial focus of these three verses.[163] The amount of attention which commentators give to this 'paean to the power of love' affirms its great significance for the poem as a whole, perhaps in crystallizing what the poet is most keen to convey.[164]

While most of vv. 5b-7 depicts love in general, abstract terms, we must not lose sight of the fact that these are words spoken by the woman to her

---

163. See Hess' analysis of the centrality of the word 'love' in these two verses (*Song of Songs*, pp. 236, 240).

164. Exum, *Song of Songs*, p. 249. See also Landy, *Paradoxes of Paradise*, p. 121, 128. Katherine Dell points out that this kind of abstract and didactic musing on love might fit in a book such as Proverbs; she argues that the Song's links with the wisdom tradition may be closer than generally thought ('Does the Song of Songs Have Any Connections to Wisdom?', in *Perspectives on the Song of Songs* [ed. Anselm C. Hagedorn; Berlin: Walter de Gruyter, 2005], pp. 8-26, particularly p. 23).

lover.[165] As in the opening words of the Song and at various moments since then, once again she is the one taking a bold initiative. She reminds him of how she first aroused his love, in the same erotic locale previously enjoyed by his mother in her own lovemaking. Here is a hint, perhaps, of her own desire to take on the role of a mother, and a reminder of successive generations which will lead on to the theme of death. She then urges him to place her as a seal on his heart and arm; her imperative could be heard as the command of one who has an irresistible call on his life, or as the urgent plea of one who is dependent and vulnerable. Further ambiguities arise concerning the seal itself: is this a reference to his own seal, or hers given to him, or just a seal in general? A seal, being skilfully carved out of precious metal or stone, would be something valuable; thus the woman is expressing a desire to be precious to her lover (a theme revisited at the end of v. 7, with its scornful dismissal of any attempt to put a monetary value on something as priceless as love). A seal was also something that was recognized as belonging to its owner; so the metaphor speaks of belonging to the other in a way that can be clearly recognized, both by the couple and the wider community. Here is an image of mutual commitment and exclusivity: the seal is unique, and belongs with one person only. Furthermore, a seal was used to express the identity and commitment of its owner, when impressed onto documents or clay; it seems that the woman longs for such a degree of intimacy with her lover that her identity is fused into his, so that the two become one in an inseparable bond.[166] Any superficial reading of the Song which sees it simply delighting in promiscuity or eroticism for their own sake is dispelled here; the Song celebrates the yearning of an individual man and woman to enjoy a bond of mutual possession (cf. Song 2.16; 6.3; 7.10).[167]

The dissolution of the self is also suggested by mention of death, which suddenly intrudes into the idyllic world of the Song, along with other disturbing images: jealousy, Sheol, fire and flood. The more congenial flowing streams, flowers, gardens, and beautiful animals found earlier in the book now give way, as glimpses of the challenges, hardships and dangers of love are presented.[168] The poet links love and death in ways that are suggestive, yet ambiguous: is this a conflict or a comparison? Clearly there are some

165. Masculine singular suffixes on 'your heart' and 'your arm' in v. 6 indicate that the man is being addressed, as he was at the end of v. 5, 'she who bore you'.

166. Landy, *Paradoxes of Paradise*, p. 122; Garrett, *Song of Songs*, p. 254; Bloch and Bloch, *Song of Songs*, p. 212; Longman, *Song of Songs*, p. 209; also Jonneke Bekkenkamp, 'Into Another Scene of Choices: The Theological Value of the Song of Songs', in *Song of Songs* (ed. Brenner and Fontaine), pp. 71, 73-74.

167. Murphy, *Song of Songs*, p. 97.

168. Cf. Weems, 'Song of Songs', p. 431; Andrew Hwang and Samuel Goh, *Song of Songs* (Asia Bible Commentary; Bangalore: Asia Theological Association, 2001), p. 164. Bloch and Bloch are right that the general 'spring-time' atmosphere of the Song

similarities between the two. Love paradoxically offers self-fulfilment in self-abandonment, by letting go of the self in order to unite with another, while death is the ultimate loss of self into the unknown.[169] Other parallels may also be suggested here between love and death, particularly regarding their insatiability. Love has an all-consuming nature; it can be argued that true love is characterized by desire for the beloved in his or her absence, rather than by satisfaction and fulfilment found when the beloved is present. 'Lovers can never be satisfied, they will always want more. They seek a total, absolute experience. The secret of true love is that it can never be satisfied.'[170] Like death, love is constantly feeding, yet always looking for more.

While death has some similarities to love, the contrasts between the two are greater. Death threatens love, by tearing away one or both of the lovers; in fact, it is the only thing that will ever separate them. Thus love and death are enemies, both tenacious and unrelenting, each vying for an exclusive and lasting hold on the loved one. The fierce passion of this struggle is emphasized by a further contrasting pair, 'jealousy' and 'Sheol', both relentless in their determination to have the loved one uniquely for themselves.[171] The phrase 'strong as death' may be simply emphasizing the demanding and ineluctable nature of love, depicting it as having a power as strong as that of death's irresistible force.[172] However, the comparison raises questions about which of the two is the stronger. Clearly, death will eventually triumph over any flesh-and-blood lovers. Yet the Song seems to proclaim that love will also triumph and live on, without clarifying how this is possible. Some might call this empty bravado; Qohelet would be among them (Eccl. 7.26; 9.5-10). Perhaps love endures in the continuing love of the mourner for the one who has died. Or it may live on in other loving relationships which the bereaved one experiences: what love builds up, death then tears

presents love as a delightful passion to be savoured rather than suffered (*Song of Songs*, pp. 7, 19); but 8.6-7 does present a more sombre, and potentially painful aspect.

169. On death as God's kiss in some medieval Jewish traditions, see Kingsmill, *Song of Songs*, pp. 197-98.

170. Assis, *Flashes of Fire*, p. 269.

171. Bergant, *Song of Songs*, p. 98; Fox, *Song of Songs*, p. 315; Bloch and Bloch, *Song of Songs*, p. 213. The word used has a wide semantic range, including envy, zeal and devotion (see G. Sauer, 'קנאה', *TLOT* 3 (Peabody, MA: Hendrickson, 2004), pp. 1145-47). Emphasizing that the correct translation is not 'passion' but 'jealousy', Fox understands the latter as 'the self-vindication of angry love' (*Song of Songs*, p. 170, cf. Delitzsch). Longman argues that 'jealousy' is sometimes seen in the Bible as a positive force, when understood as a single-minded devotion and an energy which seeks to rescue a relationship between husband and wife or God and his people—the only two relationships which are considered totally exclusive (*Song of Songs*, pp. 211-12).

172. Fox, *Song of Songs*, p. 169.

down, only for love to re-emerge sooner or later in the cycle of life. Alternatively, the willingness shown by some even to die for those they love might be a demonstration of love's immense power (see Rashi's cryptic comment on this verse). Or maybe love persists simply in the enduring vision of love presented by the poem itself.[173] None of these explanations can be proved from the text itself; such is the intriguing nature of Hebrew poetry, the way it conceals while also revealing.[174] But clearly here, as in the earlier adjurations not to 'awaken love' (Song 2.7; 3.5; 8.4), love is seen as an elemental power that will not be defeated, indeed, almost personified as a character who refuses to rest once awoken.

Surging through these few, concise lines is a broad sense of the awesome, irresistible power of love. Love is 'strong' and 'fierce', a formidable opponent; it is a 'lightening bolt' or 'raging flame' which the mightiest floods cannot quench; and even the wealthiest find themselves powerless if they are foolish enough to try to buy it. To emphasize the power of love's enemies, deities and cosmic powers are alluded to here: the Canaanite deities Mot (Death, king of the infernal realm) and Resheph, and perhaps Yamm (also known as Prince River), the god of the cosmic waters of chaos; not even these formidable mythological powers can quench the fire of love.[175]

Love itself, we are told, is *šalhebetyâ* (שלהבתיה). Commentators dispute whether the ending is a shorter form of the divine name, Yhwh, which could thus be translated 'flame of Yah', or simply an intensive form of the word 'fire'.[176] The rhythm of the verse might suggest that *yāh* (יה) should be a separate word, indicating the divine name; but where that shorter form 'Yah' is used in several psalms (e.g. Pss. 118.5, 14, 17, 18, 19; 135.1, 3, 4, 21; 149.1, 9; 150.1, 6) and other poetic texts, a mappiq is found, giving יָהּ rather than the Song's יָה.[177] Elsewhere in the Bible, not least the Psalms, flame and lightening are associated with theophany (Exod. 19.16-20; 1 Kgs

---

173. Assis, *Flashes of Fire*, pp. 239, 264; Exum, *Song of Songs*, p. 251; Provan, *Song of Songs*, pp. 373-74; Rashi, *Song of Songs*, 8.6; Keel, *Song of Songs*, p. 35.

174. 'Good poetry evokes a response as much by what is not truly expressed, as by what is given explicit expression'; Sue Gillingham (with reference to the Psalms, but equally appropriate for the Song), *Poems and Psalms*, pp. 15-17.

175. Pope, *Song of Songs*, pp. 668-69; Bergant, *Song of Songs*, pp. 98-99; Exum, *Song of Songs*, p. 253. However, Longman's translation, 'stronger than death is love' (*Song of Songs*, p. 210) seems a step too far: the -כ particle indicates a comparative, not a superlative.

176. See Gordis, *Song of Songs*, pp. 26, 44, 74; Hess, *Song of Songs*, pp. 237, 240; Davis, *Proverbs, Ecclesiastes and Song of Songs*, p. 297. This dispute goes back to the Masoretes themselves, with the Ben Asher tradition favouring the superlative (as reflected in our BHS text), while the Ben Naphtaali tradition understood the phrase as 'flame of Yah'; see Longman, *Song of Songs*, p. 212.

177. See discussion in Murphy, *Song of Songs*, pp. 191-92; 197-98.

18.36-38; Pss. 18.7-15; 50.3; 97.3-4; 105.39).[178] In addition, God's passion or jealousy (qin'â, [קִנְאָה]), the same word used in Song 8.6) may 'burn like fire' (Ps. 79.5).[179] Furthermore, the allusions to other deities in these verses suggest that a reference to Israel's own deity would not be at all out of place here, even though Yhwh is not mentioned anywhere else in the Song.[180] If such a reference is present here, we should not force it to bear too much theological weight. Yhwh is not presented as a conscious concern of the couple as they develop their sexual relationship, nor as an actor or speaker in the poem. But a passing mention of yāh at this, the crucial high point in the Song, must have some significance, particularly if we see it as a subjective genitive which depicts yāh as the cause or source of the flame.[181] It may indicate that the love which human beings can share arises from God and is a gift of God to humanity; human love is not to be deified, but is to be modelled on the love found in God, and can in turn point to that higher and ultimate love.[182] Thus the Song is seen to be singing of love, while also

178. LaCoque, *Romance She Wrote*, p. 171-76. Landy suggests a possible allusion to Gen. 3.24: the flame of God, which there excluded the couple from the paradise of Eden, now unites them in the paradise of their love (*Paradoxes of Paradise*, p. 265). Davidson suggests a parallel between the three-fold mention of flame/fire in Song 8.6 and that found in the fiery stream from the throne in Dan. 7.9-10 (*Flame of Yahweh*, p. 629).

179. Goldingay, *Psalms 42–89*, pp. 522-23. Goldingay also suggests that the divine name Yhwh is hinted at in Song 8.6 ('So What Might the Song of Songs Do to Them?', in *Reading from Right to Left* [ed. Exum and Williamson], p. 177).

180. There may also be a cryptic circumlocution for God in the adjuration of Song 2.7 and 3.5, where 'by gazelles or by the does of the field' (biṣbāôt ô bᵉaylôt haśśādeh [בִּצְבָאוֹת אוֹ בְּאַיְלוֹת הַשָּׂדֶה]) could be a word-play on Yhwh ṣᵉbāôt and El Shaddai (צְבָאוֹת and אֵל שַׁדַּי) Various scholars comment on this, and produce a diversity of speculation as to its significance. Gordis suggests this is due to a deep-seated reluctance to use the divine name in response to the injunctions of Exod. 20.7 (*Song of Songs*, pp. 26-29; see also Garrett, *Song of Songs*, p. 152, Davis, *Proverbs, Ecclesiastes and Song of Songs*, pp. 253-54). LaCocque speculatively suggests this is a deliberate and subversive parody of religious language familiar to the audience (*Romance She Wrote*, pp. 62-65); Bloch and Bloch prefer to see it as simply an artful remaking of conventional expression, to fit the Song's rural imagery (*Song of Songs*, p. 152). Keel points to ways in which gazelles and does were linked to the goddess of love in ancient Ugarit and Egypt; he argues that Yhwh's perceived strong antipathy to sexuality in the cultic-mythic arena (as evidenced in the prophetic writings) is probably behind the Song's reticence in naming him as love's protector (*Song of Songs*, pp. 34; 92-94).

181. Cf. Davidson, *Flame of Yahweh*, p. 627.

182. Hess, *Song of Songs*, p. 240; LaCocque, *Romance She Wrote*, p. 176; Landy, *Paradoxes of Paradise*, pp. 127-28; 256-57. Speaking of a mutuality of relationship within the divine Trinity, Payne suggests that 'Christians can discern the eternal dance (*perichoresis*) of divine Persons in the reciprocal love of a man and a woman' ('Song of Songs', p. 331).

whispering of God, perhaps with a deliberate ambiguity.[183] If we conclude that a reference to Yhwh cannot be clearly discerned here, we are left with a superlative which may have derived from the divine name but later lost a former association with that name, perhaps akin to the superlative use elsewhere of *el* (אל; e.g. Pss. 36.6; 80.10); thus NRSV's 'a raging flame', or, better, Exum's 'an almighty flame', which favours the superlative while preserving a hint of the ambiguity of the original.[184] Whichever we choose, the result emphasizes the irresistible strength of love.

These verses raise our eyes to see not just two lovers, but love as a whole, painted in broad brush strokes. In contrast, the Psalms do not explore 'love' in abstract or personalized terms. While, as we have seen, the verb *'āhab* is common, the noun *'ah⁽a⁾bâ* appears only twice in the Psalter (Ps. 109.4, 5), where it seems to refer to an offer of friendship which has been spurned. Love is neither personified nor portrayed as a power; it is something that both God and humanity experience and do. But the Psalms do address some of the major themes raised in Song 8.6-7, and speak of 'love' in another way, which we now need to examine.

Psalm 136
A number of the major differences between the Psalms and the Song of Songs are immediately evident when we read Psalm 136. These need to be considered at this stage.

The structural feature of this particular psalm which instantly confronts the reader is the refrain repeated at the end of each verse. This call and response approach speaks of communal worship; we may imagine a leader proclaiming the first part of each verse, and the assembled worshippers responding with the 'regular heartbeat of the congregational refrain'.[185] The opening formula ('O give thanks to Yhwh, for he is good, for his steadfast love endures forever') is associated elsewhere with the Levitical guilds of singers (1 Chron. 16.34; 2 Chron. 5.11-14; 7.1-3; 20.21; Ezra 3.10-11).[186] Here is another reminder of the nature of the Psalms, and the reason for their preservation: as a resource for worshipping communities. The Song, in contrast, shows none of the hallmarks of a text to be used in communal (or private) worship; the abandonment in recent years of speculative attempts to

---

183. Brueggemann, *Introduction to the Old Testament*, p. 328; Weems, 'Song of Songs', p. 430.
184. Exum, *Song of Songs*, p. 243, 254; cf. Bloch and Bloch, *Song of Songs*, p. 213.
185. Allen, *Psalms 101–150*, p. 234. Allen warns of the danger of overlooking the refrain in this psalm, due to its excessive repetition; curiously, he then goes on to say little about it himself. See also Kraus, *Psalms 60–150*, pp. 496-97; McCann, 'Book of Psalms' p. 1223; Schaefer, *Psalms*, p. 319.
186. Mays, *Psalms*, p. 418.

link the Song with supposed cultic rituals is to be welcomed. We may argue that passages such as Song 8.5b-7 are akin to other Wisdom texts (such as Ecclesiastes and Proverbs); but if these kinds of text were used at all in ancient Israelite worship, it would have been in a didactic setting, rather than one of declaring thanks and praise such as that indicated by Psalm 136.

Psalm 136 opens and closes with an exhortation to thanksgiving.[187] The rest of the psalm reminds worshippers of the reasons for giving thanks: the creative and saving works of Yhwh, which arise out of his 'steadfast love'.[188] Thanksgiving for all that God has done is a major and recurring theme throughout the Psalter (e.g. Pss. 7.17; 9.1; 30.4, 12; 35.18; 75.1; 86.12; 92.1; 100.4; 106.1, 47; 107: 8, 15, 21, 31; 118.1, 19, 21, 28, 29; 138.1, 2, 4; 145.10). The Song, by contrast, makes no mention of thankfulness; the lovers delight in each other, and welcome the intimacy offered by the other, but never express gratitude to each other. Even in the reflective moment of Song 8.5b-7, this theme remains absent. In the Song as a whole we find the immediate urgency of desire and delight in the pleasures of sexual intimacy; gratitude might be felt and expressed later, with the maturity of reflection, but the breathless 'now' of the Song is not such a moment.

Like the Song, Psalm 136 delights in the created world: the psalmist revels in the wonder of the heavens and their great lights, the sun, moon and stars, and also in the cycle of day and night experienced on the earth, which is spread out on the waters (vv. 5-9). However, the lovers in the Song speak of gardens, vineyards and pastures full of flowers, fragrance, spices, blossoming trees and fruit, oil and wine, along with birds, flocks and other animals. Like the psalmist, they are delighted with what they see around them. But their natural world is small, local and evocative, with occasional glimpses of hills and desert providing the furthest horizon. The psalmist, by contrast, views the cosmic vastness of the created order, looking back to its very beginnings. The natural world is seen in the psalm as the gift of a creator; the lovers in the Song simply enjoy all that is at hand, never raising the question of its origins.

Having begun with creation, the psalmist moves on to the drama of redemption, exploring certain key moments in Israel's salvation history. Once again, we are worlds away from the small, intimate setting of the

187. Unlike most English translations, Goldingay has 'Confess' rather than 'Give thanks', emphasizing the broader sense of *hôdû* (הודו) as publicly owning to the truth of something, in this case giving testimony to what Yhwh has done; he acknowledges thanksgiving as one component of this (*Psalms 90–150*, pp. 590, 753).

188. The particle *kî* (כִּי) which links the refrain to each line probably means 'because', presenting Yhwh's love as the reason for his actions; alternatively, it might be translated 'surely', with Yhwh's actions providing demonstrative evidence for his love. Cf. Brueggemann, *Israel's Praise*, pp. 78-80.

Song, where even passing glimpses of a bigger world involving city guards and a mother's house are simply the backdrop to all that really matters: you and me. The psalm pitches the reader into international power-politics, with mention of various nations and their rulers (vv. 10-22). Here is a reminder of the story of how Israel became a nation, through the formative events of the exodus. The birth of the nation, like the birth of creation itself, is entirely the work of God, who is awesome and powerful, greater than any other heavenly being as 'God of gods', 'Lord of lords' and 'God of the heavens' (vv. 2-3; 26). This God is able to strike down all manner of great and famous kings (even mighty Pharaoh is 'shaken off' as one shakes off an insect, v. 15; cf. Ps. 109.23) and to lead his people safely to their heritage in the promised land.[189] The psalmist's enthusiasm for Yhwh is matched by a sense of awe.[190] There is no hint of intimacy here; simply the 'abiding astonishment' of those who have been God's servants (v. 22), including the psalmist's own generation who are called to continue that role (vv. 23-25).[191] Mention of enemies (v. 24) unites this current generation with previous ones; the introduction of 'our/us' in vv. 23-25 makes clear that the psalm has moved its focus explicitly to its present hearers (who could be pre- or post-exilic).[192] Evidently the new generation have their own concerns about enemies, which the psalmist is seeking to allay. The theme of responding to enemies which I noted in Psalm 119 recurs throughout the Psalter (e.g. Pss. 3.7; 5.8; 9.3, 6; 18.3, 17, 37, 48; 35.1, 19; 54.5, 7; 63.9-11; 69.4, 14, 18; 89.10, 42, 51; 106.42; 119.98; 143.9, 12) which contrasts with the blissful world of the Song, where such threats are either not present or else simply ignored. Metaphors for security and protection are extensive throughout the Psalter (e.g. Psalm 18: God is rock, stronghold, refuge, fortress, strength shield, deliverer).[193] Time and again we find the psalmists yearning for a saviour, rather than a lover.

In spite of these contrasts with the Song, however, the incessant refrain of Psalm 136 ('his steadfast love endures forever') reminds us of major themes which we have already identified in Song 8.5b-7: the nature of love, and the relationship between love and death. The meaning of *hesed* (חסד)

189. Schaefer, *Psalms*, p. 320. Israel seems to be the silent and passive object of God's actions (Kraus, *Psalms 60–150*, p. 199).

190. Cf. Gunkel, *Introduction to the Psalms*, p. 49.

191. Walter Brueggemann, *Abiding Astonishment: Psalms, Modernity, and the Making of History* (Louisville, KY: John Knox Press, 1991), pp. 29-32. Brueggemann takes the phrase 'abiding astonishment' from Martin Buber, seeing it a key motif in the 'Psalms of historical recital' (Pss. 78; 105; 106; 136), where sustaining a sense of astonishment at what God has done in the past helps nurture a sense of expectation, awe and order for subsequent generations.

192. Allen, *Psalms 101–150*, p. 234; Goldingay, *Psalms 90–150*, p. 596.

193. Schaefer, *Psalms*, p. xiii.

will be considered shortly; for now, let us reflect briefly on 'forever'. Like the Song, the psalm proclaims a relationship of lasting commitment which will endure. But while the Song offers a love that is as strong as (but not stronger than) death, the psalm goes further: it declares an eternal *hesed*, giving examples of how this has been expressed in Israel's history and even from the very moment of creation. There is no clear sense here of a love which human beings can experience after death, in some kind of eternal life; the perspective is divine, rather than human, and since God never dies, God's love never dies. The relentless repetition of the refrain serves to underline the endlessness of this love and the way it has been experienced by successive generations. Neither the floods of the Red Sea nor the way-wardness of successive generations could quench God's jealous love for his people (cf. Song 8.6-7; see Exod. 20.5-6; 34.14; Deut. 4.24; 5.9; 6.15; 32.16, 19, 21).

hesed (חסד)

Clearly *hesed* is a key word for this psalm, and indeed for the Psalms as a whole: approximately half of the total occurrences of the word in the Hebrew Bible occur in the Psalter, where it is found one hundred and twenty seven times in fifty-three different Psalms. It has a significant role in a number of the Psalms I have already considered (Pss. 42.8; 63.3; 119.41, 64, 76, 88, 124, 149, 159).[194] The Psalter presents *hesed* as a characteristic of God. It is something that fills the earth (Pss. 33.5; 119.64), is as high as the heavens (36.5; 57.10), comes towards people (86.13; 117.2; 119.41), surrounds the God-fearing (32.10), follows a person (23.6), satisfies (90.14), is precious (36.7), brings deliverance (32.10; 33.18-19; 40.11; 59.16), particularly from enemies (17.7; 57.3; 143.12). God offers it, lets it be heard, and could withdraw it (42.8; 143.8; 66.20; 77.8).[195]

The richness of the word and its range of meaning is reflected in the variety of ways it is rendered in different English translations: 'steadfast love' (NRSV), 'faithful love' (NJB), 'loving kindness' (NASB), 'mercy' (KJV); or simply 'love' (NIV, REB). Not to be outdone, commentators offer 'covenant loyalty' (Anderson), 'loyal love' (Allen), 'commitment' (Goldingay), 'goodness' (Kraus), 'grace' (Weiser), 'faithfulness' (Eaton), or 'kindness' implying 'steadfast faithfulness' (Alter). *TLOT* and *TDOT* both favour 'kindness', while *DCH* begins its list of options with 'loyalty'. The

---

194. Schaefer, *Psalms*, p. 111.

195. H. Stoebe, 'חסד', *TLOT* 2, p. 461; Katherine Doob Sakenfeld, *Faithfulness in Action: Loyalty in Biblical Perspective* (Philadelphia: Fortress, 1985), pp. 83-86.

forthcoming NICOT commentary on the Psalms simply resorts to the transliteration '*ḥesed*', with an explanatory note.[196]

Katherine Sakenfeld also favours the translation 'loyalty', although she sees limitations in this as in all other attempts to render the word in English. She emphasizes that *ḥesed* in the Hebrew Bible is an attitude made manifest in action, involving persons in relationship acting loyally. It is offered to a person in need by one who has the ability to help and who freely chooses to help, but does so as part of an existing commitment to the one in need. The *ḥesed* which God gives to Israel involves God's promised yet still surprising faithfulness: an ever new and free decision to honour covenant commitments by preserving and supporting the covenant community, in spite of its waywardness. Thus divine freedom and divine self-obligation are held together in this single word.[197] Building on Sakenfeld's work, Gordon Clark adds more detailed linguistic analysis, noting the close association in the Hebrew Bible between *ḥesed*, and other words in its lexical field such as 'mercies' (*raḥᵃmîm*, רחמים), 'gracious' (*ḥannûn*, חנון) and 'faithfulness' (*ᵉmet*, אמת); frequent pairings of the latter and its cognates with *ḥesed* he regards as a hendiadys (see especially Ps. 89.1, 2, 14, 33, 49). He further notes the way *ḥesed* is frequently used with the verb of doing ('*āsâ*, עשה) which confirms that *ḥesed* is not just a sentiment or emotional reaction to a set of circumstances, but a practical activity which is beneficial to another; the deed is what really matters.[198] Psalm 136 may itself be seen as a definition of *ḥesed*: everything God does, from the epic events of creation and the redemption of his people, to ongoing faithfulness in providing daily sustenance for 'all flesh' (v.25), all displays this quality.[199]

Clearly *ḥesed* is a crucial term for understanding how God relates to God's people, particularly as depicted in the Psalter. One obvious feature of

196. Anderson, *Psalms 73–150*, p. 894; Allen, *Psalms 101–150*, p. 228; Goldingay, *Psalms 90–150*, p. 587; Kraus, *Psalms 60–150*, p. 495; Weiser, *Psalms*, p. 791; Eaton, *Psalms*, p. 451; Stoebe, 'חסד', p. 449; Hans-Jürgen Zobel, 'חסד', *TDOT* 5, p. 44; *DCH* 3, p. 277. Information on the forthcoming NICOT commentary comes from the author, Nancy L. deClaissé-Walford in her paper 'Translating the Poetry of the Psalms', given at the Conference 'Conflict and Convergence: Jewish and Christian Approaches to the Psalms', Worcester College, Oxford, 23 Sept. 2010.

197. Sakenfeld, *Faithfulness in Action*, pp. 2-3, 51, 84, 132; Schaefer, *Psalms*, p. 321.

198. Gordon Clark, *The Word Ḥesed in the Hebrew Bible* (JSOTSup, 157; Sheffield: JSOT Press, 1993), pp. 148, 186, 254. Cf. Mays, *Psalms*, pp. 33, 420. Schaefer comments that חסד is both 'trustworthy and vigorous' (*Psalms*, p. 320).

199. Goldingay, *Psalms 3*, p. 596. On v. 17-22, he comments that God's love issues in action, and 'can be terrifying' (p. 597). See also McCann, 'Book of Psalms', pp. 1224-26.

Psalm 136 is that *ḥesed* is ascribed only to God. This might lead us to wonder whether only God is capable of *ḥesed*. Is it a term borrowed from the
language of ancient Near Eastern power politics, suitable to depict only the
actions of a benevolent suzerain towards his vassals?[200] Does the complete
absence of the term *ḥesed* from the Song of Songs further suggest that it is
something human beings are not capable of?

The Hebrew Bible does present *ḥesed* as a characteristic of God rather
than humans, a tenacious commitment rooted in the divine nature (Exod.
20.5-6; 34.6-7). But it is also a quality which Yhwh expects his people to
emulate, even though their expression of it can be only a pale reflection of
Yhwh's; they are called to become *ḥasîdāyw* (חסדיו), 'his faithful ones',
expressing this quality to others (Pss. 37.27-28; 85.8; 132.9, 16; 148.14;
also 2 Chron. 32.32; 35.26-27; Neh. 13.14; Micah 6.6-8).[201] Indeed, *ḥesed*
is used elsewhere in the Hebrew Bible to describe relationships between
human beings; those involved range from an Israelite king to a desperate
widow, doing everything from lying to spying, marrying to burying, providing food to granting life, as Sakenfeld puts it.[202] Rahab of Jericho insists that
Joshua's spies swear by Yhwh to show *ḥesed* to her and her family, since
she has shown *ḥesed* to them; they agree (Josh. 2.12, 14). Jonathan urges
David to show the *ḥesed* of Yhwh to himself and his house; later David
declares his desire to show kindness (*ḥesed*) to anyone left from the house
of Saul, and seeks out Jonathan's crippled son Mephibosheth (1 Sam. 20.14;
2 Sam. 9.1-3). Micah calls people to do justice and love *ḥesed* (Micah 6.8).
If we consider sexual relationships, Esther wins the *ḥesed* of King Ahasu-
erus, when her beauty catches his eye (Est. 2.9, 17).

A common factor in most of these occurrences of *ḥesed* seems to be the
power relationship between the parties. The stronger party freely chooses to
give favour to the weaker, who is in a vulnerable position from which they
cannot save themselves.[203] Thus, in the Psalms, *ḥesed* is frequently linked

200. See Sakenfeld, 'Love', p. 379; also Zobel, 'חסד', p. 63. Kraus sees in *ḥesed* a
relationship of goodwill and conformity to the covenant between a ruler and his people,
expressing both 'affection and solidarity' (*Psalms 1–59*, p. 155).

201. Clark, *The Word Ḥesed*, p. 267; Sakenfeld, *Faithfulness in Action*, pp. 101,
123-24.

202. Sakenfeld, *Faithfulness in Action*, p. 7. On some of the more surprising relationships expressed in terms of in *ḥesed*, see Brian Britt, 'Unexpected Attachments: A
Literary Approach to the Term חסד in the Hebrew Bible', *JSOT* 27 (2003), pp. 301-306.

203. During their intimate night-time encounter, Boaz praises Ruth for showing
ḥesed (Ruth 3.10). This may mean that she has shown *ḥesed* to him, in choosing him
instead of the younger men. Perhaps more likely is the proposal that Boaz refers to the
ḥesed she has shown to her late husband and particularly to his mother Naomi, in having
concern for her future. See the discussion in Katherine Doob Sakenfeld, *Ruth* (Interpre-

with prayers for protection and deliverance from enemies. There may be an element of reciprocity in the relationship, but not symmetry.[204] So we might argue that the word *hesed* is inappropriate for the Song of Songs, where a hierarchical relationship is strikingly absent. Mutuality is a feature of the relationship depicted in the Song; both parties freely choose to give to the other. Both at times feel weak (she feels 'faint with love', he feels overwhelmed by her beauty; Song 2.5, 7; 4.9; 6.4-5); but neither has a clear status or power advantage over the other.

In the Psalms in particular, the meaning of *hesed* is expanded to include the element of forgiveness. The parallelism between *hesed* and forgiveness found in Exod. 34.6-7 is emphasized repeatedly in the Psalms; forgiveness is the particular characteristic of the God who 'abounds in *hesed*' (Pss. 25.6; 51.1; 86.5, 15; 103.8-12; also Neh. 9.17; Jonah 4.2).[205] 'In this respect especially was Yahweh's loyalty sure and abundant, far surpassing human loyalty, which in ordinary usage of the word seems never to have been extended to forgiveness.'[206]

This further dimension of forgiveness speaks to issues of power and of mutuality. As we consider the mutuality expressed in the Song of Song's vision of love, we need to be aware of its fragility. Mutuality can easily be displaced; as soon as one party feels hurt or guilty, that delicate balance is lost. If one requires an apology from the other, and this is withheld, a power struggle takes place. If one feels they have been wronged, they must decide whether to give or withhold forgiveness. Only when the issue has been resolved can a healthy mutuality be restored to the relationship. So here perhaps the Psalms ask a question of the Song: what about forgiveness? Why is this not explicit in the Song, either through use of *hesed* or some other term? Is forgiveness simply assumed and taken for granted in such an intimate relationship? Or are the lovers as yet oblivious to this dimension of intimacy? The Song seems to depict the intensity of intimate moments experienced by a young couple in love, rather than an ongoing and gradually maturing relationship. But if the love being celebrated in the Song really is going to be 'a seal upon the heart, as strong as death, a raging flame that floods cannot quench' (Song 8.6-7), then surely loyalty, faithfulness and particularly forgiveness need to be woven into the fabric of this relationship. Experiencing *hesed* from each other can touch the lovers in the deepest places, and in turn renew and deepen the passionate delight which the Song celebrates.

tation: Louisville, KY: Westminster John Knox Press, 1999), pp. 61-62; also Frederic W. Bush, *Ruth, Esther* (Word: Dallas, Texas, Word, 1996), pp. 170-72.

204. Brueggemann, *Israel's Praise*, p. 2.
205. Sakenfeld, *Faithfulness in Action*, pp. 47-51.
206. Sakenfeld, *Faithfulness in Action*, p. 132.

If human beings are able to do *ḥesed* to each other, can they also act this way to God? Occasionally the prophets suggest that the term was eventually stretched in this direction. Hosea presents God's sadness at the transience of his people's *ḥesed*; this is what God desires, rather than sacrifice (Hos. 6.4-6). In the parallelism of the line that follows, 'knowledge of God' is matched with *ḥesed* as being preferable to burnt offerings (note the similar parallel in Hos. 4.1). Jeremiah puts *ḥesed* in parallel with *aḥᵃbāh* in God's reminiscence about Jerusalem's former devotion to him when she was a youthful bride (Jer. 2.2). In both these cases, giving *ḥesed* to God is seen as an expression of Israel's free choice to preserve the covenant relationship.[207] But a human–divine mutuality of *ḥesed* is not suggested by the Psalms; here the appropriate human response to God's *ḥesed* is to give thanks, praise and obedience. Generally Yhwh seems to look for responses such as *aḥᵃbāh* from his covenant partner, rather than *ḥesed* (Exod. 20.5-6; Deut. 5.10; 6.5; Ps. 119.124, 127).[208]

Summary

In its key reflective and didactic moment (Song 8.5b-7), the Song highlights the importance and inestimable value of love, love's tenacious persistence and irresistible power, and love's exclusive claims on the other and total commitment to the other, even to the point of losing oneself. The poet presents death as a contrasting threat, to which love is apparently equal; in what sense this equality may be understood is left tantalizingly unclear. Psalms such as Psalm 136 also proclaim a love which is priceless and tenacious, and which even transcends death, because its divine source is eternal. This love is evident in God's actions of creating the world and redeeming his people, and his ongoing forgiveness of their failings. It is the love of covenant loyalty, where a stronger party fulfils promises made to one who is weaker and in need. Although both parties make commitments to each other within this covenant relationship, the kind of mutuality seen in the Song is not evident, due to the disparity of power between them. The Song's mutuality might itself be disrupted by the need for forgiveness between the lovers, but the Song does not explore this theme.

Of Lords and Lovers: Psalm 45 and Song 3.6-11

My final pairing brings together two texts which might both be described as 'mavericks', since each stands out in its literary context, puzzling the reader by its surprising and distinctive presence. Both passages are vividly visual. Both seem full of optimism about the future, while also hinting at dangers

---

207. Sakenfeld, *Faithfulness in Action*, pp. 109-16; 'Love', p. 380.
208. Clark, *The Word Ḥesed*, p. 132, 259.

which will need to be warded off. In addition, the two passages share a common theme: each gives us a glimpse of a royal wedding.

Psalm 45

Other psalms invariably speak about God, and often to God. Psalm 45, in contrast, seems to give God a fairly minor role as one of the supporting cast in a courtly drama; the main focus is on a human king at his wedding.[209] Here, uniquely in the Psalter, is a poem whose primary interest is human beings and their relationships, specifically that between a bride and groom.

This may be the only psalm to carry the ascription 'a love song' (*šîr yᵉdîdôt*, שיר ידידות) but it is a far cry from 'song of songs' (*šîr haššîrîm*, שיר השירים). Love is not mentioned at all in the psalm. Desire might be forthcoming in the future, but is indicated as arising only in the man (v.11), and may be partly connected with a desire to have children (v. 16); such a desire is never expressed in the Song, where the lovers simply delight in each other without mention of future offspring. Both the man and the woman in the psalm are praised for their beauty, using similar terms (*yāfâ*, יפה, v. 2; *yāfî*, יפי, v. 11); but the praise comes not from each other, as in the Song, but from someone else with an agenda of their own. Whereas the Song presents dialogue between the man and woman, with occasional brief interjections from the women of Jerusalem, in the psalm we hear only this third party (perhaps a court poet commissioned to produce something suitable for the wedding day). The poet expresses hyperbolic praise of the king (vv. 2-9), beginning with his physical appearance and felicity of speech, then emphasizing his military strength and royal majesty as ruler seated on what is ultimately God's throne (v. 6).[210] As the poet turns again to the king's appearance, this time depicting his clothing, the scene opens out before the reader's eyes into a grand occasion involving the fragrance of abundant spices, music from an opulent setting, noble guests and an attendant queen, dressed in gold. Language of 'king/kings', 'majesty', 'throne' and 'palace' abound throughout the psalm, emphasizing the royal setting. Only now does the reader become aware of a beautiful woman who is being brought formally from her 'father's house' to the king, suggesting a wed-

209. Other Royal Psalms give God greater prominence. Psalm 2 explores the might of human kings, but Yhwh, as king of kings, is a central character (and speaker) in the drama. In Psalm 21, the king speaks his praises directly to Yhwh. Even Psalm 72, which is strongly focussed on a king, begins by addressing God with a prayer for the king, and then continues as a combination of prayer and exhortation.

210. The much-debated v. 6a seems best translated: 'Your throne is God's for ever and ever' (Johannes Mulder, *Studies on Psalm 45* [Ph.D. dissertation; Nijmigen; Oss: Offsetdrukkerij Witsiers, 1972], p. 80; Goldingay, *Psalms 42–89*, p. 53.) See also discussion in Broyles, *Psalms,* p. 207. As in Ps. 2, the king rules on behalf of God, not simply in his own authority; cf. McCann, 'Book of Psalms', pp. 860-61.

ding.[211] The bride is probably also the queen mentioned in v. 9, although this is not entirely clear.

After this lengthy series of compliments addressed to the royal groom, we find just three lines addressed to the bride (vv. 10-12).[212] She is given no direct compliments about her appearance and character to match those given to the king. Instead she receives somewhat stern exhortations: to listen carefully, forget her people and father's house, and bow to the king who is her lord; she is to become the object of his desire, and the subject of submission.[213] Then the magnificence of her robes and joyful retinue are described as she and her companions enter the palace (vv. 13-15), before attention reverts to the king, who is promised sons and lasting renown (vv. 16-17).

The unexpected allusion to Tyre (v. 12) may suggest Jezebel, the famous royal bride of Ahab who came from that city (1 Kgs 16.31). It has been argued that, for all its generalities, this psalm is not depicting marriage in general (where bride and groom were, it is suggested, sometimes seen as 'king and queen for the day'), but instead giving specific guidance about how royal marriages should be conducted in Israel. By this argument, the psalm states that foreign royal brides are permitted (in line with the custom of using royal marriages to strengthen ties between nations). But such brides coming to Israel must break with their background and not bring with them the kind of corrupting idolatrous practices for which Jezebel became notorious (1 Kgs 16.31-34; 18.19; 19.2). King Ahab, like Solomon (1 Kgs 11.1-8), became infamous for supposedly allowing a foreign queen to lead him and his people into idolatry. Hence the severity of Ps. 45.10-11: the new queen's example must be Ruth ('your people shall be my people, and your God my God', Ruth 1.16-17), not Jezebel.[214]

211. Schaefer, *Psalms*, pp. 114-15.

212. Drawing on Akkadian and Sumerian texts, Christoph Schroeder argues that the Queen Mother becomes the speaker at this point in Ps. 45 (Christoph Schroeder '"A Love Song": Psalm 45 in the Light of Ancient Near Eastern Marriage Texts', *CBQ* 58 [1996], pp. 428-29). This is speculative, but could suggest a role for the maternal figures in royal wedding ceremonies, as hinted at in Song 3.11.

213. Tournay, 'Les Affinitiés de Ps. lxv', pp. 177, 197. Also Goldingay, *Psalms 42–90*, pp. 60-61; cf. Alter's assessment: 'The bride provides the beauty, which rouses the king's desire, but he is her master' (*Book of Psalms*, p. 160). The verb 'desire' (*āwāh* [אוה]) gets mixed reviews in the Psalms; it refers to a sinful craving for meat in the desert, yet also to God's desire for Zion (Pss. 106.14; 132.13-14).

214. Goldingay, *Psalms 2*, p. 63; McCann, 'Book of Psalms', p. 862; Terrien, *Psalms*, p. 357; Mulder proposes that Josiah is the king celebrated in the psalm (*Studies on Psalm 45*, p. 158), but for this, as for other specific proposals, the evidence is inconclusive. On the politics of Davidic royal weddings in general, see Hermann M. Niemann,

The language used in Psalm 45's address to the bride has raised questions about the psalm's intention. Would it not be offensive to the elders of foreign states with whom an alliance was sought to have their daughters told, in public (and by a mere scribe or poet), to forget their people and father's house? This and other factors have led some to argue that the poet has in mind a messianic wedding. Such an interpretation can help explain the contentious v. 6a, where (depending how the line is translated) the king may seem to be exceptionally closely identified with the person of God. It is also relevant to v. 17, where the king's name is to be celebrated by endless subsequent generations. Thus the author may be seen to present a young messianic prince, a son of David, idealized as a new Solomon, who will accomplish, through union with the bride Israel, the promises of God.[215] This traditional Jewish interpretation feeds into Christian allegorical understandings of the psalm as depicting the love between Christ and his church (see Chapter 2), but neither view is evident from the text itself.[216] It seems more appropriate to understand the psalm as a hyperbolic glimpse of court life and international relations at some point before the exile.[217] A divine–human marriage has been found in this psalm by some subsequent interpreters, but only by reading it into the text; such an understanding cannot be found in the text itself.

Song 3.6-11

Can marriage be found in the Song of Songs? Commentators offer widely differing answers to this question.[218] In a key central passage within the

'Choosing Brides for the Crown Prince: Matrimonial Politics in the Davidic Dynasty', *VT* 56 (2006), pp. 225-38.

215. See Tournay, 'Les Affinitiés de Ps. lxv', pp. 210-12 ; also Hossfeld and Zenger (*Die Psalmen* 1, pp. 278-79; 283); Richard Viladesau, *Theology and the Arts* (New York: Paulist Press, 2000), pp. 340-41.

216. See, for example, John Chrysostom, *Commentary on the Psalms* 1 (trans. Robert Charles Hill; Brookline, MS: Holy Cross Orthodox Press, 1998), pp. 257-84. Rashi, keen to rebut Christian interpretations, presents the king who is praised in the psalm as representing scholars of the Torah (*Commentary on Psalms 1–89*, pp. 212-15).

217. See Theodor H. Gaster, 'Psalm 45', *JBL* 74 (1955), pp. 239-51. Gaster's proposal that the poem was originally written for an ordinary wedding, rather than a royal one, draws particularly on Arabic and Greek traditions (plus some Ugaritic), but lacks evidence arising from ancient Jewish traditions, and gives insufficient weight to the royal language in the text of the psalm.

218. Contrast Exum's assertion that the Song is not about marriage or betrothal, although it might subtly anticipate a marriage (*Song of Songs*, pp. 79, 169-70) with Garrett, whose proposed structure for the Song centres on a wedding night in Song 3.1–6.10 (*Song of Songs*, p. vi). See also Sparks' view of the Song as a text for those who dreamed of marriage (Kenton L. Sparks, 'The Song of Songs: Wisdom for Young Jewish Women', *CBQ* 70 [2008], pp. 281-84), in contrast with Fox, *Song of Songs*, pp. 230-32.

book, the woman is repeatedly referred to by the man as 'bride' (Song 4.8, 9, 10, 11, 12; 5.1), an epithet of endearment which at least raises questions regarding marriage. Only once does the Song mention a wedding, in the passage to which I now turn.

Various puzzles tease the reader of Song 3.6-11. Who is speaking, and who is present in the envisaged procession: is it the man, or the woman, or both? Why is Solomon mentioned so prominently? If the curious reference to 'love' (3.10) is not a mistake needing emendation, then what is its significance here? What kind of 'wedding' is depicted here, and what is the role of the king's mother?

The speaker of these verses is not identified. The description focuses on the appearance of the litter and those who attend it, rather than on whoever is seated at the heart of it; this makes identification of that person difficult. However, this passage follows on from one in which it was clearly the woman who was speaking (2.8–3.5); with no indication of a change of speaker, it may be best to assume that the woman continues to speak in these verses, with the man being portrayed.[219] As in Psalm 45, visual images of royalty are prominent in this passage. Solomon is mentioned three times (twice specifically as 'king'), and is to be admired by onlookers (vv. 7, 9, 11). We also see the 'crown' with which he was 'crowned' by his mother, plus an elaborate palanquin, excessive spices and a very large retinue. But whereas the psalm presents a king static in his palace, to whom a bride is led, the Song here seems to depict a resplendent king Solomon on the move, approaching from a distance. Throughout the Song, the term 'king' is a fiction (1.4, 12; 6.8-9; 7.5), referring to the woman's lover. Here in 3.6-11, hyperbolic royal imagery is used by the woman to extol the man: he is cast as the figure of Solomon, the archetypal lover-king, and the description of a magnificent wedding procession is a tribute to him.[220] The extravagant

---

219. J. Cheryl Exum, 'Seeing Solomon's Palanquin (Song of Songs 3.6-11)', *BibInt* 11 (2003), pp. 309-13, against Garrett, who ascribes this passage to a chorus (*Song of Songs*, p. 176-77), and Hess, who ascribes it to the man (*Song of Songs*, p. 116); both see the person being carried as the woman. Although the evidence is not conclusive, I take the opening interrogative מִי, along with the feminine adjective and participle which follow, to be probably referring to the litter (a feminine noun) in v. 7; cf. NRSV, NJB, GNB, CEV; Murphy, *Song of Songs*, p. 151; Exum, *Song of Songs*, p. 145. Dirksen insists that the feminines in v. 6 must indicate that the woman is being carried, even though he emphasizes that the litter is Solomon's; Dirksen is also forced to detach v. 11 from what precedes it, which seems arbitrary (P.B. Dirksen, 'Song of Songs 3.6-7', *VT* 39 [1989], pp. 220-22).

220. Murphy, *Song of Songs*, pp. 151-52; Longman, *Song of Songs*, p. 137; Bloch and Bloch, *Song of Songs*, p. 138; also Jill M. Monro, *Spikenard and Saffron: The Imagery of the Song of Songs* (JSOTSup, 203; Sheffield: Sheffield Academic Press, 1995), p. 145. Weems suggests a modern equivalent of the 'Solomon' epithet might be

splendours of a royal pavilion are explored, perhaps in a playful way (see also 6.12–7.1). Even the 'crown' mentioned may be simply a wedding garland, although its presence on Solomon's head gives it royal status.[221]

With images of royalty come questions of power. While some see here the couple together fantasizing about their wedding, it might be more accurate (assuming that the woman is the speaker) to see this passage as the woman's fantasy: a traditional picture of a passive woman being carried on a bed to join a king's harem is reversed, as she fantasizes about him being brought to her on their wedding day, rather than vice versa.[222] Alternatively, we might emphasize the grandeur of the scene, seeing a powerful king arriving, determined to sweep all before him. Clearly the procession has an exceptionally large armed guard; here, as in Psalm 45, we find a military emphasis intruding which seems disproportionate and slightly discordant. Perhaps the many warriors depicted in Song 3.7-8 are simply decorative, adding splendour to the occasion and status to Solomon. Alternatively, they may be present in order to help ward off evil spirits which might be abroad during hours of darkness (cf. Ps. 91.5-6) and which could seek to afflict the couple on their wedding night. Yet the sheer size of the retinue apparently needed for this task seems to indicate insecurity; perhaps beneath this Solomon's grand facade lurk unspecified fears.[223] Thus we find in this passage traditional images of power, interwoven with other elements which seem to undermine traditional understandings of power, and attendant hints of vulnerability.

Allusions of Grandeur

To what extent, if any, we may identify links between Psalm 45 and Song 3.6-11 is debatable. Both paint a vivid scene of opulent royal grandeur, as thrones and garments of finest cloth are glimpsed amid abundant spices. In both, parents are at hand and military might in evidence as a bride, attended by young women, comes together in marriage with her new husband. The similarities increase further if we adopt the (less likely) view that the woman is being carried to the man in Song 3.6-11 (rather than vice versa), like the bride led to her husband in Ps. 45.10-15. A few writers argue that the con-

to call him 'Romeo' ('Song of Songs', p. 400). Solomon is also mentioned in Song 1.5 and 8.11-12; in both cases he symbolizes great wealth.

221. Fox, *Song of Songs*, pp. 127; 155-56; Garrett, *Song of Songs*, pp. 179-81. Even if we take a different view, with the woman being carried to her wedding in Solomon's palanquin, we still have a couple playing at being king and queen; perhaps she comes to her Solomon in the role of the Queen of Sheba (1 Kgs 10.1-10)?

222. Cf. Weems, 'Song of Songs', p. 399. The argument that the bed must be part of a fixed structure, not mobile, because of features such as its grand pillars (see Fox, *Song of Songs*, pp. 127, 155-56; Bloch and Bloch, *Song of Songs*, pp. 162-63), fails to give sufficient weight to the hyperbole and fantasy evident in these verses.

223. Cf. Exum, *Song of Songs*, pp. 147-48.

nections in theme and vocabulary are so strong that they cannot be ignored,[224] but many commentaries on one text make little or no reference to the other.[225] If such links are to be found, they could confirm the sense of lovers playing at royalty in Song 3.6-11 by showing that the poet has some awareness of the pageantry of royal weddings, maybe even knowledge of Psalm 45 itself. The alternative scenario (that the psalmist drew on the Song) seems less likely, for the psalm shows no interest in the playful erotic intimacy in which the Song delights, and the Song is usually dated later.

Perhaps more fruitful is the question of links between the language of Song 3.6-11 and other parts of the Hebrew Bible as a whole. Ellen Davis describes the Song as 'the most biblical of books', in the sense that the poet is in conversation with other biblical writers, constantly 'recycling' words and images taken from earlier books.[226] Song 3.6-11 seems to provide us with examples of this. The reference to 'a column of smoke' moving in 'the wilderness' above what turns out to be a crowd of people seems suggestive of the wanderings in the wilderness with the sign of God's presence, as described in the Exodus narrative (e.g. Exod. 13.21-22; 19.18; 40.34-38; Num. 10.34), even though the language used is not identical. Wilderness is also the place of divine wooing, where Hosea portrays God winning back the heart of Israel as when she was young and came out of Egypt (Hos. 2.14-15). Myrrh could suggest the smell of worship (e.g. Exod. 30.22-23). The verb translated 'perfumed' (*qāṭar* [קטר], Song 3.6) connotes burnt offerings sent up in smoke, evoking the burning of incense and sacrifices in worship (Exod. 30.1-10, 22-38; Lev. 2.1–3.17). Sacrificial worship is further hinted at by the feminine participle *'ōlâ* (עלה, Song 3.6), meaning 'coming up', which is identical to the very common feminine noun for 'burnt offering' (Gen. 22.2; Exod. 29.18, 25; Lev. 1.3). The sight of an elaborately decorated palanquin (Song 3.9, and probably v. 7) could be reminiscent of the ark of the covenant, which was also made of fine wood decorated with gold, and was carried on poles through the wilderness. References to 'wood of Lebanon' used by King Solomon to make the palanquin (3.9; cf. 1.17) would be likely to remind readers of the wood provided by the king of Tyre for the original Solomon to build the Temple (1 Kgs 5.1-10). The distinctive

---

224. Tournay, 'Les Affinitiés de Ps. lxv', pp. 171-72 ; Pfenniger, 'Bhaktin Reads the Song of Songs', pp. 348-49; see also Schroeder 'A Love Song', pp. 429-31. Schaefer points to both Song 3.6-11 and 5.10-16 as passages reminiscent of Psalm 45 (*Psalms*, p. 114).

225. Garrett, *Song of Songs*, pp. 175-84; Exum, *Song of Songs*, pp. 138-51; Murphy, *Song of Songs*, pp. 149-52; McCann, 'Book of Psalms', pp. 860-63; Goldingay, *Psalms 42–89*, pp. 52-63.

226. Davis, *Proverbs, Ecclesiastes and the Song of Songs*, pp. 231-32, 250-51, 254, 258, 261, 269, 298. See also LaCocque, *Romance She Wrote* (throughout) and Walsh, *Exquisite Desire*, pp. 92-94, 154, 210.

phrase 'terrors of the night' (Song 3.8) is almost identical to that found in Ps. 91.5. When 'columns/posts' are combined with 'silver' (Song 3.10), the construction of the Tabernacle is almost always being described (e.g. Exod. 26.32; 27.10, 11, 17; 36.36; 38.10, 11, 12, 17, 19). Mention of 'purple' in the palanquin could be simply a sign of extreme luxury; but this word is used most frequently in the Hebrew Bible of the furnishings of the Tabernacle and Temple (for example, Exod. 25.4; 26.1, 31, 36; 27.16; 28.5, 6, 8, 15, 33; 35.6, 23, 25, 35; 2 Chron. 2.14; 3.14).[227]

The density of recurrence of motifs and allusions can be an important element in recognizing intertextual links.[228] How many intertextual allusions may be identified throughout the Song is very debatable. Allusions, by their very nature, tend to be hidden and hard to verify; much depends on the eye of the beholder.[229] If André LaCocque is correct in finding such allusions in words as simple as 'dove', 'house, 'springs', 'keep', 'shepherd' and 'shade', we may wonder how much basic and stock vocabulary is left to a poet who is simply trying to write a love song, without any wider significance.[230] But the significant number of references to distinctive vocabulary which LaCocque, Davis, Kingsmill and others propose gives some cumulative weight to this argument.[231] The reference to 'honey and milk' (Song 4.11; 5.1) in the Song's central and most erotic passage, for example, seem suggestive: the praise due to the promised land given by God (Deut.

227. Garrett, *Song of Songs*, pp. 177-78, 181; LaCocque, *Romance She Wrote*, p. 98; Hess, *Song of Songs*, p. 121; Bergant, *Song of Songs*, p. 38; Davis, *Proverbs, Ecclesiastes and Song of Songs*, pp. 260-61, 278. Note also Nissinen's comment on the Song's 'network of intertextual links to other books of the Hebrew Bible' ('Song of Songs and Sacred Marriage', p. 217). Provan finds much language connoting sacrifice in Song 3.6-11; he interprets this as referring to the woman being carried to the real King Solomon, sadly to be 'sacrificed' to his lascivious desires (*Song of Songs*, p. 303).

228. Cf. Cynthia Edenburg, 'Intertextuality, Literary Competence and the Question of Readership: Some Preliminary Observations', *JSOT* 35 (2010), pp. 139, 144.

229. See Benjamin D. Sommer, 'Exegesis, Allusion and Intertextuality in the Hebrew Bible: A Response to Lyle Eslinger', *VT* 46 (1996), pp. 484-86. See also Paul R. Noble, 'Esau, Tamar and Joseph: Criteria for Identifying Inner-Biblical Allusions', *VT* 59 (2002), pp. 219-52 (although his analysis relates exclusively to biblical narrative, rather than poetry).

230. Similarly, Kingsmill's observation that there are twenty-six references in the Song to 'my beloved', and that twenty-six is also the numerical value of the divine name Yhwh seems a very tenuous and questionable connection (*Song of Songs*, p. 40).

231. The amount of shared language, and the rareness or distinctiveness of the words in question, are two significant methodological criteria which can be used in identifying allusions: see Jeffery M. Leonard, 'Identifying Inner-Biblical Allusions: Psalm 78 as a Test Case', *JBL* 127 (2008), pp. 245-56. For all his careful analysis, however, Leonard concludes that the process of identifying inner-biblical allusions includes intuitive and subjective aspects which make it 'often more art than science' (p. 164).

6.3; 31.20; Jer. 11.5; 32.22) is used of the woman's body and kisses. Even though the order of Deuteronomy's 'milk and honey' is reversed, the phrase in the Song may still be suggestive of one of Israel's most cherished national and theological *leitmotifs*. The recurring metaphor of the woman as a 'vineyard' (Song 1.6; 2.15; 8.12) is also evocative of the prophets, where God's people are described as his vineyard (Isa. 3.14; 27.2; Jer. 12.10; Ezek 19.10; also Ps. 80.8-18), most strikingly in a 'love song' which portrays Yhwh as a passionate lover (Isa. 5.1-7). The visceral churning experienced in Song 5.4 echoes God's lament over the loss of his beloved child Ephraim (Jer. 31.20; see also Isa. 63.15). The juxtaposition of fire and flood in the declaration of love's invincibility (Song 8.6) carries echoes of Isa. 43.2, where God leads his people through the most threatening of obstacles, even water and flame; they have a creator/redeemer (Isa. 43.1, 14-15) whose power to give them new life is stronger than the 'death' of the exile. The mutual belonging affirmed in Song 6.3 sounds similar to that of God and his people (Exod. 6.7; Lev. 26.12; Ezek. 36.28, 37.27). The woman's declaration that 'love is as strong as death' can be seen as a foil to Qohelet's conviction that the woman who is a trap is 'more bitter than death' (Song 8.6; Eccl. 7.26). The distinctive phrasing in the title 'Song of Songs' (Song 1.1) might perhaps remind the reader of similar plural forms in other absolute superlatives referring to God (e.g. Deut. 10.17; Ps. 148.4), particularly 'holy of holies' (Exod. 26.33; 1 Kgs 6.16; 2 Chron. 3.8), the place where God's presence was most powerfully felt. The language of exulting and rejoicing in Song 1.4, with its puzzling 'we', finds a parallel in the language of corporate worship from Ps. 118.24. Moreover, a number of readers have noted the Song's recurring garden motif. Some suggest an allusion to the Jerusalem Temple, with its abundance of cedar (cf. Song 1.16-17), decorative carvings of trees, flowers, pomegranates and creatures (1 Kgs 6–7) and associations with abundant water (Pss. 36.8; 46.4). Others find in the Song's garden the theme of Eden and 'paradise restored'; along with this comes the restoration of mutual desire in Song 7.10, where the man's desire for the woman brings contrast and balance to the woman's desire for the man depicted in Gen. 3.16.[232] There is also the possibility of an aural pun alluding to divine names 'Yhwh $\S^e b\bar{a}$ ' $\hat{o}t$' and '$\bar{E}l$ Shaddai' in the adjurations (Song 2.7; 3.5), which I considered earlier when looking at Song 8.5b-7.

---

232. LaCocque, *Romance She Wrote*, pp. 110, 126, 157, 178; Walsh, *Exquisite Desire*, pp. 92-94, 209-10; Trible, *God and the Rhetoric of Sexuality*, pp. 144-65; Landy, *Paradoxes of Paradise*, pp. 183-84; 209; 275; Davis, *Proverbs, Ecclesiastes and the Song of Songs*, pp. 231, 240, 243, 248, 251, 269, 270-71, 277-78, 283; Jenson, *Song of Songs*, pp. 3, 42-43, 50-52; Kingsmill, *Song of Songs*, pp. 6, 44, 99-108, 155-78, 255-59; also Garrett, *Song of Songs*, p. 195.

Acknowledging the presence of possible allusions is one thing; establishing their significance is another. If the Song was one of the later Hebrew Bible books to be completed in its present form, then its author may be referring to other books, rather than vice versa.[233] We might argue that some or all of the allusions are made unwittingly, simply subconscious products of a mind that is soaked in its familiar Scriptures; however, the significant number of them, combined with their potentially controversial nature in connecting God with sexual desire, still raises questions. We might speculate as to possible authorial intention. Is this a deliberate depiction of the bride Israel (cf. Jer. 2.2; Hos. 2.14-15) being brought up to her husband to offer sacrifices, indeed, to be an offering herself?[234] Alternatively, is the Song a metaphorical depiction of the exiled Israel's frustrated desire for its absent God—a theology of absence which, at the same time, celebrates human, sensual life in a vibrant creation?[235] Could the Song be an essentially mystical text intended to arouse love for God by contrasting the prophetic condemnations of Israel's adultery with glimpses of a heavenly garden-paradise, which is offered to those who choose to love God?[236] Or is the author deliberately subversive and carnivalesque, producing an irreverent and satirical pastiche of prophetic language in order to reclaim *eros* from its metaphorical use in the prophets and restore its original glory and meaning?[237] Such speculative proposals are intriguing, but can neither be proved nor disproved. Thus the value of seeking authorial intention proves very limited.

A more fruitful approach may be to ask what effect these apparent biblical allusions have on the reader. Readers who are not well-versed in the Hebrew Bible will miss them, and will continue to appreciate the Song as simply an erotic love poem. But for readers (both ancient and modern) who are familiar with the other Hebrew Scriptures, such allusions and echoes, if recognized, can resonate and intrigue. However, the various interpretations summarized in the preceding paragraph remind us that even readers who find such allusions will interpret and respond to them differently. An allusion may evoke another text, and may even guide the reader to reflect on certain aspects of the evoked text in dialogue with the alluding text. The allusion cannot, however, constrain the reader's knowledge and imagina-

---

233. The evidence regarding dating is ultimately inconclusive; see Exum, *Song of Songs*, pp. 66-67; Hess, *Song of Songs*, pp. 17-19.

234. Davis, *Proverbs, Ecclesiastes and the Song of Songs*, p. 261.

235. Walsh, *Exquisite Desire*, pp. 97, 216.

236. Kingsmill, *Song of Songs*, pp. 6, 41, 45, 199. She sees the prophets and the Song conveying God's *eros* for the people he has chosen, while the Song goes further and also portrays 'the *eros for* God of his chosen people'. (p. 39)

237. LaCocque, *Romance She Wrote*, pp. 56-58, 64, 176.

tion, both of which will affect their response. The perceived allusion may prompt a response in the reader, but cannot control it.[238]

Those who read the Song in search of (or simply open to the possibility of) connections between 'yearning for you' and 'yearning for You' may find connections hinted at in apparent allusions to other biblical texts. For such readers, allusions may suggest a blurring of distinctions between sacred and secular, spirit and flesh, human and divine, perhaps even between erotic and spiritual relationships. Those who seek to preserve such dualisms (more likely to be modern readers than ancient ones) will find them undermined if divine–human relationship can be portrayed in terms of sexual desire.[239] If the Song can yoke liturgical language to sexual desire and pleasure, readers may wonder whether it is also possible to see the spiritual responses of praise and delight as full-blooded, sensual, even verging on the sexual.[240] It seems that God, or at least rumours of God and hints of worship, will not be shut out of the Song. Different readers will, however, respond to perceived allusions in a variety of ways, while many will deny their presence altogether. The Song's ability to elicit such a diversity of responses remains one of its enduring and intriguing characteristics.

Marrying the King

The image of marriage presented in both Psalm 45 and Song 3.6-11 is patriarchal, indeed, royal, with the groom depicted as a king who has great power and authority. We might wonder why the poet portrays the woman in the Song fantasizing over such a relationship, as it seems to disrupt the mutuality of her existing rapport with her lover evident elsewhere in the Song (all the more so if he is to become 'Solomon', a king famed not for any exclusive loving relationship, but instead for his extensive harem). Perhaps, if she is to become a 'queen' through this marriage, then mutuality might be retained and consolidated. Or perhaps if she is having the man brought to her in Song 3.6-11 (rather than the woman brought to the man, as depicted in Psalm 45), this suggests a reversal of conventional roles. For all the Song's general exuberance, it is only here that the word 'joy' is used (3.11); it comes in the only part of the Song where marriage is depicted, and is ascribed to the man. Yet the same term is found in Ps. 45.15, where the poet uses it to describe the feelings of the bride and her companions on the wedding day, while 'desire' is ascribed to the man. This suggests

---

238. See Galbraith, 'Drawing Our Fish in the Sand', pp. 206-209, where similar constraints are found to apply when responding to religious allusions in contemporary music.

239. See Jenson's rejection of Nygren's distinction between *eros* and *agape* (*Song of Songs*, p. 12).

240. Cf. Walsh, *Exquisite Desire*, pp. 51-52, 191, 126.

that delight in the marriage is not totally one sided. However, if (as has been suggested) Psalm 45 was preserved in the Psalter partly in order to be used by couples at their weddings, it may have served to consolidate a view of marriage which saw the husband as dominant and lordly, by blurring the distinction between a subject who bows to the king and a woman who relates to her husband.[241]

When marital imagery is used in the Hebrew Bible to depict a relationship between God and his people, patriarchal marriage is the underlying template. Prophets such as Hosea, Jeremiah and Ezekiel all present God as a husband seeking a wayward wife (Hos. 1–3; Jer. 2.2; Ezek. 16 and 23; also Isa. 5.1-7; 54.4-8; Mal. 2.10-11). Modern readers might instinctively transfer their cultural stereotypes onto this marriage motif and see it as a poetic device enabling fantasy about romance, courtship and intimacy, but for the prophets it speaks more of God's power and Israel's punishment. This hierarchical power relationship is confirmed when we look at the other relational metaphors used by the prophets to depict divine–human relationships: shepherd and sheep, king and vassal, master and slave, father and son. Occasionally the prophets' marital imagery is tempered with striking expressions of divine tenderness and compassion (Hos. 2.14-15; Ezek. 16.9; Isa. 54.4-8; see also God's delight in his bride, Isaiah 62.3-5); but images of God's sadness, anger and punishment are more common (Hos. 2.1-13; 4.12-19; Jer. 2.20-37; Ezek. 16.15-58; 23.1-49). Woven into these prophetic texts is a powerful 'language of yearning ... both God's yearning for us and our yearning for God',[242] which carries reminders of the Song and the Psalms. However, the divine husband depicted by the prophets remains the lord; thus any sense of mutuality must be severely limited. Moreover, Israel-as-wife is repeatedly portrayed as loose, shameless and not to be trusted, in stark contrast to Yhwh-as-husband's love, generosity and forgiveness.[243]

241. Cf. Goldingay, *Psalms* 2, pp. 55, 60, 63. Davidson's view that we should see this psalm simply as 'an ode to marriage with its joyful celebration of sexuality, which is one of God's gifts to his people', is too simplistic (*Vitality of Worship*, p. 151).

242. Robert B. Robinson, 'Sing Us One of the Songs of Zion: Poetry and Theology in the Hebrew Bible', in *The Labour of Reading* (ed. Black, et al.), p. 104. Hosea places alongside אמת and חסד, 'knowledge of God' (Hos. 4.1-3, 6); דעת is another term which has overtones of relational intimacy, including sexual intimacy (cf. Sakenfeld, *Faithfulness in Action*, pp. 109-11).

243. Renita J. Weems, *Battered Love: Marriage, Sex and Violence in the Hebrew Prophets* (Minneapolis, MN: Augsburg Fortress, 1995), pp. 5, 8, 23-25, 33, 101. See also T. Drorah Setel, 'Prophets and Pornography: Female Sexual Imagery in Hosea', in *Feminist Companion to the Song of Songs*, (ed. Brenner), pp. 146-55.

Summary
The image of marriage is explicit in Psalm 45 and Song 3.6-11. Both depict the grandeur of a royal marriage, with emphasis on the king's majesty. The psalm shows concern that the bride should submit, perhaps to prevent the introduction of idolatry that could corrupt the nation. The Song here depicts a fantasy about marriage, with one or both of the lovers playing at royalty in ways which both uphold and undermine traditional power relations. Intertextual allusions to other passages in the Hebrew Bible suggested here and elsewhere in the Song hint that the erotic is far from being anathema to the spiritual; *eros* is not worshipped, but neither is God shut out from this aspect of human life. Marriage is used as a metaphor for the divine-human relationship elsewhere, particularly in the prophetic books; their model is patriarchal marriage, with commitment and obedience to the divine lord of paramount importance, while any concerns of intimacy are secondary, and mutuality is not in evidence.

Conclusion

This conversation between the Song of Songs and the Psalms reveals significant similarities between them. A yearning for encounter with the other is a recurring theme in both books, sometimes expressed in similar language. On occasions this is couched in terms of desire for intimacy, a passionate longing from deep within to find and hold tightly to the loved one. Absence and unexpected separation bring an anguished sense of loss and need, which can be resolved only by a renewed encounter. Meeting the other brings intense delight, and a desire both to hear the other's voice and to make oneself heard. Both books present love as something of infinite importance and value. Both extol a love which is tenacious and exclusive, with a covenant commitment sometimes suggested. In addition, the two books have valuable questions to ask each other about the challenge of selflessness in loving the other, the importance of forgiveness, the power relationship between two lovers, and the nature of marriage.

What of the blurring of boundaries between yearning for a human lover and yearning for a divine one, which I observed in Chapter 1? Do the Psalms and the Song also blur such boundaries? The Song presents the delights (and occasionally the challenges) of a human sexual relationship, with no overt reference to God at all. However, a sub-text or counter-melody may be rumoured intermittently, particularly in allusions to other Hebrew Bible texts and themes. These whispers of a bigger story can be heard by those who listen out for them amid the exuberant declarations of the Song's human lovers. At the very least, this suggests that sexuality and spirituality are not divorced or opposed. Perhaps it hints at more: that human love speaks of another, greater lover. Whether such a divine lover would be the type of patriarchal husband depicted elsewhere in the Hebrew Bible, or someone different and more subversive, is far from clear. Here is a suggestiveness which may intrigue and entice today's readers, including today's songwriters, and thus contribute to the blurring of boundaries which I have observed.

The Psalms present a desire for God which is not overtly expressed in the language of *eros* or romance. God is personal, and thus to be encountered in some kind of personal and relational way. Places and acts of worship involve physicality, which can even be described in terms of 'seeing', but the delights of erotic touch are not involved. The disparity in power between God and the worshipper precludes any sense of balanced mutuality in the relationship, which is often depicted in terms of master and servant. However, the language used by the psalmists can, on occasion, sound like that of romantic delight and attachment, or the assertiveness of a lover; at very least it can seem ambiguous. Contemporary songwriters who bring a romantic understanding of the meaning of 'love' (and, indeed, 'marriage') may find language in some of the Psalms which resonates with that romantic perspective. Here again, the result may be a blurring of boundaries between 'yearning for you' and 'yearning for You'. The time has come, therefore, to reconnect with the contemporary musical voices heard in my opening chapter, and to see if they and the biblical texts can engage in some worthwhile conversation.

4

'MY SOUL THIRSTS FOR YOU ... YOU ELEVATE MY SOUL': ALL THE VOICES, CONTEMPORARY AND BIBLICAL, IN CONVERSATION ABOUT YEARNING FOR you/You

For reasons of brevity, my opening chapter on contemporary music suffers from some notable omissions: artists for whom exceptional record sales and high-profile awards have been elusive, in spite of their considerable achievements and some critical acclaim. One such is Nick Cave, whose career in three bands has produced various love songs, some interwoven with religious themes. His lecture to the Vienna Poetry Festival, entitled 'The Secret Life of the Love Song', merits attention:

> Though the love song comes in many guises—songs of exultation and praise, songs of rage and of despair, erotic songs, songs of abandonment and loss—they all address God, for it is the haunted premises of longing that the true love song inhabits. ...It is the cry of one chained to the earth, to the ordinary and to the mundane, craving flight; a flight into inspiration and imagination and divinity. The love song is the sound of our endeavours to become God-like, to rise up and above the earthbound and the mediocre. ...
>
> Around the age of twenty, I started reading the Bible and I found in the brutal prose of the Old Testament, in the feel of its words and its imagery, an endless source of inspiration. The Song of Solomon, perhaps the greatest love song ever written, had a massive impact upon me. Its openly erotic nature, the metaphoric journey taken around the lovers' bodies. Its staggering imagery rockets us into the world of pure imagination. ...
>
> The Song of Solomon is an extraordinary love song but it was the remarkable series of love song/poems known as the Psalms that truly held me. I found the Psalms, which deal directly with relationship between man [sic] and God, teeming with all the clamorous desperation, longing, exultation, erotic violence and brutality that I could hope for. The Psalms are soaked in suadade [yearning of the soul], drenched in duende [mysteri-

ous sadness] and bathed in bloody-minded violence. In many ways these songs became the blue-print for much of my more sadistic love songs.[1]

Cave's experience resonates in various ways with the journey which I have traveled in the preceding chapters. I have explored contemporary songs from a variety of artists, looking for connections between desire for intimacy at the level of human relationships and desire for intimacy with God. Among the works of some of the most widely known and admired writers, I have noted various romantic songs which use religious imagery, and their mirror image in worship songs which use romantic imagery. In these songs, a blurring of boundaries is evident between human sexual desire and desire for God. Some of Cave's own songs illustrate (and perhaps have influenced) this tendency, with love of and faith in a woman seemingly fused into love of and faith in God.[2] Cave's striking claims that every love song is in some way addressed to God, and that the love song is the sound of our human endeavour to rise above earthbound mediocrity and become God-like, raise further important questions, which need to be considered in this chapter.

Like Cave, I have found myself drawn to the Hebrew Bible, where the Song of Songs and the Psalms arrest my attention with their expressions of longing and desire, one in terms of human sexual relationship, the others in terms of prayer to God. While not sharing Cave's predilection for sad or brutal songs and what he terms the experience of 'melancholy ecstasy', I share his instinct to look towards the Psalms of Lament. Both here, and also among other, more hopeful and joyful psalms, I sometimes find expressions of yearning and desire which remind me of love songs.[3]

In the preceding chapters certain parallels between the Psalms and the Song of Songs have emerged, both from their history of interpretation and from conversation between pairs of texts. From these conversations I have concluded that a longing for intimate encounter with another is a theme in both the Psalms and the Song that is sometimes expressed in passionate lan-

1. Nick Cave, *The Secret Life of the Love Song* (lecture given at the Vienna Poetry Festival, 25 Sept. 1998) [http://everything2.com/title/Nick+Cave%2527s+Love+Song+Lecture], accessed 31 Oct. 2010.

2. For example, Nick Cave's 'Into my Arms', 'Brompton Oratory', 'There is a Kingdom' and 'Are You the One that I've Been Waiting For?', all from *The Boatman's Call* (Mute Records, 1997). See also Roland Boer, 'God, Pain and Love in the Music of Nick Cave', *JRPC* 22 (2010) [http://www.usask.ca/relst/jrpc/art22(3)-god-pain-love.html], accessed 5 June 2011, paragraphs 9-17.

3. On Nick Cave, see also Anna Kessler, 'Faith, Doubt and the Imagination: Nick Cave on the Divine-Human Encounter', in *Call Me the Seeker* (ed. Gilmour), pp. 79-94; and Simon Hattenstone, 'Old Nick: Interview with Nick Cave', in *The Guardian* (London: 23 Feb. 2008); [http://www.guardian.co.uk/music/2008/feb/23/popandrock.features], accessed 22 Nov. 2010.

guage of yearning and desire. This desire can result in grievous disappointment, the anguish of absence. At other times admiration and enjoyment of the other is expressed; in the Psalms this delight is sometimes linked with the physicality of the Temple or Tabernacle and the worship which takes place there, which is depicted in opaque terms as a relational encounter, but with the language of *eros* or a lover notably absent. Hearing the voice of the other can bring great delight, although in the Psalms it may sometimes involve rebuke, which the Song of Songs lacks. Language of love is expressed very directly, but in the Psalms a master–servant or parent–child relationship seems to be indicated, in contrast to the mutuality of the Song's lovers. God's love is truly 'stronger than death', because its divine source is eternal. Although sometimes couched in terms which sound surprisingly direct and even romantic, the love expressed in the Psalms centres around *hesed,* covenant loyalty, where a stronger party fulfils promises made to one who is weaker and in need. While both parties make commitments to each other in the covenant relationship, the kind of mutuality seen in the Song is not evident, due to the disparity of power between the parties. Glimpses of marriage (in the Psalms and Song, and the prophets, where this is a metaphor for divine–human relationship) indicate royal and patriarchal marriage, where obedience, rather than intimacy, is of primary importance. However, a hint of the divine name, added to various possible allusions in the Song to other passages in the Hebrew Bible, suggest that the erotic is far from being anathema to the spiritual. *Eros* is not worshipped, nor is God shut out of this aspect of human life. Indeed, there may even be a hint that God is one who loves, and the source of all love.

In this final chapter, I seek to widen the circle of conversation, so that both the ancient and the contemporary songs may speak to each other. For example, as the chapter heading suggests, can the desperate yearning of the psalmist ('my soul thirsts for you', Ps. 42.1-2) connect with the mixture of lascivious sexual desire and ecstatic spirituality in U2's 'you elevate my soul'?[4] In this conversational or dialogical approach, I seek to keep faith with the tradition that sees biblical texts as part of an enduring framework of Christian narrative, symbols and meanings, while I also listen to expressions of popular culture for questions and corrective insights which may be relevant to those who interpret the biblical texts.[5]

On the Ambiguities of Language

A clergy colleague mentioned to me his experience when taking a wedding recently. He noticed that one of the contemporary worship songs chosen for

---

4. U2, 'Elevation', from *All That You Can't Leave Behind;* cf. Stokes, *U2,* p. 137.
5. Cf. Graham, 'What We Make of the World', p. 74.

the day was full of intimate and passionate language of love; although the intention of the song was to express a relationship with God, he felt it could easily have been interpreted by some of those present as simply words spoken to each other by the bride and groom, and by other human lovers. He felt uneasy about this ambiguity.

This experience is one of many which can highlight the inherent ambiguities of certain kinds of language. For example, a seventeen-year old poet, with no religious background, comes across George Herbert's poem 'Love', and interprets it as an amazingly exact depiction of his first good sexual encounter; thus the poem's symbolism (for example, of a meal filled with the delights of love) can register for different readers at different levels, from first adolescent sexual experience to an encounter with the divine.[6] Similarly, contemporary music can produce language full of ambiguity. When Switchfoot sing 'you can't silence my love', the listener may wonder about the phrase 'my love': does it mean 'the love I give out to others', or 'the person who loves me', or 'the person I love', or 'my experience of love'?[7]

Readers of biblical texts also puzzle over what they find to be ambiguous. I have already noted the use of *'āhab* in the Song, where it expresses the relationship between the man and the woman, as distinct from its use in the Psalms, where the same word expresses the relationship between God and human beings. In Hebrew, as in English, a wide range of meanings has been invested in one small word, 'love'. Relational language in general often seems fraught with ambiguity. Thus, in their analysis of the Hebrew Bible's understanding of 'covenant', Norbert Lohfink and Erich Zenger propose that the central idea is of a relationship with God. When it comes to the covenant formula, 'I will be your God, you will be my people' (Exod. 6.7; Deut. 26.17-19; see also Pss. 33.12; 95.7; 100.3), they conclude that it echoes the phrase 'I am his father and he is my son', used in ceremonies of the acknowledgment of a child (such as adoption); yet they also find in the formula echoes of words used in marriage: 'You are my wife and I am your husband'.[8] Simple and direct relational language is prone to such ambiguities.

The issue of ambiguity becomes particularly acute in the language of metaphor. Whereas simile makes an explicit comparison between two apparently dissimilar things, thus preserving the distinctiveness of each,

6. Sebastian Moore, 'Love Trying to Happen', *Third Way* (May 2009), p. 25. What this particular reader made of the poem's more theologically allusive lines, such as 'who made the eyes, but I?' and 'who bore the blame', is not recorded.

7. Switchfoot, 'Hello Hurricane', *Hello Hurricane* (peoplerecords/Atlantic, 2009).

8. Norbert Lohfink and Erich Zenger, *The God of Israel and the Nations* (Collegeville, MN: Liturgical Press, 2000), pp. 26, 86.

metaphor seems to collapse that distinctiveness: for simile's 'this is like that', metaphor simple states 'this is that'. I shall give more consideration to metaphor later in this chapter.

These issues of ambiguity are not to be denied, and must always be kept in mind, particularly when dealing with the language of poetry used by song-writers down the centuries. But these issues need not be deemed so problematic that further analysis and reflection is pointless. Human beings will always find meanings in words, even if they prove to be multiple and sometimes contradictory. We might align ourselves with Julia Kristeva's sense of striving 'not toward the absolute but toward the quest for a little more truth, an impossible truth, concerning the meaning of speech, concerning our condition as speaking beings';[9] but the voluminous quantity of Kristeva's own output gives encouragement that such a quest must still be pursued. So let us now turn to various options for how we read the language of desire and intimacy in songs, both old and new.

Parallels: Yearning for you as Similar to Yearning for You

Similarities between human sexual relationships and encounters with the divine have long been suggested, as we saw in Chapter 2.[10] To revisit one example, Teresa of Avila speaks of amorous intimacy with the 'bridegroom', in which the soul experiences 'a pain, keen although sweet and delicious', such that the soul trembles and even cries out. She feels that a fiery dart of divine love has been plunged into her heart, causing an ecstatic 'rapture' or 'ravishing of the soul'.[11] A more recent attempt to describe the similarities puts it like this:

> A mystical experience is geared to inward joy just as eroticism is. It is that rare moment when prayer, meditation, or life yields joy, serenity, a light, and a fullness in presence. It is when our boundaries lift for a moment and we melt into the world.[12]

Those who draw such parallels do so particularly with regard to 'peak experiences', the most intense and highly valued moments of both sexual and mystical encounters. Thus one observed similarity is a sense of internal

9. Julia Kristeva, *Desire in Language* (trans. Thomas Gora, Alice Jardine and Leon S. Roudiez; Oxford: Blackwell, 1992), p. ix.

10. For a thorough summary of these traditions, see Pope, *Song of Songs,* pp. 85-187.

11. Teresa, *Interior Castle,* particularly the 'Sixth Mansions', chapters 2, 4 and 11. See also the photo of Giovanni Bernini's sculpture in Pope, *Song of Songs,* Plate XIV (facing p. 361): here St Theresa receives the shaft of divine love, apparently fainting with ecstasy as an angel plunges the dart into her.

12. Walsh, *Exquisite Desire,* p. 196.

unity and integration, with a loss of concern for self. For mystics such as Catherine of Siena, this results in uninhibited self-giving in worship, which some have compared to a collapse of the ego in orgasm (*la petite mort*). A sense of external unity may also be experienced; for Catherine, this meant a sense of unity with Jesus and with the whole of creation, which might be compared to the sense of unity between sexual partners who trust each other. Transcendence of self may be found by a delight in the other which draws the lover out of self-absorption. Transcendence of time and space is another similarity. For mystical worshippers, as for human lovers, the past, present and future can seem to be dissolved, or at least irrelevant. For lovers and for worshippers, there may also be a sense of sacredness and reverence, and of something 'bigger than life', of reality being illuminated, of an ineffable experience, a mystery which seems beyond words. The transience of peak experiences is another common factor, with a return to normality reminding the subject of incompleteness and a need for further fulfilment. Intense feelings of ecstasy, joy, peace, wonder and awe associated with the peak experience or its afterglow are not permanent, but there may be persisting positive changes in attitude and behaviour, with increased inner strength, creativity, sensitivity, a sense of meaning and purpose, and an allaying of fears and inhibitions.[13] Sexual delight often arises from the giving and receiving of words of praise within an ongoing relationship, which involves continued devotion of the self to the other, with forgiveness and sacrifice required along the way; these are also themes which chime with religious experiences.[14]

Clearly the scope for comparison between the sexual and religious experience is significant. A number of the attitudes and intense feelings mentioned in the preceding paragraph find echoes in the biblical texts which I explored in Chapter 3. They are also evident in today's songs. Coldplay can depict human intimacy, using biblical language and rumours of old hymns. Whitney Houston sings with passion, 'I look to you' and 'I got you', with the identity of the other unclear. Delirious? sing, 'I have felt your touch, / more intimate than lovers' and 'You've come and burned me with a kiss / And my heart burns for you'. Ruth Fazal gives worshippers the words, 'How long until I see the One I love? / How long until I rest within your arms? … Beloved bridegroom, come'. Darlene Zschech sings of 'worshipping the love of my life', whose loving touch leaves her breathless as she declares, 'I am yours and you are mine forever more', while Halleluia's are heard in the

13. Chuck M. MacKnee, 'Peak Sexual and Spiritual Experience: Exploring the Mystical Relationship', *Theology and Sexuality* 5 (1996), pp. 101-110. See also Marianna Torgovonik, *Primitive Passion: Men, Women, and the Quest for Ecstasy* (New York, Alfred A. Knopf, 1996), p. 15.

14. Cf. Davis, *Proverbs, Ecclesiastes and the Song of Songs*, pp. 233-34; 248.

background.[15] In songs such as these, the similarities between experiences of worship and of romance are very evident. Now we need to delve deeper into the parallels and assess their significance, while also considering ways in which the two may differ.

Contrast: Yearning for you as Distinct from Yearning for You

Many contemporary rock and pop songs are full of 'yearning for you', while showing no obvious interest in 'yearning for You'; similarly, there are plenty of contemporary worship songs which show no interest in blurring the boundaries in the opposite direction. This silence needs to be acknowledged as part of the bigger picture. It does not imply a sense of mutual antagonism between the two kinds of yearning, any more than it suggests an implicit blurring of the two into one. It is simply silence.

Some songs, however, do seem to suggest a distinction between the two kinds of yearning. When Mumford and Sons sing, 'Serve God, love me and mend / ... Love it will not betray you / dismay or enslave you, it will set you free', they seem to make a clear distinction between a loving relationship with another human being, and a relationship with God involving service.[16] A subsequent song on the album seems to confirm the distinction between the mutuality of *eros* and the reverence of worship:

> And can you lie next to her
> and confess your love, your love,
> as well as your folly
> and can you kneel before the king
> and say 'I'm clean, I'm clean?'[17]

In a third song, the singer declares: 'Oh the shame that sent me off from the God that I once loved / was the same that sent me into your arms'. Here love for God seems to be possible, but it is not to be confused with the alternative of human intimacy.[18]

In spite of the ambiguities in some of his lyrics, U2's Bono is another singer who seems to be convinced that a distinction should be made. In

---

15. Coldplay, 'Clocks', from *A Rush of Blood to the Head*; Coldplay, 'The Message', from *X&Y*; Coldplay, 'Reign of Love', from *Viva la Vida*; Whitney Houston, 'I Look to You' and 'I Got You', from *I Look to You*; Delirious?, 'What a Friend I've Found', from *King of Fools*; Ruth Fazal, 'Maranatha', from *Joy in the Night*; Darlene Zschech, 'You Are Here', from *Change your World*.

16. Mumford & Sons, 'Sigh No More', from *Sigh No More* (Island, 2009).

17. Mumford & Sons, 'White Blank Page', from *Sigh No More*.

18. Mumford & Sons, 'Winter Winds', from *Sigh No More*.

his 'Introduction' to the Psalms, he presents as the author of some of them a David who is a 'blues-singing rock star' with a lust for power, lust for women, lust for life to match his desire for God. This connects with the singer's own experiences:

> Showbiz is shamanism, music is worship. Whether it's worship of women or their designer, the world or its destroyer, whether it comes from that ancient place we call soul or simply the spinal cortex, whether the prayers are on fire with a dumb rage or dove-like desire, the smoke goes upwards, to God or something you replace God with—usually yourself.[19]

The various antitheses in this quotation clearly suggest a distinction between the divine and the earthly. In Bono's view, it is possible to worship either yourself or God, either women or else their designer; but a distinction is being made—the two types of longing and desire are not identical or mingled.

If such a distinction exists, is there a tension between the two kinds of yearning? This theme is explored in various music videos. Eurythmics suggest that a woman must resist the hypnotic charms of a 'Missionary Man', or he will mess up her head and deprive her of the freedom to express herself sexually (expressed partly in the studded leather belt/girdle which she wears in the video version of the song).[20] The video accompanying Madonna's 'La Isla Bonita' seems to suggest that the colourful, voluptuous dancer and the colourless, prayerful devotee are two contrasting and incompatible choices for the singer (although the juxtaposition of the two may be hinting at the very opposite, a desire to blend of the two characters into one).[21] Some might see religious desire as an unhelpful displacement of sexual desire, which needs to revert to human relationships in order to find fulfilment. Yet the very use of religious imagery suggests something more, a desire for a deeper, ultimate intimacy which takes us beyond inter-human relationships and into the realm of seeking God. A more recent incarnation of these themes is Lady Gaga's 'Alejandro' video, where the woman seems to face a choice between unbridled sexual expression and the immobile restraint of a nun, dressed in full habit. Finally the nun succumbs to pressure (both from within and from those around her), swallows her rosary and strips off her

19. Bono, Introduction to *The Book of Psalms* (Cannongate, 1999); [http://www.atu2.com/news/article.src?ID=668&Key=psalms&Year=], accessed 20'June 2009.

20. Eurythmics, 'Missionary Man' [http://www.youtube.com/watch?v=GE0s6ET WraE], accessed 25 Nov. 2010.

21. Madonna, 'La Isla Bonita' [http://www.youtube.com/watch?v=opaomcV27o s&feature=PlayList&p=A43BAD8D04337FFB&index=0&playnext=1], accessed 17 June, 2009. See my earlier discussion of this song in Chapter 1.

clothes amid a group of lascivious men.[22] Put in these stark, almost carica-tured terms, *eros* seems to be not just an alternative but the very antithesis of any relationship with God.[23]

Regarding sex and spirituality as antithetical is another tradition with a long history. Building on foundations laid by Augustine, Bede and oth-ers, some medieval interpreters of the Song of Songs turned their backs on sexual love (perceiving it as inherently carnal and self-centred, or at least as particularly likely to manifest human depravity) in order to seek after the love of God. Some of the monastic orders provide examples of this. Noting that the writings of Ovid were prized in the secular literature of his own day, Bernard of Clairvaux would occasionally allude to those writings, while creating a contrast between the overt carnality and desire to possess the other which he perceived in Ovid's writings and the purity and selflessness of love for God. Sexual desire was to be sublimated by the monks to whom he preached into a different relationship, on a different plane.[24] It is evident from Bernard's writings, however, that the language of sexual desire was not to be rejected, but instead to be used in stimulating desire for God, as we shall see below.

In more recent times, Anders Nygren has argued passionately for Chris-tians, when thinking of salvation and relationship with God, to reject *eros* in favour of *agape*, which he sees as radically different. Fearing lest *eros* should be viewed as a way of salvation rivalling *agape*, Nygren compares attempts to embed *eros* in Christian thinking with Gnostic syncretism (the divine spark, seeking mystical-ecstatic liberation from the prison-house of the body). For Nygren, *agape* is not a higher and more spiritualized form of *eros*, but rather is a different kind of love, and he is determined to keep the two distinct. 'When the Eros motif invades Christianity, however, its endeavour is to drive out and supplant the Agape motif.'[25]

22. Lady Gaga, 'Alejandro', *The Fame Monster* (Streamline, 2009); [http://www.youtube.com/watch?v=niqrrmev4mA0]; see also [http://www.mtv.co.uk/artists/katy-perry/news/225577-katy-perry-lady-gaga-alejandro], both accessed 25 Nov. 2010.

23. Another of her hit singles begins, 'It doesn't matter if you love him, or capital H-I-M, / ... you were born this way'; again, a contrast between two alternative kinds of love seems to be suggested (Lady Gaga, 'Born This Way', *Born This Way* [Streamline, 2011]). See also [http://www.ladygaga.com/news/default.aspx?nid=33476], accessed 2 Mar. 2011. Antithesis between the sexual and the spiritual is also a theme presented in films such as 'Priest' and 'The Last Temptation of Christ'; see Douglas MacLeod 'The Oppressed Self: Desire, Sexuality and Religious Cinema', in *Religion and Sexuality: Passionate Debates* (ed. C.K. Robertson; New York: Peter Lang, 2006), pp. 105-108.

24. LeClercq, *Monks and Love*, pp. 66-69; 103; Matter, *Voice of my Beloved*, pp. 98-99, 181.

25. Anders Nygren, *Agape and Eros* (New York: Harper and Row, 1969), pp. 49-50, 52, 164.

Walter Brueggemann resists Nygren's conclusion, arguing that such a view can lead to excessive severity, because it negates 'human, creaturely, lustful innocence'. Brueggemann seeks to preserve a link between God's self-giving love and human delight, sensing that the Song of Songs is a love poem which calls upon our deepest responses, on every level: thus it may whisper of God even as it sings of love between humans.[26] Similarly, Catherine Osborne questions Nygren's emphasis on the possessive nature of desire in *eros,* as contrasted with the self-giving of *agape* (what C.S. Lewis terms 'need love' and 'gift love'). Osborne argues that *eros* may involve willingness to see beauty in the most unlikely candidate, a wishful hoping to find loveliness where there is little prospect of doing so, and a yearning to see that any capacity for beauty in the other is fully realized, rather than simply a desire to possess that beauty. 'In this sense *eros* is a generous-spirited love, an attitude towards the beloved, not a mean and grasping desire.' By this definition, she sees *eros* as applicable to a divine–human relationship, with each side wanting to give what is best for the other. God's love for the world may be seen as 'a devotion not so much to the goodness and beauty that the world already possesses as to the realization of his vision of what it might be'.[27] This perspective echoes the earlier Christian Neo-Platonism of Dionysius the Areopagite, who imagined God's self-giving love as 'the joyous ecstasy of living for the good of the beloved'.[28]

If we do concede that self-interest may be a part of love, the question arises whether a God who is good could have any self-interest in loving. Osborne argues that there may be some things which such a God can obtain from a loving relationship with humanity and from no other source, such as contrite hearts, fine music, upright dealings, and acts of mercy, all freely and willingly given. But the fact that such benefits may be received does not mean they are the reason why love is given; benefits can also be treasured because they come from a giver who is already loved.[29] Thus we can see that Nygren's dualism is too extreme; alongside their differences, some common ground may be found between *eros* and *agape.*

Duane Garrett is another recent writer who argues that sexual desire should not be confused with desire for God. He sees both arising out of a desire for love and significance, but argues that a particular kind of transformative experience is available through opening the inner self to sexual intimacy. Love and significance can also be sought and found through open-

26. Brueggemann, *An Introduction to the Old Testament,* pp. 327-28.

27. Osborne, *Eros Unveiled,* pp. 22-23. The way Osborne sees *eros* here is strikingly similar to U2's vision of Grace ('Grace', from *All That You Can't Leave Behind*). See also Tillich, *Love, Power and Justice,* pp. 28-33, 116.

28. Osborne, *Eros Unveiled,* p. 196.

29. Osborne, *Eros Unveiled,* pp. 65-66.

ing the self to God; but in order to function rightly, Garrett asserts, desire for God and sexual desire each need to be fulfilled in their own distinct realm.[30]

The presence of both the Psalms and the Song of Songs as separate books in the Hebrew Bible affirms for the canonical reader a positive view of both desire for God and human sexual desire. Whatever the original reasons for its inclusion in the canon (which cannot be clearly established), the Song's presence there affirms the goodness of sexual love. Indeed, in its apparent allusions to the opening chapters of Genesis, the world of the Song seems to restore, or even to enhance, the relationship between man and woman depicted in Genesis 1–2.[31] Such a relationship is never opposed to a divine–human relationship in the Genesis account, but is merely distinct from it. Nor is human sexuality presented as the particular locus of sin, either in Genesis, the Song or any other biblical texts, as some of the church fathers and medieval monastics claimed. The erotic is far from being opposed to the spiritual.[32] *Eros* is neither an idol nor an anathema; it is one of many aspects of human life created by God and affirmed by God.

The Psalms make no overt reference to human sexual relationships; the nearest they come to doing so is in declaring the value of children (Pss. 127.3-5; 128.3, 6), which must indicate, at very least, acceptance of sexual relationships. The Psalms focus on the human relationship with God, and do not refer to *eros* with reference to this. Erotic love is neither mythologized nor sacralized in ancient Israel, in contrast to some other cultures of the ancient Near East.[33] The Psalms give no hint of a female consort alongside a male Yhwh, in the way that some might have expected in light of the practices of neighbouring cultures. Thus a clear distinction is implied between human–divine relationships and human sexual relationships; but there is no suggestion of any opposition or antagonism between the two.

Agency: Yearning for you as a Means to Fulfil Yearning for You

In my Prelude I noted views recently popularized in the novel, *The Da Vinci Code*, regarding *hieros gamos*. Learned characters in Dan Brown's novel

---

30. Garrett, *Song of Songs*, pp. 100. 105, 117. In Garrett's reading of the Song, marriage is presented as the setting for this transformative experience of sexual intimacy. He also sees a significant degree of trauma involved for the woman in her loss of virginity, expressed at Song 5.2-8.

31. Trible, *God and the Rhetoric of Sexuality*, pp. 144-65; Landy, *Paradoxes of Paradise*, pp. 107, 183-84, 250-52.

32. See 'Of Lords and Lovers' in the previous chapter.

33. Dianne Bergant, *Song of Songs: The Love Poetry of Scripture* (Hyde Park, NY: New City Press, 1998), p. 162.

declare that men in ancient Israel would visit the Temple to achieve spiritual enlightenment by having sex with a priestess.

Predictably, the novel provides no evidence for this theory, and the scholarly evidence weighs heavily against it. Ziony Zevit's wide-ranging research produces evidence of various syncretistic movements in ancient Israel, and leads him to the view that Asherah was sometimes regarded as the consort of Yhwh. Yet Zevit finds no sign of any sacred marriage rites, even in settings where the worshippers were concerned about fertility. Far from being integrated with Yahwism, cults such as that of the Queen of Heaven were a challenge and alternative to it. The texts which have come to us in the Hebrew Bible make no claim to be dispassionate observations; many are promoting monotheism and overtly hostile to non-Yahwistic religion. While acknowledging this, Zevit nevertheless finds in such texts important glimpses of religious practices condemned by the prophets (e.g. Jer. 7.18; 44.15-19); these texts reveal some details of the rituals involved—and no mention is made of sexual rituals.[34] The Psalms confirm these findings, giving no indication of any sexual activity being part of worship in ancient Israel. If such practices had been present when the Psalms were written and compiled, or even previously, we might expect to find at least some allusion to them, not least in the psalmists' regular condemnations of the enemies threatening true worshippers.

Attempts by a previous generation of scholars to link the Song of Songs with liturgies used in such purported rituals have been challenged by other recent writers. Michael Fox, for example, points out that the Song makes no allusion to myth or ritual, as some Mesopotamian texts do. Nor does the Song invoke fertility; sexuality is seen as a human desire and a bond between individuals, not a source of universal plenitude, as in other ancient texts and rites. Fox further observes that '...we nowhere hear of a Sacred Marriage rite in Israel, though ritual copulation between a king and a priest-

---

34. Ziony Zevit, *The Religions of Ancient Israel: A Synthesis of Parallactic Approaches* (London: Continuum, 2001), pp. 650-53; see also Albertz, *A History of Israelite Religion*, pp. 172-73; Richard S. Hess, *Israelite Religions: An Archaeological and Biblical Survey* (Grand Rapids, MI: Baker Academic, 2007), pp. 332-35. Tilda Binger also proposes that the Asherah cult became a prominent part of official religion in Israel; however, the inscriptional and epigraphic evidence she presents is minimal and inconclusive (*Asherah*, pp. 109, 140-41). The view that Asherah was worshipped in ancient Israel from the tenth century B.C.E. until the eighth or seventh, possibly as consort of Yhwh, is argued from a limited selection of textual and archaeological evidence by Judith Hadley in *The Cult of Asherah in Ancient Israel and Judah: Evidence for a Hebrew Goddess* (Cambridge: Cambridge University Press, 2000), pp. 77-83; 209. The Psalms give no indication of a female consort for Yhwh (cf. Eaton, *Psalms*, p. 31).

ess of Astarte would hardly have escaped the prophets' notice'.[35] The Song gives no hint of sex being a means for encountering God; it simply celebrates the human sexual relationship.[36] Even when Robert Alter says of the Song, 'In a poem that never mentions God's name, love provides access to a kind of divinity', what he means turns out to be a union which recalls the primal union of baby and mother, and which links the lovers with the teeming bounty and beauty of the physical world around them.[37] Martti Nissinen concedes that it cannot be demonstrated that the Song includes poetry from any sacred marriage rite. He does, however, see the Song carrying forward an 'erotic-lyric tradition' that is firmly (though not exclusively) connected with ideas of sacred marriage in ancient Near East. But he understands 'sacred marriage' in broad terms which lean towards metaphor; I shall discuss metaphorical views shortly.[38]

Contemporary Western culture has now largely separated sexual intimacy from the concerns about fertility which are found in some ancient religious rites. But the idea of sexual relationships as a means to connect with the divine retains an attraction today. At one level, the possibility of combining two kinds of much-desired ecstasy inevitably appeals to a hedonistic culture. At a deeper level, the intensity, vulnerability, and self-giving experienced in sexual intimacy (at its best) seems to offer intimations of connection with the Other as well as the other; this can appeal to those seeking identity, purpose and fulfilment. For those striving to heal a sense of inner fragmentation, it can be attractive to think of the sexual and spiritual intertwining in 'an exhilarating embrace of what humans were meant to be—whole and complete'.[39]

Some of the contemporary songs mentioned in my opening chapter might be heard to express an understanding of sex as a means of intimacy with the divine. (The ambiguous nature of language, noted earlier, means that such an understanding can be at odds with the intention of the singer. But if beauty is in the eye of the beholder, and meaning in the ear of the listener, the significance of the author's intention is minimized; the mean-

---

35. Fox, *Song of Songs*, pp. 239-43; similarly Brenner, *Song of Songs*, pp. 72-73; Garrett, *Song of Songs*, pp. 81-83; Longman, *Song of Songs*, pp. 44-46; against Davis, who claims that the presence of the Song in Scripture suggests that genuine intimacy brings human beings into contact with the sacred: 'it is the means through which human life in this world is sanctified' (*Proverbs, Ecclesiastes and Song of Songs*, p. 235). She does not specify sexual intimacy, but implies it.
36. Bergant, *Song of Songs: The Love Poetry of Scripture*, pp. 162-63.
37. Robert Alter, 'Afterword', in *Song of Songs* (Bloch and Bloch), p. 131.
38. Nissinen, *Sacred Marriages*, pp. 1-2, 215
39. MacKnee, 'Peak Sexual and Spiritual Experience, p. 100.

ings created in the minds of the hearers becomes paramount.[40]) Thus, when Eurythmics sing, 'Love is a temple, love is a shrine', this might suggest that sexual love creates a place where the seeker truly encounters God. Madonna declares, 'Just like a prayer / your voice can take me there ... Just like a prayer / you know I'll take you there'; the sexual or romantic experience is not merely like heaven, but seems to actually lead to the divine realm. Similarly, U2's, 'Touch me, take me to that other place' may be heard as saying that human intimacy propels us into a heavenly dimension, while the phrase, 'But you're gone and so is God', blurs into one the beloved and God. As Prince's Wise One and his God-loving Muse slip into bed together, they are also falling into 'the Sensual Everafter'. Meanwhile, Trent Reznor is more crudely explicit with 'I want to fuck you like an animal / my whole existence is flawed / you get me closer to God'; here it seems that the other may be used (and abused) as means to a spiritual end.[41]

Issues of use and abuse prompt us to consider practical and ethical problems which may arise from viewing sex as an agent of spiritual encounter. If sexual intercourse is performed as part of a religious ritual by two designated priestly figures, this functional approach goes against the grain of the fundamentally relational nature of sexual intimacy. This is so particularly if the purported aim is not to benefit the couple themselves, but to release power and wisdom to the wider community which they represent.[42] If, on the other hand, the intimacy is shared between two lovers, this also proves problematic. If God can be seen when looking into the eyes of a human lover, does the human lover become of secondary interest, or even disappear from view entirely? If the loved one truly 'becomes your vehicle to God' through some kind of tantric sexual experience,[43] is this person a means to be used towards an end, rather than a human being to be loved for their own sake? The depth and intimacy of the relationship between the two human lovers will surely be compromised by this further agenda of seeking spiritual fulfilment. Moreover, if the divine is personal, not simply abstract,

---

40. Commenting on one listener's response to his song 'No Pussy Blues', Nick Cave acknowledges the artist's lack of control over the way songs are received: 'You know, people can listen to this stuff without an imagination. They take the whole thing literally. It's playing around with ideas. It's not a diary of my sex life. None of my records are that.' (Interview with Nick Cave and Jim Sclavunos, *Q Magazine*, [Nov. 2010], p. 85).

41. Eurythmics, 'You Have Placed a Chill on My Heart', from *Ultimate Collection*; U2, 'Beautiful Day', from *All That You Can't Leave Behind*; U2, 'A Man and a Woman, from *How to Dismantle an Atomic Bomb*; Prince, 'The Sensual Everafter' and 'Mellow', from *The Rainbow Children*; Nine Inch Nails, 'Closer', from *The Downward Spiral*.

42. As suggested in Wagar, 'The Wiccan "Great Rite"', paragraph 23.

43. Anand Veereshwar, 'Love', *Journal of Humanistic Psychology* 19 (1979), pp. 12-13.

then a human connection with God needs to be directly relational, not one step removed through inter-human relationships, which are likely to distract attention from the God who is being sought.

There are also implications for those who are unable to experience a sexual relationship (for example, through disability, relationship breakdown, or not finding a suitable partner). Are they then excluded from a meaningful encounter with God? All these considerations chime with the unwillingness of the biblical texts to countenance relationship with God through the agency of human sexual activity. Attempting to fulfil the 'yearning for You' by means of expressing 'yearning for you' proves highly problematic.

Sacrament: Yearning for you as an Expression of Divine Yearning

'Eros is the "sacrament" of the divine love'.[44] André LaCocque provocatively chooses this theological language for his interpretation of the Song of Songs. In Song 3.6-11 he sees the man and woman being compared to the sacred chariot carrying the ark of the covenant. Asserting that no human being can live without love, LaCocque further concludes that no one is ignorant of God or deprived of God's care, since God is love. In this view, wherever there is love between two humans, God is present, for 'the manifestations of human love are the privileged loci where the miraculous intimacy between God and humans is experienced as habitual'. Human love is seen as the incarnation of God's love.[45]

Sacramental language can be somewhat slippery, being linked from earliest times with the Greek word *mystērion* ('mystery'), as well as the Latin term for a sacred oath.[46] Church history testifies to various debates about the nature and significance of the sacraments. Some have followed Augustine in defining 'sacrament' broadly, as an outward physical expression of an inward, spiritual reality. For Augustine, sacrament could include the Lord's Prayer and aspects of the liturgy, the sign of the cross, the font used for baptism, blessing, foot-washing, the reading and exposition of Scripture, and prayers.[47] Others have developed Augustine's view that sacraments do not simply signify grace, but in some way also evoke and enable what

44. LaCocque, *Romance She Wrote*, p. 55.

45. LaCocque, *Romance She Wrote*, pp. 55-58, 66, 207.

46. On Tertullian's presentation of these terms, and ways in which the sacred oath terminology was later explored by Zwingli, see Alister E. McGrath, *Christian Theology: An Introduction* (4th edition; Oxford: Blackwell, 2007), pp. 420-21, 429-30.

47. See Ann Loades, 'Sacrament', in *The Oxford Companion to Christian Thought* (ed. Adrian Hastings, Alistair Mason and Hugh Pyper; Oxford: Oxford University Press, 2000), p. 635.

they signify. Thus it is argued that sacramental action brings grace to those participating in it, as created things become vehicles of God's blessing.[48] Sacraments can be seen as 'effective signs', not merely signifying, but also effecting that which is signified, especially by sanctifying, or by strengthening faith.[49]

Traditionally theologians have limited the number of sacraments (to two or seven), and many have retained a Christocentric view that a sacrament must in some way represent the work of Jesus Christ and be authorised by Christ. Emphases on sacraments as means of strengthening faith in Christ, and of enhancing unity and commitment within Christ's church, have also been significant, particularly since the Reformation.[50] A sacramental understanding of *eros* is not evident in these definitions and discussions.

In more recent times, however, it has been proposed that the whole of life is 'sacramental', with innumerable human actions expressing God's grace. Paul Tillich denies a sacred–secular divide, arguing that 'the universe is God's sanctuary', and so 'every work day is a day of the Lord ... every joy a joy in God'. Thus the sacramental is seen to include everything in which the divine presence had been experienced.[51] In less prosaic terms, 'Earth's crammed with heaven / and every common bush aflame with God'.[52] When LaCocque uses the language of 'sacrament', it is safe to assume that he is using it in a broad sense, although just how broad is not clear. One problem with a very broad understanding is that it reduces the distinctiveness of sacraments, blurring them into the wider semantic field of figurative language in general, which I shall consider shortly. Broad understandings also neglect the significance of words, which play a crucial role in sacraments as understood in the traditional, narrower sense.[53]

Francis Landy avoids the language of 'sacrament', but presents views which echo some sacramental understandings. Focussing on the suggestive word *šalhebetyâ* (שלהבתיה), Landy chooses the translation, 'Flame of Yah'.

---

48. J. Martos, 'Sacrament', in *A New Dictionary of Christian Theology* (ed. Alan Richardson and John Bowden; London: SCM Press, 1983), pp. 514-15; E.J. Yarnold, 'Sacramental Theology', in *A New Dictionary of Christian Theology*, p. 516.

49. Patrick Sherry, 'The Sacramentality of Things', *New Blackfriars* 89 (2008), p. 580.

50. See McGrath, *Christian Theology*, pp. 421-24, 426-30. Regarding a recent renewed emphasis on Christ as the paradigm of what is truly sacramental, see Daniel L. Migliore, *Faith Seeking Understanding: An Introduction to Christian Theology* (Grand Rapids, MI: Eerdmans, 2nd edn, 2004), pp. 279-82.

51. Paul Tillich, *Theology of Culture* (New York: Oxford University Press, 1959), p. 41; Loades, p. 635.

52. Elizabeth Barrett Browning, *Aurora Leigh*, 7.1. 820-21; see [http://digital. library.upenn.edu/women/barrett/aurora/aurora.html#7], accessed 2 Dec. 2010.

53. See Sherry, 'Sacramentality of Things', pp. 579, 580-81, 587.

He sees this word as the apex of the Song's credo (Song 8.5b-7), and thus of the whole book. The resonance of *yâ* (יה) with the verb 'to be' suggests to him 'an imageless intangible energy in everything evanescent', while the final open vowel, disappearing into momentary silence, emphasizes the divine mystery. Thus, for Landy, 'in the Song of Songs, the flame of God is that of sexuality'; in the erotic drive between them, the lovers generate the divine creative flame. He compares this to 'a kind of hieros gamos', but crucially without a religious ritual context devoid of human affections. Fire is an image of the fusion of the lovers, in which they are destroyed and recreated as a single flame.[54] Similarly, Alicia Ostriker suggests a spiritually elevating, divine power inherent in human love. For her, God can be present in the interaction of the lovers in the Song, as they recognize, honour and celebrate the divine in each other; through love for another person, humans are sanctified and uplifted.[55]

As in the discussion of Agency or Means in the previous section, so also here we find the Psalms eloquent in their silence. Psalm 136 is one of those which shows God's love being expressed: this is done through creation and redemption, forgiveness and covenant loyalty, even through physical practicalities such as supplying food, but sexuality is not mentioned. Psalm 139 shows God's intimate knowledge of and concern for the speaker, but again, sexuality is not in focus. Even Psalm 45, which celebrates a marriage, makes no link between God's love and human sexual intimacy. If we look at Psalms which express human love for God, such as Psalms 84 and 119, the pattern is similar: pilgrimage, worship, praise, hearing and obeying God's Torah are all expressions of that love, but the sexual is never indicated, even if some of the language used may be desirous and romantic. Some kind of intimacy with God is sought, as seen in Psalm 63, but nowhere is it suggested that God's love is inherently present and expressed in human sexual relationships.

A sacramental understanding of *eros* is occasionally hinted at in contemporary songs, such as Leonard Cohen's 'Hallelujah'. The innumerable verses explore different aspects of intimacy, but each in turn comes round the same simple chorus, with its unmistakable suggestion of a divine presence: 'Hallelujah, hallelujah'. One verse says 'And remember when I moved in you / The holy dove was moving too / And every breath we drew was Hallelujah'. We could be simply in the realm of metaphor, but the religious tone of the whole suggests more than this taking place in the beauty and mystery of the sexual experience. However, other verses explore the darker sides of human intimacy; one of these concludes that 'love is not a victory march / It's a cold and it's a broken Hallelujah', the latter line also

54. Landy, *Paradoxes of Paradise*, pp. 126-28, 256-57.
55. Ostriker, 'Holy of Holies', p. 41.

featuring in a subsequent verse. Cohen's song as a whole is full of evidence of human fragility and the various ways in which sexual relationships can bring pain and disappointment, as well as a sense of the transcendent.[56]

Cohen's ambivalence raises important questions about any sacramental understanding of sex. Most obviously, what does such an understanding say about bad sex? The human capacity for abusive sexual relationships needs no rehearsing here. Sacraments have traditionally been seen as having efficacy *ex opere operato*, independent of the merits of those who administer them.[57] This view may be acceptable with regard to the administration of baptism and the eucharist by morally flawed Christian ministers; but considering an abusive sexual relationship in this light is another matter. Is God's grace inevitably received by one or more of those involved in such a relationship, provided at least one of them has a receptive attitude? Applying such an understanding to cases of rape or child abuse has profoundly disturbing consequences.

A sacramental understanding raises further questions of integrity. It sees the love expressed in a sexual relationship as God's love, whether or not the couple acknowledge this. But if God is perceived to be somehow present and active within an intimate relationship, yet the human parties involved do not recognize it, are they then being abused by this God? If God's love is flowing through them, are they really puppets with little or no autonomy? We might argue that they simply need to be liberated from their blindness, so that they can understand the deeper nature of the relationship into which they have entered. Yet if we pursue an understanding of God as one who gives dignity to human beings, we must surely resist any idea of God as a manipulative intruder in the most intimate of moments, uninvited and unwelcome.

Therefore, if human love is to be seen as in some way expressing the divine, an alternative model may be needed. Rather than seeing human love as a sacrament which expresses the love of God, it seems preferable to regard human love as a gift which expresses the image of God, in which humanity is created (Gen. 1.27); the echo of Genesis 1 in Oasis' 'Let there be love' seems quite appropriate.[58] By this understanding, human beings instinctively seek to express aspects of the divine image (i.e. character), such as creativity, order, and love, whether or not they believe in a creator, but a degree of independence from the creator is preserved, and with it, both human and divine integrity. Those who believe in a loving God may then also choose to see their sexual relationships as an expression of the image

56. Leonard Cohen, 'Hallelujah', from *Leonard Cohen: Live in London*.
57. See McGrath, *Christian Theology*, pp. 424-25.
58. Oasis, 'Let There Be Love', from *Don't Believe the Truth*.

of God within them, and as a reflection of the love they have received from God.

Figurative: Yearning for you
as a Metaphor for Yearning for You

Although less elusive than the word 'sacrament', the term 'metaphor' can also seem slippery, with different people using it in different ways. A narrow definition presents metaphor as of a trope of resemblance in which one thing is identified with another, usually by replacement of the more usual word or idea with another. The literal reference of a particular word or phrase is suspended, in order that a second-degree reference may be released. The similar is seen in the dissimilar.[59] Some writers, however, speak of metaphor in broader terms, equating it with figurative and referential language in general. In this approach, all language, and all renderings of reality, can be seen as metaphorical.[60] In what follows, I refer sometimes to a narrower definition, but generally incline towards a broader understanding of metaphor as figurative and referential language.[61]

The authors of the Song of Songs and the Psalms are clearly familiar and at home with figures of speech such as metaphor, sometimes intermingling it with its cousin, simile. Examples abound in the Song; one of the passages already discussed in Chapter 3 will suffice. 'Your eyes are doves' (Song 1.15) is a metaphoric statement, while 'our couch is green' (v. 16) presumably blends a literal description of the grass they lie on ('green') with a metaphorical image which transforms that grass into a 'couch'. The subsequent phrase, 'the beams of our house are cedar' (v. 17) seems to mix the literal image of cedar trees overhead with the metaphor of house, while in the following verses we find two metaphors ('I am a rose of Sharon, a lily of the valleys') leading into two similes (she is 'like a lily', he is 'like an

---

59. Cohen, *Three Approaches to Biblical Metaphor*, p. 17; Paul Ricoeur, *The Rule of Metaphor* (trans. Robert Czerny; London: Routledge, 2003), pp. 2-5. See also Fernando Balbachan, '"Killing Time": Metaphors and Their Implications in Lexicon and Grammar', *metaphorik.de* 10 (2006), pp. 7-13.

60. Sallie McFague, *Models of God: Theology for an Ecological, Nuclear Age* (Philadlphia PA: Fortress Press, 1987), pp. 23-27 (note her reference to Derrida); Ellen Van Wolde, 'Sentiments as Culturally Constructed Emotions: Anger and Love in the Hebrew Bible', *BibInt* 16 (2008), pp. 2-4; Murphy, *Song of Songs*, p. 41. On metaphor identification, see Peter Crisp, 'Metaphorical Propositions: A Rationale', *Language and Literature* 11 (2002), pp. 7-16.

61. Ricoeur himself presents both narrow understandings of metaphor (based on individual words) and much broader ones at the level of poetic discourse. He explores the possibility that any shift from literal to figurative sense can be called a metaphor, and emphasizes metaphor's 'iconic' element (*Rule of Metaphor*, pp. 222-25).

apple tree'). Her experience of sitting 'in his shadow' could then be either literal or metaphorical, while tasting his sweet 'fruit' is clearly a metaphor for sexual intimacy. Meanwhile the Psalms also incline towards simile and particularly metaphor. We find that God's Torah is 'a lamp to my feet' (Ps. 119.105); alongside metaphor comes simile, such as 'I rejoice in your word like one who finds great spoil' (Ps. 119.162). Elsewhere, the speaker 'thirsts' for God 'as a deer longs for flowing streams' (Ps. 42.1-2). God is 'my rock' (Ps. 42.9). In Ps. 84 we find that Yhwh is 'a sun and a shield' to the faithful (Ps. 84.11). The language of pilgrimage and dwelling in God's 'house' in these psalms could itself be metaphorical for drawing close to God.[62]

The tradition of metaphor remains alive and well among contemporary songwriters. Beyoncé declares, 'You are my heaven on earth, / you are my hunger, my thirst', while Annie Lennox sings, 'You are a shining light'. Florence Welch explores an intimate relationship through the metaphorical image of a sacrificial offering being raised up, while Whitney Houston laments that 'my levees are broken (oh Lord), / my walls have come (coming down on me)'. Madonna seems to prefer simile ('Like a Prayer'), but also offers the invitation, 'I'll be the garden, you'll be the snake, / All of my fruit is yours to take'. In broader, figurative terms, Coldplay explore the 'heavy heart, made of stone', and the 'reign of love'. U2 offer 'Grace', 'the the name for a girl, / but also a thought that changed the world', that travels outside of karma and makes beauty out of ugly things. They also depict a girl on the dance floor wearing a cross who 'has Jesus round her neck', and an intimate moment in which 'we set ourselves on fire / Oh God, do not deny her'. Delirious? also use the image of fire ('You've come and burned me with a kiss / And my heart burns for you'), and that of falling ('Falling into you / I'm drawn to the gravity of love'). Stuart Townend declares, 'Your fragrance is lovely, / your radiance fills my gaze', while Matt Redman is one of many who favour the language of the heart, saying 'You've become the ruler of my heart', and desiring to look upon God's 'heart'.[63]

62. On metaphors in the Psalms, see Brown, *Seeing the Psalms,* pp. 15-53; also Hunter, *Psalms,* p. 15.

63. Beyoncé, 'Ave Maria', from *I Am . . . Sasha Fierce;* Lennox, 'Shining Light', from *Annie Lennox Collection;* Florence and the Machine, 'Rabbit Heart', from *Lungs;* Whitney Houston, 'I Look to You', from *I Look to You;* Madonna, 'Like a Prayer', from *Like a Prayer;* Madonna, 'Like it or Not', from *Confessions on a Dance Floor;* Coldplay, 'The Message', from *X&Y;* Coldplay, 'Reign of Love', from *Viva la Vida;* U2, 'Grace', from *All That You Can't Leave Behind;* U2, 'Vertigo', from *How to Dismantle an Atomic Bomb;* U2, 'Moment of Surrender', from *No Line on the Horizon;* Delirious?, 'Obsession', from *Live and In the Can;* Delirious?, 'My Soul Sings', from *Kingdom of Comfort;* Stuart Townend, 'Your Fragrance is Lovely', from *Personal Worship;* Matt Redman, 'Intimacy', from *Intimacy.*

This inclination towards the figurative, found among ancient poets and songwriters and continued by contemporary ones, does not reveal to us the mind and intention of the original author. But it does at least suggest an invitation to look beyond the surface of the text, beyond literal understanding of words, in search of meaning. The fact that such a search has contributed to the excesses of the allegorical interpretations of the Song of Songs will encourage caution as to how deep we 'delve' for hidden meanings. Nonetheless, the figurative nature of poetic language needs to be explored, rather then resisted.

In spite of the demise of allegorical approaches to the Song, various contemporary scholars argue for broadly metaphorical understandings, in addition to the overtly erotic. Carey Walsh sees sexual pleasure functioning in the Song as a metaphor (rather than an allegory); within the range of its metaphoric meanings is the expression of spiritual yearning. While allegory would replace other meanings, she argues that metaphor allows meanings to co-exist.[64] Alicia Ostriker proposes that the love celebrated in the Song can be understood as both natural and spiritual; she sees it as no accident that 'every mystical tradition on earth speaks of God as the beloved, and that everyone in love sees the beloved's face and form as holy'.[65] Tremper Longman notes the use of marriage as a metaphor elsewhere in the biblical canon, and proposes that we can learn from the Song about the emotional intensity, intimacy and exclusivity of a relationship with God.[66] Commenting on Song 3.6-11, Renita Weems argues that marriage is an apt metaphor for the divine–human relationship, because it captures the vicissitudes of trying to live both faithfully and spontaneously with the Other.[67] Meanwhile Roland Murphy sees human love and divine love mirroring each other. For him, the 'flame of Yah' (Song 8.6) 'implies that the varied dimensions of human love described in the Song—the joy of presence and pain of absence, yearning for intimate partnership with the beloved, and even erotic desire—can be understood, *mutatis mutandis*, as reflective of God's love'. This might sound closer to a sacramental understanding; but Murphy goes on to explain that sexual love and marriage is used as a 'grand metaphor' to express the loving relationship which God initiates and pursues with the community of faith (cf. Isa. 62.4-5).[68] None of these interpretations deny that the Song

64. Walsh, *Exquisite Desire,* pp. 211-12

65. Ostriker, 'Holy of Holies', p. 37. More consideration will be given to her views below.

66. Longman, *Song of Songs,* p. 70.

67. Weems, 'Song of Songs', p. 401.

68. Murphy, *Song of Songs,* p. 104. See also Nissinen, 'Song of Songs and Sacred Marriage', pp. 215, 217-18; Provan, *Song of Songs,* pp. 344-45. Davidson seems to be thinking in terms of metaphor, although he talks of a 'typological' interpretation of the

is, first and foremost, an erotic poem expressing love and desire between human beings; they simply suggest that a further layer of (metaphorical) meaning is also possible.

As for the Psalms, metaphorical readings are more rare. Certain psalms have traditionally been allegorized, in order to make them speak of Jesus Christ (the ways in which Pss. 2, 45 and 110 are used in the book of Hebrews are obvious examples; see Heb. 1.5-13). But the eclipse of allegory by historical critical interpretation has seen the demise of such readings in scholarly circles. Today the Psalms are rightly accepted at face value, as a collection of ancient songs and prayers collected for use in worship, particularly in the Second Temple period. The language and imagery used in many Psalms, however, is sufficiently general and stereotypical to be applicable to a variety of situations; the symbolic and metaphorical potential has long been noted.[69] As observed in my previous chapters, some of the psalms use passionate language, expressing a longing to find and cling tight to God which arises from the desirous inner being. Some agonize at God's absence, while others delight to 'see' God, usually in the context of worship at the Temple/ Tabernacle. God's voice, heard in the Torah, is a source of joy and delight which Psalm 119 expresses, using language of personal relationship which at times seems to border on that of romance. The relationship with God expressed in some psalms also involves stern rebuke at times, from both sides; this fact could still be reconciled with a marital relationship between God and humanity, particularly when a royal and patriarchal marriage is envisaged. Similarly, declarations of the unending nature of God's love, as expressed in Psalm 136, could be appropriate for a marriage in which persistent faithfulness to each other is promised. The divine love is understood in this psalm in terms of forgiveness and covenant loyalty; both of these can have an important place in a marital relationship. However, this psalm also sees divine love expressed in awesome acts of creation and redemption. The asymmetry of power between the two parties is highlighted here, as it is by the recurrent language of master and servant in a number of psalms. When marriage is clearly depicted, in Psalm 45, it is a patriarchal marriage, where the majesty and power of the king is contrasted with the submission of the bride. Perhaps most significantly for this discussion, none of the psalms use the language of *eros* with regard to worship; God is never depicted as a divine lover. Thus, while some elements in the Psalms seem open to a metaphorical interpretation which resonates with the romance/*eros* motif,

---

Song, with human love typifying the divine as it points beyond itself to the divine Lover (*Flame of Yah,* p. 632). Hess sees sex as a 'signpost' pointing to a greater love (*Song of Songs,* p. 35).

    69. McCann, 'Book of Psalms', p. 646.

there is also plenty in the psalter that will resist such a reading. Some of the implications of that resistance will be explored shortly.

Many of the worship songs featured in my first chapter make good sense if viewed through the lens of metaphor. When Jamieson and Townend write, 'My lover's breath is sweetest wine / I am His prize and He is mine', they seem to be adapting metaphors from the Song of Songs and presenting a metaphorical picture of God and the singer as lovers. When Jeremy and Connie Sinott sing: 'Embrace me in your arms, / Hold me close and never let me go / I want to fall in love with you again', they use language of falling-in-love drawn from their own culture figuratively to depict a relationship with God. Similar things could be said of Redman's 'Jesus, I am so in love with you', Delirious?'s 'You're all over me / I'm all over you' and 'We are God's romance', and Zschech's delight in the 'kiss of heaven', 'embrace of heaven' and a love which is 'heaven on earth'.[70] It seems most appropriate to understand these images figuratively. Even if the songwriter is portraying an experience of the Holy Spirit which had a powerful effect on them physically as well as emotionally, the comparison with an erotic relationship remains limited. A literal interpretation of this relationship as romance or *eros* does not work with a non-physical divine partner.

In rock and pop songs, the 'direction' of metaphor is often reversed: here we find human intimacy described using the metaphor of a mystical or 'heavenly' experience. Thus Beyoncé's lover is her 'saving grace'; she can see his 'halo', and prays it won't fade away. Lennox's lover is 'a shining light, / a constellation once seen / over Royal David's city, / an epiphany you burn so pretty'. Bono sings, 'you elevate my soul /...Love, won't you lift me out of these blues, / let me tell you something new, / I believe in you', and elsewhere, 'your love is teaching me how to kneel'; here the human lover seems to be both elevated and humbled. But as often with U2's songs, the ambiguity means the metaphor could be taken to move in a different direction, so that the lover is lifted into another dimension, learning how to repent and pray. Similar ambiguity can be heard from Oasis ('you hold the key to the shrine') and Prince ('Love if u're there come save me / From all this cold despair'): is the religious language simply a figurative expression for human experience, or does human love depict an encounter with God? Only occasionally is such ambiguity clarified, as when Bono sings, 'Take this mouth, give it a kiss', in a song which is a very overt prayer to

---

70. Jamieson and Townend, 'The King of Love'; Sinott, *Come Away my Beloved*; Redman, 'Let my Words Be Few', from *The Father's Song*; Delirious?, 'Inside, Outside', from *World Service*; Delirious?, 'God's Romance, from *Glo*; Darlene Zschech, 'Kiss of Heaven' and 'Heaven on Earth' from *Kiss of Heaven*.

'Yahweh'. In other songs, the direction of the metaphor is in the mind of the listener.[71]

Yes, But ... : Issues Raised by a Metaphorical Understanding

Of the various options considered in this chapter, metaphor (understood broadly as figurative language) seems the most promising in helping us make sense of the blurring of boundaries previously observed between 'yearning for you' and 'yearning for You'. Further consideration now needs to be given to some of the implications of a metaphorical view. I shall begin with literary critical concerns, and then move to issues arising from contemporary culture.

A Range of Meanings

One obvious feature of metaphor is ambiguity: what is this unexpected word or image saying? Is it saying one thing, or more than one? How far can its meaning be stretched? The metaphor of the woman as 'garden' in Song 4.12–5.1 provides a good example. As Landy points out, this metaphor has not one but multiple potentiality. It can speak of something private and secure; of something cultivated, indeed, beautiful; of something created, perhaps by one's self, perhaps with help from others, such as a mother; of sensitivity; of fertility; of capacity for growth; and of uniqueness.[72] Similarly, if romance or *eros* is accepted as a metaphor for divine–human relationship, different possibilities arise as to how the metaphor may be understood. John Searle argues that metaphorical meaning is always the same as 'speaker's utterance meaning', and therefore that discerning the speaker's

71. Lennox, 'Shining Light', from *The Annie Lennox Collection*; U2, 'Elevation', from *All That You Can't Leave Behind*; U2, 'Vertigo', from *How to Dismantle an Atomic Bomb*; Oasis, 'Love Like a Bomb', from *Don't Believe the Truth*; Prince, 'Thieves in the Temple', from *The Very Best of Prince*; U2, 'Yahweh', from *How to Dismantle an Atomic Bomb*. The lyrics of these songs present the other, rather than the self, in divine terms. More rarely, with bands such as the Stone Roses, song lyrics consciously adopt a divine or messianic persona; see James G. Crossley, 'For EveryManc a Religion: Biblical and Religious Language in the Manchester Music Scene, 1976-1994', *BibInt* 19 (2011), pp. 163-66.

72. Landy, *Paradoxes of Paradise*, pp. 104-105; also pp. 189-210; cf. Cohen, *Three Approaches to Biblical Metaphor*, p. 2. Speaking of the movement from symbol to sign in novelistic discourse, Julia Kristeva understands the sign as not referring to a single unique reality, but evoking a collection of associated images and ideas; she sees signs articulated in the creation of metaphors ('From Sign to Symbol', *The Kristeva Reader* (ed. Toril Moi; trans. Seán Hand; Oxford: Blackwell, 1986), pp. 70-72.

intentions is crucial for understanding metaphor.[73] We may agree with him that detecting the speaker's intentions could be helpful in unravelling the mysteries of metaphor, but whether this can truly be achieved is very questionable. Moreover, a metaphor may offer meaning of which the author was unaware; detaching ourselves from perceived authorial intention can open up new avenues of understanding.

However, for all the openness and ambiguity of metaphor, there will nonetheless be limits to the possible range of meanings. If we reflect further on our example, a garden can be dry, fetid and barren; but these are not the understandings being conveyed by the metaphor in Song 4.12–5.1, as can be seen from the references to flowing water, abundant fruit and spices, and a fragrant smell. Gardens can also be unkempt, neglected, unattractive and even dangerous; there is nothing in the wording of Song 4.12–5.1 which clearly contradicts this kind of picture, but it cannot be appropriate in what is presented as a complimentary metaphor.[74]

If the metaphor of 'God as lover' or 'God as husband' is adopted, a broad range of possible meanings opens up for exploration. If we expand the conversation to include the Prophets, this will include disturbing questions about whether the divine lover is abusive, in light of passages such as Hosea 2 and Ezekiel 16 and 23.[75] But still there will be limits to the range of meanings: pictures of God as a lover who is indifferent, or promiscuously chasing after other partners, for example, will not fit what is presented in these texts.

Tension: 'Is' and 'Is Not'

Another important aspect of any metaphor is the tension inherent within it. Concluding that the ultimate abode of metaphor is the copula of the verb 'to be', Paul Ricoeur notes that the metaphorical 'is' at once signifies both 'is like' and 'is not'. Within the metaphorical 'is' always lies the 'is not', implied by the impossibility of a literal interpretation; the literal submits to the metaphorical interpretation, even while resisting it. Sometimes this tension leads on to elaboration in the form of simile, 'is like'. This narrower understanding of metaphor helps to highlight the tension between the metaphorical meaning and the literal meaning. The tension is always

73. John R. Searle, *Expression and Meaning: Studies in the Theory of Speech Acts* (London: Cambridge University Press, 1979), p. 77.

74. Fiona Black takes a notably different view, arguing that the Song's metaphors are often not complimentary but an exaggerated mixture of the comic and the terrifying (see 'Beauty or the Beast?', pp. 302-23.)

75. On the portrayal and treatment of women in Hosea, see Van Dijk-Hemmes, 'The Imagination and the Power of Imagination', pp. 173-87; Setel, 'Prophets and Pornography', pp. 149-55; Brenner, *Intercourse of Knowledge*, pp. 153-74.

retained, since the borders of meaning are transgressed by metaphor, but not abolished; seeing X as Y thus encompasses 'X is not Y'.[76]

Ricoeur's emphasis on the tension between 'is' and 'is not' helps preserve a clear distinction between 'yearning for You' and 'yearning for you', in contrast with a tendency to collapse the distinction if the two kinds of yearning are understood in terms of 'sacrament' or 'means'. In my previous chapter, significant differences were observed between the two kinds of yearning as expressed in the Psalms and the Song of Songs; in light of these differences, it seems important to preserve a distinction between the two kinds of yearning, in the way that Ricoeur's analysis makes possible.

Interaction: Seeing As

Metaphor poses a rhetorical problem, which is also highlighted by Ricoeur. Exploring what it means to 'see X as Y', he asks: 'if metaphor consists in talking about one thing in terms of another, does it not consist also in perceiving, thinking, or sensing one thing in terms of another?'[77] How far does 'seeing as' go? Ricoeur goes on to argue that metaphor works at the level of feelings, infusing the feelings attached to the situation of the symbol into the heart of the situation being symbolized. This extends the power of double meaning from the cognitive realm to the affective. Here the distinction between the 'is' and 'is not' of a metaphorical statement seems to diminish, as the two intertwine in the mind of the hearer. For example, to some of those in the religious mystical traditions, it seems that, through use of metaphorical language, the soul is not simply compared to a bride but actually *is* the divine bride in their emotional understanding.[78] In Sallie McFague's terminology, we might regard this as an example of a metaphor which has, over time, lost its power to create a 'shock of recognition' which disorients and reorients the reader, and has subsequently hardened into a definition.[79]

Further questions about these distinctions are raised by the debates among literary critics and philosophers of language regarding the nature of the duality inherent in metaphor. A movement can be noted in recent years away from a traditional 'substitution' view (in which a literal paraphrase can be substituted for the metaphorical term; thus, in Song 1.16, 'the ground on which we lie' might be substituted for 'couch') in favour of 'interaction'. Here a metaphor is understood to result from an interaction between two ideas in the mind of reader, namely, the tenor or referent (what is meant) and the vehicle or image (the way it is said). In this fairly precise understanding

76. Ricoeur, *Rule of Metaphor*, pp. 6, 253, 293-98, 302. See also McFague, *Models of God*, pp. 32-33.
77. Ricoeur, *Rule of Metaphor*, pp. 97, 224.
78. See Riehle, *Middle English Mystics*, p. 3.
79. McFague, *Models of God*, pp. 35, 63.

of metaphor, meaning is derived by perceiving the tenor through the lens of the vehicle. Accordingly, the vehicle is neither incidental nor arbitrary; exchanging it for another—or expressing the tenor in literal language, such as a paraphrase—would alter the meaning of the metaphor. According to this view, the meaning of a metaphor cannot be reproduced or paraphrased by using literal language.[80]

Debates over the nature of metaphor and the principles by which a metaphor is to be interpreted continue.[81] But however we choose to understand it, it is clear that the nature of the interaction between tenor and vehicle is an essential part of the way metaphor functions. This has implications for the way we read texts in general, and for this study in particular. If romance or *eros* can be a vehicle through which a tenor (relationship with God) is perceived, what does the interaction between the two do to our understanding of that divine–human relationship? If God is 'seen as' lover, what happens as these two words interact in our mind?

The rhetoric of Bernard of Clairvaux provides some interesting examples of this interaction. Using hermeneutical approaches which seem to sway between metaphor and full-blown allegory, he revels in the erotic language of the Song. While others of his era are concerned to spiritualize the carnal in the Song, Bernard seems more committed to eroticizing the spiritual for his hearers. It is not enough for them to be instructed; he wants them also to be affected, with hearts moved and seized by God's love, souls inebriated with love, rather than wine.[82] His comment that only a man whose years make him ripe for marriage is truly prepared for nuptial union with the divine partner raise questions about Bernard's intended audience.[83] For a particular group of men committed to a life of celibacy, many of whom were brought up on traditions of sensuality and romantic courtly love, Bernard creates a kind of 'alternative love literature', in which he seems to be using images of erotic desire in order to prompt and stir up spiritual desire. The vehicle of *eros* is used to transform understanding of the tenor (relationship with God), and, indeed, to stimulate desire for it. We might see this as a kind of 'speech act', with Bernard's words, framed in terms of *eros*, actually achieving the effect of stimulating desire for God in the hearer.[84] Certainly

---

80. Cohen, *Three Approaches to Biblical Metaphor*, pp. 17-23.

81. Searle critiques both theories (which he terms 'comparison' and 'interaction'). He concludes that there is no single principle on which metaphor works (*Expression and Meaning*, pp. 86, 104).

82. See Corneille Halflants' 'Introduction' to Bernard of Clairvaux, *On the Song of Songs* 1, pp. xxii-xxiv.

83. Bernard, *On the Song of Songs* 1, Sermon 1, p. 7.

84. Cf. Turner, *Metaphor or Allegory?*. Also LeClercq, *Monks and* Love, pp. 22-23, 103. Carey Walsh also notes the Song's ability not just to elicit our sympathy for the lovers, but also to ignite the reader's own desires (*Exquisite Desire*, p. 79). Regarding

it is an illustration of the powerful ways in which tenor and vehicle may interact in a metaphor.

Cutting God Down to Size

Another aspect of this interaction between tenor and vehicle is seen in the way it may change our view of God. Ostriker, who revels in the Song's wealth of metaphor, explores possibilities of understanding it spiritually as well as literally. The absence of hierarchy, control and submission in the Song's depiction of the lovers provides for her a striking and welcome contrast to how relationship with the divine is normally viewed. Reflecting on ways in which, in her own experience, 'glimpses of holiness' have always involved a sense of 'powerful connection which is not subordination', she finds the same to be true of any relationship with any beloved or friend, when the connection feels blessed. These 'heavenly' experiences lead her to ask whether 'God's love of us, and ours of God, might ideally be as tenderly ardent and as free of power-play as the love enacted in this Song'. She finds herself wondering if God can be seen as friend, companion, co-creator, and also as lover—one who 'yearns towards us, as we yearn back, unconditionally?'[85] For Ostriker, the mutuality expressed between the lovers in the Song interacts with her desire for relationship with God, resulting in a divine lover who is accessible, tender and unthreatening.

One obvious difficulty with this approach is working out just how limited God can become, particularly in terms of power. The singer Sinéad O'Connor begins her version of Psalm 130 with the words of the psalm itself, as a needy suppliant crying out from the depths for mercy from the powerful Lord. But she then moves away from the biblical text, to explore her own unease about 'religion', which is seen as a human construct devising rules that imprison God. She wonders whether God will ever get free from this prison, and asks, 'Is it bad to think you might like help from me?' The servant suppliant has become indignant and compassionate, seeking to help liberate one who is wrongfully being held hostage. In place of the powerful Lord, here is a God who is vulnerable, and very much cut down to human size.[86]

---

the identification of 'speech acts', Searle observes similarities between metaphor and 'speech acts', but concludes that ultimately these categories cut the linguistic pie from different directions (Searle, *Expression and Meaning,* p. x.).

85. Ostriker, 'Holy of Holies', pp. 48-50.

86. Sinéad O'Connor, 'Out of the Depths', from *Theology.* It would be interesting to hear a conversation on this subject between O'Connor and her compatriot, Bono, since one of his recent songs includes the line 'Stop helping God across the road like a little old lady' (U2, 'Stand Up Comedy', from *No Line On the Horizon*).

Suggesting that God can be this vulnerable has significant consequences, particularly in prompting human beings who seek relationship with God to be active and assertive, rather than passive, in that relationship. However, this kind of view of God will be resisted by numerous psalms; indeed, Psalm 130 itself features an unusual amount of 'Lord' language.[87] As I have already noted, in some psalms we find speakers who are remarkably assertive (e.g. Pss. 13.1-4; 22.1; 44.23; 59.4). However, it is God's apparent unwillingness to act, rather than any supposed weakness, that is the source of frustration in these cases. Only by excluding the voices of many of the Psalms, with their imagery of a divine king or master and his human servants (and other, similar voices, such as those of the prophets),[88] can any sense of relaxed mutuality in a relationship with God be argued.

A Christian understanding of divine incarnation can significantly affect the way a divine–human relationship is understood, particularly with regard to distance and mutuality. If God chooses to be reduced to human size, then God becomes visible, approachable and even vulnerable as never before. The New Testament Gospels present Jesus Christ as one who moves among human beings and shares their experiences. Even John's Gospel, with its high Christology, emphasizes aspects of the divine Word's humanity, referring to him by his name, Jesus, and depicting him as son of a human mother, tired, thirsty, disturbed and weeping, troubled, unclothed, physically active, sharing in meals and celebrations (e.g. Jn 2.1-2; 4.6-7, 31; 11.33-35; 12.27; 13.4-5; 19.28; 21.12). In addition to this is his experience of suffering, which is a major emphasis in all four Gospels as they focus on the cross. Here human beings may find a divine figure with whom a degree of friendship and unthreatening mutuality seems possible.

However, there is still much that sets the Jesus of the Gospels apart, in his ongoing authoritative teaching and numerous miraculous signs, not to mention his resurrection from the dead. Alongside his humanity, the narratives uphold his greatness and uniqueness. Commenting on the phrase, 'in the shadow of your wings I sing for joy', in Ps. 63.7, Augustine relates it to Matt. 23.37, where Jesus speaks of wanting to gather Jerusalem's children together like a hen gathering her brood under her wings. Augustine then reflects:

> Little ones we are: therefore may God protect us under the shadow of His wings. What when we shall have grown greater? A good thing it is for us

---

87. Note the threefold use of אדני (Ps. 130.2, 3, 6), in addition to four uses of יהוה (vv. 1, 5, 7), which is rendered as 'LORD' in most English translations, even though strictly a proper name.

88. Hosea 2, for example, depicts God as a husband who divorces and severely punishes his wife, as well alluring her back; Hosea 11 shows God as a compassionate parent, who is nonetheless holy and all-powerful (vv. 9-11).

that even then He should protect us, so that under Him the greater, always we be chickens. For always he is greater, however much we may have grown.[89]

The parental image of a mother hen with her chicks may have scope for an understanding of loving tenderness in the divine–human relationship, but an asymmetry of power is unavoidable if God is always the protective mother bird. As noted in Chapter 2, Bernard of Clairvaux is another who senses this power issue, even as he delights in the erotic language of the Song. On Song 1.2, he comments, 'He is the one at whose glance the earth trembles, and does she demand that he give her a kiss?', and admonishes the soul that is 'called to holiness' to make sure its attitude is respectful.[90] Bernard, like Augustine, cannot conceive of a God who is 'cut down to size'.

The Sacred Self

The tension between Ostriker's reflections and those of Augustine and Bernard raise questions of eisegesis: to what extent do readers impose their own understanding and experience, and their own cultural norms, onto texts? Perhaps all of us who read the Song and the Psalms instinctively project our deepest longings and desires onto them; their history of interpretation provides evidence of this. Jacob Neusner asserts that 'no one can read the Song of Songs without seeing the poetry as an analogy for the love he or she holds most dear'; thus, he argues, Jewish sages who deeply loved Israel and loved God found it 'self-evident' that the Song supplied metaphors for that kind of love.[91] Readers of the Song sometimes develop a quasi-personal relationship with this particular text, which may produce a version of it that bears a strong (or even distorting) resemblance to its creator.[92] The same might be said of the Psalms, which have been so treasured down the centuries and have stirred such passions in successive generations who have read and prayed them.[93]

---

89. Augustine, 'Expositions on the Psalms', p. 262.

90. Bernard, *On the Song of Songs* I, Sermon 7, p. 40; Sermon 8, p. 52.

91. Neusner, *Israel's Love Affair with God*, p. 4.

92. Constanze Güthenke, 'Do Not Awaken Love Until It Is Ready: George Seferis's *Asma Asmaton* and the Translation of Intimacy', in *Perspectives on the Song of Songs* (ed. Anselm C. Hagedorn; Berlin: Walter de Gruyter, 2005), pp. 339, 354-55. Cheryl Exum wryly comments that 'something about the Song turns even the most hardened of feminist critics into a bubbling romantic' ('Ten Things Every Feminist Should Know about the Song of Songs', in *Song of Songs* [ed. Brenner and Fontaine], p. 25).

93. A deep emotional engagement with the Psalms is clear in the comments cited in Chapter 2 from Chrysostom, Athanasius, Jerome, Augustine, Cassiodorus, Luther, Calvin, Francis de Sales and Teresa of Avila. Equally passionate are contemporary songs using the Psalms which were cited in Chapter 1, by the likes of Leonard Cohen, Sinéad O'Connor, U2, Matt Redman and Stuart Townend.

Each reader of a text brings their own emotional agenda, which will in some ways reflect the concerns of the era and culture which has shaped that reader. Those of us coming from contemporary Western culture are likely to bring to the text a focus on the individual. Paul Heelas and Linda Woodhead speak of a pervasive cultural trend in the UK over recent decades which they call a 'massive subjective turn'. The 'turn' is to what they refer to as 'subjective life'; that is, life lived in accordance with the individual's own inner experience, needs, desires, in order to discover and become who one truly is, the unique 'me'.[94] Gordon Lynch refers to one of the defining features of contemporary societies as 'the sacralization of the self, in which the struggles, growth and interior life of the individual have developed a sacred quality without any reference to a transcendent sacred or external religious authority'.[95]

It is therefore no surprise that popular songs arising from such a culture should have a repeated emphasis on the fulfilment of the individual, particularly in terms of romantic or sexual intimacy. Nor does it surprise us to find contemporary spirituality showing similar concerns, since it too is moulded by its culture. Thus, for example, when one glances through any book of contemporary worship songs, it can be revealing to note what a large proportion of them begin with the word 'I'. The spirituality of the individual is highlighted.[96]

Some of the songs on O'Connor's 'Theology' album also provide illustrations of these contemporary concerns. In ending her version of Psalm 130, she omits the psalm's final two verses, which speak words of reassurance to the wider community of Israel about God's faithfulness and power to redeem (perhaps indicating that this Psalm was designed for corporate worship rather than individual prayer). Instead she takes vv. 5-6, with their striking repetition ('I wait for Yhwh, my soul waits for the Lord, / more than those who watch for the morning, / more than those who watch for the morning'), and amplifies that repetition still further. She changes 'I wait for Yhwh / the Lord', which has a certain confidence and hopefulness, into 'I long for you', which she sings repeatedly. The sensuous tone of this finale suggests a deep-rooted yearning for intimacy, wistful and tenacious. But

94. Heelas and Woodhead, *The Spiritual Revolution*, pp. 2-4.
95. Lynch, 'What is this "Religion"', p. 136. As an example of what Lynch is referring to, see Margarita L. Simon's focus on connectivity, self-actualization and lived experience in 'Intersecting Points: The "Erotic as Religious" in the Lyrics of Missy Elliott', *Culture and Religion* 10 (March 2009), pp. 85-88.
96. Of the 130 songs in *Spring Harvest Praise 2005–06* (Eastbourne: Spring Harvest, 2005), for example, 42 have 'I/me/my' in the opening line of the verse or chorus; the number using 'we/us/our' is 22. *Survivor Songbook 7* (Kingsway Music, 2010) reveals similar figures, with an increase in the second category (43 'I/me/my', 26 'we/us/our', out of 126 songs in total).

will the longed-for 'you' respond to her cry? We do not know. Unlike the psalmist, O'Connor offers no final word of assurance. Similarly, her version of the Song of Songs departs from the original in significant ways. The mutuality of the Song's dialogue is missing, as her version gives us only the woman's voice. Indeed, the 'he' of O'Connor's Song seems to be not simply silent but actually absent. The words she sings are to a third party, the 'daughters of Jerusalem' (as in Song 5.8–6.3); 'he' is not addressed directly. Where is he? Why are they separated? Does she not know where to find him? O'Connor's version ends, 'Tell him that love isn't done, / tell him don't leave me alone'. 'Alone' is the last word, raising a note of uncertainty, perhaps anxiety. The biblical Song ends with words spoken directly to 'him', which, for all their teasing ambiguity, seem to be inviting him to return to 'the mountain of spices'; that is, to the woman herself. O'Connor's version of the Song seems to reframe the original in terms of absence and loneliness, while her version of Psalm 130 seems to emphasize a sense of unfulfilled 'yearning for You'.[97] Here is the agenda of today's culture, the anxiety of the individual who seeks fulfilment in intimate personal relationships, subtly reshaping the biblical text.

Words in Context

I proposed earlier that Bernard of Clairvaux may have tailored his message to the situation of his contemporaries and their particular cultural background. Is this simply an example of 'contextualization', that is, adjusting your proclamation so that it resonates most strongly with your intended audience? A similar question could be asked of singers such as Delirious? and Zschech: when they provide the language and atmosphere of romance for a live audience whom they are encouraging to worship God, is this an example of contextualization for today's world?[98]

Attempting to establish authorial intention is a perilous undertaking which I have largely avoided (see the earlier discussion in Chapter 1). But the significance of the interface between any writer and their cultural con-

---

97. Sinéad O'Connor, 'Out of the Depths' and 'Dark I Am Yet Lovely', from *Theology*. We might ask whether, in these songs, O'Connor is back where she was twenty years ago, with the grief over lost love expressed in her first big hit, 'Nothing Compares 2 U'. However, that earlier song was particularly about the sudden death of her mother, rather than any romantic loss; and some of the recent songs have an assured tone deriving from their biblical lyrics, such as 'vast floods can't quench love, no matter what love did, / rivers can't drown love no matter where love's hid'.

98. As a band, Delirious? were musicians rather than preachers; but it is clear from their songs and publicity that they had 'got a message to bring, / well I can't preach but I can sing', and wanted to be 'a history maker in this land /...a speaker of truth to all mankind' ('Revival Town' and 'History Makers, from *King of Fools*). See also [www. delirious.co.uk].

text is undeniable. Indeed, one of the major challenges faced by those who proclaim anything is the interaction between the message and the context. Preachers and singers, as products of their own culture, are shaped by that culture, sometimes in ways of which they are only dimly aware. This will affect the words they choose, and the emphasis placed on particular ideas. What results may be quite different from the words chosen by previous generations, even on similar subject matter.

Singers and preachers may also attempt quite intentionally to acculturate their words and songs so that they resonate with the sensitivities of their audience. Sallie McFague urges that such an intentional approach is essential in theology, particularly in an era when the new crises of potential nuclear and ecological catastrophe have arisen. Arguing that all linguistic renderings of reality are metaphorical, rather than literal, she insists that each generation needs the freedom to embrace new metaphors and, if need be, to discard some of the older, inherited ones. In her view, if former metaphors for God (particularly hierarchical and triumphalist ones, such as 'king' or 'father') are allowed to petrify and take on the status of exclusive definitions, they become idolatrous and destructive, prisons rather than open, impermanent houses. So she bids us avoid 'the tyranny of the absolutizing imagination, which suggests that current metaphors are the only or permanent ones'.[99] For our day, she proposes a new 'trinity', with Mother, Lover and Friend as her preferred models (by which she means metaphors with 'staying power') for God. Ideas of intimacy, mutuality and relatedness are prominent in each of these models, along with the persuasive power of love, rather than the power of domination evident in traditional monarchical models of God.[100]

A metaphor of 'God as lover' is likely to resonate with a culture in which sexual relationships have a high profile and are a major concern. But this raises questions about how both biblical tradition and the culture in question should be understood, and how the two should best relate to each other. McFague's preference for the language of 'love' and 'lover' may be undermined by a cognitive linguistic approach which compares contemporary English with biblical Hebrew. Sexual love is today prototypically conceptualized among English speakers as a reciprocal romantic relationship involving mutuality, whereas in biblical Hebrew the semantic values attached to the word love incline towards a hierarchical way of thinking.[101] These distinct, culturally defined ways of understanding the word need to be acknowledged if confusion is to be avoided.

99. McFague, *Models of God*, p. 63; also pp. ix-xii, 26-27, 39.
100. McFague, *Models of God*, pp. 65-69, 84-85.
101. See Ellen van Wolde, *Reframing Biblical Studies*, pp. 45-50; also Weems, *Battered Love*, pp. 5, 9-10, 33.

McFague gives few clues as to how and by whom decisions should be made to adopt a new metaphor, or to discard an old one, or to seek the mutual enrichment through multiple metaphors, which she also proposes. Discarding the old in favour of something different risks producing a theology which has little or no connection with its roots. McFague's desire to find 'demonstrable continuities' within the Christian paradigm is in tension with her insistence that theology needs to be 'free' and willing to play with possibilities. She does insist that, when making such decisions, 'the theologian is constrained to return to the paradigmatic story of Jesus for validation and illumination', but fails to explain why this story must remain paradigmatic when other metaphors may be discarded.[102]

Connecting theology with contemporary context, as McFague strives to do, is vital for those seeking to commend ancient wisdom for today's needs. Embracing a metaphor primarily because it resonates strongly with one's culture is attractive, but also carries significant risks. Reflecting on his interaction with conservative Christians from the USA, southern Africa and Korea at the seminary where he teaches, John Goldingay notes that many of them continue to understand the Song of Songs allegorically. He suggests that some of them, as individuals, may be looking for an emotional love relationship with God as a form of displacement, a way of avoiding the risk and vulnerability inherent in seeking sexual intimacy within human relationships. While empathizing with the painful experiences which may have generated such an attitude, Goldingay warns against this 'cheap form of intimacy', particularly when it focuses on achieving good feelings, rather than on the sacrifices and commitments involved in any loving relationships. Human sexual relationships may be painful at times and risky, but 'the Song invites readers to summon up the strength to take the risk'.[103] Here is a warning that attempting to contextualize a relationship with God through the metaphor of *eros* or romance may simply highlight, or even increase, some of the problems inherent in that context. To sing 'Jesus, I am

---

102. McFague, *Models of God,* pp. 37, 39, 49. McFague also proposes a metaphor of 'the world as God's body' (pp. 69-77), which raises questions of self-serving narcissism: does God loving the world actually mean God loving God's own body?

103. John Goldingay, 'So What Might the Song of Songs Do to Them?', pp. 175, 180. (Some of the above draws on an initial, unedited draft of this article, supplied by the author.) Graham Ward depicts the emergence in Western culture of an eclectic spirituality looking for 'good vibrations', a collection of people who are 'unable to tell the difference between orgasm, an adrenalin rush and an encounter with God'. ('The Future of Religion', *JAAR* 74 [2006], p. 185.). Others have noted with concern the scarcity of lament in contemporary worship songs: see Andy Walton, 'Worship is More Than Intimacy: Interview with Graham Kendrick', in *Christianity Today* (Carol Stream, Illinois; April, 2010), pp. 24-29; cf. Walter Brueggemann, 'The Costly Loss of Lament', in *The Poetical Books* (ed. Clines), pp. 84-97.

so in love with you' or 'Feel his pleasure / We are God's romance'[104] may simply detract from the importance of human sexual intimacy.

This discussion raises questions about the direction of a metaphor. I am focussing on the idea that *eros* or romance might provide a metaphor for relationship with God. But can the reverse be true: can worship be a metaphor for human sexual relationships? Can those who actively explore relationship with God discover, in so doing, insights which are valuable for people experiencing a human sexual relationship? Some of the rock songs cited earlier in this chapter may unwittingly hint at this, in their use of religious language about human lovers. The romantic element in the songs of Redman or Zschech could serve to inspire worshippers to enter into romance or marriage with a delight and self-giving love fuelled by their understanding of God's love. Worshippers may experience transcendent moments, when a vision is grasped of a different reality and new possibilities. They may sense that God delights in them, in spite of their failings, enabling them to develop and blossom as people; this in turn can become a model for how they view their human beloved, enabling the other to grow and flourish. If the visionary moment of worship does not last, this might help prepare the worshipper for the way the heady delirium of romance fades in time, and needs to develop into something more stable.[105] Questions also arise regarding liturgies used for marriage: is it appropriate to promise to 'worship' one's spouse, as has sometimes been done in wedding vows?[106] There is potential in this area for further research.

Intent on Intimacy
Another expression of the subjective turn in Western culture is a preoccupation with intimacy. When the Corrs sing, 'Everybody's searching for intimacy, / Everybody's hurting for intimacy'[107], they express a widespread anxiety. This desire for intimacy begs an important question: 'what kind of intimacy?' If we ask the Corrs this question, the answer found in their songs, as in those of many other contemporary singers, is clearly romantic and sexual intimacy. It is in such relationships, above all others, that the

---

104. Redman, 'Let my Words Be Few', from *The Father's Song*; Delirious?, 'God's Romance, from *Glo*.

105. Cf. Gavin Ashden, 'In Love With Love', *Third Way* (June, 1997), pp. 10-12.

106. In the vows introduced in the Anglican church in 1980, the couple may choose an alternative whereby the groom promises to 'love, cherish and worship', while the bride promises to 'love, cherish and obey' (see Anonymous, *The Alternative Service Book* [Colchester: William Clowes, 1980]; pp. 290-91). The more recent *Common Worship* wedding service no longer offers this option.

107. The Corrs, 'Intimacy', from *Talk on Corners* (Atlantic, 1998).

identity and fulfilment of the individual is sought, and the 'sacralization of
the self' most clearly focussed.

But is intimacy confined to romantic relationships? Human experience
indicates that other kinds of intimacy are also possible, between friends, for
example, or between parents and children. Immersing oneself in cultures
less saturated by sexuality than Western ones can help highlight these other
types of intimacy, as my own experiences of living in India and Ethiopia
testify. There, for example, friends (or even colleagues) commonly embrace
and hold hands, without any romantic connotations. When Diane Bergant
claims that 'sexuality is the physiological and psychological grounding of
the human ability to love', she seems to betray a Western perspective which
is wide of the mark.[108] Surely it is our humanity, rather than sexuality, that
is the grounding of our ability to love. We who experience and express that
love are obviously sexual beings, but preoccupation with our sexuality may
distract us from broader aspects of being human.

Some of the hints of intimacy found in the biblical texts may be seen in
these broader terms: for example, parent and child, or even benevolent master and servant. Thus the soul that clings to God is in the shadow of God's
wings, and is helped by a protective and powerful divine hand (Ps. 63.7-8).
The living God to whom the worshipper's heart and soul sing for joy is also
'my king' (Ps. 84.2-3), while the one who loves Yhwh's Torah and finds it
'sweeter than honey to the mouth' is also Yhwh's servant (Ps. 119.97, 103,
124-25, 135, 140, 176). We find other glimpses of parental intimacy in texts
such as Hosea, where Yhwh is depicted teaching Ephraim to walk, leading
them with chords of human kindness and love, like one who lifts the yoke
(or the infant, NRSV) and bends down to feed them (Hos. 11.3-4; see also
v. 11).

A recent best-selling novel sets a human being in a remote old shack
for a few days with the members of the Trinity. The three divine characters
interact in relaxed and sometimes intimate ways, kissing each other on the
cheek and once on the lips. The human character, Mack, has an intimate
encounter with the (apparently female) Holy Spirit figure, whom he invites
to touch him:

> As she reached her hands toward him, Mack closed his eyes and leaned
> forward. Her touch was like ice, unexpected and exhilarating. A delicious
> shiver went through him and he reached up to hold her hands to his face.[109]

Here we might find hints of sexuality, but the intimacies presented in the book
are generally more familial. The novel explores some of the implications of

108. Bergant, *Song of Songs: The Love Poetry of Scripture*, pp. 10-11.
109. William P. Young, *The Shack* (London: Hodder & Stoughton, 2008), pp. 208;
also 138, 220.

a Christian understanding of incarnation: God is not 'cut down to size' but rather chooses to become like us, embracing at least some of humanity's limitations in the person of Jesus. The novel creates an atmosphere of intimacy, but at the expense of majesty; there is no real sense of transcendence.[110]

Goldingay warns that seeing God through the lens of romance may become displacement, deflecting people from the challenge of human sexual relationships. There may also be an alternative danger which mirrors this: a culture which is excessively preoccupied with human sexual relationships may displace onto those relationships needs which should be met elsewhere. A desire for a guiding parent figure, or an affirming companion, or for physical touch, need not always be fulfilled by a sexual partner; indeed, projecting all these desires onto one's sexual partner may put excessive strain on the relationship. Moreover, a desire to find someone who is always available, always understanding, always forgiving, is a desire for perfection which no human being can fulfil; projecting this kind of desire onto a human partner means asking them to 'be God', which is too big a job for them to take on. If the biblical 'God is love' (1 John 4.16) becomes inverted into 'love is God' (with a Beatlesque subtext, 'all you really need is romantic love'), then the expectations placed on romantic relationships become too great. Attitudes such as these may be contributing to the fragility of sexual relationships in contemporary Western culture; a wider understanding of intimacy, and where to find it, is needed.[111]

Multiple Metaphors, and How to Handle Them

Embracing Multiplicity

It seems clear that various kinds of relationship are a feature of a healthy human life. I have further argued that, within these different relationships, different types of intimacy are needed for emotional balance and well-being. It is likely, therefore, that we also need a variety of different metaphors in order to deepen our understanding of something as complex as human rela-

---

110. This approach also raises questions of difference among human beings, as well as between them and God. Others have proposed that human 'attraction-in-difference' (particularly between the sexes) reflects the 'divine dance' or 'difference-in-relation' of a Trinitarian God: see Graham Ward, 'The Erotics of Redemption—After Karl Barth', *Theology and Sexuality* 8 (1998), p. 55; Payne, 'Song of Songs', p. 331; Provan, *Song of Songs*, pp. 345-46.

111. The phenomenally successful Harry Potter series of books and films may be a sign and cause of a broader appreciation of love in Western culture. Romance emerges towards the end of the series, but it is friendship, parental love and self-sacrifice that provide the most intimate and fulfilling moments for the main character, and ultimately bring about the triumph over evil.

tionship with the divine.[112] The foregoing discussion seems to confirm this
view, as a variety of such metaphors (using a broad understanding of the
term) have emerged from a study of the Psalms, Song of Songs and contemporary music. These can be summarized briefly as follows:

1. *Eros/romance*. This metaphor for divine–human relationship is not
   found explicitly in the Psalms, in spite of occasionally romantic-
   sounding language. It is prominent in the history of interpretation of
   the Song, and may be hinted at in the text itself. It features intermittently in contemporary songs, including some worship songs.
2. *Patriarchal marriage*. Although used in particular prophetic books,
   this does not feature as a metaphor for divine–human relationship in
   either the Song or the Psalms, even though both briefly allude to it.
   Nor do we find it in contemporary pop and rock music, although it is
   suggested in some recent worship songs.
2. *Master–servant* or *king–subject*. This kind of image is common in the
   Psalms, but is not used in the Song (a royal fiction is found there, but
   it does not depict hierarchy between the lovers). Contemporary worship songs regularly favour this type of metaphor, while pop and rock
   songs show little or no interest in it.
4. *Parent–child*. The Song does not explore this metaphor in the relationship between the lovers. The Psalms occasionally do suggest it,
   and it is found in the prophetic books. Worship songs regularly favour
   the metaphor of 'Father', while pop and rock songs will occasionally
   explore literal, rather than metaphorical, family relationships.

Other metaphors might also be considered: friendship, for example, is a
notable absentee from the above list, due to its scarcity in my chosen texts,
where it tends to be subsumed under *eros*/romance.[113] Therefore I limit my
attention to these four. Since a multiplicity of metaphors is acknowledged,
how is this to be handled? Various options can be suggested.

112. Phyllis Trible highlights the mixture of diverse and partial metaphors for God
in the Hebrew Bible, some featuring male imagery (father, king, warrior, husband) and
others occasionally using female imagery (pregnant woman [Isa. 42.14]; mother [Isa.
66.13]; midwife [Ps. 22.9] and mistress [Ps. 123.2]; *God and the Rhetoric of Sexuality*,
p. 22), although some of these should perhaps be termed similes.
113. The Psalms give no suggestion of humans being friends with God. The Song
occasionally depicts the lovers as friends (Song 5.1, 16), but this is clearly part of the
overarching romantic relationship. *Eros*/romance is also the preoccupation of contemporary rock and pop songs. Worship songs occasionally present Jesus as a friend (Delirious?, 'What a Friend I've Found', from *King of Fools*; YFriday, 'Saviour and Friend',
from *Great and Glorious* [Survivor Records, 2009]).

U2: Suggestive Metaphors

'It could be about God, it could be about your father or your friends. Or the audience.'[114] This comment from Adam Clayton (U2's bass player) is a reflection on the words of one particular song, 'All because of you, I am'. Placed at the centre of an album full of references to the recent death of the singer's father, the song suggests relationship with a parent, perhaps a mother, when it speaks of 'being born', having 'just arrived, I'm at the door / of the place I started out from / and I want back inside'. Yet these lyrics, coming as they do from an adult, could also suggest biblical language of needing rebirth through encounter with God (Jn 3.3-4). The song begins with the declaration 'I was born a child of grace', and ends with the repeated refrain, 'all because of you / I am'. Here a sense of personal identity blurs into a rumour of the divine name, 'I am', as revealed to Moses (Exod. 3.14); later the album will highlight another of the Hebrew Bible's divine names, in a prayer to 'Yahweh'.[115] Yet this chorus, 'all because of you / I am' could also suggest that identity is found in relationship with a human lover, or one's family, or with the song's audience.

In the passionate impressionism of their music, U2's instinct seems to be to embrace suggestiveness and ambiguity. Examples abound, as seen in Chapter 1; those found in the remaining songs on this one album, *How to Dismantle an Atomic Bomb*, will suffice here. They articulate longing for intimacy as they explore familiar human relationships, between parents and children, lovers, husbands and wives, rich and poor, powerful and power- less. Yet rumours of God, and of relationship with God, persist throughout, in a glimpse of the cross of Jesus and clear allusions to his teaching, repeated references to prayer and to the importance of kneeling, mention of the soul and faith, phrases such as 'God I need your help tonight'. As Bono, in his own words, segues between human and divine love, sometimes confusing them, it seems that all kinds of human relationships may be highly sugges- tive: they can provide metaphors for relationship with God.[116] The choice of figurative language arises largely from the experience of the songwriter; on this particular album, romantic and parental images are to the fore, as Bono reflects on his relationship with his wife and with his father. Near the

114. Adam Clayton, quoted in *Blender* (17th October 2004) [http://u2_interviews. tripod.com/id179.html], accessed 21 May, 2009. He was referring to the song 'All Because of You', from *How to Dismantle an Atomic Bomb*.

115. The book supplied with one edition of the album hints that an original or alter- native lyric might have been: 'Take off your shoes / Who are you, said Moses to the burning bush / I am the great I am / All because of you / All because of you'; see Steve Stockman, *Walk On: The Spiritual Journey of U2* (Orlando: Relevant Books, 2005), pp. 224-26.

116. Assyas, *Bono on Bono*, pp. 120, 128. See the full quotation in Chapter 1.

end of the album overt prayer to 'Yahweh' finally emerges, couched in the
language of complete self-offering to a God who can love, kiss and make
the singer clean, interwoven with a chorus depicting the pain of childbirth
as part of this process. Is this the nakedness of self-giving *eros*, or of childbirth? Let the hearer decide.

'The goal is soul', as Bono repeatedly proclaimed to the crowds on the
aptly named 'Elevation' tour, during which he would also read to them
words of explicit gratitude and self-offering to God from Ps. 116.12-14.[117]
U2's songs explore the fullness of relational life, with a spiritual dimension interwoven. Sometimes the songs use the most intense and intimate of
human experiences, those which bring the most delight and the most pain,
to suggest the possibility of encounter with God.[118] At times this can seem
to present *eros* as a means of connecting with the divine, as noted earlier.
But more generally, these songs seem to be in the realm of suggestive metaphor: they whisper of and hint at another level of meaning. In the struggle to
express the inexpressible, they embrace language which blurs boundaries,
as if to say, 'Vive l'ambiguïté!'

A problem may arise from this ambiguity when the audience seeks a
shared experience, both in a worship context and in everyday life. To revert
to my earlier illustration, if Homer feels that a song is about human romance,
while Marge hears it as about God, are the two able to have a shared experience as they listen and sing along to it?[119] A similar question may arise, even
if two listeners agree that a relationship with God is suggested by the figurative language in a song: what if one of them understands it as a relationship
with a divine lover, while the other hears of a relationship with a divine
parent? Each of the hearers may be happy to explore their understanding of
what the song suggests about relationship with God, but doing so together
is likely to prove difficult, since relating to a lover is different from relating
to a parent. This will not be a problem during the euphoric 'church' event of
the live concert, where the powerful shared experience of the music creates
a profound sense of unity. But it may become more of a problem after the
show is over, as people return to everyday life and seek to build a sense of
community based on some shared beliefs.

117. Stockman, *Walk On*, p. 166. The catch phrase 'The Goal is Soul' was also
emblazoned prominently on Bono's guitar during the subsequent 'Vertigo' tour (see
photos in Bono *et al*, *U2 by U2*, p. 338.)

118. Cf. Sallie McFague's conclusion that 'when people are attempting to express
the inexpressible, they use what is nearest and dearest to them: they invoke the most
important human relationships'. (McFague, *Models of God*, pp. 84, 126).

119. See Prelude, p. 4.

Delirious? Mingled Metaphors

One of many bands influenced by U2 was Delirious? Differences between the two are evident, however, in the more overt worship content of Delirious? songs and in their approach to metaphor.[120]

The songs of Delirious? tend to set various figurative expressions for divine–human relationship alongside and parallel to one another, with no apparent interest in any connections or dissonance between them. Examples abound in their album *The Mission Bell*. Here we find romantic, marital, parental and royal metaphors all placed alongside one other and sometimes intermingled. After the rousing opening chorus of 'I love you from the depths of my heart, / ... and I'm living just to say that 'I love you'', the following song celebrates 'precious Jesus, king of lights', while the third one looks to 'a tower on a hill'. The fifth song stands 'at the feet of the miracle maker', 'who was and is, and is to come, holy, saviour', while the seventh takes on the role of Jesus' bride, who is glorious, on fire with 'great desire' for him who will 'come and take us home / ... your home is where my heart is'. We might argue that a distinction between particular metaphors is being preserved by their presence in separate songs. However, in the eighth song, God is both a king who reigns and a father who loves, while, in the song that follows, God is the 'love of my life', yet also the one who 'took hold of my hand / and taught me to walk' (echoes of the parental figure in Hos. 11.3-4). The penultimate song again speaks of God as 'love of my life', but also of 'my king and I'; the singer is 'in the arms of my beautiful one', singing, 'Hold me, saviour of heaven and earth, king forever'.[121] Throughout the album, metaphors abound and intermingle, with no apparent concern about disparities among them.

Intermingling metaphors is hardly a new idea. It might be argued that this approach is canonical, since a variety of metaphors for the divine–human relationship are found in the biblical canon, with no attempt made to interrelate them. In the psalms which I considered in Chapter 3, God is portrayed in the same verse as both a rock and a person (Ps. 42.9; 43.2), a sun and a shield (Ps. 84.11). Within a few verses, Psalm 119 can depict God's Torah as delicious to the taste, a source of understanding, and a light for the journey (Ps. 119.103-105). The speaker in Psalm 63 can thirst for God and feast on God, yet also cling to and be upheld by God (vv. 1, 5, 8); God can be mighty and glorious to behold, yet also provide wings that give shelter (vv. 2, 7). Turning to the Song, we find that the man is happy to produce a

120. See Martin Smith and Stuart Garrard, 'Cutting a Deeper Groove', Interview, *Third Way* (June 1997), p. 13.

121. Delirious?, *Mission Bell*. A similar pattern can be seen in their previous album, *World Service*.

string of unrelated metaphors, describing the body of his lover in terms of animals, thread, fruit, military might, and then animals again (Song 4.1-5). She returns the compliment in her description of him, laced with metaphors and similes (Song 5.10-16). The juxtaposition of these diverse images in the Song's 'praise songs' require a degree of mental agility from the reader which can feel bewildering, yet the effect is also quite dazzling and almost intoxicating.[122]

We might argue that some distance is kept between particular biblical metaphors by their presence in separate books: thus *eros* is evident in the Song, but not the Psalms, while the royal metaphors found in the Psalms are not used in the Song. But occasionally such distinctions become blurred, particularly when we venture into the prophets. Hosea offers a marital metaphor in ch. 2, but a parental one in ch. 11. In Ezekiel 16, we find both parental and marital metaphors in the same oracle, as Yhwh changes role from father to husband when the orphan child grows to maturity. Rather more succinctly, Isaiah declares to the exiles, 'For your maker is your husband, / Yhwh of hosts is his name' (Isa. 54.5). The use of parallel or mingled metaphors can help express multiple understandings of the divine–human relationship, perhaps reminding us yet again that no human language can do justice to something so mysterious and ineffable.[123] But this approach risks bringing confusion and contradiction, rather than integration, within the psyche of those seeking to relate to God. If God is seen as king and lover and father and husband all at once, how then should God be spoken to? Can I respond to my lover as I would to my lord?

YFriday: Favoured Metaphors
Another option may be to adopt different metaphors, but to favour some more than others. YFriday provide examples of this approach. While to some extent following in the slipstream of Delirious?, YFriday built their success as a rock/worship band around a distinctive sound; they also brought a somewhat different emphasis in their lyrics. The absence of this band from my first chapter is evidence of this different emphasis: they showed a much greater reluctant to use the language of romance in their worship songs than some of their contemporaries.[124]

YFriday's most successful songs are far more likely to be addressed to a 'great and glorious God almighty', a mighty creator who is 'all sufficient,

---

122. Single, sustained metaphors can also be found in the Song, such as at Song 4.12–5.1, where the woman is depicted as a garden.

123. Sallie McFague's new 'trinity' of metaphors for God, as mother, lover and friend, is a contemporary proposal of mingled or parallel metaphors (*Models of God*, pp. 23; 84-85).

124. YFriday disbanded in 2010, hence my use of the past tense.

powerful' and 'our God incredible, immortal saviour', than to a divine lover. God is the 'majesty' who is invited to 'reign in me', the 'God who needs no other yet / you long to share eternity with us'. A divine 'saviour and friend' can be found, but his depiction in pain on the cross prompts grief and gratitude in the singer, rather than any sense of intimacy.[125] When the image of the church as 'bride' is acknowledged, it comes only briefly, in a song called 'Holy, Holy, Holy', which emphasizes the glory and holiness of God. When a kiss is given, it is to the hope-filled morning, rather than to God. The worshipper can sing, 'I love and adore you', yet the song qualifies this with 'I long for you, my king'. Occasionally a more overtly romantic song is found, such as 'I Love You', which says, 'I love you more each day, / with all my heart can give'. But even here, the beloved turns out to be 'my saviour, my lover, my king'—two more traditional biblical metaphors bracket and implicitly qualify the romantic one.[126]

Thus a mixture of metaphors can sometimes be found in the YFriday canon, and rumours of romantic intimacy may be heard at times, but these tend to be overwhelmed by images of a majestic, omnipotent creator and saviour. This seems to reflect the overall balance of the biblical material which I have been examining: the Psalms abound in such imagery with regard to God, while both Psalms and the Song offer at best only occasional hints at a more romantic understanding of relationship with God. For those who understand the Bible as authoritative Scripture, seeking to retain a biblical balance in this way may be attractive. A multiplicity of metaphors can be retained, but some will be presented and explored much more regularly and thoroughly than others. On the other hand, those whose most pressing concern is to respond to today's culture, particularly its desire for intimacy and mutuality, might adopt a similar approach in the sense of favouring certain metaphors above others. But they will probably choose to minimize some of the more dominant biblical metaphors, such as the mighty king and awesome creator, in favour of the less common and more intimate pictures, in order to give a different overall emphasis.

Paul Ricoeur: Intersecting Metaphors
Precision is not required of poets; nor are their close cousins, songwriters, expected to be specific. Prose-writing theologians, however, may still strive for greater clarity when boundaries have been blurred. So I return

---

125. YFriday, 'Great and Glorious', 'Creation', 'You Are Great', 'Come Let Us Worship', 'Reign in Me', 'Saviour and Friend', from *Great and Glorious*.
126. YFriday, 'Holy, Holy, Holy', 'Praise', 'Start of the Summer', 'I Love You', from *Everlasting God: The Very Best of YFriday* (Kingsway, 2010).

to Ricoeur's idea of 'intersecting metaphors', mentioned in my Prelude.[127] It seems clear that multiple metaphors are needed, in order to reflect the depth and breadth of both the biblical texts and human experience. In light of this, rather than simply ignoring the issues raised, it can be helpful to look intentionally for points of intersection between different metaphors. These intersections may serve to clarify the nature of each metaphor, while also highlighting either convergence or conflict between them. Sparks may indeed fly at these points of friction, as Ricoeur puts it; a spark can itself be a metaphor for antagonism, or for creative insight.

Intersecting metaphors may agree with each other. For example, the disparity of status and power between God and human beings emerges strongly in the master–servant/king–subject metaphor. Here is a point of intersection and convergence with the metaphor of patriarchal marriage, where the husband is also lord of the wife. However, the degree of inequality between husband and wife could vary, as some husbands behave differently from others. This scenario also raises questions about a master–servant metaphor, since some masters are more compassionate than others: to what extent might this relationship be benevolent, rather than simply autocratic and oppressive? Meanwhile, the parent–child metaphor can intersect and converge with the romantic one to some extent over the issue of intimacy, since affection, tenderness and compassion can be experienced in both these kinds of relationship, although in different ways. However, if the parent–child relationship is formal and distant, as might be imagined in some cultures between father and children, this convergence is diminished and the inequalities of a hierarchy come to the fore.

As for points of intersection which highlight conflict between metaphors, 'husband' and 'lover' provide a clear example. When exploring a romantic metaphor of 'God as lover', some of today's readers may instinctively think in terms of mutuality and intimacy, from their own understanding of how lovers are expected to relate to each other. But when this metaphor is confronted with the biblical understanding of patriarchal marriage, ideas of mutuality and intimacy are challenged, since one of the prominent concerns in this biblical metaphor is for the wife's obedience to the husband.[128] Or to take another example, the hierarchy of a traditional parent–child relationship in the ancient world could be set in contrast with the mutuality of romance enjoyed by the idealized lovers in the Song: relating to God as a parent is very different to relating to God as a lover. However, the latter

127. Ricoeur proposes that various biblical texts which use sexual or marital metaphors should be allowed to project themselves onto one another 'and let us gather those sparks of meaning that fly up at their points of friction' (LaCocque and Ricoeur, *Thinking Biblically*, pp. 296, 301-303).

128. Cf. Weems, *Battered Love*, pp. 5, 8, 23-25, 33, 101.

conflict might move towards convergence if the parent–child relationship involves a grown-up child, rather than a young one. In this case, it is possible to imagine a degree of mutuality, with the child having a more mature relationship with their parents as an adult than they did when they were younger. Human relationships offer a rich variety of scenarios which can help us explore these different metaphors.

Another interesting point of intersection is found if *eros* or romance intrudes in the master–servant relationship. The hierarchical nature of the latter relationship may then be subverted and ignored, to a greater or lesser extent, particularly if both parties have fallen in love with each other. Here the boundaries between two metaphors can become blurred, as the two kinds of relationship seek to combine. A further blurring could take place if the romance leads on to a formal marriage, thus blending two of our relational metaphors into a third. On the other hand, if only one party in a master–servant relationship has fallen in love with the other, subversion of hierarchy seems less likely, and manipulation may be an outcome.

Thus points of both convergence and conflict can prompt fruitful reflection on the nature of a divine–human relationship, when these metaphors are allowed to intersect and a conversation among them ensues. This 'intersecting' approach neither erases nor reconciles the real differences between the various metaphors. But it can bring clarity and honesty in highlighting these differences, through a conscious focus on points of intersection. It can also claim to be canonical, by acknowledging the variety of metaphors within Scripture, and refusing simply to suppress one while privileging another. In addition, this approach can remind us of the limitations of language: multiple metaphors, 'far from reducing God to what we understand, underscore by their multiplicity and lack of fit the unknowability of God'.[129]

Conclusion

As the circle is widened to make room for all four of my chosen 'voices', a conversation can be opened up between the ancient songs and the contemporary ones. The language of 'yearning for you/You' is found, in different degrees, among all of them. The ambiguity inherent in such language is part of its fascination, and can easily result in a blurring of boundaries.

An opposition, or even hostility, between sexual desire and desire for God is suggested in some recent songs. This attitude proves to have a long tradition behind it: various monastic groups and theologians have emphasized the distinctions between the two kinds of desire, with some suggesting an irreconcilable antithesis between them. Certain contemporary songs

129. McFague, *Models of God*, pp. 97, 181.

reject a sense of suspicion and repression of sexuality which they perceive in Christian tradition, while other songs may be reacting against a sense of asymmetry and lack of mutuality in the divine–human relationship, such as that observed earlier in the Psalms. But the biblical texts themselves affirm both sexual desire and desire for God as good.

In contrast to the oppositional view, parallels between sexual desire and desire for God are hinted at in the language of various contemporary songs. Here again today's songwriters follow in a long tradition which features theologians and mystics, and more recently psychologists. Peak experiences (both religious and sexual) can evince certain similarities, such as intense feelings of ecstasy, joy, peace, and wonder, along with a sense of integration, unity and transcendence, and a sense of sacredness and reverence for an ineffable reality which is being illuminated. The transience of these experiences leads to desire for more, but they may also bring persisting positive changes in attitude and behaviour, such as an inclination away from concern for self and towards generous self-giving. Many of these sentiments find echoes in the Psalms and Song of Songs, and in the language of desire, reverence and romance heard in today's songs.

The idea that sexual experience might actually be used as a means to achieve union with God is a tradition which finds no support in the Hebrew Bible, in spite of a renewed recent interest in it which may be reflected in some contemporary songs. The relational and ethical problems raised by such a view are serious. Ethical objections also arise from an understanding which uses the language of sacrament in depicting human sexual encounter as an expression of God's love. This finds no support in the Psalms, and suggestions that the Song may hint at it lack substance. Seeing human *eros* as a reflection of the image of God is preferable. The presence of both the Psalms and the Song in the Hebrew Bible encourages canonical readers to see desire for God and sexual desire as neither identical nor opposed, but clearly distinct from each other.

The conversation leads most fruitfully into the realm of the figurative, particularly metaphor (understood in broad terms). In the language of sexual desire we find potential metaphors for relationship with God, and in the language of religious worship possible metaphors for human relationships. The imagery in various contemporary songs can be understood metaphorically, although the direction of the metaphor is at times debatable. The ubiquity of metaphor in the Psalms and Song indicates an openness to figurative understandings in these texts which need not preclude literal approaches. However, while the sexual imagery of the Song might be seen as a metaphor for divine–human relationships, we must note that the Psalms avoid the imagery of romance or marriage when depicting divine–human relationships.

Embracing metaphor raises various issues. A range of meanings becomes possible, although this has limits. A distinction between tenor and vehicle is preserved, although it may become blurred when the two are seen as interactive (for example, if the metaphor of *eros* is used to stimulate human desire for God). If God is seen as lover or husband, this can cut God down to human size in our understanding, creating a sense of mutuality in the divine–human relationship. This idea will be resisted by the Psalms and by much of theological tradition, but is attractive to some in today's culture, and also resonates with aspects of a Christian understanding of divine incarnation.

Contemporary culture raises further issues for a metaphorical approach. If readers of the Song and the Psalms instinctively project their deepest desires onto these texts, this will inevitably affect any metaphorical understanding. The subjective turn in today's culture will foreground the spirituality of the individual. Attempts to relate biblical metaphors to culture can lead to a distorted picture of both, not least in understanding the nature of intimacy, which extends beyond *eros* into other relationships. Negation of human sexual relationships in favour of relationship with God can prove destructive, as can any idolizing of sexual intimacy at the expense of all other kinds of intimacy.

The songs which I have examined, both ancient and contemporary, remind us that various different kinds of relationship are a feature of healthy human life. A corresponding variety of relational metaphors may be needed in exploring human relationship with the divine. The metaphors I have highlighted, which arise from my chosen biblical and contemporary texts, are *eros/ romance*, patriarchal marriage, master–servant/king–subject, and parent–child. While it can be attractive to reject certain of these metaphors entirely and to propose alternatives, there is value in engaging with what we have inherited. One approach available to songwriters and other writers today is ambiguity, whereby a depiction of different human relationships is interlaced with suggestions that these provide metaphorical glimpses of a relationship with God. Another approach is simply to mingle the various metaphors in songs of worship, setting them in parallel alongside each other and giving no attention to discrepancies or imbalances between them. A more nuanced alternative is to use a mixture of metaphors, but with some favoured above others; this is done in an effort to reflect the overall balance of the biblical material, or else to subvert the biblical balance in favour of a different emphasis. For those seeking more clarity in analysis, a fruitful option is to keep the metaphors distinct, while also looking for points of intersection between them; this leads to reflection on how they converge and conflict at those points. In this way conversation continues, as the metaphors interact.

FINALE

'YOU'VE GOT THE LOVE I NEED TO SEE ME THROUGH'

The importance and power of music, particularly of song, is a timeless mystery acknowledged by people of every culture and era. Its connection with what human beings hold most dear is repeatedly evident.[1] As one novelist muses, 'maybe we are just creatures in search of exaltation. …Song shows us a world that is worthy of our yearning, it shows us our selves as they might be, if we were worthy of the world.'[2] Here are echoes of a songwriter's more overtly religious reflection, already mentioned in the previous chapter, that 'the love song is the sound of our endeavours to become God-like, to rise up and above the earthbound and the mediocre'.[3] Songs can express our deepest hopes and desires, as we long to become more than we are and strive for something greater. Often that longing is couched in relational terms, as a 'yearning for you/You'.

A blurring of boundaries between these two kinds of yearning in contemporary culture has been examined in the preceding chapters. The song cited at the head of this Finale and mentioned in my opening chapter provides one of many examples. 'You Got the Love' was initially recorded by Candi Staton in 1986. In this gospel version the 'Lord' and the 'saviour's love' in the lyrics clearly speak of a divine You; the official video of her version of the song depicts a benevolent angel stepping off the roof of St Paul's cathedral to bring grace to needy people on the streets of London. During the 1990s, the song went through various incarnations, repeatedly becoming a hit single and a favourite on the UK club and rave circuits. It re-emerged briefly in

---

1. When the Voyager space probes were launched in 1977, they carried messages designed to express human identity and values to any other life form which might eventually intercept them. These messages featured a selection of vocal and instrumental music on a 'Golden Record'; see [http://voyager.jpl.nasa.gov/spacecraft/music.html]; accessed 12 April 2011.

2. Salman Rushdie, *The Ground Beneath Her Feet* (London: Random House, 1999), pp. 19-20. Rushdie's poem, with the same title, became one of the U2 songs cited in Chapter 1.

3. Nick Cave, *Secret Life of the Love Song* (see the opening of Chapter 4). In West Papua, the human soul is sometimes called the 'seed of singing'; see Jay Griffiths, 'Land of the Freedom Singers', in *The Guardian Weekly* (London: 1 Apr. 2011), p. 30.

2004 as a soundtrack for the 'Sex in the City' television series, and then again emphatically in 2009 as 'You've Got the Love', a hit single for Florence and the Machine. In all these versions it remains a gospel song, declaring that 'I know my saviour's love is real'. It has fed into the corporate spirituality of the rave scene in ways that cannot be quantified. Now it stands as the climax to an album by Florence Welch full of songs about human intimacy and particularly romance, many of them addressed to 'you'. To some listeners, this final song on the album might speak of romance by using religious imagery; to others, it might suggest that romance, or the language of romance, offers a way to connect with the divine. Who is this 'you', the one who has 'got the love to see me through'?[4] It is left to the listener to decide.

In my opening chapter, I observed ambiguities in the language of some of the most popular songs of the past decade in the UK. The language of romance is evident in various songs which are popular in certain churches, where they are used as vehicles for understanding and worshipping God. This presents a mirror image of mainstream culture, where the language of worship and the divine is to be found in a host of rock (and some pop) songs. All this results in a blurring of the boundaries between human sexual desire ('yearning for you') and desire for God ('yearning for You') in popular culture.

A conversation was begun in Chapter 2 between these contemporary songs and particular biblical songs, namely, the Psalms and Song of Songs. A selective examination of the history of interpretation of both these biblical texts revealed various developments in the ways in which they have been understood. Both the Song and the Psalms have been treasured and much discussed down the centuries. At times, both have been read as expressing desire for intimacy with God, and some commentators have linked the two books in this regard. Others have avoided sexual or romantic imagery, while still affirming that passion for God is expressed in both texts. Understanding love poetry in religious terms proves to be a longstanding tradition; the demise of this view with regard to the Song of Songs is quite recent, and reflects developments in the culture of modern and postmodern interpreters. In recent times the Song's lyric earthiness has been reclaimed, a thoroughly human, sexual 'yearning for you'. Yet its resonance with understandings of a divine–human relationship is also being rediscovered, giving a sense that it may still have something to say about humanity's 'yearning for You'.

---

4. See Sophie Heawood, *I Was So Drunk I Fell Onto the Stage*, Interview with Candi Staton in *The Guardian*, London: 24 Mar. 2006); [http://www.guardian.co.uk/music/2006/mar/24/popandrock], accessed 13 Apr. 2011; Heikki Suasalo, 'Interview with Candi Staton' [http://www.soulexpress.net/candistaton.htm], accessed 12 Apr. 2011. See also [http://www.youtube.com/watch?v=wMNVrW2kNF0] and [http://www.youtube.com/watch?v=fhrmtqXeZWw&feature=related], both accessed 14 Apr. 2011. The song 'You Got the Love' was written by Anthony B. Stephens, Arnecia Michelle Harris and John Bellamy; see also [http://en.wikipedia.org/wiki/You_Got_the_Love].

In Chapter 3 the dialogue between the two biblical texts was taken further. Particular Psalms were set in conversation with particular passages
from the Song of Songs. Similarities were noted in the language of passionate desire, and in deep distress felt at times of separation from the other. A
relationship between persons is indicated; intimacy between them is evident in the Song, and sometimes in the Psalms. Both texts indicate that
encountering the beloved other is possible, as is hearing and speaking, and
even seeing (although what the latter means for the Psalms is unclear). Both
books extol the value and importance of love, using terms which sometimes
sound similar; this ambiguity in language might be attractive to some of
today's songwriters. However, the Psalms generally present a divine figure
who loves, but whose majesty, greatness and holiness sets him apart from
human beings. The disparity of power evident in the Psalms' regular use of
master–servant imagery weighs against any sense of balanced mutuality, as
seen between the two lovers in the Song.

Having observed language of yearning in the biblical songs, I welcomed
the contemporary songs to rejoin the conversation in Chapter 4, so that ancient
and modern voices could be heard together. Some recent songs suggest that
sexual desire is a very distinct alternative which is opposed to desire for God,
or at least opposed to Christian tradition. In contrast to this, however, similarities between these two kinds of desire and their outcomes are regularly
indicated in today's songs, and have been explored by religious mystics in the
past. Suggestions can be heard in some songs and other contemporary voices
that human sexual experience may be a means of encounter with God; these
are resisted by the biblical voices. The idea that sexual love between humans
may be a sacrament of such an encounter is also problematic. A figurative
understanding, however, finds more common ground among the ancient and
contemporary voices. Thus the language of worship can provide metaphors
for human sexual relationships, expressing in heartfelt and hyperbolic terms
just how valuable the other person and the relationship itself is. Moreover,
relationship with God can be explored using metaphors which draw on the
language of human sexual relationship and intimacy.

The resistance to sexual metaphor observed in the Psalms, however,
alerts us to issues raised by this approach. A God who is seen as 'lover'
or 'husband' may be cut down to a more approachable, human size than is
possible with the majestic figure of the Psalms, despite the attraction of this
view to some people today. An obsession with sexual intimacy in today's
culture may distract from the value of other kinds of intimacy, while a pro-
jection of romance onto a relationship with God may distract people from
the value and demands of human sexual intimacy.

Nonetheless, while taking these reservations into account, I conclude
that *eros*/romance may serve as a metaphor for relationship with God, provided it is used alongside a variety of other metaphors. If these metaphors

are simply mingled, the result may be a breadth and richness of understanding; but this mingling can also bring confusion about how to relate to God. Ambiguity will always remain in the realm of poetry and song lyrics, but clarity can also be sought through theological reflection focussed on points at which metaphors intersect. Some of these different metaphors will need to be balanced in tension with each other, with particular attention given to areas of conflict and convergence between them. There may also be times to favour certain metaphors above others, in order to meet the pastoral needs of contemporary culture, but those who value the Bible as authoritative will want to explore, rather than abandon, the biblical metaphors.

As I conclude my writing, various events have been taking place to mark the four hundredth anniversary of the publication of the King James Bible. A number of commentators note the profound influence of this Bible translation, not only in the churches, but far more broadly, on the language and culture of the English speaking world (including its music). Some lament the demise of the King James Version, both in popular culture and in the churches, and wonder what, if anything, may succeed it. What kind of words will shape our values, beliefs and public discourse in the years that lie ahead? Which texts will people use to make sense of their lived experience and so construct their lives?[5]

Amid the multiplicity of voices to be heard in today's information and media-saturated world, I contend that popular music is one of the more significant, and will continue to be so. Music provides entertainment, but it also contributes to many people's meaning-making: it reflects and shapes the way they perceive and speak about important aspects of their life, including the relational and the spiritual. Those of us who want to understand and connect with our culture, particularly its desire for intimacy, need to continue listening to the voices of today's songs.

Many of us who value the Bible will want to listen afresh to these ancient texts in the light of contemporary voices. Those such as myself, who see the Bible as a part of divine revelation, will give particular weight to what we find in its pages as authoritative. We will allow the Scriptures to ask searching questions of our culture and its voices, as part of our commitment to shaping that culture for a healthy future. But we also need to hear the cultural voices, and to allow them to ask searching questions of the biblical texts. In so doing, we can come to understand both the ancient texts and today's world more deeply. Today's songs can speak to yesterday's. Conversation between different voices, in all its messiness, subtlety and fruitfulness, must be a continuing feature of the way ahead.

---

5. Cf. Worton and Still, 'Introduction', in *Intertextuality* (ed. Worton and Still), p. 19.

BIBLIOGRAPHY

Ackerman, Susan, 'The Personal Is Political: Covenantal and Affectionate Love ('āhēb, 'ahăbâ) in the Hebrew Bible', *VT* 52 (2002), pp. 437-458.

Adams, Guy, 'Beyoncé—Born to Be a Star, *The Independent*, (6 Feb. 2011), [http://www. independent.co.uk/news/people/profiles/beyonc-born-to-be-a-star-1890924. html], accessed 14 Mar. 2011.

Adorno, Theodor W., 'On Popular Music', in *On Record* (ed. Frith and Goodwin), pp. 301-14.

Aichele, George (ed.) *Culture, Entertainment and the Bible* (JSOTSup, 309; Sheffield: Sheffield Academic Press, 2000).

Albertz, Rainer, *A History of Israelite Religion in the Old Testament Period* (2 vols.; trans. John Bowden; London: SCM Press, 1994).

Alexander, Philip S., 'The Song of Songs as Historical Allegory: Notes on the Development of an Exegetical Tradition', in *Targumic and Cognate Studies* (ed. Kevin J. Cathcart and Michael Maher; Sheffield: Sheffield Academic Press, 1996), pp. 14-29.

—*The Targum of Canticles* (The Aramaic Bible, 17a; London: T. & T. Clark, 2003).

Alkier, Stefan K., 'Intertextuality and the Semiotics of Biblical Texts', in *Reading the Bible Intertextually* (ed. Hays *et al.*), pp. 3-21.

Allen, Leslie C., *Psalms 101-150* (Word Biblical Commentary, 21; Waco, TX: Word, 1983).

—'Psalm 73: an Analysis', *TynB* 33 (1982), pp. 93-118.

Alter, Robert, 'Afterword', in *The Song of Songs* (Bloch and Bloch), pp. 119-31.

—*The Book of Psalms: A Translation and Commentary* (New York: W.W. Norton, 2007).

—*The Art of Biblical Poetry* (New York: Basic Books, 1985), pp. 3-26.

Ambrose of Milan, *Concerning Virgins* [http://www.ccel.org/ccel/schaff/npnf210.iv. vii. ii.vii.html?scrBook=Ps&scrCh=45&scrV=9#iv.vii.ii.vii-p11.1], accessed 5 June 2009.

Anderson, A.A., *Psalms 1-72* (New Century Bible Commentary; London: Marshall, Morgan and Scott, 1972).

—*Psalms 73-150* (New Century Bible Commentary; London: Marshall, Morgan and Scott, 1972).

Anonymous, *Gita Govinda* [http://en.wikisource.org/wiki/Gita_Govinda], accessed 12 June 2010.

—*Hymns and Psalms* (London: Methodist Publishing House, 1983).

—*Spring Harvest Praise 2005-06* (Eastbourne: Spring Harvest, 2005).

—*Survivor Songbook 7* (Kingsway Music, 2010).

—*The Cloud of Unknowing* [http://www.ccel.org/ccel/anonymous2/cloud.xxxii.html], accessed 25 Aug. 2009.

—*The Midrash on Psalms* (2 vols.; trans. William G. Braude; New Haven, CT: Yale University Press, 1959).

—*Zohar: Bereshith to Lekh Lekha* (trans. Nuro de Manhar) [http://www.sacred-texts.com/jud/zdm/index.htm], accessed 27 Aug. 2009.

Anselm, *Meditations,* X [http://www.ccel.org/ccel/anselm/meditations.html], accessed 25 Aug. 2009.

Aqiba, Rabbi, *Tosefta, Sanhedrin* (trans. Herbert Danby; London: SPCK, 1919), [http://www.toseftaonline.org/seforim/tractate_sanhedrin_mishna_and_tosefta_1919.pdf], accessed 7 May 2010.

Arbel, Daphna V., 'My Vineyard, my Very Own, is for Myself', in *The Song of Songs* (ed. Brenner and Fontaine), pp. 90-101.

Ashden, Gavin, 'In Love With Love', *Third Way* (June, 1997), pp. 10-12.

Assayas, Michka, *Bono on Bono: Conversations with Michka Assayas* (London: Hodder & Stoughton, 2005).

Assis, Eliyahu, *Flashes of Fire: A Literary Analysis of the Song of Songs* (London: T. & T. Cark, 2009).

Astell, Ann W., *The Song of Songs in the Middle Ages* (Ithaca, NY: Cornell University Press, 1990).

Astor, Peter, 'The Poetry of Rock: Song Lyrics Are Not Poems But the Words Still Matter', *PopMus* 29 (2010), pp. 143-48.

Athanasius of Alexandria, *Letter to Marcellinus, Concerning the Psalms* [http://www.fisheaters.com/psalmsathanasiusletter.html], accessed 30 June 2009.

Attridge, Harold W. and Margot E. Fassler (eds.), *Psalms in Community: Jewish and Christian Textual, Liturgical and Artistic Traditions* (SBL Symposium, 25; Atlanta, GA: Society of Biblical Literature, 2003).

Augustine of Hippo, *Confessions* (trans. Albert C. Outler; Philadephia, PA: Westminster Press, 1955), [http://www.ccel.org/ccel/augustine/confessions.xii.html], accessed 22 June 2009.

Augustine of Hippo, *Expositions on the Psalms* (trans. A. Cleveland Coxe; ed. Philip Schaff; A Select Library of the Nicene and Post-Nicene Fathers of the Christian Church, VIII; New York: Christian Literature Company, 1888).

—*St Augustine on the Psalms, II* (trans. Scholastica Heben and Felicitas Corrigen; London: Longmans, Green and Co, 1961).

Bach, Alice, *Religion, Politics, Media in the Broadband Era* (Sheffield: Sheffield Phoenix Press, 2005).

Balbachan, Fernando, '"Killing Time": Metaphors and Their Implications in Lexicon and Grammar', *metaphorik.de* 10 (2006), pp. 6-30.

Barthes, Roland, 'The Grain of the Voice', in *On Record* (ed. Frith and Goodwin), pp. 293-300.

Barton, John, 'The Canonicity of the Song of Songs', in *Perspectives on the Song of Songs* (ed. Anselm C. Hagedorn; Berlin: de Gruyter, 2005), pp. 1-7.

Beaudoin, Tom, 'Popular Culture Scholarship as a Spiritual Exercise', in *Between Sacred and Profane* (ed. Lynch), pp. 94-110.

Beckwith, Jeremy, 'God Gave Rock and Roll to You' (Channel 4 broadcast, 23 Dec. 2006).

Begbie, Jeremy, *Resounding Truth: Christian Wisdom in the World of Music* (Grand Rapids, MI: Baker Academic, 2007).

Bekkenkamp, Jonneke, 'Into Another Scene of Choices: The Theological Value of the Song of Songs', in T*he Song of Songs* (ed. Brenner and Fontaine), pp. 55-89.

Bellinger, W.R. Jr, *Psalms: Reading and Studying the Book of Praises* (Peabody, MA: Hendrickson, 1992).

Bergant, Dianne, *Song of Songs: The Love Poetry of Scripture* (Hyde Park, NY: New City Press, 1998).

—*The Song of Songs* (Berit Olam: Collegeville, MN: Liturgical Press, 2001).

Bernard of Clairvaux, *On the Song of Songs,* (2 vols.; trans. Kilian Walsh; Kalamazoo, MI: Cistercian Publications, 1977).

—*Sermons on Conversion* (trans. Marie-Bernard Said; Kalamazoo, MI: Cistercian Publications, 1981).

—*The Song of Songs: Selections from the Sermons of Bernard of Clairvaux* (trans. and ed. H.C. Backhouse; London: Hodder & Stoughton, 1990).

Berryman, John, 'Eleven Addresses to the Lord', in *Collected Poems* [http://www.pan-hala.net/Archive/Eleven_Addresses_1.html], accessed 14 Nov. 2010.

Binger, Tilda, *Asherah: Goddesses in Ugarit, Israel and the Old Testament* (JSOT Sup. 232; Sheffield: Sheffield Academic Press, 1997).

Björnberg, Alf, 'Structural Relationships of Music and Images in Music Video', in *Reading Pop* (ed. Middleton), pp. 246-78.

Black, Fiona C., 'Beauty or the Beast? The Grotesque Body in the Song of Songs', *BibInt* 8 (2000), pp. 302-23.

—*The Artifice of Love: Grotesque Bodies in the Song of Songs* (London: T. & T. Clark, 2009).

—'Unlikely Bedfellows: Allegorical and Feminist Readings of Song of Songs 7:1-8', in *The Song of Songs* (ed. Brenner and Fontaine), pp. 104-129.

—'What is my Beloved? On Erotic Reading and the Song of Songs', in *The Labour of Reading* (ed. Black *et al.*), pp. 35-52.

—and J. Cheryl Exum, 'Semiotics in Stained Glass: Edward Burne-Jones' Song of Songs', in *Biblical Studies/Cultural Studies: The Third Sheffield Colloquium* (ed. J. Cheryl Exum and Stephen D. Moore; JSOTSup, 266; Sheffield: Sheffield Academic Press, 1998), pp. 315-42.

—Roland Boer and Erin Runions (eds.), *The Labour of Reading: Desire, Alienation and Biblical Interpretation* (Semeia Studies, 36; Atlanta, GA: Society of Biblical Literature, 1999).

Blanski, Tyler, *Mud and Poetry: Love, Sex and the Sacred* (Nashville, TN: Fresh Air Books, 2010).

Bloch, Ariel and Chana Bloch, *The Song of Songs: A New Translation* (London: University of California Press, 1998).

Bloom, Harold, *Kabbalah and Criticism* (New York: Seabury Press, 1975).

Boer, Roland, 'God, Pain and Love in the Music of Nick Cave', *JRPC* 22 (2010) [http://www.usask.ca/relst/jrpc/art22(3)-god-pain-love.html], n.p. accessed 5 June 2011.

—*Knockin' on Heaven's Door: The Bible and Popular Culture* (London: Routledge, 1999) [http://resolver.shef.ac.uk/?http://www.netLibrary.com/urlapi.asp?action=summary&v=1&bookid=60770], accessed 14 Apr. 2011.

—'Under the Influence? The Bible, Culture and Nick Cave', *JRPC* 11 (2006), [http://www.usask.ca/relst/jrpc/art12-nickcave.html], n.p., accessed 12 Apr 2009.

Bonheoffer, Dietrich, *Psalms: The Prayer Book of the Bible* (trans. James H. Burtness; Minneapolis: Augsburg, 1970).

Bono, Interviewed by Niall Stokes, *Hot Press Annual 2002* [http://www.atu2.com/news/article.src?ID=2082], accessed 20 May 2009.

—'Introduction', *The Book of Psalms* (Edinburgh: Cannongate, 1999) [http://www.guardian.co.uk/theobserver/1999/oct/31/featuresreview.review2?INTCMP=SRCH], accessed 29 Mar. 2011.

—The Edge, Adam Clayton, Larry Mullen Jr, with Neil McCormick, *U2 by U2* (London: Harper Collins, 2006).

Bradby, Barbara and Brian Torode, 'Pity Peggy Sue', in *Reading Pop* (ed. Middleton), pp. 203-227.

Bray, Elisa, 'Hallelujah—A Song with a Life of its Own', in *The Independent* (5 Dec 2008), [http://www.independent.co.uk/arts-entertainment/music/features/hallelujah-a-song-with-a-life-of-its-own-1052178.html], accessed 14 Apr. 2011.

Brenner, Athalaya, '"Come Back, Come Back the Shulammite" (Song of Songs 7.1-10): A Parody of the *wasf* Genre', in *A Feminist Companion to the Song of Songs* (ed. Brenner), pp. 234-57.

—'Introduction', in *Culture, Entertainment and the Bible* (ed. Aichele), pp. 7-12.

—'My Song of Songs', in *The Song of Songs* (ed. Brenner and Fontaine), pp. 154-68.

—*The Intercourse of Knowledge: On Gendering Desire and 'Sexuality' in the Hebrew Bible* (Biblical Interpretation Series, 26; Leiden: Brill, 1997).

—*The Song of Songs* (OT Guides Series; Sheffield: JSOT Press, 1989).

—(ed.), *A Feminist Companion to the Song of Songs* (Sheffield: Sheffield Academic Press, 1993).

—and Carole R. Fontaine (eds.), *The Song of Songs* (A Feminist Companion to the Bible, Second Series, 6; Sheffield: Sheffield Academic Press, 2000).

Bridge, Edward J., 'Loyalty, Dependency and Status with YHWH: The Use of '*bd* in the Psalms', *VT* 59 (2009), pp. 360-78.

Britt, Brian, 'Unexpected Attachments: A Literary Approach to the Term חסד in the Hebrew Bible', *JSOT* 27 (2003), pp. 289-307.

Brown, Dan, *The Da Vinci Code* (London: Corgi, 2003).

Brown, William P., *Seeing the Psalms: A Theology of Metaphor* (Louisville, KY: Westminster John Knox Press, 2002).

Browning, Elizabeth Barrett *Aurora Leigh,* pp. 820-21; see [http://digital.library.upenn.edu/women/barrett/aurora/aurora.html#7], accessed 2 Dec. 2010.

Broyles, Craig C., *Psalms* (New International Bible Commentary; Peabody, MA: Hendrickson, 2002).

—*The Conflict of Faith and Experience in the Psalms: A Form-Critical and Theological Study* (JSOTSup, 52; Sheffield : JSOT Press, 1989).

Brueggemann, Walter, *Abiding Astonishment: Psalms, Modernity, and the Making of History* (Louisville, KY: John Knox Press, 1991).

—*An Introduction to the Old Testament: The Canon and Christian Imagination* (Louisville, KY: Westminster John Knox Press, 2003).

—*An Unsettling God: The Heart of the Hebrew Bible* (Minneapolis, MN: Fortress, 2009).

—*Finally Comes the Poet* (Minneapolis, MN: Fortress Press, 1989).

—*Israel's Praise: Doxology Against Idolatry and Ideology* (Philadelphia, PA: Fortress Press, 1988).

—'Psalms and the Life of Faith: A Suggested Typology of Function', in *The Poetical Books* (ed. Clines), pp. 35-66.

—*Praying the Psalms,* (Minneapolis, MN: St Mary's Press, 1986).

—*Spirituality and the Psalms* (Minneapolis, MN: Fortress Press, 2002).

—'The Costly Loss of Lament', in *The Poetical Books* (ed. David J.A. Clines; Sheffield: Sheffield Academic Press. 1997), pp. 84-97.

—*The Message of the Psalms: A Theological Commentary* (Minneapolis: Augsburg, 1984).

Burrus, Virginia and Stephen D. Moore, 'Unsafe Sex: Feminism, Pornography, and the Song of Songs', *BibInt* 11 (2003), pp. 24-52.

Burstein, Dan (ed.), *Secrets of the Code: The Unauthorized Guide to the Mysteries behind The Da Vinci Code* (London: Orion, 2005).

Bush, Frederic W., *Ruth, Esther* (Word Biblical Commentary, 9; Dallas, TX: Word, 1996).

Butler, Cuthbert, *Western Mysticism* (London: Constable,1967).

Byassee, Jason, *Praise Seeking Understanding: Reading the Psalms with Augustine* (Grand Rapids, MI: Eerdmans, 2007).

Cahn, Walter, 'Illuminated Psalter Commentaries', in *Psalms in Community* (ed. Attridge and Fasler), pp. 241-64.

Calvin, John, *Commentary on the Psalms* (Library of Christian Classics, 23; London: SCM, 1958); [http://www.ccel.org/ccel/calvin/calcom08.html], accessed 10 Aug. 2009.

Carr, David, 'Gender and the Shaping of Desire', *JBL* 119 (2000), pp. 233-48.

Carr, G. Lloyd, *Song of Songs* (Leicester: Inter-Varsity Press, 1984).

Carroll, Robert P., 'Removing an Ancient Landmark: Reading the Bible as a Cultural Production', in *Borders, Boundaries and the Bible* (ed. Martin O'Kane; JSOTSup, 313; London: Sheffield Academic Press, 2002), pp. 6-14.

Cassiodorus, *Explanation of the Psalms,* I (trans. P.G. Walsh; New York, Paulist Press, 1990).

Cave, Nick, *The Secret Life of the Love Song,* Lecture given at the Vienna Poetry Festival, 25 Sept. 1998, [http://everything2.com/title/Nick+Cave%2527s+Love+Song+Lecture], accessed 31 Oct. 2010.

Cave, Nick and Jim Sclavunos, Interview in *Q magazine* (London, Nov. 2010), pp. 82-85.

Ceresko, Anthony R., 'A Note on Psalm 63: A Psalm of Vigil', *ZAW* 92 (1980), pp. 435-36.

Childs, Brevard S., 'Critique of Recent Intertextual Canonical Interpretation', *ZAW* 115 (2003), pp. 173-84.

Chrysostom, John, *Commentary on the Psalms,* I (trans. Robert Charles Hill; Brookline, MA: Holy Cross Orthodox Seminary Press, 1998).

Clark, Gordon, *The Word* Hesed *in the Hebrew Bible* (JSOTSup, 157; Sheffield: JSOT Press, 1993).

Clines, David J.A., 'Why Is There a Song of Songs and What Does It Do to You If You Read It?', in *Interested Parties: The Ideology of Writers and Readers in the Hebrew Bible* (David. J.A. Clines; JSOTSup, 205, GTC 1; Sheffield: Sheffield Academic Press, 1995), pp. 94-121.

—(ed.), *The Poetical Books: A Sheffield Reader* (Sheffield: Sheffield Academic Press, 1997).

Clement of Alexandria, *The Instructor (Paedagogus),* II [http://www.ccel.org/ccel/schaff/anf02.vi.iii.ii.iv.html], accessed 9 May 2011.

Cohen, Mordechai Z., *Three Approaches to Biblical Metaphor: From Abraham Ibn Ezra and Maimonides to David Kimhi* (Leiden: Brill, 2003).

Cohn-Sherbrook, Dan and Lavinia Cohn-Sherbrook, *Jewish and Christian Mysticism: An Introduction* (New York: Continuum, 1994).

Coldplay, Interview in *Q magazine*, (London: June 2005), pp. 66-75.

—Interview in *Q magazine* (London: July 2008), pp. 34-46.

Connor, Alan, 'Just Whose Hallelujah Is It Anyway?', *BBC News Magazine* (17 December, 2008) [http://news.bbc.co.uk/1/hi/magazine/7787355.stm], accessed 30 June 2009.

Considine, J.D., 'Madonna—Like a Prayer', *Rolling Stone Magazine* (6 April 1989) [http://www.rollingstone.com/artists/madonna/albums/album/185201/review/5940859/like_a_prayer], accessed 18 June 2009.

Cousland, J.R.C., 'God, the Bad, and the Ugly: The *Vi(t)a Negativa* of Nick Cave and P.J. Harvey', in *Call Me the Seeker* (ed. Gilmour), pp. 129-57.

Craigie, Peter C., *Psalms 1-50* (Word Biblical Commentary, 19; Waco TX: Word, 1983).

Crisp, Peter, 'Metaphorical Propositions: A Rationale', *Language and Literature* 11 (2002), pp. 7-16.

Croft, Steven J.L., *The Identity of the Individual in the Psalms* (JSOTSup, 44; Sheffield: JSOT Press, 1987).

Cross, F.L. and E.A. Livingstone (eds.), *The Oxford Dictionary of the Christian Church* (3rd edition; Oxford: Oxford University Press, 1997).

Crossley, James G., 'For EveryManc a Religion: Biblical and Religious Language in the Manchester Music Scene, 1976-1994', *BibInt* 19 (2011), pp. 151-80.

Cubitt, Sean, '"Maybellene": Meaning and the Listening Subject', in *Reading Pop* (ed. Middleton), pp. 141-59.

Dahood, Mitchell, *Psalms 1-50* (Anchor Bible, 16; Garden City, NY: Doubleday, 1966).

—*Psalms 51-100* (Anchor Bible, 17; Garden City, NY: Doubleday, 1968).

—*Psalms 101-150* (Anchor Bible, 17a; Garden City, NY: Doubleday, 1970).

Daley, Brian, 'Finding the Right Key: The Aims and Strategies of Early Christian Interpretation of the Psalms', in *Psalms in Community* (ed. Attridge and Fasler), pp. 189-205.

Daley, M., 'Patti Smith's Gloria: Intertextual Play in a Vocal Performer', *PopMus* 16 (1997), pp. 235-53.

Dante (Alighieri), *The Divine Comedy* (trans. Geoffrey L. Bickersteth: Oxford; Blackwell, 1981).

Davidson, Richard M., *Flame of Yahweh: Sexuality in the Old Testament* (Peabody, MA; Hendrickson, 2007).

Davidson, Robert, *The Vitality of Worship: A Commentary on the Book of Psalms* (Cambridge, UK: Eerdmans, 1998).

Davies, Andrew, 'The Bible under the Joshua Tree: Biblical Imagery in the Music of U2', *SBL Forum* (Jan 2009) [http://www.sbl-site.org/Publications/article.aspx?articleId=795], accessed 28 Apr. 2009.

Davis, Ellen F., 'Exploding the Limits: Form and Function in Psalm 22', in *The Poetical Books* (ed. Clines), pp. 135-46.

—*Proverbs, Ecclesiastes and the Song of Songs* (Louisville, KY: Westminster John Knox Press, 2000).

Day, John, *Psalms* (Old Testament Guides; Sheffield: Sheffield Academic Press, 1990).

Deckers, M., 'The Structure of the Song of Songs and the Centrality of *nepheš*', in *A Feminist Companion to the Song of Songs* (ed. Brenner), pp. 172-96.

Delirious?, Interview in *The Mag*, (24 Apr. 2008) [http://www.the-mag.me.uk/Music/Articles/Item/Delirious-Interview], accessed 9 May 2009.

Dell, Katherine J., 'Does the Song of Songs Have Any Connections to Wisdom?', in *Perspectives on the Song of Songs* (ed. Anselm C. Hagedorn; Berlin: de Gruyter, 2005), pp. 8-26.

—'Wisdom in Israel', in *Text in Context* (ed. A.D.H. Mayes; Oxford: Oxford University Press, 2000), pp. 348-75.

Dionysius the Areopagite, *On the Divine Names and the Mystical Theology* [http://www.ccel.org/ccel/rolt/dionysius.v.html], accessed 25 Aug. 2009.

Dirksen, P.B., 'Song of Songs 3:6-7', *VT* 39 (1989), pp. 219-25.

Doelman, James, 'Song of Songs', in *A Dictionary of Biblical Tradition in English Literature* (ed. David Lyle Jeffrey; Grand Rapids, MI: Eerdmans, 1992), pp. 727-30.

Doerksen, Brian, *Make Love, Make War: Now Is the Time to Worship* (London: David C. Cook, 2009).

Donne, John, *Devotions* [http://www.ccel.org/ccel/donne/devotions.toc.html], accessed 25 Aug. 2009.

—*Selected Poems of John Donne* [http://rpo.library.utoronto.ca/poet/98.html], accessed 25 Aug. 2009.

Dove, Mary, 'Sex, Allegory and Censorship: A Reconsideration of Medieval Commentaries on the Song of Songs', *Literature and Theology* 10 (1996), pp. 317-28.

Drane, John, *Celebrity Culture* (Edinburgh: Rutherford House, 2005).

Eaton, John, *The Psalms: A Historical and Spiritual Commentary with an Introduction and New Translation* (London: T. & T. Clark, 2003).

Edenburg, Cynthia, 'Intertextuality, Literary Competence and the Question of Readership: Some Preliminary Observations', *JSOT* 35 (2010), pp. 131-48.

Evans, G.R., *Bernard of Clairvaux* (Oxford: Oxford University Press, 2000).

Exum, J. Cheryl, 'How Does the Song of Songs Mean? On Reading the Poetry of Desire', *Svensk Exegetisk Årsbok* 64 (1999), pp. 33-50.

—'In the Eye of the Beholder: Wishing, Dreaming and *Double Entendre* in the Song of Songs', in *The Labour of Reading* (ed. Black, Boer and Runions), pp. 71-86.

—'Seeing Solomon's Palanquin (Song of Songs 3:6-11)', *BibInt* 11 (2003), pp. 301-16.

—*Song of Songs: A Commentary* (Old Testament Library; Louisville: Westminster John Knox Press, 2005).

—'Ten Things Every Feminist Should Know about the Song of Songs', in *The Song of Songs* (ed. Brenner and Fontaine), pp. 24-36.

—'"The Voice of my Lover": Double Voice and Poetic Illusion in Song of Songs 2:8-3:5', in *Reading from Right to Left: Essays on the Hebrew Bible in Honour of David J.A. Clines* (ed. J. Cheryl Exum and H.G.M. Williamson; JSOTSup, 373; London: Sheffield Academic Press, 2003).

Falk, Marcia, *The Song of Songs: A New Translation and Interpretation* (San Francisco, CA: Harper San Francisco, 1993).

Farmer, Kathleen A., 'Psalms', *The Woman's Bible Commentary* (ed. Carol A. Newsom and Sharon H. Ringe; London: SPCK, 1992), pp. 137-44.

Fewell, Danna N. (ed.), *Reading Between Texts: Intertextuality and the Hebrew Bible* (Louisville, KY: Westminster/John Knox Press, 1992).

Fiori, Umberto, 'Listening to Peter Gabriel's "I Have the Touch"', in *Reading Pop* (ed. Middleton), pp. 183-91.

Fishbane, Michael, *The Exegetical Imagination: On Jewish Thought and Theology* (Cambridge, MA: Harvard University Press, 1998).

Fox, Michael V., *The Song of Songs and the Ancient Egyptian Love Songs* (Madison, WI: University of Wisconsin Press, 1985).

Francis de Sales, *Treatise on the Love of God* [http://www.ccel.org/ccel/desales/love. html], accessed 13 Aug. 2009.

Franken, H.J., *The Mystical Communion of JHWH in the Book of Psalms* (Leiden: Brill, 1954).

Frith, Simon, 'Listen! Hear! The Uneasy Relationship of Music and Television', *PopMus* 21 (2002), pp. 277-290.

—*Performing Rites: Evaluating Popular Music* (Oxford: Oxford University Press, 1998).

—'Popular Culture', in *A Dictionary of Cultural and Critical Theory* (ed. Michael Payne; Oxford: Blackwell, 2005), pp. 415-17.

—and Angela McRobbie, 'Rock and Sexuality', in *On Record* (ed. Frith and Goodwin), pp. 371-89.

—and Andrew Goodwin (eds.), *On Record: Rock, Pop and the Written Word* (London: Routledge, 1990).

—Andrew Goodwin and Lawrence Grossberg (eds.), *Sound and Vision: The Music Video Reader* (London: Routledge, 1993).

Froese, Brian, 'Comic Endings: Spirit and Flesh in Bono's Apocalyptic Imagination, 1980-83', in *Call Me the Seeker* (ed. Gilmour), pp. 61-78.

Frost, Michael, *Exiles: Living Missionally in a Post-Christian Culture* (Peabody, MA: Hendrickson, 2006), pp. 301-323.

Frow, John, 'Intertextuality and Ontology', in *Intertextuality* (ed. Worton and Still), pp. 45-55.

Galbraith, Deane, 'Drawing Our Fish in the Sand: Secret Biblical Allusions in the Music of U2', *BibInt* 19 (2011), pp. 181-222.

Garrett, Duane and Paul R. House, *Song of Songs/Lamentations* (Word Biblical Commentary, vol 23B; Nashville, TN: Thomas Nelson, 2004).

Garrett, Greg, *We Get to Carry Each Other: The Gospel According to U2* (Louisville, KY: Westminster John Knox, 2009).

Gaster, Theodor H., 'Psalm 45', *JBL* 74 (1955), pp. 239-51.

Gerstenberger, Erhard S., *Psalms* Part I (Grand Rapids, MI; Eerdmans, 1988).

Gilbert, Jeremy and Ewan Pearson, *Discographies: Dance Music Culture and the Politics of Sound* (London: Routledge, 1999).

Gillingham, Susan E., *Psalms Through the Centuries,* I (Blackwell Bible Commentaries; Oxford: Blackwell, 2008).

—*The Poems and Psalms of the Hebrew Bible* (Oxford: Oxford University Press, 1994).

Gillmayr-Bucher, Susanne, 'Body Images in the Psalms', *JSOT* 28 (2004), pp. 301-26.

Gilmour, Michael J., *Gods and Guitars: Seeking the Sacred in Post-1960s Popular Music* (Waco, TX: Baylor University Press, 2009).

—'They Refused Jesus Too: A Biblical Paradigm in the Writing of Bob Dylan', *JRPC* 1 (Spring 2002) [http://www.usask.ca/relst/jrpc/article-dylan.html], n.p., accessed 22 Feb. 2009.

—(ed.), *Call Me the Seeker: Listening to Religion in Popular Music* (New York: Continuum, 2005).

Goldingay, John, *Psalms 1-41* (Grand Rapids, MI: Baker Academic, 2006).

—*Psalms 42-89* (Grand Rapids, MI: Baker Academic, 2007).

—*Psalms 90-150* (Grand Rapids, MI: Baker Academic, 2008).

—'So What Might the Song of Songs Do to Them?', in *Reading from Right to Left: Essays on the Hebrew Bible in Honour of David J.A. Clines* (ed. J. Cheryl Exum and H.G.M. Williamson; JSOTSup, 373; London: Sheffield Academic Press, 2003), pp. 173-83.

Gordis, Robert, *The Song of Songs and Lamentations* (New York: Ktav, 1954).

Goulder, Michael, *The Psalms of David (Psalms 51-72)* (JSOTSup, 102; Sheffield: JSOT Press, 1990).

—*The Song of Fourteen Songs* (JSOT Sup. 36; Sheffield: JSOT Press, 1986).

Graham, Elaine, 'What We Make of the World: The Turn to 'Culture' in Theology and the Study of Religion', in *Between Sacred and Profane* (ed. Lynch), pp. 63-81.

Gregory of Nyssa, 'Letters and Select Works', in *A Select Library of the Nicene and Post-Nicene Fathers of the Christian Church*, 5 (ed. P. Schaff and H. Wace; 2nd Series; Oxford, Parker, 1893).

Grelot, Pierre, *The Language of Symbolism* (trans. Christopher R. Smith; Peabody, MA: Hendrickson, 2006).

Griffiths, Jay, 'Land of the Freedom Singers', *The Guardian Weekly* (London: 1 Apr. 2011), p. 30.

Grohmann, Marianne, 'Psalm 113 and the Song of Hannah (1 Samuel 2:1-10): A Paradigm for Intertextual Reading?', in *Reading the Bible Intertextually* (ed. Hays *et al.*), pp. 119-135.

Grossberg, Lawrence, 'The Media Economy of Rock Culture: Cinema, Post-Modernity and Authenticity', in *Sound and Vision* (ed. Frith *et al.*), pp. 159-79.

Gunkel, Hermann, *Introduction to the Psalms* (completed by Joachim Begrich; trans. James D. Nogalski; Macon, GA: Mercer University Press, 1998).

Gunn, David M., 'Yearning for Jerusalem: Reading Myth on the Web', in *The Labour of Reading* (ed. Black *et al*), pp. 123-40.

Güthenke, Constanze, 'Do Not Awaken Love Until It Is Ready: George Seferis' *Asma Asmaton* and the Translation of Intimacy', in *Perspectives on the Song of Songs* (ed. Anselm C. Hagedorn; Berlin: Walter de Gruyter, 2005), pp. 338-55.

Guyon, Jeanne Marie, *Autobiography of Madame Guyon* (Chicago, IL: Moody Press, 1960).

Hadley, Judith, *The Cult of Asherah in Ancient Israel and Judah: Evidence for a Hebrew Goddess* (Cambridge: Cambridge University Press, 2000).

Hagedorn, Anselm C., 'Of Foxes and Vineyards: Greek Perspectives on the Song of Songs', *VT* 53 (2003), pp. 337-52.

Häger, Andreas, 'Under the Shadow of the Almighty: Fan Reception of Some Religious Aspects in the Work and Career of the Irish Popular Musician Sinéad O'Connor', in *Call Me the Seeker* (ed. Gilmour), pp. 215-25.

Hand, Seán, 'Missing You: Intertextuality, Transference and the Language of Love', in *Intertextuality* (ed. Worton and Still), pp. 79-91.

Harding, Kathryn, '"I sought him but I did not find him": The Elusive Lover in the Song of Songs', *BibInt* 16 (2008), pp. 43-59.

Hattenstone, Simon, 'Old Nick: Interview with Nick Cave', *The Guardian* (23 Feb. 2008) [http://www.guardian.co.uk/music/2008/feb/23/popandrock.features], accessed 22 Nov. 2010.

Hawkins, Peter S., 'Singing a New Song: The Poetic Afterlife of the Psalms', in *Psalms in Community* (ed. Attridge and Fasler), pp. 381-94.

Hays, Richard B., Stefan Alkier and Leroy A. Huizenga (eds.), *Reading the Bible Intertextually* (Waco, Texas: Baylor University Press, 2009).

Heawood, Sophie, 'I Was So Drunk I Fell onto the Stage: Interview with Candi Staton', *The Guardian* (24 Mar. 2006); [http://www.guardian.co.uk/music/2006/mar/24/popandrock], accessed 13 Apr. 2011.

Heelas, Paul, *Spiritualities of Life: New Age Romanticism and Consumptive Capitalism* (Malden, MA: Blackwell, 2008).

—and Linda Woodhead, *The Spiritual Revolution: Why Religion is Giving Way to Spirituality* (Oxford: Blackwell, 2004).

Herbert, George, *Selected Poetry of George Herbert* [http://rpo.library.utoronto.ca/poet/159.html], accessed 25 Aug. 2009.

Hess, Richard S., *Israelite Religions: An Archaeological and Biblical Survey* (Grand Rapids, MI: Baker Academic, 2007).

—*Song of Songs* (Grand Rapids, MI: Baker Academic, 2005).

Heyward, Carter, *Staying Power: Reflections on Gender, Justice and Compassion* (Cleveland, OH: Pilgrim Press, 2000).

Hilary of Poitiers, 'Homilies on the Psalms', in *The Nicene and Post-Nicene Fathers*, IX (ed. P. Schaff and H. Wace; Oxford: Parker and Company, 1899).

Hoffman, Lawrence A. 'Hallels, Canon and Loss: Psalms in Jewish Liturgy', in *Psalms in Community* (ed. Attridge and Fasler), pp. 33-57.

Holden, Stephen, 'Diana Ross Flirts with a Willing Audience', *New York Times* (16 June 1989) [http://www.nytimes.com/1989/06/16/arts/review-pop-diana-ross-flirts-with-a-willing-audience.html], accessed 10 Dec. 2009.

Horrobin, Peter and Greg Leavers (eds.), *Mission Praise* (London: Marshall Pickering, 1990).

Horton, D., 'The Dialogue of Courtship in Popular Song', in *On Record* (ed. Frith and Goodwin), pp. 14-26.

Hossfeld, Frank-Lothar and Erich Zenger, *Die Psalmen*, I (Neue Echter Bibel; Würzburg: Echter Verlag, 1993).

—*Psalms 2: A Commentary on Psalms 51-100* (Hermeneia; Minneapolis, MN; Augsburg Fortess Press, 2005).

Hughes, Timothy R., *Holding Nothing Back* (Eastbourne, UK: Kingsway, 2007).

Hunter, Alastair G., *Psalms* (London: Routledge, 1999).

Hwang, Andrew and Samuel Goh, *Song of Songs* (Asia Bible Commentary; Bangalore: Asia Theological Association, 2001).

Jayadeva, *Gita Govinda* [http://en.wikisource.org/wiki/Gita_Govinda], accessed 7 July 2009.

Jeffrey, Peter, 'Philo's Impact on Christian Psalmody', in *Psalms in Community* (ed. Attridge and Fasler), pp. 147-88.

Jenni, Ernst, 'אהב', *TLOT*, I (Peabody, MA: Hendrickson, 2004), pp. 45-54.

Jenson, Robert W., *Song of Songs* (Interpretation: Louisville, KY: John Knox Press, 2005).

Jerome, *Homilies on the Psalms*, I (The Fathers of the Church, 48; trans. Marie L. Ewald; Washington DC, Catholic University of America Press, 1981).

—'Letters and Select Works', in *A Select Library of the Nicene and Post-Nicene Fathers of the Christian Church*, VI (trans. W.H. Fremantle; ed. P. Schaff and H. Wace; 2nd Series; Oxford: Parker and Company, 1893).

Joffe, Laura, 'The Answer to the Meaning of Life, the Universe and the Elohistic Psalter, *JSOT* 27 (2002), pp. 223-235.

Kaplan, James, 'Life after the Da Vinci Code: Interview with Dan Brown' [http://www.parade.com/news/2009/09/13-dan-brown-life-after-da-vinci-code.html], accessed 14 Apr. 2011.

Keel, Othmar, *The Song of Songs* (trans. Frederick J. Gaiser; Continental Commentary: Minneapolis, MN: Fortress Press, 1994).

Kessler, Anna, 'Faith, Doubt and the Imagination: Nick Cave on the Divine-Human Encounter', in *Call Me the Seeker* (ed. Gilmour), pp. 79-94.

Kidner, Derek, *Psalms 1-72* (Tyndale; Leicester: Inter-Varsity Press, 1973).

—*Psalms 73-150* (Tyndale; Leicester: Inter-Varsity Press, 1975).

King, Roberta R., 'Toward a Discipline of Christian Ethnomusicology: A Missiological Paradigm', *Missiology* 33 (2004), pp. 293-306.

Kingsmill, Edmée, *The Song of Songs and the Eros of God* (Oxford: Oxford University Press, 2009).

Knight, Diana, 'Roland Barthes: An Intertextual Figure', in *Intertextuality* (ed. Worton and Still), pp. 92-107.

Kramer, Samuel N., *The Sacred Marriage Rite* (Bloomington: Indiana University Press, 1969).

Kraus, Hans-Joachim, *Psalms 1–59* (trans. Hilton C. Oswald; Minneapolis, MN: Augsburg Fortress, 1989).

—*Psalms 60–150* (trans. Hilton C. Oswald; Minneapolis, MN: Augsburg Fortress, 1993).

Kristeva, Julia, *Desire in Language* (trans. Thomas Gora, Alice Jardine and Leon S. Roudiez; Oxford: Blackwell, 1992.

—'From Sign to Symbol', in *The Kristeva Reader* (ed. Toril Moi; trans. Seán Hand; Oxford: Blackwell, 1986).

LaCocque, André, *Romance She Wrote: A Hermeneutical Essay on Song of Songs* (Harrisburg, PA: Trinity Press International, 1998).

—and Paul Ricoeur, *Thinking Biblically: Exegetical and Hermeneutical Studies* (trans. David Pellauer; Chicago, IL: University of Chicago Press, 1998).

Landy, Francis, *Paradoxes of Paradise: Identity and Difference in the Song of Songs* (Sheffield: Almond Press, 1983).

LeClercq, Jean, *Monks and Love in Twelfth-Century France* (Oxford: Clarendon Press, 1979).

—*The Love of Learning and the Desire for God: A Study of Monastic Culture* (New York: Fordham University Press, 1982). [http://quod.lib.umich.edu.eresources. shef.ac.uk/cgi/t/text/pageviewer-idx?c=acls;cc=acls;rgn=full%20text;idno=heb0 1061.0001.001;didno=heb01061.0001.001;view=image;seq=41;node=heb01061 .0001.001%3A7;page=root;size=s;frm=frameset], accessed 4 Mar. 2009.

Leneman, Helen, 'Portrayals of Power in the Stories of Delilah and Bathsheba: Seduction in Song', in *Culture, Entertainment and the Bible* (ed. Aichele), pp. 139-55.

Lennox, Annie, Interview in *The Sunday Times* (20 Mar. 2009), http://www.sabotage newmedia.com/AL/TALC/Annie%20Lennox%20STM%2022%20March.JPG], accessed 12 May 2009.

Leonard, Jeffery M., 'Identifying Inner-Biblical Allusions: Psalm 78 as a Test Case', *JBL* 127 (2008), pp. 241-65.

Levenson, Jon D., *Esther: A Commentary* (Old Testament Library; Louisville, KY: Westminster John Knox Press, 1997).

Lewis, C.S., *Reflections on the Psalms* (London: Collins, 1973).

—*The Four Loves* (London: Geoffrey Bles, 1960).

Loades, Ann, 'Sacrament', in *The Oxford Companion to Christian Thought* (ed. Adrian Hastings, Alistair Mason and Hugh Pyper; Oxford: Oxford University Press, 2000), pp. 634-37.

Löbert, Anja, 'Cliff Richard's Self-Presentation as a Redeemer', *PopMus* 27 (2008), pp. 77-97.

Lohfink, Norbert and Erich Zenger, *The God of Israel and the Nations* (Collegeville, MN: Liturgical Press, 2000).

Longman, Tremper, III, *Song of Songs* (New International Commentary on the Old Testament; Cambridge, UK: Eerdmans, 2001).

Lucas, Ernest, *Exploring the Old Testament: The Psalms and Wisdom Literature* (London: SPCK, 2003).

Luther, Martin, 'Word and Sacrament', in *Luther's Works*, XXXV (trans. Herbert J.A. Bouman; ed. E. Theodore Bachmann; Philadelphia, PA: Fortress, 1960).

—'Devotional Writings', in *Luther's Works*, XLII (trans. Martin H. Bertram; ed. Martin O. Dietrich; Philadelphia, PA: Fortress, 1969).

—'First Lectures on the Psalms', in *Luther's Works*, X and XI (trans. Herbert J.A. Bouman; ed. Hilton C. Oswald; St Louis, MO: Concordia, 1974, 1976).

—'Lectures on the Song of Solomon', in *Luther's Works*, XV (trans. Ian Siggins; ed. Jaroslav Pelikan; St Louis, MO: Concordia, 1972), pp. 189-264.

—'Letters 1', in *Luther's Works*, XLVIII (trans. and ed. Gottfried G. Krodel; Philadelphia, PA: Fortress, 1963).

—'Selected Psalms 1', in *Luther's Works*, XII (trans. E.B. Koenker; ed. Jaroslav Pelikan; St Louis, MO: Concordia, 1955).

Lynch, Gordon (ed.), *Between Sacred and Profane: Researching Religion and Popular Culture* (London: I.B. Tauris, 2008).

Lyons, William J., 'The Apocalypse of John and Its Mediators, or Why Johnny Cash Wrote a Better Apocalypse than John of Patmos!', *SBL Forum*, [http://www.sbl-site.org/Publications/article.aspx?articleId=806], accessed 28 April 2009.

MacKnee, Chuck M., 'Peak Sexual and Spiritual Experience: Exploring the Mystical Relationship', *Theology and Sexuality* 5 (1996), pp. 97-115.

MacLeod, Douglas, 'The Oppressed Self: Desire, Sexuality and Religious Cinema', in *Religion and Sexuality: Passionate Debates* (ed. C.K. Robertson; New York: Peter Lang, 2006), pp. 94-110.

Madonna, 'Madonna on Madonna', Interview in *Time Magazine* (27 May, 1985) [http://www.time.com/time/magazine/article/0,9171,957025-10,00.html], accessed 17 June 2009.

—'Madonna's Hard Candy—Material Woman Restoring Her Brand', Interview with John Pareles, *New York Times* (27 Apr. 2008); [http://www.nytimes.com/2008/04/27/arts/music/27pare.html?pagewanted=2&_r=1], accessed 17 June 2009.

Martos, J., 'Sacrament', in *A New Dictionary of Christian Theology* (ed. Alan Richardson and John Bowden; London: SCM Press, 1983), pp. 514-15.

Matter, E. Ann, *The Voice of my Beloved: The Song of Songs in Western Medieval Christianity* (Philadelphia, PA: University of Pennsylvania Press, 1990).

Mays, James Luther, *Psalms* (Interpretation; Louisville, KY: John Knox Press, 1994).

—*The Lord Reigns: A Theological Handbook of the Psalms* (Louisville: Westminster John Knox Press, 1994).

McCann, J. Clinton, Jr, *Great Psalms of the Bible* (Louisville, KY: Westminster John Knox Press, 2009).

—'The Book of Psalms: Introduction, Commentary and Reflections', in *New Interpreter's Bible*, IV (ed. Leander E. Keck; Nashville, TN: Abingdon Press, 1996), pp. 641-1280.

—(ed.) *The Shape and Shaping of the Psalter*, (JSOTSup, 159; Sheffield: JSOT Press, 1993).

McClary, Susan and Robert Walser, 'Start Making Sense! Musicology Wrestles with Rock', in *On Record* (ed. Frith and Goodwin), pp. 277-92.

McCormick, Neil, 'Leonard Cohen: Hallalujah!', *The Daily Telegraph* (20 June 2008) [http://www.telegraph.co.uk/culture/music/3554289/Leonard-Cohen-Hallelujah.html], accessed 30 June 2009.

McFague, Sallie, *Models of God: Theology for an Ecological, Nuclear Age* (Philadelphia, PA: Fortress Press, 1987).

McGrath, Alister E., *Christian Theology: An Introduction* (Oxford: Blackwell, 4th edn, 2007).

McKay, J.W., 'Psalms of Vigil', *ZAW* 92 (1979), pp. 229-47.

Middleton, Richard (ed.), *Reading Pop: Approaches to Textual Analysis in Popular Music* (Oxford: Oxford University Press, 2003).

Migliore, Daniel L., *Faith Seeking Understanding: An Introduction to Christian Theology* (Grand Rapids, MI: Eerdmans, 2nd edn, 2004).

Miscall, Peter D., 'Isaiah: New Heavens, New Earth, New Book', in *Reading Between Texts* (ed. Fewell), pp. 41-56.

Mitchell, David C., "God Will Redeem my Soul from Sheol': The Psalms of the Sons of Korah', *JSOT* 30 (2006), pp. 365-84.

Monro, Jill M., *Spikenard and Saffron: The Imagery of the Song of Songs* (JSOTSup, 203; Sheffield: Sheffield Academic Press, 1995).

Moore, Sebastian, 'Love Trying to Happen', *Third Way* (May 2009), pp. 24-27.

Morgan, David, 'Studying Religion and Popular Culture', in *Between Sacred and Profane* (ed. Lynch), pp. 21-33.

Morgan, Huw, 'Just Some Joseph Looking for a Manger', *Third Way* (Dec. 2009), pp. 8-12.

Motion, Andrew, Interview in *Third Way* (April 2009), [http://www.thirdwaymagazine.co.uk/editions/no-edition/high-profile/still-wondering.aspx], accessed 11 June 2011.

Mowinckel, Sigmund, *The Psalms in Israel's Worship* (2 vols.; trans. D.R. Ap-Thomas; Oxford: Blackwell, 1962).

Mulder, Johannes S.M., *Studies on Psalm 45* (Ph.D. dissertation; Nijmigen; Oss: Offsetdrukkerij Witsiers, 1972).

Murphy, Roland E., *The Song of Songs* (Hermeneia; Minneapolis, MN: Augsburg Fortress Press, 1990).

Neusner, Jacob, *Israel's Love Affair with God: Song of Songs* (Valley Forge, PA: Trinity Press International, 1993).

Niehoff, Maren R., 'The Symposium of Philo's Therapeutae: Displaying Jewish Identity in an Increasingly Roman World', *Greek, Roman, and Byzantine Studies* 50 (2010), pp. 95-116.

Niemann, Hermann M., 'Choosing Brides for the Crown Prince: Matrimonial Politics in the Davidic Dynasty', *VT* 56 (2006), pp. 225-38.

Nissinen, Martti, *Homoeroticism in the Biblical World: A Historical Perspective* (Minneapolis, MN: Fortress Press, 1998).

—'Song of Songs and Sacred Marriage', in *Sacred Marriages: The Divine-Human Sexual Metaphor from Sumer to Early Christianity* (ed. Martti Nissinen and Risto Uro; Winona Lake, IN: Eisenbauns, 2008), pp. 173-218.

—and Risto Uro (eds.), *Sacred Marriages: The Divine-Human Sexual Metaphor from Sumer to Early Christianity* (Winona Lake, IN: Eisenbauns, 2008).

Noble, Paul R., 'Esau, Tamar and Joseph: Criteria for Identifying Inner-Biblical Allusions', *VT* 59 (2002), pp. 219-52.

Norris, Richard A., Jr, *The Song of Songs Interpreted by Early Christian and Medieval Commentators* (The Church's Bible; Cambridge, UK: Eerdmans, 2003).

Nygren, Anders, *Agape and Eros* (New York: Harper and Row, 1969).

Obama, Barack, *The Audacity of Hope* (Canongate, 2008).

O'Brien, Lucy, *Madonna—Like an Icon* (London: Corgi, 2007).

—*She Bop II—The Definitive History of Women in Rock, Pop and Soul* (London: Continuum, 2003).

Olaveson, Tim, 'Transcendent Trancer: The Scholar and the Rave', in *Call Me the Seeker* (ed. Gilmour), pp. 189-214.

Origen, *The Song of Songs: Commentary and Homilies* (London: Longman, Green & Co, 1957).

—*Commentaire sur le Cantique des Cantiques*, I (Sources Chrétiennes, 375; Paris: Éditions du Cerf, 1991).

—*Homélies sur les Psaumes 36 à 38* (Paris : Éditions du Cerf, 1995).

Osborne, Catherine, *Eros Unveiled: Plato and the God of Love* (Oxford: Clarendon Press, 1994).

Ostriker, Alicia, 'A Holy of Holies: The Song of Songs as Countertext', in *The Song of Songs* (ed. Brenner and Fontaine), pp. 36-54.

Paas, Stefan, 'A Textual Note on Psalm 143,6', *ZAW* 113 (2001), pp. 415-18.

Palmer, James, 'Exodus and the Biblical Theology of the Tabernacle', in *Heaven on Earth: The Temple in Biblical Theology* (ed. T. Desmond Alexander and Simon Gathercole; Carlisle, UK: Paternoster, 2004), pp. 11-22.

Patmore, Hector, '"The Plain and Literal Sense": On Contemporary Assumptions about the Song of Songs', *VT* 56 (2006), pp. 239-50.

Payne, Robin, 'The Song of Songs: Song of Woman, Song of Man, Song of God', *Expository Times* 107 (1996), pp. 329-33.

Pfenniger, Jennifer, 'Bhaktin Reads the Song of Songs', *JSOT* 34 (2010), pp. 331-49.

Philo of Alexandria, 'On the Contemplative Life', in *Philo* (Loeb Classical Library vol. 9; translated by F.H. Colson; London, Heinemann, 1941).

Pinn, Anthony B., 'On a Mission from God: African American Music and the Nature/Meaning of Conversion and Religious Life', in *Between Sacred and Profane* (ed. Lynch), pp. 143-56.

—and Monica R. Miller, 'Introduction: Intersections of Culture and Religion in African-American Communities', *Culture and Religion* 10 (March 2009), pp. 1-9.

Piper, John, *Desiring God: Meditations of a Christian Hedonist* (Nottingham: Inter-Varsity Press, 2004).

Pisa, Nick, 'Vatican Fury at 'Blasphemous' Madonna, *The Daily Telegraph* (4 Aug. 2006) [http://www.telegraph.co.uk/news/1525587/Vatican-fury-at-blasphemous-Madonna.html], accessed 19 June 2009.

Plank, Karl A., 'By the Waters of a Death Camp: An Intertextual Reading of Psalm 137', *Literature and Theology* 22 (2008), pp. 180-94.

Plato, *Lysis* [http://classics.mit.edu/Plato/lysis.html], accessed 10 Nov. 2009.

—*Symposium* [http://classics.mit.edu/Plato/symposium.1b.txt], accessed 10 Nov. 2009.

Polaski, Donald C., '"What Will Ye See in the Shulammite?": Women, Power and Panopticism in the Song of Songs', *BibInt* 5 (1997), pp. 64-81.

Pope, Marvin H., *Song of Songs* (Anchor Bible, 7c; New York: Doubleday, 1977).

Porter, Wendy J., 'The Composer of Sacred Music as an Interpreter of the Bible', in *Borders, Boundaries and the Bible* (ed. Martin O'Kane; JSOTSup, 313; London: Sheffield Academic Press, 2002), pp. 126-53.

Prince, 'Prince Epilepsy Cured by an Angel', Interview with Travis Smiley, *Hollywood Grind* [http://www.hollywoodgrind.com/prince-epilepsy-cured-by-an-angel], accessed 23 Dec. 2009.

—'Prince Says He Wants Less Explicit Lyrics', *Freemuse* 16 July 2004; [http://www.freemuse.org/sw6611.asp], accessed 23 Dec. 2009.

Provan, Iain W., *Ecclesiastes, Song of Songs* (NIV Application Commentary; Grand Rapids, MI: Zondervan, 2001).

Rashi, *Commentary on Psalms 1-89* (trans., Introduction and Notes by Mayer I. Gruber; Atlanta GA, Scholars Press, 1998).

—*Commentary on the Tanakh,* [http://www.chabad.org/library/bible_cdo/aid/16263/showrashi/true], accessed 17 June 2009.

Redman, Matt, Interview with *Christianity Today* (2 May 2007), [http://www.christianitytoday.com/ct/music/interviews/2007/mattredman-mini-0207.html], accessed 21 Apr. 2009).

—and Beth Redman, *Blessed Be your Name: Worshipping God on the Road Marked with Suffering* (London: Hodder & Stoughton, 2005).

Reinhartz, Adele, 'To Love the Lord: An Intertextual Reading of John 20', in *The Labour of Reading* (ed. Black *et al*), pp. 53-69.

Reuter, E. 'קנא', *TDOT*, XIII (Grand Rapids, MI: Eerdmans, 1974), pp. 47-58.

Richard of Rolle, *The Fire of Love,* [http://www.ccel.org/ccel/rolle/fire.pdf], accessed 6 Mar. 2011.

Ricoeur, Paul, *The Rule of Metaphor* (trans. Robert Czerny; London: Routledge, 2006).

Ridderbos, N.H., 'Response to Alonso Schökel', in *The Poetical Books* (ed. Clines), pp. 28-34.

Riehle, Wolfgang, *The Middle English Mystics* (trans. Bernard Standring; London: Routledge, 1981).

Riffaterre, Michael, 'Compulsory Reader Response: The Intertextual Drive', in *Intertextuality* (ed. Worton and Still), pp. 56-78.

Robinson, A, 'Three Suggested Interpretations in Psalm 84', *VT* 24 (1974), pp. 378-81.

Robinson, F.N. (ed), *The Works of Geoffrey Chaucer* (Oxford: Oxford University Press, 1977).

Robinson, Robert B., 'Sing Us One of the Songs of Zion: Poetry and Theology in the Hebrew Bible', in *The Labour of Reading* (ed. Black, *et al*), pp. 87-106.

Rodger, Gillian, 'Drag, Camp and Gender Subversion in the Music and Videos of Annie Lennox', *PopMus* 23 (2004), pp. 17-29.

Rogerson, John, 'Music', in *The Blackwell Companion to the Bible and Culture* (ed. John F.W. Sawyer; Oxford: Blackwell, 2006), pp. 286-98.

—'The Use of the Song of Songs in J.S. Bach's Church Cantatas', in *Biblical Studies/Cultural Studies: The Third Sheffield Colloquium* (ed. J. Cheryl Exum and Stephen D. Moore; JSOTSup, 266; Sheffield: Sheffield Academic Press, 1998), pp. 343-51.

—and J.W. McKay, *Psalms 1-50* (Cambridge, UK: Cambridge University Press, 1977).

—and J.W. McKay, *Psalms 51-100* (Cambridge, UK: Cambridge University Press, 1977).

—and J.W. McKay, *Psalms 101-150* (Cambridge, UK: Cambridge University Press, 1977).

Roncace, Mark and Dan W. Clanton Jr, 'Introduction: Teaching the Bible with Music' in *Teaching the Bible through Popular Culture and the Arts* (ed. Mark Roncace and Patrick Gray; Atlanta, GA: SBL, 2007), pp. 7-13.

Rushdie, Salman, *The Ground beneath Her Feet* (London: Random House, 1999).

Sabourin, L.J., *The Psalms: Their Origin and Meaning* (2 vols.; Staten Island, NY: The Society of St Paul, 1969).

Sakenfeld, Katherine Doob, *Faithfulness in Action: Loyalty in Biblical Perspective* (Philadelphia, PA: Fortress, 1985).

—'Love', *ABD*, IV (New York: Doubleday, 1992), pp. 375-81.

—*Ruth* (Interpretation: Louisville, KY: Westminster John Knox Press, 1999).

Sauer, G., 'קנאה', *TLOT*, III (Peabody, MA: Hendrickson, 2004), pp. 1145-47.

Savan, Leslie, 'Commercials Go Rock', in *Sound and Vision* (ed. Simon Frith et al.), pp. 85-90.

Savran, George, 'Seeing is Believing: On the Relative Priority of Visual and Verbal Perception of the Divine', *BibInt* 17 (2009), pp. 320-61.

Schaefer, Konrad, *Psalms* (Berit Olam; Collegeville, MN: Liturgical Press, 2001).

Scharen, Christian, *One Step Closer: Why U2 Matters to Those Seeking God* (Grand Rapids, MI: Brazos, 2006).

Scherzinger, Martin and Steven Smith, 'From Blatant to Latent Protest (and Back Again): On the Politics of Theatrical Spectacle in Madonna's "American Life"', *PopMus* 26 (2007), pp. 211-29.

Schneider, Laurel C., 'Yahwist Desires: Imagining Divinity Queerly', in *Queer Commentary and the Hebrew Bible* (JSOTSup, 334; ed. Ken Stone: Sheffield, Sheffield Academic Press, 2001), pp. 210-27.

Schofield Clark, Lynn, 'Why Study Popular Culture?', in *Between Sacred and Profane* (ed. Lynch), pp. 5-20.

Schökel, Alonso, 'The Poetic Structure of Psalm 42-43', in *The Poetical Books* (ed. Clines), pp. 16-23.

Scholem, Gershom, 'Kabbalah', *Encyclopaedia Judaica*, 10 (Jerusalem: Keter Publishing House, 1971), pp. 490-654.

Schroeder, Christoph, '"A Love Song": Psalm 45 in the Light of Ancient Near Eastern Marriage Texts', *CBQ* 58 (1996), pp. 417-32.

Schroer, Silvia, 'Under the Shadow of your Wings: The Metaphor of God's Wings in the Psalms, Exodus 19:4, Deuteronomy 32:11 and Malachi 3:20, as Seen through the Perspectives of Feminism and the History of Religion', in *Wisdom and Psalms* (ed. Athalaya Brenner and Carol Fontaine; A Feminist Companion to the Bible, Second Series; Sheffield: Sheffield Academic Press, 1998), pp. 264-82.

Schunck, Klaus-Dietrich, 'Wanting and Desiring', *ABD*, VI (New York: Doubleday, 1992), pp. 866-67.

Scott, Alan P., 'Talking about Music', [http://home.pacifier.com/~ascott/they/tamildaa.htm], accessed 2 Mar. 2011.

Searle, John R., *Expression and Meaning: Studies in the Theory of Speech Acts* (London: Cambridge University Press, 1979).

Seebass, Horst, 'נפשׁ', *TDOT*, 9 (Grand Rapids, MI: Eerdmans, 1974), pp. 497-519.

Setel, T. Drorah, 'Prophets and Pornography: Female Sexual Imagery in Hosea', in *A Feminist Companion to the Song of Songs* (ed. Brenner), pp. 143-55.

Seybold, Klaus, *Introducing the Psalms* (trans. R. Graeme Dunphy; Edinburgh: T. & T. Clark, 1990).

Sheriffs, Deryck, *The Friendship of the Lord: An Old Testament Spirituality* (Carlisle, UK: Paternoster, 1996).

Sherry, Patrick, 'The Sacramentality of Things', *New Blackfriars* 89 (2008), pp. 575-90.

Simon, Margarita L., 'Intersecting Points: The 'Erotic as Religious' in the Lyrics of Missy Elliott', *Culture and Religion* 10 (March 2009), pp. 81-96.

Smith, Mark S., '"Seeing God" in the Psalms: The Background to the Beatific Vision in the Hebrew Bible', *CBQ* 50 (1988), pp. 171-83.

Smith, Martin, Interview with *LouderThanTheMusic.com*, 2 Oct. 2009 [http://www.louderthanthemusic.com/document.php?id=771], accessed 14 Jan. 2010.

—Interview with *Premier.tv* [http://player.premier.tv/#&&index3=a68eb002-34b0-42b1-a790-24b5a6e6e1fc&indexVideoTitle=Compassionart], accessed 14 Jan. 2010.

—and Craig Borlase, *Delirious: My Journey with the Band, a Growing Family and an Army of Historymakers* (Colorado Springs, CO: David C. Cook, 2011).

—and Stuart Garrard, 'Cutting a Deeper Groove', Interview with *Third Way* (June 1997), p. 13.

Snaith, John G., *Song of Songs* (New Century Bible Commentary; London: Marshall Pickering, 1993).

Sommer, Benjamin D., 'Exegesis, Allusion and Intertextuality in the Hebrew Bible: A Response to Lyle Eslinger', *VT* 46 (1996), pp. 479-498.

Soulen, Richard N., 'The *wasfs* of the Song of Songs and Hermeneutic', *JBL* 86 (1967), pp. 183-90.

Sparks, Kenton L., 'The Song of Songs: Wisdom for Young Jewish Women', *CBQ* 70 (2008), pp. 277-99.

Spurgeon, Charles H., *Treasury of David* [http://www.ccel.org/ccel/spurgeon/treasury3.i.xxx.html], accessed 29 Mar. 2010.

Starbird, Margaret, 'God Does Not Look Like a Man', in *Secrets of the Code*, (ed. Burstein), pp. 62-66.

Steinholt, Yngvar B., 'You Can't Rid a Song of its Words: Notes on the Hegemony of Lyrics in Russian Rock Songs', *PopMus* 22 (2003), pp. 89-108.

Stockman, Steve, *The Rock Cries Out* (Orlando: Relevant Books, 2004).

—*Walk On: The Spiritual Journey of U2* (Orlando: Relevant Books, 2005).

Stoebe, H., 'חסד', *TLOT*, II (Peabody, MA: Hendrickson, 2004), pp. 449-464.

Stokes, Niall, *U2: The Story Behind Every U2 Song* (London: Carlton Books, 2009).

Susaalo, Heikki, Interview with Candi Staton [http://www.soulexpress.net/candistaton.htm], accessed 12 Apr. 2011.

Taft, Robert F., 'Christian Liturgical Psalmody: Origins, Development, Decomposition, Collapse', in *Psalms in Community* (ed. Attridge and Fasler), pp. 7-32.

Tanner, Beth LaNeel, *The Book of Psalms through the Lens of Intertextuality* (SBL Monographs 26; New York: Peter Lang, 2001).

Tate, Marvin E., *Psalms 51-100* (Word Biblical Commentary, 20; Dallas, TX: Word, 1990).

Tatusko, Andrew, 'Transgressing Boundaries in the Nine Inch Nails: The Grotesque as a Means to the Sacred', *JRPC* 11 (2005), n.p.

Teresa of Avila, *The Interior Castle, or the Mansions* [http://www.ccel.org/ccel/teresa/castle2.txt], accessed 27 Aug 2009.

Terrien, Samuel, *The Psalms: Strophic Structure and Theological Commentary* (Eerdmans Critical Commentary; Cambridge, UK: Eerdmans, 2003).

Tertullian, *The Apology (Apologeticum)* [http://www.tertullian.org/articles/mayor_apologeticum/mayor_apologeticum_07translation.htm], accessed 9 May 2011.

Theodoret of Cyrus, *Commentary on the Psalms* (2 vols.; trans. Robert C. Hill; Washington DC: Catholic University of America Press, 2000).

Tillich, Paul, *Love, Power and Justice,* (New York: Oxford University Press, 1960).

—*Theology of Culture* (New York: Oxford University Press, 1959).

Torgovonik, Marianna, *Primitive Passion: Men, Women, and the Quest for Ecstasy* (New York, Alfred A. Knopf, 1996).

Tournay, Raymond J., 'Les Affinités de Ps. lxv Avec le Cantique des Cantiques et Leur Interpretation Messianique', in *Congress Volume: Bonn, 1962* (VT Sup., 9: Leiden: Brill, 1963), pp. 168-212.

—*Seeing and Hearing God in the Psalms: The Prophetic Liturgy from the Second Temple in Jerusalem* (trans. J. Edward Crowley; JSOTSup, 118; Sheffield: Sheffield Academic Press, 1991).

Traherne, Thomas, *Centuries, Poems and Thanksgivings,* II (ed. H.M. Margoliouth, Oxford: Clarendon, 1958).

Trible, Phyllis, *God and the Rhetoric of Sexuality* (Philadelphia, PA: Fortress, 1978).

Tull, Patricia K., 'Bakhtin's Confessional Self-Accounting and Psalms of Lament', *BibInt* 13 (2005), pp. 41-55.

Turner, Denys, *Metaphor or Allegory? Erotic Love in Bernard of Clairvaux's Sermons on the Song of Songs* (Paper presented to the Catholic Biblical Association, Newman College, 28 April 1998), n.p.

Turner, Steve, *Cliff Richard: The Bachelor Boy* (London: Carlton, 2008).

—*Hungry for Heaven: Searching for Meaning in Rock and Religion* (London: Hodder & Stoughton, 1995).

Twomey, Jay, 'The Biblical Man in Black: Paul in Johnny Cash/Johnny Cash in Paul', *BibInt* 19 (2011), pp. 223-252.

U2, Interviewed in *Q Magazine* (London, Feb. 2009), pp. 40-68.

Urbanski, Dave, *The Man Comes Around: The Spiritual Journey of Johnny Cash* (Lake Mary, FL: Relevant Books, 2005).

Vagacs, Robert, *Religious Nuts, Political Fanatics: U2 in Theological Perspective* (Eugene, OR: Cascade, 2005).

Van Dijk-Hemmes, Fokkelien, 'The Imagination and the Power of Imagination: An Intertextual Analysis of Two Biblical Love Songs: The Song of Songs and Hosea 2', in *The Poetical Books* (ed. Clines), pp. 173-87.

Van Wolde, Ellen, *Reframing Biblical Studies: When Language and Text Meet Culture, Cognition and Context* (Winona Lake, IN: Eisenbrauns, 2009).

—'Sentiments as Culturally Constructed Emotions: Anger and Love in the Hebrew Bible', *BibInt* 16 (2008) pp. 1-24.

Veereshwar, Anand, 'Love', *JHP* 19 (1979), pp. 3-13.

Vernalis, Carol, 'The Aesthetics of Music Video: An Analysis of Madonna's "Cherish"', *PopMus* 17 (1998), pp. 153-85.

—'The Functions of Lyrics in Music Video', *JPMS* 14 (2002), pp. 11-31.

Viladesau, Richard, *Theology and the Arts* (New York: Paulist Press, 2000).

Wagar, Samuel, 'The Wiccan "Great Rite"— *Hieros Gamos* in the Modern West', *JRPC* 21 (2009) [http://www.usask.ca/relst/jrpc/art21(2)-HierosGamos.html], n.p., accessed 5 June 2011.

Wagner, Siegfried, 'בקש', *TDOT,* II (Grand Rapids, MI: Eerdmans, 1974), pp. 229-41.

Wallis, Gerhard, 'אהב', *TDOT,* I (Grand Rapids, MI: Eerdmans, 1974), pp. 99-118.

Walsh, Carey E., *Exquisite Desire: Religion, the Erotic, and the Song of Songs* (Minneapolis, MN: Fortress, 2000).

Waltke, Bruce K., and James M. Houston, with Erika Moore, *The Psalms as Christian Worship: A Historical Commentary* (Grand Rapids, MI: Eerdmans, 2010).

Walton, Andy, 'Worship is More Than Intimacy: Interview with Graham Kendrick', in *Christianity Today* (April, 2010), pp. 24-29.

Ward, Graham, 'The Erotics of Redemption—After Karl Barth', *Theology and Sexuality* 8 (1998), pp. 52-72.

Ward, Graham, 'The Future of Religion', *JAAR* 74 (2006), pp. 179-86.

Ward, Pete, *Selling Worship: How What We Sing Has Changed the Church* (Milton Keynes, UK: Paternoster, 2005).

—'The Eucharist and the Turn to Culture', in *Between Sacred and Profane* (ed. Lynch), pp. 82-93.

Watson, Greg, 'The Bedroom Blues: Love and Lust in the Lyrics of Early Female Blues Artists', *Language and Literature* 15 (2006), pp. 331-56.

Watson, W.G.E., 'Hebrew Poetry', in *Text in Context: Essays by Members of the Society for Old Testament Study* (ed. A.D.H. Mayes; Oxford: Oxford University Press, 2000), pp. 253-85.

Weems, Renita J., *Battered Love: Marriage, Sex and Violence in the Hebrew Prophets* (Minneapolis, MN: Augsburg Fortress, 1995).

—'The Song of Songs', in *New Interpreter's Bible,* IV (ed. Leander E. Keck; Nashville, TN: Abingdon Press, 1997), pp. 363-434.

Weiser, A. *The Psalms* (OTL; London: SCM, 1962).

Welch, Florence, Interview with Francesca Ryan, *The Daily Telegraph* (4 June 2009) [http://www.telegraph.co.uk/culture/music/rockandpopfeatures/5443013/Florence-and-the-Machine-interview-sound-and-vision.html], accessed 22 Nov. 2010.

Westermann, Claus, 'נפש', *TLOT,* II (Peabody, MA: Hendrickson, 2004), pp. 743-59.

—*The Living Psalms* (trans. J.R. Porter; Edinburgh: T. & T. Clark, 1989).

Whedbee, J. William, *The Bible and the Comic Vision* (Cambridge: Cambridge University Press, 1988), pp. 263-77.

White, John B., *A Study of the Language of Love in the Song of Songs and Ancient Egyptian Poetry* (SBL Dissertation Series; Missoula, MT: Scholars Press, 1978).

Worton, Michael and Judith Still (eds.), *Intertextuality: Theories and Practices* (Manchester: Manchester University Press, 1990).

Wright, Chris, *The Message of Ezekiel* (Nottingham, UK: Inter-Varsity Press, 2006).

Yarnold, E.J., 'Sacramental Theology', in *A New Dictionary of Christian Theology* (ed. Alan Richardson and John Bowden; London: SCM Press, 1983), p. 516.

Yorke, Thom, Interview, *Third Way* (Dec. 2004), pp. 16-21.

Young, Francis, *Biblical Exegesis and the Formation of Christian Culture* (Cambridge: Cambridge University Press, 1997).

Young, William P., *The Shack* (London: Hodder & Stoughton, 2008).

Zevit, Ziony, *The Religions of Ancient Israel: A Synthesis of Parallactic Approaches* (London: Continuum, 2001).

Zobel, Hans-Jürgen, 'חסד', *TDOT,* V (Grand Rapids, MI: Eerdmans, 1974), pp. 44-64.

Zschech, Darlene, *The Kiss of Heaven: God's Favor to Empower your Life Dream* (Grand Rapids, MI: Baker, 2003).

DISCOGRAPHY

Arcade Fire, *Neon Bible* (Merge, 2007).

Arctic Monkeys, *Whatever People Say I Am, That's What I'm Not* (London, Domino, 2006).

Barnett, Marie 'This Is the Air I Breathe' (Mercy/Vineyard Publishing, 1996).

Beyoncé, *I Am . . . Sasha Fierce* (Music World, 2008).

Bush, Kate, *The Kick Inside* (EMI, 1983).

Cash, Johnny, *Personal File* (Legacy/ Columbia, 2006).

—*Love, God, Murder* (Legacy/Columbia, 2000).

—*The Gospel Music of Johnny Cash* (Gaither, 2008).

Cave, Nick, *The Boatman's Call* (Mute Records, 1997).

Cohen, Leonard, *Leonard Cohen: Live in London* (Sony, 2009).

Coldplay; *A Rush of Blood to the Head* (Parlophone, 2002).

—*Viva la Vida* (Parlophone, 2008).

—*X&Y* (Parlophone, 2005).

Corrs, The, *Talk on Corners* (Atlantic, 1998).

Delirious?, *Cutting Edge 1 & 2* (Furious? Records, 1994).

—*Cutting Edge 3 & Fore* (Furious? Records, 1995).

—*Glo* (Furious? Records, 2000).

—*History Makers: Greatest Hits* (Furious? Records, 2009).

—*Kingdom of Comfort* (Furious? Records, 2008).

—*King of Fools* (Furious? Records, 1997).

—*Live and in the Can* (Furious? Records, 1996).

—*The Mission Bell* (Furious? Records, 2005).

—*World Service* (Furious? Records, 2003).

Dido, *Safe Trip Home* (Sony BMG, 2008).

Eurythmics, *Ultimate Collection* (Arista, 2005).

Evanescence, *Fallen* (Wind Up Records, 2004).

Fazal, Ruth, *Joy in the Night* (Tributary Music, 2007).

Florence and the Machine, *Lungs* (Island Records, 2009).

Gorrillaz, *Plastic Beach* (EMI Records, 2010).

Hillsong, *For This Cause,* (Hillsong Music Australia, 2000).

—*One* (Hillsong Music Australia, 1999).

—*Overwhelmed* (Hillsong Music Australia, 2000).

Houston, Whitney, *I Look to You* (Arista, 2009).

—*One Wish: The Holiday Album* (Arista, 2003).

—*The Preacher's Wife* (Arista, 1996).

—*Ultimate Collection* (Arista, 2007).

Hughes, Tim, *When Silence Falls* (Survivor Records, 2004).

Jamieson, Kevin and Stuart Townend, 'The King of Love' (Thankyou Music, 1997).

Jars of Clay, *Furthermore* (Essential Records, 2003).
Jenkins, Katherine, *Sacred Arias* (Universal Music: 2008).
Killers, The, *Sam's Town* (The Island Def Jam Music Group, 2006).
Lady Gaga, *Born This Way* (Streamline, 2011).
—*The Fame Monster* (Streamline, 2009).
Lennox, Annie, *The Annie Lennox Collection* (Sony BMG, 2009).
Madonna, *American Life* (Warner Brothers, 2003).
—*Confessions on a Dance Floor* (Warner Brothers, 2005).
—*Hard Candy* (Warner Brothers, 2008).
—*Like a Prayer* (Warner Brothers, 1989).
—*Ray of Light* (Warner Brothers, 1998).
Mitchinson, Steve, 'Divine Romance' (ION, 2007).
Morgan, Reuben, *Extravagant Worship: The Songs of Reuben Morgan* (Hillsong Music
    Australia, 2002).
Mumford & Sons, *Sigh No More* (Island, 2009).
Musseau, Craig, 'Here I Am Once Again' (Mercy/Vineyard Publishing, 1994).
Nine Inch Nails, *The Downward Spiral* (Nothing Records, 1994).
Oasis, *Dig Out your Soul* (Big Brother Recordings, 2008).
—*Don't Believe the Truth* (Big Brother Recordings, 2005).
—*Heathen Chemistry* (Big Brother Recordings, 2002).
—*Stop the Clocks* (Big Brother Recordings, 2005).
O'Connor, Sinéad, *Theology* (Rubyworks, 2007).
Prince, *The Rainbow Children,* (NPG Records, 2001).
—*The Very Best of Prince* (Rhino Records, 2001).
—*3121* (Universal/NPG Records, 2006).
Queen, *Sheer Heart Attack* (EMI, 1974).
Quilala, Chris, Kim Walker and Melissa How, *Your Love Never Fails* (jesusculture
    music, 2008).
Radiohead, *In Rainbows* (Self-released, 2007).
Redman, Matt, *Blessed Be your Name: The Songs of Matt Redman vol. 1* (Survivor
    Records, 2005).
—*Facedown* (Survivor Records, 2004).
—*Intimacy* (Survivor Records, 1998).
—*The Father's Song* (Survivor Records, 2000).
—*Wake Up my Soul* (Kingsway Records, 1993).
Richard, Cliff, *Forever the Young One* (Topaz, 2010).
—*Love ... the Album* (EMI, 2007).
—*Something's Goin' On* (Decca, 2004).
—*Wanted* (Papillon, 2001).
Rivera, Alberto and Kimberly, *Captured* (Integrity Music, 2009).
Sinott, Jeremy and Connie, *Come Away my Beloved* (Brampton, Canada: Rejoice Pub-
    lishing and Productions, 2006).
Switchfoot, *Hello Hurricane* (peoplerecords/Atlantic, 2009).
Townend, Stuart, *Creation Sings* (Kingsway Music, 2009).
—*Lord of Every Heart* (Kingsway Music, 2002).
—*Personal Worship* (Kingsway Music, 1999).
Tunstall, K.T., *Eye to the Telescope* (Virgin Records, 2006)
U2, *Achtung Baby* (Island Records, 1991).
—*All That You Can't Leave Behind* (Island Records, 2000).

—*Boy* (Island Records, 1980).
—*How to Dismantle an Atomic Bomb* (Island Records, 2004).
—*No Line on the Horizon* (Rhino Records, 2009).
—*October* (Island Records, 1981).
—*The Joshua Tree* (Island Records, 1987).
—*War* (Island Records, 1983).
Various Artists, *Love, Lift Us Up—40 Legendary Love Songs* (Universal Classics & Jazz, 2009).
—*10 Years of Vineyard UK Worship—Live* (Vineyard Music, 2009).
West, Kayne, *The College Dropout* (Roc-a-Fella, 2004).
YFriday, *Everlasting God: The Very Best of YFriday* (Kingsway Music, 2010).
—*Great and Glorious* (Survivor Records, 2009).
Yussuf, *An Other Cup* (Atlantic Records, 2006).
—*Roadsinger* (Island, 2009).
Zschech, Darlene, *Change your World* (INO Records, 2005).
—*Kiss of Heaven* (INO Records, 2003).

Details of certain song lyrics were found at http://www.lyricslook.com and http://www.lyricsfreak.com

INDEX OF BIBLICAL REFERENCES

References in **bold** refer to sections where a particular passage is studied in some detail. Specific verses from these sections are not itemized in this index.

When a reference includes multiple verses, the biblical chapter (or Psalm) number alone may be given here.

HEBREW BIBLE

Genesis	95, 105, 139,	20.7	163	38.17, 19	178
	195	21.5	156	40.34-38	177
1	17, 37, 202	25.4	178		
1.27	202	26.1	178	*Leviticus*	
1–2	195	26.31	178	1.3	177
2–3	7, 8, 110	26.32	178	2.1–3.17	177
2.7	122	26.33	179	26.12	179
2.23-24	9, 124	26.36	178		
3	33	27.10	178	*Numbers*	
3.16	179	27.11	178	10.34	177
3.24	163	27.16	178	36.7, 9	124
8.10-12	44	27.17	178		
9.12-17	44	28.5	178	*Deuteronomy*	
22.2	177	28.6	178		149, 156,
31.23	123	28.8	178		179
34.8	158	28.15	178	4.24	167
35.18	131	28.33	178	4.29	122
39.12	81	29.18	177	5.9	167
44.30	122	30.1-10	177	5.10	171
		30.22-23	177	6.3	178-79
Exodus	142	30.22-38	177	6.5	122, 171
3.14	24, 223	33.11	142	6.15	167
6.7	179, 188	33.20	141, 142	7.7	158
13.21-22	177	33.23	142	10.12	122, 156
15.1-18	74	34.6-7	169, 170	10.17	179
19.4	151	34.14	167	10.20	124
19.16-20	162	34.23	141	11.13	156
19.18	177	35	178	11.22	124
20.5-6	167, 169,	36.36	178	13.4	105, 124
	171	38.10-12	178	15.16	156

21.11	158	6.16	179
26.17-19	188	8.48	122
30.2	122	10.1-10	176
30.6	122, 156	11.1-8	173
30.10	122	11.2	124
30.20	124	16.31-34	173
31.20	179	18.6	124
32.11	151	18.19	173
32.16	167	18.36-38	162-63
32.19	167	19.2	173
32.21	167		
33.12	140	*2 Kings*	
34.1-43	74	18.6	124
		23.25	122
Joshua			
2.12-14	169	*1 Chronicles*	
22.5	122	16.34	164
		29.1-9	143
Judges			
6.22-23	141	*2 Chronicles*	
15.3-5	91	2.14	178
18.22	123	3.8	179
20.45	123	3.14	178
		5.11-14	164
Ruth		7.1-3	164
1.14	124	20.21	164
1.15	20	32.32	169
1.16-17	173	35.26-27	169
2.8	124		
2.21	124	*Ezra*	
2.23	124	3.8-13	143
3.10	169	3.10-11	164
		6.13-22	143
1 Samuel			
1.17	87	*Nehemiah*	
2.1-10	38	9.17	170
2.23	123	13.14	169
20.14	169		
31.2	123-24	*Esther*	
		2.9, 17	169
2 Samuel			
1.6	124	*Job*	152
9.1-3	169		
		Psalms	57, 71-73,
1 Kings			74-75, 77,
2.4	122		80, 82,
5.1-10	177		83-84, 86-88,
6-7	179		99, 112-13,
6-8	143		115-16, 126-

	28, 137, 143,
	151, 183-84,
	185-87, 192,
	195, 196,
	206, 214,
	222, 230-31
1	148, 150
2	172, 206
2.7	144, 151
2.7-9	154
3.7	166
4.5	120
4.6	145
5.8	166
6.1	144
7.6	144
7.12-13	96, 144
7.17	165
9.1	165
9.3	166
9.6	166
10.1	129
10.3	122
10.12-14	144
11.4	143
11.5	123
11.7	142, 144
12.5	154
13.1-2	129
13.1-4	213
16.7	118
16.11	99
17.7	124, 144,
	151, 167
17.15	142
18	166
18.1	84, 158
18.3	154
18.7-15	163
18.19	144
18.35	124
19	148, 149
19.7	122
19.10	149
19.14	144
20.4	101
21	172
21.6	142
22.1	151, 213

Psalms (cont.)

22.1-2	129
22.9	222
22.14	131
23.3	122
23.5-6	146
24	142
24.6	121
24.7-10	143, 144
25.1	122
25.6	170
25.14	145
27	58
27.4	76, 121, 141, 142, 146
27.4-6	143
27.8	99, 121
27.10	144
27.12	123
27.13	76
29.3-9	154
29.10	144
30.4	165
30.5	144
30.12	165
31	79
31.16	145
32.8-9	144
32.10	167
33	38
33.5	144, 167
33.6	144
33.9-10	144
33.12	188
33.18-19	167
34.2	122
34.8	101
34.15-18	144
35.1	166
35.3	154
35.4	121
35.10	144
35.18	165
35. 19	166
35.23	151
35.25	122
36.5	167
36.6	164
36.6-8	151

36.8	100, 179
37	93
37.3-4	61
37.4	101
37.13	154
37.24	61
37.27-28	169
37.28	144
38.7	101
39	93
39.13	145
40.8	131
40.11	167
40.14	121
40.16	121
41.11	144
41.12	124, 144
42–43	85, 122, **125-29**, 139-40, 154
42–83	115
42.1-2	59, 76, 84, 98, 101, 104, 122, 123, 146, 187, 204
42.2	141
42.3	85, 102, 141
42.4	142
42.5	130
42.8	167
42.9	204, 225
42.11	130
43.2	225
43.3-4	142
43.5	130
44.2	144
44.3	145
44.23	151, 213
45	79, 80, 83, 84, 88, 93, 98, 140, **172-74**, 201, 206
45.3	78
45.7	144
45.10-15	176
45.11	79, 98
45.12	76

45.15	181
46.1	142
46.4	179
46.5-7	142
46.6	154
46.10	154
47	144
47.5	143
48.12	96
48.12-14	142
50	154
50.2	142
50.3	163
51.1	170
51.12	99
51.18	144
51.19	144
54.5	166
54.7	166
55.12-14	95
55.14	145
57.1	151
57.3	167
57.10	167
59.4	151, 213
59.16	167
60.5	140
61.4-5	151
62.1	122
62.7-8	145
63	82, **118-25**, 139-40, 145-46, 201, 225
63.1	79, 98, 115, 122, 126
63.1-2	78
63.1-3	76
63.1-8	58
63.2	142
63.2-5	127
63.3	83, 141, 167
63.5	136, 147
63.7	61, 213, 220, 151
63.8	77, 86, 99, 220
63.9-10	91
63.9-11	166
66.20	167

67.1	145	84.10	146
68.1	143, 145	84.11	204, 225
68.5	151	85.1	144
68.18	143	85.8	169
69.4	166	86.5	170
69.14	166	86.10	144
69.17	145	86.12	165
69.18	166	86.13	167
69.24	144	86.15	170
70.4	121	88.13	101
70.4-5	144	88.14	144, 151
71.13	121	89	154, 168
71.23	122	89.10	166
71.24	121	89.21	124
72	172	89.25-26	144, 151
72.1-3	144	89.42	166
73	79, 81	89.51	166
73.23	125	90.8	144
73.25	70	91	38, 81
73.25-26	86, 97	91.1-4	151
73.28	99, 145	91.2	145
74.12-14	144	91.5	178
75.1	165	91.5-6	176
76	142	91.9	145
77.8	167	91.14	158
77.17-18	154	91.14-15	154
78	178, 144,	91.15	81
	166	92.1	165
78.18	121	92.2	118
78.34	121	93.3-4	154
78.65-66	144, 151	94.9-11	144
79.5	163	94.12-13	144
80.3	145	95.7	96, 188
80.7	145	95.8-11	154
80.8-18	179	96-100	61
80.10	164	96.1-3	61
80.16	145	96.6	142, 144
80.17	124	96.13	145
80.19	145	97.3-4	163
81	154	97.10	144
83.1	144	97.11-12	61
83.4	144	98.9	145
84	77, 82, **139-**	99	144
	42, 146, 201	99.5	143
84.1-2	84	100	61
84.1-7	146	100.3	188
84.2	122	100.4	165
84.2-3	220	102.13	144
84.3	145	102.25-27	144

103	104
103.1	122
103.2	122
103.8-12	170
103.13-14	144, 151
103.22	122
104	38
104.32	100
105	166
105.3-4	131
105.39	163
106	166
106.1	165
106.4	144
106.14	173
106.42	166
106.47	165
107	165
107.9	121
107.18	121
108.6	140
109.4-5	164
109.23	166
110	206
110.5	124
111.1	145
112	8
115.2-8	144
116.5	144
116.12-14	224
117.2	167
118	142, 162,
	165
118.15-16	144
118.24	179
119	**148-51**, 167,
	201, 206,
	220
119.4-5	144
119.8-10	144
119.20	122
119.31	124
119.41	167
119.64	167
119.81	122
119.98	166
119.103	104
119.103-105	225
119.105	204

Psalms (cont.)
119.124   171
119.127   171
119.162   204
119.176   121
120–134   115
121.7   96
122   78, 142
122.7   96
123.2   222
127   79
127.2   140
127.3-5   195
128.3   105, 195
128.6   195
130   38, 212-13, 215
130.2   213
130.3   213
130.6   213
131.2-3   144
132   143
132.9   169
132.13-14 173
132.16   169
134.1   118
135   143, 162
136   **164-67**, 201, 206
136.12-15 144
137   9, 38
138.1   165
138.2   165
138.4   165
139   104, 121, 131, 201
139.10   125
139.13-16 61
143   77, 135
143.6   84, 122, 126
143.7   98
143.8   122, 167
143.9   166, 167
143.12   166, 167
145.4-5   61
145.10   165
146.2   72
146.8   144
147.1   72

147.9-11   144
147.15-20 144
148.4   179
148.14   169
149.1   72, 162
149.3   72
149.9   162
149.4   144
149.5   120
150.1   162
150.3-5   72
150.6   162

Proverbs
6.30   121
7.18   155, 157
13.2   122
24.13-14   149

Ecclesiastes 165
7.26   161, 179
9.5-10   161

Song of Songs
           38, 54, 57, 64, 69, 70, 74-75, 85, 88-90, 98, 101-102, 106, 107-14, 116-17, 133-34, 180-81, 185, 196-97, 212-14
1.1   179
1.2   70, 78, 80, 81, 90, 93, 94, 99, 104, 105, 126, 137, 152, 155, 214
1.3   79, 120, 137, 155
1.4   76, 117, 179, 155, 175, 179
1.5   137, 176
1.6   179
1.7   77, 95, 121, 122, 137, 155
1.8   137
1.9–2.7 **136-39**, 155
1.12   175
1.13   86, 115
1.15   117, 120
1.15-16   120, 154, 179, 203
1.16   210
1.17   177
2.1   67
2.1-3   154
2.1-7   120
2.3   120, 149
2.3-7   92, 117, 155
2.4-5   96
2.5   79, 104, 107, 131, 140, 170
2.5-6   127
2.6   96, 97, 106
2.7   118, 162, 170, 179, 133
2.8-9   133
2.8-17   117, 118, 121, **152-53**, 154
2.10-12   76
2.10   45, 59, 137, 155
2.13   45, 59, 137, 155
2.14   103
2.15   91, 124, 179
2.16   139, 160
3.1   77
3.1-5   99, **117-18**, **120-25**, 130, 155
3.1-5.1   133
3.3   133
3.4   86
3.5   155, 162, 179
3.6-11   94, **174-78**, 199, 205
4.1   137
4.1-5   137, 226

4.1–5.1	154	6.3	139, 160,	42.1	123		
4.1-8	94, 96, 120		179	42.6	124		
4.3	137	6.4	137	42.14	222		
4.7	77, 137	6.4-5	170	43.1	87, 179		
4.8	175	6.4-7	137	43.2	179		
4.9	138, 170	6.4–7.9	154	43.14-15	179		
4.9-11	104, 175	6.4-10	120	49.2	92		
4.10	137, 155	6.5	138	54.4-8	134, 182		
4.10	126	6.8-9	61, 175	54.5	226		
4.10-11	117	6.9	80	62.3-5	182		
4.11	104, 149,	6.10	137	62.4-5	134, 205		
	178	6.12	121	63.15	179		
4.12–5.1	80, 129, 138,	6.12-13	104	66.13	222		
	154, 175,	7.1-5	137				
	208-209, 226	7.5	175	*Jeremiah*			
4.15	126	7.6	155	2.1-2	134		
4.16	33	7.6-9	120	2.2	171, 180,		
4.16–5.1	51, 132	7.8	80, 124		182		
5.1	104, 120,	7.9	126, 137,	2.20-37	182		
	126, 133,		149	2.24	122		
	135-36, 149,	7.10	160, 179	4.19	131		
	155, 178,	7.10-13	154	6.8	123		
	222	7.11	45	7.4	143		
5.2	104, 120,	7.12	155	7.18	196		
	121, 152	8.1-2	104	7.23	124		
5.2-3	154	8.2	126	11.5	179		
5.2-8	94, 99, 102,	8.3	120	11.15	140		
	120, **129-34**,	8.4	118, 155,	12.10	179		
	195		162	13.11	124		
5.2–6.3	118, 132	8.5	76, 79, 97	17.10	121		
5.4	179	**8.5b-7**	63, 120, 155,	31.20	131, 179		
5.4-5	104		**159-64**, 165,	32.22	179		
5.6	121		166, 170,	32.41	123		
5.7	81		179, 201	33.3	44		
5.8	85, 92, 138,	8.6	96, 179, 205	44.15-19	196		
	155	8.11-12	176	51.14	123		
5.8–6.3	216	8.12	179				
5.9	137	8.14	117, 133	*Lamentations*			
5.9-16	134			1.10	143		
5.10-16	120, 137,	*Isaiah*	110	1.20	131		
	177, 226	1.14	123	2.11	131		
5.14	131	3.14	179				
5.16	143, 149,	5.1	140, 155	*Ezekiel*	157		
	222	5.1-7	38, 179	16	134, 182,		
6.1	97, 121,	6.5	141		209, 226		
	133	26.9	121	16.8	155		
6.1-3	120	27.2	179	16.9	182		
6.1	137	38.17	158	16.15-58	182		
6.2	80, 132	40.31	43, 141	16.27	122		

Ezekiek (cont.)
19.10   179
23   182, 209
23.1-49   182
23.17   155
24.15   143
24.21   143
24.25   143
36.28   179
37.27   179
40–48   143

Daniel   97
7.9-10   163

Hosea
1–3   182
2.1-13   182

2.5-7   7
2.14-15   177, 180,
             182
4.1   171
4.1-3   182
4.6   182
4.12-19   182
5.15   121
6.4-6   171
9.16   143
11.1   157
11.3-4   220, 225

Joel
3.5   143

Amos
6.8   123

Jonah   128
4.2   170

Micah
6.8   169

Habakkuk
3   74

Zephaniah
3.17   59

Haggai
2.1-9   143

Malachi
2.10-11   182

New Testament

Matthew
5.48   94
13.44-45   46
22.1-14   107
23.37   213
25.1-13   64, 107
25.35-40   34

Mark
14.51-52   81

John
2.1-2   213
3.3-4   223
4.6-7   213
4.14   93
4.31   213
6.33   93
6.41   93
8.12   20
11.33-35   213
12.3   2
12.27   213
13.4-5   213
14.6   20
19.28   213
21.12   213

1 Corinthians
6.17   101
10.1-12   91
10.11   95
13.1-3   16
15.45   92

2 Corinthians
5.13-14   79
12.2   79

Galatians
4.21-24   91
6.8   93

Ephesians
5.18-20   72
5.32   95

Colossians
3.16-17   72

2 Timothy
4.7   24

Hebrews
1.5-13   206
5.14   92
12.1   24

James
4.8   94

1 John
4.8   91
4.16   91, 221
4.18   48

Revelation
1.9-16   57
21-22   64

Index of Authors

Ackerman, S. 156, 157
Adorno, T. 5
Aichele, G. 5, 157
Albertz, R. 128, 196
Alexander, P. 90
Alkier, S. 8
Allen, L. 149, 150, 164, 166, 167, 168
Alter, R. 122, 123, 125, 126, 138, 139,
        140, 158, 167, 173, 197
Anderson, A. 119, 124, 127, 148, 149,
        151, 167, 168
Aqiba 88, 89
Arbel, D. 132
Assis, E. 117, 121, 133, 161, 162
Astell, A. 99 100, 104
Athanasius 74, 75, 214
Attridge, H. 70, 71, 72, 73, 78
Augustine (of Hippo) 77, 78, 79, 80, 83,
        95, 96, 115, 124, 193, 199, 213,
        214

Barton, J. 89, 90
Begbie, J. 3, 5, 11, 12, 13, 14, 67, 82,
        84, 133
Bellinger, W. 128
Bergant, D. 114, 123, 131, 133, 137, 161,
        162, 178, 195, 197, 220
Bernard (of Clairvaux) 70, 81, 98, 99,
        100, 101, 193, 211, 214, 216
Björnberg, A. 15
Black, F. 8, 9, 13, 108, 130, 132, 138,
        182, 209
Bloch, A. and C. 118, 131, 132, 134,
        137, 138, 152, 155, 160, 161, 163,
        164, 175, 176, 197
Bloom, H. 67
Boer, R. 130, 186
Bonhoeffer, D. 127
Brenner, A. 5, 105, 109, 122, 132, 151,
        156, 160, 182, 197, 209, 214

Brown, D. 1, 2, 195
Brown, W. 116, 144, 204
Broyles, C, 87, 88, 119, 120, 126, 128,
        129, 137, 143, 151, 172
Brueggemann, W. 73, 87, 88, 129, 142,
        143, 144, 145, 147, 148, 150, 154,
        158, 164, 165, 166, 170, 194, 218
Burrus, V. 111
Byassee, J. 78, 79

Calvin, J. 71, 83, 84, 85, 108, 124, 149,
        214
Carr, D. 111, 112
Cassiodorus 72, 80, 214
Chrysostom 72, 174, 214
Clark, G. 168, 169, 171
Clines, D. 7, 109, 126, 153, 218
Cohen, M. 97, 126, 203, 208, 211
Craigie, P. 126
Croft, S. 86, 128

Dahood, M. 123, 148
Dante (Alighieri) 101
Davidson, R. 156, 163, 205
Davidson, R. 119, 182
Davis, E. 110, 126, 162, 163, 177, 178,
        179, 180, 190, 197
Day, J. 116, 119, 128, 143, 146, 148
Dell, K. 159
Dionysius (the Areopagite) 103, 194
Dirksen, P. 175
Donne, J. 104

Eaton, J. 6, 74, 119, 120, 124, 142, 143,
        151, 167, 168, 196
Exum, C. 8, 9, 73, 80, 105, 107, 108,
        109, 116, 118, 123, 125, 127, 130,
        131, 132, 133, 134, 137, 138, 139,
        141, 152, 153, 154, 159, 162, 163,
        164, 174, 175, 176, 177, 180, 214

Falk, M. 138
Fewell, D. 8, 115
Fishbane, M. 105
Fox, M. 9, 118, 131, 132, 138, 139, 141,
    153, 154, 161, 174, 176, 196, 197
Francis (de Sales) 66, 70, 85, 86, 89, 91,
    133, 200, 214
Franken, H. 87, 145, 146
Frith, S. 3, 6, 11, 12, 13, 14, 15, 16, 35,
    68

Galbraith, D. 49, 181
Garrett, D. 69, 77, 91, 107, 108, 109,
    117, 118, 123, 131, 138, 152, 153,
    160, 163, 174, 175, 176, 177, 178,
    179, 194, 195, 197
Gerstenberger, E. 128, 158
Gilbert, J. 6, 12, 14
Gillingham, S. 6, 69, 72, 74, 84, 87, 98,
    128, 129, 162
Gilmour, M. 4, 14, 43, 67, 68, 186
Goldingay, J. 70, 86, 88, 116, 119, 120,
    123, 124, 125, 127, 129, 139, 140,
    141, 142, 143, 146, 147, 148, 150,
    151, 158, 163, 165, 166, 167, 168,
    172, 173, 177, 182, 218, 221
Gordis, R. 132, 153, 162, 163
Goulder, M. 117, 119
Graham, E. 2, 3, 26, 35, 187, 218, 221
Gregory (of Nyssa) 92, 94
Gunkel, H. 86, 87, 88, 118, 119, 127,
    129, 135, 166

Hand, S. 208
Harding, K. 133
Heelas, P. 215
Herbert, G. 70, 82, 83, 89, 104, 188
Hess, R. 117, 118, 123, 130, 131, 133,
    139, 152, 154, 157, 159, 162, 163,
    175, 178, 180, 196, 206
Hossfeld, F.-L. 116, 119, 123, 124, 125,
    126, 127, 140, 141, 143, 146, 147,
    174
Hunter, A. 3, 7, 118, 204

Jerome 75, 76, 77, 90, 93, 214

Keel, O. 111, 122, 162, 163
Kidner, D. 121, 140

Kingsmill, E. 110, 120, 129, 161, 178,
    179, 180
Kramer, S. 109
Kraus, H.-J. 123, 135, 141, 145, 149,
    150, 164, 166, 167, 168, 169
Kristeva, J. 7, 189, 208

LaCocque, A. 9, 108, 110, 112, 119, 129,
    134, 138, 139, 163, 177, 178, 179,
    180, 199, 200, 228
Landy, F. 89, 118, 134, 135, 139, 153,
    159, 160, 163, 179, 195, 200, 201,
    208
LeClercq, J. 99, 101, 193, 211
Lewis, C. 136, 146, 158, 194
Longman, T. 89, 90, 92, 107, 116, 122,
    131, 132, 137, 152, 160, 161, 162,
    175, 197, 205
Lucas, E. 88, 91, 116
Luther, M. 71, 82, 83, 84, 106, 107, 118,
    214
Lynch, G. 3, 215

MacKnee, C. 190, 197
Matter, A. 14, 91, 93, 95, 101, 104, 106,
    193
Mays, J. 118, 128, 143, 146, 164, 168
McCann, C. 78, 86, 88, 116, 121, 123,
    124, 126, 148, 149, 150, 158, 164,
    168, 172, 173, 177, 206
McCormick, N. 22, 44
McFague, S. 125, 137, 203, 210, 217,
    218, 224, 226, 229
McGrath, A. 199, 200, 202
McKay, J. 119, 124, 150
Middleton, R. 5, 12, 15
Moore, S. 9, 107, 111
Motion, A. 16, 17
Mowinckel, S. 86, 87, 128
Murphy, R. 91, 96, 99, 108, 109, 112,
    118, 123, 132, 137, 152, 153, 160,
    162, 175, 177, 203, 205

Neusner, J. 89, 90, 157, 214
Nissinen, M. 89, 112, 137, 178, 197,
    205
Norris, R. 69, 91, 93, 94, 95, 96, 100,
    102, 117
Nygren, A. 92, 181, 193, 194

Obama, B. 4
O'Brien, L. 30, 32, 34, 35
Origen 90, 91, 92, 93, 94, 95, 101
Osborne, C. 92, 135, 136, 194
Ostriker, A. 105, 110, 111, 132, 201, 205, 212, 214

Payne, R. 137, 163, 221
Pfenniger, J. 9, 177
Philo (of Alexandria) 73, 74, 91
Pinn, A. 3
Plato 91, 92
Pope, M. 69, 89, 91, 94, 103, 105, 109, 121, 137, 138, 162, 189
Provan, I. 130, 139, 152, 162, 178, 205, 221

Rashi 70, 96, 97, 98, 140, 162, 174
Ricoeur, P. 9, 108, 112, 129, 203, 209, 210, 227, 228
Riehle, W. 98, 103, 104, 113, 210
Rogerson, J. 2, 107, 124, 150
Rolle, R. 103, 104
Rushdie, S. 46, 232

Sabourin, L. 140, 148
Sakenfeld, K. 156, 167, 168, 169, 170, 171, 182
Schaefer, K. 116, 119, 120, 125, 129, 140, 141, 150, 164, 166, 167, 168, 173, 177
Scharen, C. 45, 46, 47, 48
Schökel, A. 126, 127, 134
Searle, J. 208, 209, 211, 212
Seybold, K. 71, 82, 128
Smith, M. 144, 146
Spurgeon, C. 139
Stockman, S. 223, 224
Stoebe, H. 167, 168
Stokes, N. 17, 48, 187

Tate, M. 119, 124, 142
Teresa (of Avila) 86, 104, 189, 214
Terrien, S. 6, 72, 124, 146, 148, 149, 173
Tertullian 73, 199
Theodoret (of Cyrus) 72, 79, 94, 122, 124
Tillich, P. 125, 194, 200
Tournay, R 71, 88, 173, 174, 177
Traherne, T. 104
Trible, P. 7, 8, 110, 139, 179, 195, 222
Turner, D. 100, 211
Turner, S. 42, 67

van Dijk-Hemmes, F. 7
van Wolde, E. 157, 217
Veereshwar, A. 198
Vernalis, C. 15

Walsh, C. 11, 132, 133, 177, 179, 180, 181, 189, 205, 211
Waltke, B. 71, 72, 81
Ward, G. 218, 221
Weems, R. 114, 135, 160, 164, 175, 176, 182, 205, 217, 228
Weiser, A. 87, 119, 128, 145, 146, 148, 167, 168
Westermann, C. 87, 122, 129
Whedbee, W. 138, 139
Woodhead, L. 215
Worton, M. 7, 134, 235

Young, F. 91
Young, W.P. 220

Zenger, E. 116, 119, 122, 123, 124, 125, 126, 127, 140, 141, 146, 147, 174, 188
Zevit, Z. 144, 196
Zobel, H.-J. 168, 169

Index of Musicians

Arcade Fire 68
Arctic Monkeys 19

Bach, J.S. 3, 48, 107
Barnett, Marie 64
Beyoncé 17-18, 204, 207
Bono 17, 43-49, 191, 192, 207, 212,
    223-24
Bush, Kate 13

Cash, Johnny 41, 49, 67
Cave, Nick 185-86, 198, 232
Cohen, Leonard 6, 19-23, 61, 201-202,
    214
Coldplay 8, 23-24, 68, 190-91, 204
Corrs, The 219

Delirious? 51-55, 190-91, 204, 207, 216,
    219, 222, 225-26
Dido 16

Eurythmics 28-30, 192, 198
Evanescence 49-50

Fazal, Ruth 64, 190-91
Florence and the Machine 24-26, 204,
    233
Francis, Samuel Taylor 66

Gorrillaz 50

Hillsong 59-62
Houston, Whitney 26-28, 190-91, 204
Hughes, Tim 63-64

Jamieson, Kevin 57
Jars of Clay 64-65
Jenkins, Katherine 22-23

Killers, The 50

Lady Gaga 192-93
Lennox, Annie 28-30, 192, 198, 204,
    207-208

Littledale, R.F. 65

Madonna 15, 30-35, 192, 198, 204
Mitchinson, Steve 63
Morgan, Reuben 62
Mumford & Sons 191
Musseau, Craig 64

Nine Inch Nails 50-51, 198

Oasis 8, 17, 36-38, 202, 207, 208
O'Connor, Sinéad 24, 38-39, 212, 214,
    215-16

Prince 38, 39-41, 198, 207-208

Queen 67
Quilala, Chris 63

Radiohead 8, 16
Redman, Matt 55-57, 204, 207, 214,
    219
Richard, Cliff 41-43
Rivera, Alberto and Kimberly 62

Sinott, Jeremy and Connie 59, 207
Smith, Martin 54, 225
Switchfoot 188

Townend, Stuart 57-58, 204, 207, 214
Tunstall, K. T. 8

U2 8, 15, 17, 43-49, 187, 191-92, 194,
    198, 204, 207-208, 212, 214, 223-
    24, 225, 232

Wesley, Charles 66
West, Kayne 66

YFriday 222, 226-27
Yussuf 41

Zschech, Darlene 59-62, 190-91, 207,
    216, 219